MINORITY MENTAL HEALTH

MINORITY MENTAL HEALTH

Edited by

Enrico E. Jones

and

Sheldon J. Korchin

PRAEGER

PRAEGER SPECIAL STUDIES • PRAEGER SCIENTIFIC

If we want humanity to advance a step further...
then we must invent and we must make discoveries

—F. Fanon

Library of Congress Cataloging in Publication Data
Main entry under title:

Minority mental health.

Includes bibliographies and index.
1. Minorities—Mental health—United
States. 2. Minorities—United States—
Psychology. I. Jones, Enrico E., 1947-
II. Korchin, Sheldon J. [DNLM: 1. Minority
groups—Psychology. WA 305 M6664]
RC451.5.A2M564   362.2′0880693   82-396
ISBN 0-03-047056-0 (hb)   AACR2
        0-03-061912-2 (pbk.)

Published in 1982 by Praeger Publishers
CBS Educational and Professional Publishing
A Division of CBS, Inc.
521 Fifth Avenue, New York, New York 10175 U.S.A.

© 1982 by Praeger Publishers

23456789   145   987654321

Printed in the United States of America

Contents

v

PREFACE

This volume brings together the concepts, findings, and experiences of a number of social scientists and mental health professionals concerned with understanding the particular mental health problems of minority communities and with contributing to their solution. With few exceptions the writers are themselves members of ethnic minorities and are, therefore, able to bring to their work not only professional expertise but rich backgrounds of firsthand experience in their cultures of origin. We hope that by bringing these chapters together, all of them written expressly for this volume, we can give readers, whether professionals or students, the opportunity to study in one place contemporary thinking that exemplifies some of the better work in the field. Students who are themselves of minority background may also find models for their future development as serious professionals applying psychological and social theory and research methods to the understanding and solution of keenly felt social problems.

Though clearly oriented toward discovering means of improving the psychological well-being of minority peoples, these are scholarly papers that avoid polemic and go beyond protesting the inequities of a racist society. As we develop in Chapter 1, the thinking of many who work in the area of ethnicity and mental health reflects a "political perspective," which emphasizes the oppression and powerlessness of minority groups and sees solution mainly in terms of major social change. While valuable ideas have emerged from this perspective, we also see as fruitful a "cross-cultural perspective," one that views the behavior and problems of minority persons as expressions of their history and life conditions and that can best be understood in terms of the customs and values of each of their cultures in a pluralistic society. Each author, obviously, writes from within his own intellectual and value orientation, but a number of common themes run through the several chapters: psychological functioning and dysfunctioning of minorities cannot be understood by simply attributing the meanings of the larger society—rather they need to be viewed in their own terms; similarly, the work of helping professionals and the intervention methods employed must be adapted to the particular needs and values of minority groups; toward these ends, greater numbers of well-trained bicultural and bilingual mental health professionals are needed if the mental health problems of minorities are to be seriously attacked.

Part I of the volume begins with general overviews of concepts and issues of ethnic psychology that may be applicable to all minority group members in our society and then moves to more specific consideration of particular issues in each of several minority groups. In Chapter 1, as already noted, we attempt to distinguish in historical and theoretical terms political and cross-cultural perspectives and to consider their implications for clinical and community intervention. S. Sue in Chapter 2 looks broadly at the field from the vantage of research strategies and methods. C. Banks (Chapter 3) with the scalpel of philosophical analysis calls into questions the appropriateness of traditional theoretical models for understanding black behavior and, by implication, that of other ethnic minorities. By "deconstructive falsification" he shows that premises taken for granted in the research literature can be overthrown. G. DeVos (Chapter 4), from an anthropological perspective, argues that for any minority group adaptation in the larger society may depend on the internal stability of family roles and community cohesiveness in the particular group rather than being directly related to external oppression and poverty. H. Myers (Chapter 5) demonstrates the value of a stress model for considering dysfunctional behavior in black individuals. From the close examination of epidemiological findings, H. Kitano (Chapter 6) argues that the apparently low incidence rates probably more reflect underutilization of services because of cultural barriers than any genuine lack of psychological problems in the Japanese-American community. In a unique study, R. Lum (Chapter 7) describes mental health attitudes in San Francisco's Chinatown, a community in which social research is notoriously difficult to conduct. In a second part of his chapter, he examines the impact on Chinese families of having a son psychiatrically hospitalized.

Part II examines more closely issues of intervention (clinical testing, psychotherapy, community interventions) with minority populations. L. Snowden and P. Todman (Chapter 8) critically analyze the utility of personality and clinical assessment instruments, developed and widely used in white society, from a cross-cultural perspective. N. Boyd (Chapter 9) addresses psychosocial problems of the black family and the ways in which family therapy can be modified to better serve its needs. Similarly, C. Carrillo (Chapter 10) highlights the importance of a familiarity with culturally determined sex-role attitudes and family structure in treating the Hispanic family. In A. Franklin's chapter (11), the emphasis shifts to a particularly vulnerable group in black society, the adolescent. He examines their therapeutic needs and shows the advantages of a "psychoeducational" model of therapy. Nor are those in later life free of human problems, as J. Sczapocznik, et al. (Chapter 12) show in their analysis of a new "Life Enhancement Counseling" for Cuban elders in the United States. In addition to describing the problems of this group and his therapeutic intervention, he brings forth empirical evidence of its effectiveness. A. Meadow (Chapter 13), who has had the unique experience of conducting therapy with Hispanic clients both in the United States and in Latin America, provides us with a rich set of clinical material, which is examined from the vantage of a Spanish-speaking Anglo. R. Muñoz (Chapter 14) analyzes in detail the workings of a community mental health system relevant to the needs of Spanish-speaking clients. In his chapter, he also helps clarify the distinction among the various groups described by such terms as Hispanics, Latinos, Chicanos, among others.

This volume evolved from the editors' long-standing interest in minority mental health. Over the past dozen years, we at Berkeley made a serious commitment to recruit and train high-quality minority students. We also initiated a research program aimed at increasing the psychological understanding of minority groups and improving their mental health care, in which a number of these students worked. We are grateful to the National Institute for Mental Health for Research Grant #RO1 MH26104-01, which supported this project and helped launch this volume. In the course of these activities, we came to know the work of all of the contributors to this volume, many of whom visited with us to present and exchange ideas. The Psychology Department and, more particularly, the Psychology Clinic, which houses the graduate program in clinical psychology, have been supportive settings for our work, for our concern with minority issues is widely shared by faculty and students alike. We are grateful to our colleagues both for moral support and for more tangible contributions to the area, as, for example, in encouraging the development of new courses and funding a colloquium series.

A particular contribution was made by an unusually thoughtful and concerned group of ten Berkeley undergraduates, many of minority heritage, who worked with one of us (EEJ) reading and criticizing drafts of each chapter, thereby clarifying ambiguities that might have escaped more jaded professional eyes. We are grateful to Lew Abrams, Patrick (Gunther) Fahey, Brent Ferm, Susan (Kichea) Gautreaux, Corinne Kong, Winnie Lam, Derrick Lim, Beckie Masaki, Katherine Walker, and Ronnie Walker.

Finally, Kathie Stout and Norma Partridge-Wallace were of enormous help in typing this manuscript and otherwise helping to lighten the load of preparing this book for publication.

Any volume of this sort is necessarily selective. Many issues of personality, psychopathology, evaluation, and intervention are not touched upon; not all ethnic minorities are represented in these chapters. However, we believe that the themes treated by the authors do have applicability in other areas and to other groups. The selective nature of this book truly represents the state of this young, though important field; these chapters provide an overview of emerging trends. We hope that they contribute to its further growth.

Enrico E. Jones
Sheldon J. Korchin

Berkeley, California

June, 1980

PART I
THEORY AND RESEARCH

1   Minority Mental Health: Perspectives

Enrico E. Jones and Sheldon J. Korchin

INTRODUCTION

The aim of this chapter is to examine the status of ethnicity in mental health. It attempts to understand how ethnic groups, minorities in the United States, differ from or correspond with both each other and the majority group in the ways they experience and respond to stress and generate or resist psychopathology. It examines what factors in each group dispose toward greater receptivity or opposition to change-oriented interventions and how individual psychological change processes are set into motion, as well as how group and organizational structures evolve. This is a very major and difficult task. This discussion begins to address this broad and unwieldy topic through the generation of some rudimental elements of a conceptual framework within which matters relevant to ethnicity can productively be considered.

Generally speaking, two fundamental perspectives on ethnicity can be distinguished, two basic orientations along which thinking in the field has been directed. While these perspectives overlap in certain particular regards, they remain by and large contending points of view. On the one hand, there is a political orientation, which takes as its basic tenet that the mental health, as well as social and economic status, political power, personal dignity, and other facets of well-being of minority group members, depends on the acquisition of power and control over their personal and collective destinies. Within this viewpoint, which will be termed a "political" or "social action" orientation, a number of different versions exist. In common, however, all assert that true change can only occur when the conditions of oppression in the larger society are eliminated.

In contrast to this, we would propose that there is a "cross-cultural" point of view, which begins from the assumption that there are indeed differences among all of the participant groups in U.S. society, each with its own unique tradition, culture, ways of living, and, in some cases, language. And, that each of these more-or-less distinct cultures generate among individual members specific behaviors consonant with the main cultural themes. These behaviors are comprehensible only if one understands, and understands sympathetically, the ethnic culture. This point of view also stands in contradistinction to the old idea of U.S. society as a "melting pot" (Glazer and Moynihan, 1975), which holds that various cultural groups surrender their ethnic heritage within the span of a few generations after arrival on U.S. shores, assimilating with the dominant culture, adopting its values and forms of behavior and, while contributing to the overall cultural blend, no longer remaining distinct from it. The application of this concept is actually quite limited, particularly with respect to racial minorities. The "cross-cultural" perspective posits that there are real and fundamental differences in values, role concepts, behavioral patterns, forms of expression, and cognitive styles that must be acknowledged before effective understanding can occur. Any specific behavior that in the context of the majority society would appear to have specific meaning cannot be prejudged unless one knows the framework of the minority culture. Without the understanding of the cross-cultural framework of individual behaviors (whether symptomatic, attitudinal, or treatment related), efforts at the development and utilization of more effective means of change-oriented interventions are at the very least limited, if not destined to failure.

Before considering how these alternate perspectives conceptualize the problems of minority communities, particularly in the mental health sphere, it would be useful to consider concretely the mental health problems of ethnic minorities and the reasons traditional medical and clinical practices have fallen short of serving their needs, thereby requiring new paradigms to be developed.

MENTAL HEALTH NEEDS

It is generally agreed that ethnic minorities have unmet mental health needs. Epidemiological surveys, whether based on clinical statistics or field surveys, consistently show more psychological disorder in the lowest socioeconomic classes (Hollingshead and Redlich, 1958; Dohrenwend and Dohrenwend, 1969, 1974). The poor, which includes a disproportionate number of nonwhites, needs more and receives less good clinical care. Compared to white Americans, blacks clearly are overrepresented on the rosters of public psychiatric hospitals (Kramer, Rosen, and Willis, 1973). However, studies of Hispanics (Padilla and Ruiz, 1973; Padilla, Ruiz, and Alvarez, 1975), Japanese Americans (Kitano, 1969), and Chinese Americans (Brown, et al., 1973; Sue and Kitano, 1973; True, 1975) all show that these groups are less likely to be found in psychiatric facilities. It is sometimes argued that there exist factors in these cultures that help avert gross psychiatric symptoms (e.g., indigenous support systems or cultural values concerning work). It is more frequently claimed, however, that the relatively small numbers of members of these ethnic groups that appear in public mental health facilities indicate underutilization rather than any lack of problems. In this volume, two well-known workers in the field assume contrasting positions on this issue with respect to the Japanese American. G. DeVos (Chapter 4) proposes that the family integration and community cohesiveness that frequently typifies the Japanese minority has helped serve as a deterrent to psychological disorder, while H. Kitano (Chapter 6) claims that underutilization by this group is a symptom demonstrating that it remains apart from the mainstream and is being deprived of what the community has to offer. It is very possible that the data on utilization of mental health facilities represents lower rates of mental illness among some groups and underutilization among others. Nevertheless, it is in fact true that there are greater barriers to mental health care for all ethnic groups. These obstacles include language differences, a greater concern with stigma, fear of contact with the bureaucracies of local and federal governments, and less access to resources. It has also been pointed out that for a variety of historical and social reasons, minorities hold less favorable attitudes toward mental health care than whites (Thomas and Sillen, 1972).

Minority patients often have inferior clinical services available to them. Blacks are more likely to be offered custodial care and medication, less often psychotherapy, than whites (Hollingshead and Redlich, 1958). When seen in psychiatric facilities, blacks, Hispanics, and Asians are more likely to be assigned to supportive than intensive therapy and to be discharged more rapidly (Yamamoto, James, and Palley, 1968). In a study of nearly 14,000 clients seen in 17 community mental health centers in the greater Seattle area over a three-year period, Sue (1977) found that about half of all ethnic-group clients failed to return after one session, significantly more than whites, although in his sample there was no difference in the type of service offered minority clients. Even when economic status is controlled statistically, the difference between minority and white clients in nonreturn rate remained statistically significant.

Arguments as to why minorities have a great need and yet benefit less from mental health services and what can be done to remedy the situation usually proceed from one of two fundamental assumptions. The first of these is that the concepts, institutions, and practices developed by the mental health establishment are ill-adapted to ethnic problems and needs and that, because of important cultural differences, traditional methods of psychotherapy are inadequate for the ethnic client (Weems, 1974). There is a lack of sensitivity to the ethnic Weltanschauung and life style, and the ways of minority peoples are as a result misunderstood. Clinical assessment techniques sometimes tend to underestimate their strengths and overemphasize their weaknesses. There is a desperate need for minority professionals in the field, and white mental health workers frequently hold unreceptive attitudes towards ethnic clients (Jones, 1974). Mental health settings are often alien and inaccessible to members of minority groups. In psychotherapy, the expectations of ethnic clients may not mesh with those of white therapists, and they are less likely to continue in treatment. Many minority individuals, especially the less well-educated, may need and want more direct intervention—explicit advice, financial counseling, vocational help—than is offered by traditional therapies. Various devices have been developed by community/clinical psychologists in an attempt to respond to these concerns—decentralized services, crisis intervention, and other brief and more active therapies, among others.

THE POLITICAL PERSPECTIVE

Origins of a Third World Psychology

The political or social change perspective in ethnicity and mental health includes a number of important themes, primary among them a deep and wide-ranging critique of traditional mental health practices, attitudes, research methods, and intervention techniques. This view derives from, or at least has been powerfully influenced by, progressive elements in minority communities, the Civil Rights Movement, and other important political and social change action undertaken by ethnic minorities in the last two decades. A manifestation of this social movement has been the challenge mounted by black intellectuals on prevailing conceptualizations of black social life (Billingsley, 1968) and their attack on the notion of black intellectual inferiority (Guthrie, 1976). Traditional social science scholarship has assumed that the personality and social structure of ethnic minorities derived from historical isolation and continued economic and cultural deprivation (Pettigrew, 1964; Deutsch, 1960; Rainwater, 1966). An expression of the political perspective can be found in the revisionist trend in social science thinking that is taking a fresh look at the circumstances and nature of ethnic minority history and culture in the context of the dominant culture and is asserting that the conventional misconceptions of ethnic social life and character have caused inherent strengths and adaptive qualities to be largely overlooked (Hays and Banks, 1980; Clark, 1973).

The political or social change perspective has also been profoundly critical of the adequacy of prevailing mental health practices for serving the needs of minority communities. Despite the strenuous effort on the part of community/clinical psychology to develop new approaches to intervention suited to the mental health needs of minority clients, those who espouse the political perspective still despair about the ultimate efficacy of such approaches for contributing to the improvement of health and well-being in minority communities. This reaction stems from the second assumption, i.e., that the problems of ethnic minority people arise from the massive social stresses of a racist society and can only be rectified through social action aimed at revolutionary change. Mental health care, especially as developed by white professionals, is at best a palliative; at worst, it detracts from recognizing the true source of the problem. The patient is not sick, society is, it is argued, and "blaming the victim" (Ryan, 1971) for difficulties caused by a social order that distorts his life locates the problem incorrectly and leads to misguided and ultimately futile attempts at intervention. The locus of the problem is instead the social context or system. The reality of social stress, economic disadvantage, and racial discrimination is self-evident. This is the context in which mental health interventions must occur and, as a result, will often fail. The individual who may in fact have benefitted substantially from a psychotherapy is forced to return to a pathogenic environment of poverty, community disorganization, and racism. The political perspective emphasizes the psychological damage of oppression and advocates broad social change as the only ultimate prevention and cure for psychological problems, which spring from oppression. In this view, social action is seen as the vehicle for psychological health, and social change is seen as a necessary precondition for personal change.

This theme within the political perspective has been influenced by revolutionary thinking in the Third World, as these nations around the globe struggle to achieve greater political and economic independence. Some minority scholars have noted the similarities in attitude and behavior of oppressed people of widely different cultural traditions and history as well as racial composition. Howard (1980) in a review of psychological studies of oppressed groups ranging from Algerians and South African blacks to Native Americans, Chinese Americans, and black Americans shows that many individuals among these groups view their world as hostile, frequently manifest symptoms of depression, and sometimes suffer from a sense of alienation, self-negation, and ambivalence about personal identity. The explanation seems to lie in the reciprocity between personality and social setting. The psychologically and economically colonized have been removed from history. There is frequently too little sense of continuity with the past, traditional cultural systems of reference have been destroyed, and historical values and social forms have lost their power to govern social relations and superintend personality organization.

No one has written more cogently or insightfully about the psychological problems that emanate from the loss of culture than A. Memmi (1967), a Jew born in Tunisia, and F. Fanon (1967, 1968), a black Martiniquean educated in France who experienced the Algerian revolution as a practicing psychiatrist. Both of these writers stress above all the destruction of the indigenous culture of those peoples colonized by the Europeans. In Rieff's (1966) terms, this entails the destruction of a compelling set of personal and cultural symbols. Culture provides the symbolic system, the moral demand system, which superintends the organization of personality. Such symbols include folk heroes, political legends, religious beliefs and rituals, and language, a most powerful carrier of culture. When the symbols of a culture lose their legitimacy, their power to compel, disruption occurs, not only within the culture, but within personalities within the culture. (DeVos in Chapter 4 also comments on this problem). The debilitating effects of the destruction of culture upon personalities within that culture is especially keen when the symbol system that attempts to usurp, or is superimposed upon, the traditional system of integrating symbols is antithetical to, or antagonistic towards, the values and symbols deeply rooted in traditional culture. Western culture and its symbols have tended to invalidate, and indeed denigrate, fundamental and important aspects of non-Western personality. This destroys not only the culture of the people it oppresses but also imposes a set of symbols, the acceptance and legitimization of which requires the rejection of part of the personality, part of the self. That is to say, because the ethnic minority's culture and its system of symbols is frequently vitiated or lost, a culture member may internalize negative stereotypes attributed to him by those of the dominant culture; in a sense, this becomes the new cultural superego. He may even begin to see himself in all those stereotypic fashions: he's weak, dependent, and so on—and he may even begin to act in ways that validate those stereotypes. Or, alternatively, he begins to reject himself and strives to become as much like those of the dominant culture as possible.

The conflicts surrounding identity for the ethnic person, and the critical relationship between ethnic identity, sense of self, mental health, and an individual's stance toward society have been frequently pointed out (DeVos, 1978; Erikson, 1968). Indeed, the problem of identity and the internal constraints that arise from it have been considered a prerequisite for all other solutions of personal conflicts (Essien-Udom, 1962). A variety of strategies have been adopted in an attempt to resolve this conflict: movement toward the dominant culture (assimilation), movement away (separation), and movement against (aggressive reactions) (Pettigrew, 1964; Gibbs, 1974). Cross (1978) has delineated several distinct stages of identity transformation detected in those who move away from a usually unstable and conflicted identification with the dominant culture to a more truly integrated sense of self that includes elements of ethnicity. Invariably, rejection of a more complete identification with the dominant culture to a sense of self that includes cultural and racial elements is associated with greater psychological well-being.

Rieff (1966), as well as contemporary community psychologists such as Sarason (1972), contends that psychological well-being depends upon membership in a community. Some sort of positive community is necessary that offers meaningfulness and hope through participant membership, and within which the individual can merge himself. All cultures serve such a function in so far as they are systems of symbolic integration, religious, philosophical, or ideological. The political perspective holds, then, that the remedial response of oppressed minorities to the devitalization of the traditional culture and the mass pathology this entails is a communal or commitment therapy. This is the therapy of choice because it offers the possibility of revitalizing some cultural form. Revitalization occurs when the traditional cultural symbol system becomes relegitimized in a social-change oriented framework, in which it reacquires its compelling quality. Memmi (1967) details the process in North Africa through which the young, formerly disaffected from traditional religion, returned to Islam during the Algerian revolution. Old rituals and religious forms were reintroduced and adapted to present-day needs.

A clear analogue to this phenomenon can be seen in the rise of the Nation of Islam in America (Essien-Udom, 1962). In attempting to explain this and other black nationalistic movements, scholars repeatedly return to the theme of alienation and the hopeless frustration that black Americans experience in trying to identify themselves and their aspirations with white society. The Nation of Islam in America can be seen as a positive community, which offers some kind of salvation, a community with which participating members can identify themselves and transform themselves in the classic mode of commitment therapy. Fanon (1968) points out how blacks the world over sought cultures that existed before the colonial era and describes their delight when they discovered not barbarism, but complex social and economic systems, sophisticated art forms, and personal dignity. The claim to a national culture not only rehabilitates a people, but serves as the hope of a future community. This symbolic activity aids the destruction of the identity with the oppressor and helps overcome alienation from self and society.

Efforts to infuse the old cultural symbolic with new meaning have found their expression not only in movements of cultural nationalism, but also in a renewed interest among minority communities in historical roots and ethnic cultures, a heightened sense of identification and affinity with group of origin as well as with other minority group members, and an emphasis on community solidarity and group action. They have also led to a reawakening of the painful dilemma over whether integration or separation, with all their symbolic meanings and implications for personal identity, is the more appropriate route to achieve more equal standing; and they have given rise to a number of groups and organizations powerfully committed to social change as well as quasi-therapeutic in orientation.

Related developments are the creation of psychologies specific to an ethnic group, e.g., an African Psychology (Khatib and Nobles, 1977), a Chinese psychology (Tong, 1971), and *a La Raza* psychology Martinez,

1977). More than substantive content areas, or coherent intellectual systems, these psychologies are in the line of a system of symbols or an ethos, an attempt to return to historical cultural symbols and infuse them with new meaning. According to African psychology, for example, the black American differs from whites especially in his retention of the (historically African) sense of being a communal person, one who subordinates personal goals and desires to the survival and well-being of the group (Nobles, 1980). This stands in direct contrast to the democratic, rugged individualism that represents the U.S. ethos and offers clear alternatives for identity and the potential for group-oriented social change action. (Another view of "Black Psychology" and its task of "deconstructive falsification" is presented by C. Banks in Chapter 3 of this volume). In a similar fashion, there has been a movement among Hispanics toward dissimilation, return to cultural roots, reassertion of ethnicity, to become politicized and active and proud of cultural differences (Padilla and Ruiz, 1973). The resurrection of myths and symbols in this fashion represents of broad social intervention in and of itself, with clear therapeutic possibilities.

Commitment therapies operate by returning the individual to a community, or they retrain him for membership in a new community with a more effective pattern of symbolic integration. They are transformative, often involving conversion experiences, usually authoritarian, and tend to take on religious or mythical symbolism. Most contemporary psychotherapies stand in contrast to commitment therapies and can be considered functional alternatives to them. Modern therapies historically arose in the era of democratic individualism and do not depend for their effects on a symbolic return to a positive community. The therapeutic experience is less transformative and committed than it is informative and neutral, and it tends to be antiauthoritarian.

From the political perspective, the psychotherapies that constitute the primary armamentarium of contemporary mental health professionals are inimical. Psychotherapy tends to promote individual, rather than group, solutions to the problems of alienation and identity conflict. Indeed, from the point of view of commitment therapies, the resolutions achieved in psychotherapy may be considered a symptom of illness, since the individual in some sense assumes a stance that is detached from the community. Commitment therapies generally belong to the classical tradition of moral demand systems and are culturally conservative while socially revolutionary. The antagonism of the political perspective to conventional treatment techniques results, then, not only from their inadequcy in meeting the needs of ethnic patients, but also because they represent a rival, and in this view inferior, therapeutic mode.

The renewal of old symbol systems unquestionably has had a major impact in ethnic minority communities. Still, these symbol systems are entirely compelling to only a small number, partly because they compete with traditional U.S. values, such as democratic individualism, equality under the law, and equal opportunity to advance, which have historically been powerful and appealing. The culturally conservative ideals represented by commitment therapies also conflict at points with other currents of social change, such as the Women's Liberation Movement. Nevertheless, the political perspective and the therapeutic of commitment will continue to have an important and by and large positive impact on minority social life. This movement, deeply rooted in history, and reflected widely in developments throughout the Third World today, is a vital manifestation of the efforts of ethnic minorities to achieve personal and social change.

Ethnic Communities and Community Control

The community mental health (community psychology, community psychiatry) movement grew in the same social matrix as the struggle for civil rights, economic and social equality, and racial pride and identity among ethnic people (Levine and Levine, 1970; Sarason, 1972; Goldenberg, 1971). It is linked to the political perspective through its core premise: that social-environmental factors create psychopathology and social systems change is needed for effective treatment. Attention shifted from factors within the individual to those of the social system. One stance within this movement, most frequently held by those in professional circles, emphasizes preventively oriented programs involving, for example, consultation to schools or other community facilities, or alterations in clinical programs to make them more accessible, more harmonious with community values, and more relevant to culturally diverse people. The community mental health centers, as mandated by federal legislation, were intended to facilitate care of the poor and ethnic groups by decentralizing psychiatric services and by providing outreach services, shorter term therapies, crisis intervention, 24-hour care, mental health education, community consultation, and the like. Programs were to be run with the collaboration of community people and to utilize indigenous nonprofessionals.

From the political perspective, however, the element within the community psychology movement that contained the greatest potential for large-scale social change was the concept of community control. Indeed, essential to this "bold, new approach" to mental health care was the concept of citizen participation in various aspects of the community mental health center, especially as official community representatives in decision-making processes. Various attempts (Kaplan and Roman, 1973) to assign purposes to citizen participation cluster into two categories. The first category, both less controversial and less political, concerns (1) service (organizational) objectives addressed to the problem of maximizing the provision of direct benefits to consumers, (2) informing clients and residents about services, and (3) gaining program legitimacy through greater utilization rates. The secondary category is explicitly addressed to political issues, particularly to the realignment of local community power. The ultimate goal is direct representation in the formal control of service programs, both government and private, by those community interests typically excluded from such positions.

Important ideological differences over treatment orientations, which parallel the health service delivery vs. systems intervention models (the health science idiom for an essentially political perspective) of community psychology, were from the very beginning a major problem in implementing treatment control. The traditional mental health view held, of course, that psychological problems are analogous to phsycial problems, psychological problems should be recognized and accepted, and treatment should be made available. Psychotherapy is therefore valued and respected. The more radical view holds that mental disorders are largely the result of such forces as poverty and social and racial oppression, and that the psychotherapist is an agent of society who attempts to adjust the "sick" individual to a profoundly disturbed social system, thereby serving to maintain the status quo. In the disease model, citizen involvement is minimized. More importantly, the disease model carries a treatment implication that directly contradicts the wishes of ethnic minority groups who no longer want services done to them, but who prefer that services are rendered for and with their collaboration.

In the systems intervention or institutional change model, citizen involvement is essential to achieve a solution to the problem. Many social activists began to regard the concept of community control as the ultimate means by which the poor and disenfranchised could finally achieve equality and a more responsive social welfare system. "What citizen participation does mean is participation in every dimension of our culture, our political system and our decision-making processes. It means full enfranchisement with respect to the totality of society's activities" (Cahn and Cahn, 1970). Darley (1974), too, writes that ethnic minorities are widely convinced of their inability to influence their own lives and that they adapt to that belief. He construes community psychology as a *therapeutic,* a means through which an individual or group may learn more clearly the reality of his or their situation and may acquire as much control over his life or their lives as is possible. Mogulof (1974) justifies community control as a means to decrease alienation and to engage the "sick" individual in a process that will contribute to his own healing. Also, Pierce notes: "The process of community involvement, that is participation and control,...is healthy for the community" (1975, p. 42).

The political perspective stressed that community mental health delivery systems should function as social action programs. In the mental health delivery system, efforts at social change were to reflect the priorities and sense of urgency of the ethnic community served, and the system was to take an active, aggressive role in that change (Hodges and Mahoney, 1970). In order to achieve this, control was to be taken out of the hands of the professional mental health worker and invested in community representatives. Even though community control has a more direct relationship to the operation of the mental health delivery system itself, it nevertheless provided a forum that community leaders could control and begin to organize and that could serve as a base for *political* action.

It is enormously telling that the impulse for institutional control in ethnic communities found its most direct focus in mental health care rather than in hospitals, or public schools, or community colleges. Although in some communities other institutions, especially public schools, became the target of community control efforts, community mental health centers were the most common battle grounds for this issue. It might be considered an historical accident, since mental health centers were institutions whose administrative and control structures had not yet become rigid and that seemed as a result of this as well as the democratic spirit in which they were conceived as potentially more pregnable to control by community people.

A perhaps more potent force was the intuitive recognition of the fact that a sense of empowerment, of group effort and belonging, and of being able to take greater control over one's destiny was an important source of positive morale and psychological well-being. The institution that purported to be concerned with the enhancement of emotional well-being became symbolically invested with this ideal and the struggle to achieve it.

Although community psychology emerged from a general sense of disillusionment in the field with the efficacy of conventional treatment approaches and traditional medical concepts (Korchin, 1976), the community control element within it must be credited more to ethnic minority leaders than to any other social influence (Altschuler, 1970). Indeed, most ethnic civil rights leaders considered control of social institutions essential to psychological and economic liberation (Carmichael and Hamilton, 1967). However, along with controlling social institutions in ethnic communities, there was at least an equal emphasis on developing a new consciousness. In the sense that it involved developing a healthier self and racial image and infusing ethnic cultural symbols with new, personal, and social change oriented meanings, the community control impulse can be viewed as the direct expression of a communal therapeutic.

The evaluation of the concept of community control obviously assumes a political and racial dimension. Various studies (Chu and Trotter, 1974; Flynn, 1973) have noted only modest citizen participation, especially with regard to autonomous decision-making power on important issues. The most prevalent form of citizen participation appears to be an advisory and consultative arrangement with seriously circumscribed power to influence policy (Tischler, 1971). Moreover, as long as actual sources of power remain unchallenged, acquisition of control of local mental health centers cannot significantly induce a realignment of power and resources either in the community or society at large. Community control has had the impact of creating more responsive and accessible health care systems and has given community members an unprecedented voice in resource allocation and determining program priorities. However, in the sense of formal control of mental health delivery systems, or with respect to the redistribution of power in the community, the community control thrust has largely failed. Its great success has been as a *therapeutic,* as a vehicle for action directed at personal and social change. As an expression of the need for greater self-determination and autonomy, it has been one of the more vigorous political components of a commitment therapy.

Attitudes toward Research

An important component of the political or social change perspective has been a powerful antagonism towards research conducted in minority communities (Sue and Sue, 1972). The general objection is that the results of this kind of research are biased in favor of the technological and white world. Much of this research has been comparative in nature, and minority groups have more often than not been conceptualized as deviant in respect to the dominant culture. Regardless of the aspect of psychological functioning on which the ethnic minority and whites are compared, the ethnic group is usually found to be deficient in some regard, be it in terms of psychological adjustment, self-concept, intellectual functioning, family structure, or linguistic styles (Katz, 1974; Nobels, 1973; Billingsley, 1968; Baratz and Baratz, 1970; Ramirez and Castaneda, 1974). Positive psychological factors have often been overlooked, while pathological elements have been emphasized.

Even where no bias exists, the product of the research is considered of no value to the people concerned; it is thought that such research does no more than perpetuate an industry for its own behalf. Researchers have failed to promote community involvement in their own activities and have failed to incorporate community service considerations in the design of investigations. There has been a failure to respond to the answers sought by those being studied; the problems have been structured in terms of theoretical concerns and not those of the people being investigated (Vargus, 1971; Hsu, 1973; Clark, 1973).

The antipathy toward empiricism, however, extends beyond a sense of being exploited and of being unfairly portrayed by research findings. It stems also from the view that the researcher is not an impartial observer, or seeker of truth, but an agent of the political and social status quo. This notion, intuitively grasped by community leaders, was best articulated by Marcuse (1964). It was the sense that the scientific world view involved a relatively uncritical submission to presumably objectively derived facts. Scientific formalism represented a preoccupation with a neutral mode of abstraction, statistics, mathematical models, and the like, to the exclusion of other, potentially critical modes, such as political theory. There was a realization that this perspective inhibited a genuinely critical view of our social system. From this perspective, not only does empiricism appear to have an anticritical bias, but it seems to contribute positively to the ideology of domination and manipulation. The ethnic minority understood, even if inchoately, that through the subordination of nature by scientific technology, the domination of man by man becomes increasingly effective. The minority population that is the target of research, often poor and powerless, becomes in this view the subject of prediction and control, to its ultimate disadvantage.

A Critique

The political or social change perspective in ethnicity and mental health has laid the groundwork for a number of critical developments in the field. Perhaps one of the most important contributions of this perspective has been the shift of focus away from the individual and the tendency to locate the source of all psychological problems within the person. It has alerted us to the fact that the disease or medical model contributes to the avoidance of social issues that are involved in the individual's malaise about himself and can in this sense contribute to the maintenance of the status quo. The political perspective has addressed and in part corrected an imbalance that existed in the traditional conceptions of psychopathology and its treatments by formally acknowledging the impact of socioeconomic issues and racism on the mental health of ethnic minority people.

Moreover, the communal therapeutic has served as a vital vehicle for personal and social change efforts. Indeed, greater numbers of minority people have undoubtedly been helped in their struggles with alienation, identity, self-respect, and an inner sense of debilitation by this social movement than those aided by conventional forms of mental health care. The political perspective has raised morale, contributed to community cohesiveness, and brought into sharper focus the social change goals that minority groups must pursue. It has engendered a sense of affinity with Third World peoples, and has reacquainted many minority individuals with the richness of their cultural heritage.

Nevertheless, there are some important limitations inherent in this point of view. One shortcoming of the political perspective lies in its unqualified antagonism toward contemporary mental health practices. Psychotherapy that improves the internal functioning of the individual does not necessarily adapt him to the existing social order, preempting his desire for social change. On the contrary, he may indeed become more effective in focusing on the insufficiencies of his social environment and become increasingly effectual in reaching out in some way to change his condition. The problem is that too many individuals in fact defeat themselves in reaching out for desirable and proper social objectives. The idea, then, that psychotherapy promotes only individual solutions to psychological dilemmas, thereby diverting the impulse for social system change, is seriously shortsighted.

Another limitation of the political perspective is its very strong propensity toward a kind of social reductionism, i.e., the notion that all psychological problems derive, in some way, from social conditions in every instance. This view neglects to take into account that ethnic minority individuals can suffer from psychological conflicts that are associated not at all, or only minimally, with social conditions. Psychological therapies are clearly needed to deal with problems of psychological (cognitive and emotional) structure. Within the political perspective, too, lies a danger that the individual may externalize his problems and fail to assume responsibility for dysfunctional patterns of behavior that, if changed and corrected, could result in greater personal efficacy and satisfaction in living despite an unfavorable social context. In this way, the political perspective diminishes the importance of the individual asserting what control he can over his personal existence, however limited this control might be by external social forces.

A related issue is the problem of short-term strategies. While the ultimate goal for ethnic minorities must be large-scale social change, experience suggests that this will require unremitting effort over an extended period of time, perhaps even generations. There remains the problem of treating ethnic individuals who are in psychological distress now, and existing forms of mental health care can clearly contribute here. It must be kept in mind, too, that even in a more ideal society there are likely to be psychological casualties, for whom the treatment of choice would seem to be some form of psychotherapy.

Finally, the hostility of the political perspective to research in minority communities, while understandable and justifiable, may well be self-defeating in the long term. As S. Sue points out in Chapter 2 of this volume, good, nonbiased research is needed if we are to anticipate properly the mental health and medical needs of ethnic communities. Though much of the research of the past has been patronizing, even damaging, this does not obviate the need to know how things are. The problems inherent in research being conducted from outside the ethnic community can in part be remedied today by work done by members of ethnic groups seeking to discover not only what *is not* functioning well in individuals and communities, but also what *is* working well. Those who hold the political viewpoint would, of course, argue that just as current mental health practices are not suited for the minority person, so too research strategies, assessment techniques, and other tools of empirical investigation are irrevocably biased, and that no matter what the ethnicity of those who employ these methods, biased results are a foregone conclusion. However, we would propose that a *cross-cultural* view of ethnicity and mental health will prove very useful in addressing many of the difficult problems in clinical intervention and research with minority populations that have been identified and highlighted by the political perspective.

THE CROSS-CULTURAL PERSPECTIVE

Another perspective on the topic of ethnicity and mental health might be termed a cross-cultural approach. Just as anthropologists attempt to understand the meaning of the behaviors of people of different nationalities in terms of their values, norms, life conditions, their history and heritage, and the adaptive problems they face, the field would gain greatly if ethnic groups of our society were viewed in similar fashion (Korchin, 1980). The cross-cultural framework is sympathetic to the relatedness of particular behaviors to the larger pattern of the ethnic culture, rather than being based simply on the imposition of dominant culture values. It is culturally pluralistic. This is not to exaggerate differences among peoples, but to understand their meaning in terms of the cultures in which they are discovered. From a scientific standpoint, this conceptual model has important heuristic promise. The recognition of differences is the first step toward the development of a theory and a research method appropriate to the understanding of cultural diversity. Within the cross-cultural framework proposed here, the crucial issue is to understand functioning or particular behaviors as they make sense within a particular culture, though with a readiness to evaluate and propose change in terms of more universal standards. Moreover, the cross-cultural perspective fosters a greater sensitivity to the role that values play in the study of ethnic peoples.

Ethnicity and the Concept of Subjective Culture

What, more precisely, is meant by a cross-cultural approach to understanding the status of ethnicity in mental health? Cross-cultural psychology has more generally been defined as "the empirical study of members of various culture groups who had different experiences that lead to predictable and significant differences in behavior" (Brislin, Lonner, and Thorndike, 1973, p. 5). It has been a matter of some debate whether the study of minority groups within a society can be properly considered "cross-cultural." Until recently, most cross-cultural comparisons were of groups who speak different languages and are governed by different political units. Some (e.g., Frijda and Jahoda, 1966) have even attempted to make a distinction between "cross-national" and cross-cultural studies. Cross-national refers to comparing nations of Western culture to each other, while cross-cultural studies are those that compare Western populations with traditional, usually preliterate societies, or comparisons of subjects from these societies to one another. (See also G. DeVos, Chapter 4 of this volume, for another view on this debate).

However, as Price-Williams (1975) points out, the problem with these perhaps too facile definitions is that they imply a comparison of two or more cultures, thereby excluding studies in which only one culture is investigated. First of all, this suggests that a given culture is relatively homogeneous, which, as Schwartz (1978) notes, can be more than a little misleading. Moreover, the construct of culture as defined by geography, anthropology, or political science need not necessarily have psychological relevance. The issue is tying the psychology of behavior with the cultural element, and in this respect the distinctions between "intracultural" "cross-cultural," and "cross-national" investigations are of secondary importance, since no fundamental difference in methodology is involved. Moreover, as Lonner (1980a) has noted, studies of culturally distinct groups within a nationality are increasingly given the status of legitimate cross-cultural investigations.

Given the complexities of defining culture (Kroeber and Kluckhohn [1952] list 150 definitions) the hypothesis is that ethnic minority groups in the United States have separate and distinct cultures is, given the historical, anthropological, and sociological data, a tenable hypothesis. The case for Chicano and Asian-American groups is perhaps more readily apparent, though the argument for distinct cultural elements among black Americans has also been made (DuBois, 1908; Herskovitz, 1958) and more recently, with greater frequence (e.g., Price-Williams, 1975; Word, 1979; Billingsley, 1968). The problem of whether or not racial minorities have separate cultures and whether or not it is appropriate to consider comparisons between these groups and white samples as essentially cross-cultural comparisons can be circumvented through the notion of "subjective culture" (Osgood, 1965; Triandis, 1972). Subjective culture is a group's characteristic way of perceiving its social environment. It can be analyzed by referring to already well-established concepts such as attitudes, roles, and values. For example, people who live near one another, speak the same dialect, and engage in similar activities are likely to share the same subjective culture. Propinquity, a common language, and similar activities tend to lead to high rates of interaction among members of human groups. Frequent interaction usually leads to similar norms, attitudes, and roles and hence to similar subjective cultures. Ethnic similarity also leads to high rates of interaction and hence to similarities in subjective culture (Triandis, 1976).

Implications for Research

Research reports have generally portrayed ethnic minorities in a negative fashion, finding them with unremitting regularity to be disadvantaged or deficient in some way (Katz, 1974). Such findings have led to a "deficit hypothesis," which, stated briefly, rests on the assumption that a community subject to poverty and oppression is a disorganized community, and this disorganization expresses itself in various forms of psychological deficit in realms ranging from intellectual performance (Kamin, 1974; Guthrie, 1976) to personality functioning (Proshansky and Newton, 1968) and psychopathology (Kardiner and Ovesey, 1951; Baughman and Dahlstrom, 1972). These sorts of misconceptions about the psychology and social functioning of minority persons arose from a "psychology of race differences" tradition. Studies typically involved the comparison of ethnic and white groups on measures standardized on white, middle-class samples, administered by examiners of like background, intended to assess variables conceptualized on the basic U.S. population.

The "deficit hypothesis" has increasingly been challenged, and serious question has been raised concerning the methodological adequacy of ethnic research in the United States (Gynther, 1972; Cole and Bruner, 1971). Minority investigators in particular are alert to the questionable validity of research involving ethnic subjects; they are acutely aware of the limitations and culture bound nature of the many commonly employed measurement techniques; they know only too well the dangers in interpreting the frequently easily obtained significant findings derived from these instruments. Indeed, minority psychologists have played an instrumental role in expressing community concerns about the potentially harmful effects of such studies and have led the revolt against unrestrained research in minority communities (Williams, 1974). They have proclaimed the preeminent right to conduct studies of ethnic people, claiming, among other things, that they alone are sensitive enough to the issues and that ethnic status is essential for the appropriate interpretation of the data, since this requires an intimate knowledge and subjective understanding of the cultural context that only racial membership can confer (Clark, 1973). However, ethnic researchers have not assumed a leadership role in conducting research on their groups of origin, primarily because of the very formidable methodological barriers that are immediately encountered. It is, then, not only ideological and political resistance that has stymied minority research efforts; it is also an uncertainty as to correct method and technique, a failure to move beyond a challenge to the assumptions underlying prevailing approaches and models and to actively assert a more appropriate methodology. The following discussion will attempt to delineate the difficulties inherent in attempting to apply conventional methods of investigation to ethnic populations and to point the way toward a more appropriate (cross-cultural) conceptualization of technique for such studies.

Among the problems confronting the researcher conducting research with ethnic populations are: the influence of race of the experimenter or the tester on subjects, the effect of socially related motivational and situational factors associated with test-taking behavior on dependent variables (i.e., differences in levels of anxiety generated by the experimental situation, familiarity with test materials, etc.), as well as the more strictly methodological issues of control groups and the validity of commonly used measurement instruments for cultural minorities.

One of the foremost problems is the existence of adequate control groups. Regardless of whether ethnic groups alone are studied (e.g., Griffin and Korchin, 1980) or comparisons of ethnic and white subjects are made, nomothetic research requires control over such gross variables as education and socioeconomic status if the more subtle aspects of psychological functioning are to be teased out. Control of the socioeconomic variable presents particularly vexing difficulties. Although the economic position of ethnic minorities has somewhat improved over the past three decades in absolute terms, the ratio of incomes of minority groups to that of whites has not changed dramatically (Valdes and Steiner, 1972). As a result, the distribution of economic levels for whites and ethnic minorities is not equivalent.

An example of the problems that ensue from this fact can be found in the body of research that has concerned itself with the comparison of black and white MMPI (Minnesota Multiphasic Personality Inventory) profiles. One such study (Butcher, Ball, and Ray, 1964) was explicitly designed to investigate the effects of socioeconomic level on MMPI differences in black and white college students. Although the researchers found that differences emerged between black and white subjects who were matched on socioeconomic status (SES), they are, unlike most investigators, careful to point out the difficulties in equating SES for black and white subjects. They claim that while college subjects can be matched reasonably well on the basis of their parents' occupation, there is no guarantee that black subjects are of the same SES as white subjects since both income and job conditions differ for blacks and whites. They point to yet another difficulty that arose after the subjects had been assigned to socioeconomic levels. The lowest SES level, level 5 according to their classification system, could not be considered equivalent for whites and blacks since this was the modal level for black subjects and the lowest level for the white group. Thus, in the matched comparison, low status white subjects were being compared with blacks who were in the modal SES level for their group. The researchers were, as a result, forced to conclude that any differences that they discovered may well have been an artifact of the inadequate control over the socioeconomic variable.

Careful indices of socioeconomic status (e.g., Hollingshead and Redlich, 1958) devised on all-white populations frequently do not transfer easily to black populations because the definition of the *status* (i.e., how you are perceived in the eyes of the other) aspects of SES may be different in different populations. A possible remedy for this problem was attempted by Parker and Kleiner (1964) in their study of black status, mobility, and identity. They developed an SES index based on the various criteria of social status mentioned by members of the Philadelphia black community in which they worked. These criteria included education, area of residence, income, family background, occupation, membership in organizations, and influence in the community. The result of their efforts was a seven-step occupation scale and a formula that relatively weighed education, income, and occupation in a manner far different from Hollingshead's procedure.

Another issue relevant to the problem of contrast groups, especially with Hispanic and Asian-American populations, is level of acculturation. Ramirez and Castaneda (1974), for example, found that children and their mothers from a Mexican-American community that was largely acculturated were more field dependent than mothers and children from "dualistic" communities whose members were influenced by both the Anglo and Mexican culture. Among Hispanics, too, level of acculturation has been shown to be related to patterns of conflict resolution (Kagan, Zahn, and Gealy, 1977), sex-role standards and behaviors (Tharp, et al., 1968) and alcohol abuse (Madsen, 1964). More acculturated individuals have also been shown to have a greater likelihood of continuing, and succeeding, in psychotherapy (Miranda, et al., 1976; Padilla, Carlos, and Keefe, 1976). It would, then, appear to be critical for studies of many ethnic populations to attempt to control for, or at least assess in some fashion, acculturation level.

The problem of controls highlights the potential for error in the tendency to view a given ethnic group as a homogenous population. The enormous variance associated with differences in environmental context, geographic region, acculturation, or education is often underestimated. Generalizations about ethnic groups need to be qualified with reference to the specific characteristics of the population under investigation.

There has already been a good deal of controversy around the theme of cultural bias in measurement instruments. Not surprisingly, this problem is one of the most difficult confronted by cross-cultural researchers (Dawson, 1971). Almost all psychological measures have been validated on majority populations, and consequently their validity for minority groups may be quite different from that for their standardization and validation groups. Discussions of IQ tests have made this clear (Cole, et al., 1971). Yet another example can be drawn from projective techniques. The definitive standardization information provided on the location, accuracy, determinants, and content of Rorschach responses was obtained from white middle-class samples (Beck, et al., 1961). Little information exists as to how ethnic groups might differ in their responses. The essential problem is one of establishing whether experimental stimuli are equivalent for different cultural groups. There are clear differences among cultural groups in cognitive categories, especially in response to visual stimuli (Triandis, 1972). Nonnormative responses by ethnic subjects to the Rorschach could possibly reflect attention to subtly different aspects of stimulation, as well as different meaning categories, rather than perceptual or cognitive distortions (e.g., Padilla and Ruiz, 1975). Until more is known about the influence of ethnic cultures on responses to the Rorschach, it is only reasonable that standard scoring categories be applied with caution. But perhaps even more important than the cautious application of scoring categories is the very nature of the interpretation of responses. Inferences about the meaning of responses to projective techniques are particularly vulnerable to cultural bias.

Another example is the fairly extensive work that has been done on racial differences on the MMPI. Studies have shown that blacks are consistently more elevated on certain MMPI scales than whites (Gynther, 1972). Despite the fact that these elevations are relative to majority population norms, and the fact that the pattern that emerges reflects no readily apparent clinical picture, still many white researchers have interpreted these differences to mean that blacks suffer from more pathology than whites (Baughman and Dahlstrom, 1972). More objective investigators view the consistent differences between blacks and whites that emerge even when such variables as education and socioeconomic status are relatively well controlled as a manifestation of cultural differences and have called for the construction of separate black and white norms.

However, this may be insufficient remedy, since it appears that MMPI *items* differ in their psychological significance for blacks and whites. A number of attempts have been made to explore the sources of variance that underlie the race variable by performing item analyses. One such study found that MMPI items are much more sensitive to racial differences than are the scales (Harrison and Kass, 1967). A similar analysis of items (Jones, 1978a) drawn from both the MMPI and the California Personality Inventory found significant differences in the nature of black and white subjects' response to more than 80 percent of the item pool and, moreover, determined that ethnic differences in responses could in many cases be readily understood in terms of differences in life style, demography, and culture. In short, ethnic differences on measures of psychopathology like the MMPI are less likely due to differences in actual level of adjustment than to differences in the *meaning* of items from one group to another. This, of course, implies that a different set of validation studies must be established for minority subjects (L. Snowden and P. Todman provide an excellent discussion of problems of psychological assessment from a cross-cultural perspective in Chapter 8 of this volume).

A very important, but less recognized, difficulty in studies of ethnic subjects is the influence of the race of the experimenter or tester on subjects of another race and culture. Numerous studies have extensively documented the differential effects of white and black interviewers, experimenters, or testers on the interview responses, projective test responses, IQ test performance, manual dexterity test performance, and even the galvanic skin responses of black subjects (Sattler, 1970). There is some evidence, too, that black and white experimenters and testers have a differential effect on white subjects (Riess, Schwartz, and Cottingham, 1950). While evidence demonstrates the existence of a race-of-experimenter effect, the existing data are inconsistent and do not yield sufficient information to provide a basis from which definitive statements can be made as to what that effect is. Although it appears that in certain experimental situations white experimenters can have a positive effect on black subjects' performance on a particular task (Katz, Henchy, and Allen, 1968), in general, blacks interact more comfortably and function more effectively with other blacks (Allen, Dubanowski, and Stevenson, 1966). Interviewers, experimenters, and testers who are of the same ethnicity as their subjects are more likely to obtain fewer biased responses and better performance than those who are of a different race than their respondents. However, this must be stated with some qualifications, since the race of the experimenter can differentially affect subjects depending on the nature of the experimental situation and that of the experimental task; motivational and situational factors can strongly influence dependent measures, and these factors may interact with the race of tester to produce a pronounced biasing effect (see Sattler, 1970; Katz, 1968).

Studies show that blacks tend to become resistant and underproductive when asked to solve problems cooperatively with whites (Katz and Cohen, 1962), perform less well on tasks that are described as intellectual tests, especially when comparison with whites is anticipated, and though they usually perform better with a black tester, in some instances perform better with a white tester (Kennedy and Vega, 1965). It appears that for black subjects, a white environment (i.e., being among a group of white subjects with a white tester) is more stressful than is a black environment. If the stress is not too great, it may actually enhance black subjects' performance. However, if stress is beyond an optimal level, performance is lowered, particularly if the perceived probability of success is small (Katz, Roberts, and Robinson, 1965). Intellectual testing situations in particular appear to create high stress conditions for black subjects, and they tend to perform more poorly when a task is described as a test of intelligence as opposed to, say, a test of motor coordination (Katz, Epps, and Axelson, 1964). In any case, these findings enormously complicate attempts to delineate specifically the "race of tester" effect, for it is clear that a complex interaction effect exists between the race of tester, the race of other subjects in the experimental setting, and the perceived nature of the experimental task. This in turn suggests that the dynamics of the interracial experimental situation must be considered within the context of the more general social psychology of the relationship dynamics between the races.

Another aspect of the experimental situation that has been largely overlooked is the very means by which data are gathered. In ethnic communities the approaches that researchers typically employ may appear to be completely novel or even threatening. R. Lum, in Chapter 7 of this volume, notes that Asian Americans are often very reluctant to respond to interviewers or surveys, and a number of investigators have commented on the discomfort of many ethnic subjects when confronted with paper and pencil measures (Cole and Bruner, 1971) and with psychological assessment procedures in general (Triandis, 1976).

Yet another related element is that of language. Especially among Hispanics and Asian Americans, English may not be the most commonly used or familiar language. And among many blacks, particularly in the youth culture, "black English" is the predominant mode of expression (Labov, 1972; Ervin-Tripp, 1972). It has been argued that black English, which varies from standard English in important and systematic ways, is a precise language with a history and grammar of its own (Dillard, 1972). There is some evidence, too, that suggests minorities describe others in their environment with greater specificity and differentiation when they use an idiom that is most familiar (Labov, 1970; Smith, 1973). It is possible, then, that when many ethnic subjects are asked to perceive or describe themselves in some fashion, a task essential to most clinical assessment procedures, they may attain greater specificity and finer discrimination if they do so in a familiar idiom and, conversely, may lose subtlety and complexity if they are required to do so in standard English.

The attitudes that ethnic subjects bring with them to an assessment situation are very important, though largely overlooked and poorly understood. Clearly, they are often likely to be very different from those that majority group subjects bring to such situations. It does seem quite possible that ethnic subjects view most assessment situations as a means for whites, but not themselves, to get ahead in society (Pettigrew, 1964). This has certainly been true generally of testing; from literacy tests used to determine voter eligibility to those used to determine qualifications for employment, tests have been designed to, or have effectively resulted in, keeping minorities down and out. It would make sense, then, that ethnic subjects would approach the assessment situation differently, i.e., with a different interpretive framework from that of whites. The import of this for motivational differences is not difficult to discern. Certainly empirical data can be obtained from both minorities and whites, but the *meaning* of the procedures for subjects of different ethnic groups, and hence the meaning of the data, may differ drastically.

The problems discussed here stem from the failure of investigators to conceptualize studies of ethnic groups as cross-cultural comparisons, from an unwillingness to recognize such efforts as being legitimately and appropriately cross-cultural enterprises. They are likely to be better managed if a cross-cultural research paradigm were systematically applied. Admittedly, a standard method for cross-cultural research has not yet been systematized (Triandis, Malpass, and Davidson, 1973). Nevertheless, adherence to the *principles* of a cross-cultural approach will help to avoid all-too-common and serious errors and will aid as a guide to the eventual development of an appropriate methodology.

Berry (1969) has proposed a promising strategy for cross-cultural comparisons. He points out that a researcher necessarily begins a study of a different culture by employing categories of experience and instruments derived from his own culture, which are, to a greater or lesser degree, alien to the culture being studied. A commonality in the problems discussed above is that such categories are presumed to be universal (or etic). However, most often these are indigenous (or emic) to the majority culture. Forcing aspects of the culture into this framework often leads to a comparison of incomparables, i.e., a lack of equivalence of meaning.

A first step in developing an etic methodology is determining whether the behavior of interest has functional equivalence, i.e., whether or not similar activities have similar or different functions across ethnic groups. If certain behaviors appear similar on the surface, but their meanings or functions differ, then they cannot be used for comparative purposes. The behavior must have similar psychological meaning. Second, an appropriate descriptive framework must be constructed that describes the behavior in terms that are meaningful to members of the ethnic culture, which at the same time allows comparison with that behavior in the majority culture. Almost all studies of ethnic groups have assumed universal descriptive categories, but which have been in fact "pseudoetic" (Triandis, 1972), i.e., not genuinely universal. In fact, there has been a long standing debate as to the existence of cultural universals. Cultural relativists argue that meaningful interpretation and comparisons across cultures cannot be based on universal categorization; rather, each culture must be understood in it own terms. A detailed examination of this issue is beyond the scope of this chapter (see Lonner, 1980b for a summary of perspectives on this topic). In any case, culture-bound categories must be modified until they are truly descriptive of the behavior of a given ethnic culture. There may be some categories that are in fact universal, or at least equivalently descriptive across cultures. But some basic categories, such as notions of intelligence (Cole and Bruner, 1971) and deviance (Edgerton, 1978), may require substantial modification.

A particularly serious problem is in the cross-cultural use of tests and scales. When scales are applied outside the population in which they were developed, differences between cultural groups are essentially uninterpretable. Triandis (1972) has suggested that one approach to this dilemma is to start with a construct that appears to have universal status and to develop emic (culturally specific) ways to measure it. Again, however, a universal or "culture-free" construct may be an illusory abstraction since it does not take into account person-culture interaction. More modestly, if the instrument can be modified to reflect categories of experience relevant to ethnic cultures and still retain some semblance of its original nature, it would tap elements common to both cultures. From this transcultural framework, valid comparison could then be made. This model has been successfully used in comparisons of U.S. ethnic minorities with subjects of foreign cultures (Jones and Zoppel, 1979) and U.S. whites (Jones, 1979). (See L. Snowden and P. Todman, Chapter 8, for an extended discussion of this topic).

Implications for Clinical Interventions

A cross-cultural approach is far more congenial with current mental health practices than is a political perspective. Indeed, it contributes a great deal to mental health work with minorities by providing another, potentially very fruitful way of thinking about clinical problems and therapeutic interventions with ethnic clients. As noted earlier in this chapter, studies of Hispanics, Japanese Americans, and Chinese Americans show that these groups are less likely to be found in psychiatric facilities. While some argue that low utilization rates result from institutional policies that discourage entry by these ethnic groups and deter continuation in treatment once initiated (see H. Kitano, Chapter 6, as well as R. Muñoz, Chapter 14, in this volume), others maintain that elements of these cultures (e.g., family structure or parental roles) provide a certain immunity from the stress and social degradation inherent in minority status, which in turn leads to lower frequency and severity of mental illness (e.g., G. DeVos, Chapter 4). A cross-cultural perspective, that is, an acknowledgment of cultural differences in social forms, traditions, and world view, would promote a more effective investigation and understanding of epidemiology, mental health utilization, and naturally occurring therapeutic forces (such as social support networks) within ethnic communities.

A cross-cultural approach would also promote a greater interest in, and understanding of, the use and efficacy of folk healing traditions. There is evidence that indigenous therapists—whether curanderos, herbalists, Puerto Rican spiritualists, faith healers, or religious men—can relieve psychological distress (Kiev, 1964; Lebra, 1976). The investigation of indigenous treatment approaches in a cross-cultural framework may help inform about the circumstances in which these treatments can be effective and could, furthermore, lead to the identification of aspects of conventional treatment methods that sometimes render them less effective with ethnic clients.

Another realm in which a cross-cultural perspective is essential is in making judgments about the presence and extent of psychopathology in ethnic clients. Most mental health workers proceed on the assumption of the pancultural (i.e., etic) generality of categories, criteria, and theories of psychopathology originated in Western cultures. Minority clinicians have long objected that standard psychiatric nomenclature does not recognize cultural variation in symptomatology. This position is quite consistent with a growing view among cross-cultural psychologists that problems of identifying cases of psychopathology in clients from different cultures, and comparing incidence and forms of psychopathology across cultures, need to be reconsidered. The discussion concerning whether established nosological categories of description and explanation are fully appropriate for studying other cultures is simply an extension of the etic–emic distinction into the realm of psychopathology.

The question of what criteria should be used for assessing psychological disorder is clearly as much an ethical and value issue as it is a technical and scientific one. The problem becomes somewhat complicated in view of the fact that ethnic cultures are contained in the majority culture, for the question then arises: according to which cultural standard ought deviant behavior be assessed? From the standpoint of clinical intervention, the answer is clear— the culture from which the client comes must be seen in its own terms. In order to justify an interpretation of behavior as an instance of psychopathology, it must be established that there is intersubjective agreement among members of the culture that the behavior in question represents an exaggeration or distortion of culturally acceptable behavior and belief.

A most obvious example is culture-specific syndromes, such as *ataque,* which is found primarily among Puerto Ricans (Levine and Padilla, 1980). This syndrome, somewhat akin to hysterical conversion reactions, is characterized by psychomotor seizures during which the victim cries or screams, falls to the ground, and flails extremities. While fairly common among this ethnic group, it is virtually unknown in the majority population and hence is prone to be misdiagnosed as a more severe form of illness than it actually is. A somewhat similar syndrome, termed "falling out," which has been observed among southern blacks and West Indian immigrants, is frequently misdiagnosed as epilepsy or a form of psychosis (Weidman, 1979). Yet another example is the pathological significance of hallucinations among Hispanics. Torrey (1972) has demonstrated that Mexican Americans associate hearing voices significantly less with psychological disturbance than Anglo subjects. Hearing voices is more culturally sanctioned among Hispanics and hence is a highly unreliable index of pathology; nevertheless, hallucinations are often employed as a standard of maladjustment of equal import for Hispanics and whites (see A. Meadow, Chapter 13, for an interesting clinical discussion of this issue). In short, behavior that may be misjudged as severely disturbed may be reinterpreted as merely culturally different, or less seriously pathological, when it is evaluated in terms of the cultural milieu in which it appears.

Although culture-specific syndromes are particularly dramatic in calling attention to the utility of a cross-cultural framework, there are more subtle examples that are perhaps of greater import because of their wider generality. In a recent study, a large sample of black and white clinicians were asked to assess the level of adjustment of black psychotherapy patients on a number of rating scales (Jones, in press). White therapists tended to view black patients as significantly more disturbed than did black therapists, particularly in their assessments of symptomatology and ratings of the quality or nature of family relationships. It is very likely that these different ratings of adjustment level represent differences in culturally influenced notions about what constitutes psychopathology and what characterizes good family relationships. The fact that differences emerged in the areas of symptoms and family life is hardly surprising, since it is precisely around these issues that there has been a fair amount of controversy. It has been shown that, especially in the domain of less severe psychological disturbance, blacks and whites hold varying conceptions of mental illness (Crawford, 1969) and that certain forms of behavior frequently considered signs of disturbance by majority clinicians may in fact serve adaptive functions among blacks (Grier and Cobbs, 1968). In a similar vein, the characteristics of the black family, its health and its stability, has been a source of debate among social scientists, with blacks and whites usually assuming conflicting points of view (e.g., Billingsley, 1968). It seems likely, then, that judgments about psychological disturbance will vary between ethnic minority and majority clinicians at points of divergence between their cultures.

It would be wise, however, to be cautious about rejecting conventional psychiatric diagnostic categories as completely culturally irrelevant. Particularly in the realm of very severe disturbance, they may have a good deal of utility since such disorders as psychosis or addictive behavior tend to be recognized as deviant in cultures throughout the world (Murphy, 1976). What is important is to attempt to evaluate and understand behavior in the social and cultural context in which it occurs.

The importance of a cross-cultural perspective for the development of accommodations or adjustments in psychological intervention strategies to improve their efficacy for ethnic minorities has now begun to be explored. It cannot be assumed that the tools and techniques that are effective with majority group clients will be applicable to the same degree with ethnic clients. The cultural adaptiveness of each technique must be investigated. An early step in this direction is the pluralistic counseling model developed by Levine and Padilla (1980). In their terms, pluralistic counseling requires a special awareness of the client's cultural beliefs, values, and behaviors and is concerned with the client's adaptation to his cultural milieu. It is important for the therapist to be aware of both minority and majority cultures, points of contact between them, and the process by which cultural standards influence the individual. Without such familiarity, it is often exceedingly difficult to empathize accurately and distinguish the realities of the client's experiences from psychologically determined distortions. In short, therapists must assume an emic posture when working with ethnic clients, one that allows an empathetic grasp of how culture and social position influence their phenomenology (Devereaux, 1978). Indeed, there is growing evidence that traditional psychotherapies, when conceived in a cross-cultural framework, can be successful with minority clients (Jones, 1978b; Griffith and Jones, 1978; Lorion, 1978; Lerner, 1972).

Much of this volume is dedicated to the task of further extending and elaborating the implications of a cross-cultural perspective for intervention. In the realm of family therapy, for example, C. Carrillo (Chapter 10) emphasizes the importance of an awareness of both traditional Mexican-American family structure and sex roles, as well as the evolution they undergo when contact with U.S. culture is made. Similarly, N. Boyd (Chapter 9) discusses the importance of including members of the extended family in the treatment of black families, as well as the utility of strengthening ties with community support networks. R. Muñoz (Chapter 14) makes clear the critical importance of a staff familiar with the language and values of their clientele for a community mental health center serving Hispanic populations. In the realm of special populations, A. Franklin (Chapter 11) provides important insights on the treatment of black adolescents and encourages an awareness not only of black culture, but of youth mores and life styles in the treatment of this group, while Szapocznik, et al. (Chapter 12) demonstrates that even when new techniques are devised for a population such as the aged, they must be culturally sensitive to be effective. These chapters, as well as others, are abundant documentation of the value of a cross-cultural perspective in guiding intervention strategies with ethnic minority clients.

CONCLUSION

This introductory chapter has attempted to sort through the varied, and sometimes tangled and conflicting, strands of thought current in the field of ethnicity and mental health. Two major themes have been identified: the political and the cross-cultural. It often seems that those who work in the area of minority mental health are caught in a continuing intellectual and ethical struggle between those two points of view, perspectives that appear to present opposing ways of conceptualizing critical issues in the field. We know all too well that our efforts at helping individuals can be vitiated by psychologically unfavorable social conditions, and we are keenly aware that our endeavors pale against the enormity of the task. Yet, we are concerned with how to more effectively intervene with those who are now suffering, in an immediate way, from psychological distress. As community/clinical psychology begins to pursue the goal of primary prevention, we must address the issue of whether our means of intervention are adequate for the task of the institutional, and even broader social change, that prevention demands. And there remains the troublesome question of whether research can ultimately become a tool for change and better health care, or whether it will continue to primarily reflect an imbalance in political and economic power.

Those who are committed to the field of minority mental health must continue to contend with these dilemmas. There are no easy answers. This discussion has simply attempted to address the dialectic between these two basic orientations to the field, the political and the cross-cultural, and to suggest, in the end, that if the issues are clarified, and points of conflict and harmony are uncovered, the two can coexist. Through the application of the principles of a cross-cultural psychology, intervention and research strategies can be strengthened and rendered more effective. Nevertheless, at the same time this work must remain highly attuned to the political and social change context in which it must be carried out.

REFERENCES

Allen, S.A., Dubanowski, N.A., and Stevenson, H.W. Children's performance as a function of race of E, race of S, and type of verbal reinforcement. *Journal of Experimental Child Psychology* 4 (1966):248-56.

Altschuler, A. *Community Control: The Black Demand for Participation in Large American Cities.* New York: Pegasus, 1970.

Baratz, S. and Baratz, J. Early childhood intervention: The social science base of institutional racism. *Harvard Educational Review* 40 (1970):29-50.

Baughman, E. and Dahlstrom, W.G. Racial differences on the MMPI. In *Black Psyche: The Modal Personality Pattern of Black Americans,* edited by S. Guterman. Berkeley, Calif.: Glendessory Press, 1972.

Beck, S., Beck, A., Levitt, E., and Molish, H. *Rorschach's Test.* New York: Grune and Stratton, 1961.

Berry, J.W. On cross-cultural comparability. *International Journal of Psychology,* 4 (1969):119-28.

Billingsley, A. *Black Families in White America.* Englewood Cliffs, N.J.: Prentice-Hall, 1968.

Brislin, R.W., Lonner, W.J., and Thorndike, R.M. *Cross-Cultural Research Methods.* New York: John Wiley & Sons, 1973.

Brown, T.R., Stein, K.M., Huang, K., and Harris, D.E. Mental illness and the role of mental health facilities in Chinatown. In *Asian-Americans: Psychological Perspectives,* edited by S. Sue and N. Wagner. Palo Alto, Calif: Science and Behavior Books, 1973.

Butcher, J., Ball, B., and Ray, E. Effects of socio-economic level on MMPI differences in Negro-White college students. *Journal of Counseling Psychology* 11 (1964): 83-87.

Cahn, E. and Cahn, J. Maximum feasible participation: A general overview. In *Citizen Participation: A Case Book in Democracy,* edited by E. Cahn and B. Dassett. Princeton, N.J.: Community Action Training Institute, 1970.

Carmichael, S. and Hamilton, C. *Black Power.* New York: Random House, 1967.

Chu, F. and Trotter, S. *The Madness Establishment.* New York: Center for the Study of Responsive Law, 1974.

Clark, C. The role of the white researcher in black society. *Journal of Social Issues* 29 (1973):109-18.

Cole, M. and Bruner, J.S. Cultural differences and inferences about psychological processes. *American Psychologist* 26 (1971):867-76.

Cole, M., Gay, J., Glick, J.A., and Sharp, D.W. *The Cultural Context of Learning and Thinking.* New York: Basic Books, 1971.

Crawford, F. Variations between Negroes and whites in concepts of mental illness, its treatment and prevalence. In *Changing Perspectives in Mental Illness,* edited by S. Plog and R. Edgerton. New York: Holt, Rinehart and Winston, 1969.

Cross, W.E. The Thomas and Cross models of psychological nigrescence: A literature review. *Journal of Black Psychology* 5 (1978):13-31.

Darley, D. Who shall hold the conch? Some thoughts on community control of mental health programs. *Community Mental Health Journal* 10 (1974):185-91.

Dawson, J.L.M. Theory and research in cross-cultural psychology. *Bulletin of British Psychology* 24 (1971):291-306.

Deutsch, M. Minority groups and class status as related to social and personality factors in scholastic achievement. *Society for Applied Anthropology Monographs* No. 2 (1960).

Devereaux, G. *Ethnopsychoanalysis.* Berkeley: University of California Press, 1978.

DeVos, G. Selective permeability and reference group sanctioning: Psychocultural continuities in role degradation. In *Major Social Issues,* edited by J.M. Yinger and S.J. Cutler. New York: The Free Press, 1978.

Dillard, J. *Black English: Its History and Usage in the United States.* New York: Random House, 1972.

Dohrenwend, B.P. and Dohrenwend, B.S. Social and cultural influences on psychopathology. *Annual Review of Psychology* 25 (1974):417-52.

_____ *Social Status and Psychological Disorder.* New York: John Wiley & Sons, 1969.

DuBois, W.E.B. *The Negro American Family.* Atlanta: Atlanta University Press, 1908.

Edgerton, R.B. The study of deviance—marginal man or everyman? In *The Making of Psychological Anthropology,* edited by G. Spindler. Berkeley: University of California Press, 1978.

Essien-Udom, E.U. *Black Nationalism.* Chicago: University of Chicago Press, 1962.

Erikson, E. *Identity, Youth and Crisis.* New York: W.W. Norton, 1968.

Ervin-Tripp, S.M. Children's sociolinguistic competence and dialect diversity. In *Seventy-First Yearbook of the National Society of the Study of Education,* pp. 123-60, 1972.

Fanon, F. *Black Skin, White Masks.* New York: Grove Press, 1967.

Fanon, F. *The Wretched of the Earth.* New York: Grove Press, 1968.

Flynn, J. Local participants in planning for comprehensive community mental health centers: The Colorado experience. *Community Mental Health Journal* 2 (1973): 3-10.

Frijda, N. and Jahoda, G. On the scope and methods of cross-cultural research. *International Journal of Psychology* 1 (1966):109-27.

Gibbs, J. Patterns of adaptation among Black students at a predominately white university: Selected case studies. *American Journal of Orthopsychiatry* 44 (1974):728-40.

Glazer, N. and Moynihan, P., eds. *Ethnicity: Theory and Experience.* Cambridge, Mass.: Harvard University Press, 1975.

Goldenberg, I. *Build Me a Mountain: Youth, Poverty and the Creation of New Settings.* Cambridge, Mass.: The M.I.T. Press, 1971.

Grier, W.H. and Cobbs, P.M. *Black Rage.* New York: Basic Books, 1968.

Griffith, M.S. and Jones, E.E. Race and psychotherapy: Changing Perspectives. In *Current Psychiatric Therapies,* volume 18, edited by J.H. Masserman. New York: Grune & Stratton, 1978.

Griffin, Q.D. and Korchin, S.J. Personality competence in black male adolescents. *Journal of Youth and Adolescence* 9 (1980):211-27.

Guthrie, R. *Even the Rat Was White.* New York: Harper & Row, 1976.

Gynther, M. White norms and Black MMPI's: A prescription for discrimination? *Psychological Bulletin* 78 (1972):386-402.

Harrison, H. and Kass, E. Differences between Negro and white pregnant women on the MMPI. *Journal of Consulting Psychology* 31 (1967):454-63.

Hayes, W. and Banks, W. The nigger box or a redefinition of the counselor's role. In *Black Psychology,* edited by R.L. Jones. New York: Harper & Row, 1980.

Herskovitz, M.L. *The Myth of the Negro Past.* Boston: Beacon Press, 1958.

Hodges, A. and Mahoney, S. Expectations for the comprehensive mental health center: The community. *Community Mental Health Journal* 6 (1970):75-77.

Hollingshead, A. and Redlich, F. *Social Class and Mental Illness.* New York: John Wiley & Sons, 1958.

Howard, J.H. Toward a social psychology of colonialism. In *Black Psychology,* edited by R.L. Jones. New York: Harper & Row, 1980.

Hsu, F. Lo, K. Prejudice and its intellectual effect on American anthropology: An ethnographic report. *American Anthropologist* 75 (1973):1-19.

Jones, E.E. Social class and psychotherapy: A critical review of research. *Psychiatry* 37 (1974):307-20.

Jones, E.E. Black-white personality differences: Another look. *Journal of Personality Assessment* 42 (1978a):244-52.

Jones, E.E. Effects of race on psychotherapy process and outcome: An exploratory investigation. *Psychotherapy: Theory, Research and Practice* 15 (1978b):226-36.

Jones, E.E. Personality characteristics of Black youth: A cross-cultural investigation. *Journal of Youth and Adolescence* 8 (1979):149-59.

Jones, E.E. Psychotherapy outcome as a function of client-therapist race. *Journal of Clinical Psychology,* in press.

Jones, E.E. and Zoppel, C.L. Personality differences between Blacks in Jamaica and the United States. *Journal of Cross-Cultural Psychology* 10 (1979):435-56.

Kagan, S., Zahn, G.L. and Gealy, J. Competition and school achievement among Anglo-American and Mexican American children. *Journal of Educational Psychology* 69 (1977):432-41.

Kamin, L. *The Science and Politics of IQ.* Potomac, Md.: Lawrence Erlbaum Associates, 1974.

Kaplan, S. and Roman, M. *The Organization and Delivery of Mental Health Services in the Ghetto: The Lincoln Hospital Experience.* New York: Praeger, 1973.

Kardiner, A. and Ovesey, L. *The Mark of Oppression.* Cleveland: World, 1951.

Katz, I. Factors influencing Negro performance in the desegregated school. In *Social Class, Race and Psychological Development,* edited by M. Deutsch, I. Katz, and A. Jensen. New York: Holt, Rinehart and Winston, 1968.

_____ Alternatives to a personality-deficit interpretation of Negro underachievement. In *Psychology and Race,* edited by P. Watson. Chicago: Aldine, 1974.

Katz, I. and Cohen, M. The effect of training Negroes upon cooperative problem solving in biracial teams. *Journal of Abnormal and Social Psychology* 64 (1962):319-25.

Katz, I., Epps, E., and Axelson, L. Effect upon Negro digit symbol performance of anticipated comparison with whites and other Negroes. *Journal of Abnormal and Social Psychology* 69 (1964):77-83.

Katz, I., Henchy, T., and Allen, H. Effects of race of tester, approval-disapproval, and need on Negro children's learning. *Journal of Personality and Social Psychology* 8 (1968):38-42.

Katz, I., Roberts, S.O., and Robinson, J.M. Effects of task difficulty, race of administrator, and instructions on digit-symbol performance of Negroes. *Journal of Personality and Social Psychology* 2 (1965):53-59.

Kennedy, W.A. and Vega, M. Negro children's performance on a discrimination task as a function of examiner race and verbal incentive. *Journal of Personality and Social Psychology* 2 (1965):839-43.

Khatib, S.M. and Nobles, W.W. Historical foundations of African psychology and their philosophical consequences. *Journal of Black Psychology* 4 (1977-78): 91-101.

Kiev, A., ed. *Magic, Faith and Healing.* New York: The Free Press, 1974.

Kitano, H.L. Japanese-American mental illness. In *Changing Perspectives on Mental Illness,* edited by S. Plog and R. Edgerton. New York: Holt, Rinehart and Winston, 1969.

Korchin, S.J. *Modern Clinical Psychology.* New York: Basic Books, 1976.

Korchin, S.J. Clinical psychology and minority problems. *American Psychologist* 35 (1980):262-69.

Kramer, M., Rosen, B.M., and Willis, E.M. Definitions and distributions of mental disorders in a racist society. In *Racism and Mental Health,* edited by C.V. Willie, B.M. Kramer, and B.S. Brown. Pittsburgh: University of Pittsburgh Press, 1973.

Kroeber, A. and Kluckhohn, C. Culture: A critical review of concepts and definitions. *Papers of the Peabody Museum of American Archaeology and Ethnology* 47 (1952): No. 1.

Labov, W. The logic of nonstandard English. In *Language and Poverty: Perspectives on a Theme,* edited by F. Williams. Chicago: Markham, 1970.

Labov, W. *Language in the Inner City: Studies in the Black English Vernacular.*

Philadelphia: University of Pennsylvania Press, 1972.

Lebra, W.P. *Culture-Bound Syndromes, Ethnopsychiatry, and Alternative Therapies.* Honolulu: University Press of Hawaii, 1976.

Lerner, B. *Therapy in the Ghetto.* Baltimore: The John Hopkins University Press, 1972.

Levine, E. and Padilla, A. *Crossing Cultures in Therapy: Pluralistic Counseling for the Hispanic.* Monterey, Calif.: Brooks/Cole, 1980.

Levine, M. and Levine, A. *A Social History of Helping Services: Clinic, Court, School and Community.* New York: Appleton, 1970.

Lonner, W.J. A decade of cross-cultural psychology: JCCP, 1970-79. *Journal of Cross-Cultural Psychology* 11 (1980a):7-34.

Lonner, W.J. The search for psychological universals. In *Handbook of Cross-Cultural Psychology,* edited by H.C. Triandis and W.W. Lambert. Boston: Allyn and Bacon, 1980b.

Lorion, R.P. Research on psychotherapy and behavior change with the disadvantaged: Past, present and future directions. In *Handbook of Psychotherapy and Behavior Change: An Empirical Analysis,* 2nd ed., edited by S.L. Garfield and A.E. Bergin. New York: John Wiley & Sons, 1978.

Madsen, W. *The Mexican-Americans of South Texas.* New York: Holt, Rinehart and Winston, 1964.

Marcuse, H. *One-Dimensional Man.* Boston: Beacon Press, 1964.

Martinez, J.L., Jr., ed. *Chicano Psychology.* New York: Academic Press, 1977.

Memmi, A. *The Colonizer and the Colonized.* Boston: Beacon Press, 1967.

Miranda, M.R., Andujo, E., Caballero, I.L., Guerrero, C.C. and Ramos, R.A. Mexican-American dropouts in psychotherapy as related to level of acculturation. In *Psychotherapy with the Spanish Speaking: Issues in Research and Service Delivery,* edited by M. Miranda. Monograph Number 3. Spanish Speaking Mental Health Research and Development Program, UCLA, 1976.

Mogulof, M. Advocates for themselves: Citizen participation in federally supported community organization. *Community Mental Health Journal* 10 (1974):66-76.

Murphy, J.M. Psychiatric labeling in a cross-cultural perspective. *Science* 193 (1976):1019-28.

Nobles, W. Psychological research and black self-concept. Journal of *Social Issues* 29 (1973):11-31.

Nobles, W. Extended self: Rethinking the so-called Negro self-concept. In *Black Psychology,* edited by R.L. Jones. New York: Harper & Row, 1980.

Osgood, C.E. Cross-cultural comparability in attitude measurements via multilingual semantic differentials. In *Current Studies in Social Psychology,* edited by I.D. Steiner and M. Fishbein, pp. 95-107. Chicago: Holt, Rinehart and Winston, 1965.

Padilla, A.M., Carlos, M.L., and Keefe, S.E. Mental health service utilization by Mexican Americans. In *Psychotherapy with the Spanish-Speaking: Issues in Research and Service Delivery,* edited by M. Miranda. Monograph Number 3. Spanish Speaking Mental Health Research and Development Program, UCLA, 1976.

Padilla, A.M. and Ruiz, R.A. *Latino Mental Health: A Review of Literature.* Washington, D.C.: U.S. Government Printing Office, 1973.

Padilla, A.M. and Ruiz, R.A. Personality assessment and test interpretation of Mexican-Americans: A critique. *Journal of Personality Assessment* 39 (1975): 103-9.

Padilla, A.M., Ruiz, R.A., and Alvarez, R.A. Community mental health services to the Spanish-speaking/surnamed population. *American Psychologist* 30 (1975): 892-905.

Parker, S. and Kleiner, R. Status position, mobility and ethnic identification of the Negro. *Journal of Social Issues* 20 (1964):85-102.

Pettigrew, T.F. *A profile of the Negro American.* Princeton, N.J.: Van Nostrand, 1964.

Pierce, W. The concept of community control in community mental health delivery systems. *Journal of Black Psychology* 2 (1975):35-43.

Price-Williams, D.R. *Explorations in Cross-Cultural Psychology.* San Francisco: Chandler & Sharp, 1975.

Proshansky, H. and Newton, P. The nature and meaning of Negro self-identity. In *Social Class, Race and Psychological Development,* edited by M. Deutsch, I. Katz and A. Jensen. New York: Holt, Rinehart and Winston, 1968.

Rainwater, L. Crucible of identity: The Negro lower-class family. *Daedalus* 95 (1966):172-217.

Ramirez III, M. and Castaneda, A. *Cultural Democracy: Bi-Cognitive Development and Education.* New York: Academic Press, 1974.

Rieff, P. *The Triumph of the Therapeutic.* New York: Harper & Row, 1966.

Riess, B.F., Schwartz, E.K., and Cottingham, A. An experimental critique of the Negro version of the TAT. *Journal of Abnormal and Social Psychology* 45 (1950):700-9.

Ryan, W. *Blaming the Victim.* New York: Random House, 1971.

Sarason, S.B. *The Psychological Sense of Community: Prospects for a Community Psychology.* San Francisco: Jossey-Bass, 1972.

Sattler, J. Racial "experimenter effects" in experimentation, interviewing and psychotherapy. *Psychological Bulletin* 68 (1970):347-60.

Schwartz, T. Where is the culture? In *The Making of Psychological Anthropology,* edited by G.D. Spinder. Berkeley: University of California Press, 1978.

Smith, M. Differences in social perception among blacks and whites. Unpublished manuscript, University of California, Berkeley, 1973.

Sue, D.W. and Sue S. Ethnic minorities: Resistance to being researched. *Professional Psychology* 3 (1972):11-16.

Sue, S. Community mental health services to minority groups. *American Psychologist* 32 (1977):616-24.

Sue, S. and Kitano, H.L., eds. Asian Americans: A success story? *Journal of Social Issues* 29 (1973): Whole No. 2.

Tharp, R.G., Meadow, A., Lenhoff, S.G., and Satterfield, D. Changes in marriage roles accompanying the acculturation of the Mexican-American wife. *Journal of Marriage and the Family* 30 (1968):404-12.

Thomas, A. and Sillen, S. *Racism and Psychiatry.* New York: Brunner/Mazel, 1972.

Tischler, G.L. The effects of consumer control on delivery of services. *American Journal of Orthopsychiatry* 41 (1971):501-5.

Tong, B. The ghetto of the mind: Notes on the historical psychology of Chinese

America. *Amerasia Journal* 1 (1971):28.

Torrey, E.F. *The Mind Game: Witchdoctors and Psychiatrists.* New York: Emerson Hall, 1972.

Triandis, H.C. *The Analysis of Subjective Culture.* New York: John Wiley & Sons, 1972.

Triandis, H.C. *Variations in Black and White Perceptions of the Social Environment.* Urbana: University of Illinois Press, 1976.

Triandis, H., Malpass, R., and Davidson, A. Psychology and culture. *Annual Review of Psychology* (1973):355-78.

True, R.H. Mental health services in a Chinese American community. In *Service Delivery in Pan-Asian Communities,* edited by W.H. Ishikawa and N.H. Archer. San Diego: Pacific Asian Coalition, 1975.

Valdes, L. and Steiner, S., eds. *Aztlan: An Anthology of Mexican-American Literature.* New York: Random House, 1972.

Vargus, B.S. On sociological exploitation: Why the guinea pig sometimes bites. *Social Problems* 19 (1971):238-48.

Weems, L. Awareness: The key to black mental health. *Journal of Black Psychology* 1 (1974):30-37.

Weidman, H.H. Falling-out: A diagnostic and treatment problem viewed from a transcultural perspective. *Social Science and Medicine* 13B (1979):95-112.

Williams, R.L. From dehumanization to black intellectual genocide: A rejoinder. In *Clinical Child Psychology: Current Practices and Future Perspectives,* edited by G.J. Williams and S. Gordon. New York: Behavioral Publications, 1974.

Word, C.O. Cross cultural methods for survey research in Black urban areas. In *Research Directions of Black Psychologists,* edited by A.W. Boykin, A.J. Franklin and J.F. Yates. New York: Russell Sage Foundation, 1979.

Yamamoto, J., James, O., and Palley, N. Cultural problems in psychiatric therapy. *Archives of General Psychiatry* 19 (1968):45-49.

2   Ethnic Minority Research: Trends and Directions

Stanley Sue, Joanne Ito, and Carla Bradshaw*

Psychology, as well as other social sciences, has attempted to address the needs of various ethnic minority groups. The importance of research in pointing to these needs and to possible solutions was underscored by the President's Commission on Mental Health: "...research should be undertaken to understand the needs and problems of underserved populations, such as Asian Americans, Blacks, Hispanic Americans, and Native Americans. These groups represent about 17 percent of the United States population and suffer disproportionately from the alienation and fear, depression and anger which accompany prejudice, discrimination, and poverty" (*Report to the President,* 1978, pp. 75-76).

While there is a strong consensus among policy makers, researchers, and the public that substantial time, effort, and funding should be focused upon ethnic minority research, two problems immediately come to mind. First, ethnic minority groups such as American Indians, Asian Americans, blacks, and Hispanics have similar as well as different mental health research needs and experiences. In order to speak of ethnic minority research, it is to some extent necessary to draw out general trends applicable to all groups and at the same time to refer to each group's concerns. Second, ethnic minority research has generated a great deal of controversy and rhetoric because research is not simply a scientific task but, rather, a process involving scientific methodology, values, needs, philosophical perspectives, politics, and funding. The purpose of this chapter is to examine trends for ethnic research and to offer suggestions for research directions. Several questions and issues are discussed.

---

*An earlier version of this paper was an invited address at the National Conference on Minority Group Alcohol, Drug Abuse, and Mental Health Issues sponsored by the Alcohol, Drug Abuse and Mental Health Administration (ADAMHA), Denver, May 1978.

1. What are the research themes and trends that have evolved with respect to minority groups?
2. What themes or areas in mental health, drug, and alcohol research should we focus upon?
3. What is the value of research for minority groups?
4. Who should conduct research on what populations?
5. What methods should we use in research?
6. What is the relationship between researchers, various communities, and consumers?
7. How can we obtain funds for ethnic research?

THEMES AND TRENDS

It is impossible to appreciate the current status of ethnic research without reference to past research themes. Three general themes can be identified: (1) the inferiority model, (2) the deficit model, and (3) the bicultural or multicultural model. In the Foreword to the book *Racism and Psychiatry* by Thomas and Sillen (1972), Kenneth Clark, past president of the American Psychological Association, indicates that social scientists often reflect the trends of society. He states that "Probably the most disturbing insight obtained from the relentless clarity with which this book documents the case of racism in American Psychiatry is the ironic fact that the students, research workers and professionals in the behavioral sciences—like members of the clergy and educators—are no more immune by virtue of their values and training to the disease and superstitution of American racism than is the average man" (p. xii). Indeed, Thomas and Sillen document the historical theme perpetuated by research that blacks are psychologically and intellectually inferior to whites. Society was largely held unaccountable for the plight of ethnics since the victims themselves were to blame. We do not want to dwell on this point except to say that early research aimed at the perceived inferiority of certain ethnic minority group individuals.

More recently, there has been greater movement in a direction that attributes the plight of ethnic minority groups to society and social conditions. Investigators attempted to study societal racism and its effects on ethnic minorities. The victim was blamed less, for it was believed that society was the culprit. Gordon Allport (1954) in his classic book *The Nature of Prejudice* laid the groundwork for the view that prejudice and discrimination could not solely be attributed to abnormal personalities or to "rednecks." Rather, social psychological processes in society were responsible, a theme reiterated by Jones (1972) and greatly elaborated by Pettigrew (1973). The assumption was that prejudice and discrimination created stress for minority groups. Consequently, many minority group individuals were deficient, underprivileged, pathological, or deviant. Kramer, Rosen, and Willis (1973) went so far as to say that "Racist practices undoubtedly are key factors—perhaps the most important ones—in producing mental disorders in Blacks and other underprivileged groups...."(p. 355). Many studies documented the social, economic, and mental health conditions of minority groups. Blacks were presumed to have high rates of drug addiction; American Indians were prone to alcoholism and suicide; Hispanics were described as having tendencies toward drunkenness, criminal behavior, and undependability (see Fischer, 1969; Kitano, 1974; Padilla and Ruiz, 1973). Interestingly, Asian Americans were believed to have few problems since they were supposedly free from prejudice and discrimination (Sue, Sue, and Sue, 1975). Most ethnic minorities were assumed to have serious problems involving self-identity and self-esteem because of culture conflict.

The deficit model was helpful in focusing on society rather than the individual ethnic minority in explaining the status of minority groups. The implication was that analysis of institutional factors is necessary. Racism does affect the physical, social, economic, and psychological well-being of minority groups. Because of discrimination and unresponsiveness of services to minority groups, mental health treatment and service delivery systems are inadequate. The deficit model, therefore, stimulated research into societal factors, the effects of racism, and the adequacy of treatment services.

The deficit model, while valuable in certain respects, also raised grave concerns.

1. The emphasis on deficits neglected strengths, competencies, and skills found in ethnic families, communities, and cultures (Jones, 1972; Thomas and Sillen, 1972).

2. There was a tendency to focus upon treatment or remediation of "deficiencies," rather than upon the institutional roots for the deficiencies, as means of resolving problems.

3. The deficit model implied that certain ethnic group behaviors were psychopathological if they deviated from mainstream norms (Padilla and Ruiz, 1973), so that a strict assimilation model was deemed appropriate.

4. Conceptual and methodological challenges were made concerning the adequacy of research findings. For example, in the areas of ethnic identity and self-esteem (Banks, 1976; Brand, Ruiz, and Padilla, 1974), family structure (Jones, 1972), and rates of psychopathology (Fischer, 1969), many investigators felt that previous research strategies were inadequate. Similarly, the view that Asian Americans are free from, or immune to, the effects of prejudice and discrimination is inaccurate (Sue, Sue and Sue, 1975).

These criticisms stimulated bicultural or multicultural research. In this kind of research, the status of minority groups is viewed as a function of (1) ethnic values, (2) U.S. or Western values, and (3) the interaction of the two sets of values. Bicultural research can be contrasted with cross-cultural research in that the former includes the dynamic interplay of ethnic and Western values, while the latter is predominantly interested in the similarities and differences of individuals from different cultures. Thus, in the case of black Americans and American Indians who have had hundreds of years of experience in the United States, it would be inappropriate to say that their status is simply the result of cultural differences or culture conflict. Rather, exploitation, discrimination, prejudicial attitudes, etc. have also accompanied and have interacted with their history. Bicultural or multicultural research considers not only the differences in cultural backgrounds but also the interaction of cultures. Furthermore, culture conflict and racism, while creating stress, are also viewed as providing seeds for growth and the development of competencies. Ethnic minority groups have evolved unique means of coping with these stressors, and bicultural research includes the examination of these coping and adaptive strategies.

In summary, research on ethnic minority groups has moved, first, from an inferiority model to a deficit model and, now, to a bicultural model. Obviously, these are trends rather than distinct, nonoverlapping stages. It should also be noted that we are still at elementary stages in terms of knowing mental health status, causes of mental health and needs, and solutions.

DIRECTIONS FOR RESEARCH

Let us now turn to directions that we should take in ethnic minority research and, in doing so, propose a model by which we can systematize research efforts. One is tempted to say that we need more research in almost all areas involving minority groups: essential demographic data, needs assessment, culture, education, ethnic identity, mental health, community functioning, discrimination, the costs of racism not only upon minority groups but upon all Americans, family structure, psychopathology, sex roles, mental health delivery systems, and ethnic resources to name a few. Where, among these and other areas, should we begin in our research priorities? We would like to introduce a four-stage cycle of research and to indicate important areas upon which to focus, as indicated in Figure 2.1. The four stages are: (1) status of ethnic minorities, (2) causes of psychological well-being or disturbance, (3) solutions to mental health problems, and (4) implementation of solutions. These four areas are intimately related. If we do not know the status and situation of minority groups, then it is fruitless to look for causal factors. If we do not know the causes for mental health status, then it is exceedingly difficult to plan for solutions. Finally, knowing solutions to problems is of no value unless we can implement programs and policies that in turn affect the status and well-being of ethnics. Let us briefly discuss the four stages.

Figure 2.1. Research Directions.

Status of Ethnic Groups

1. Needs assessment, epidemiology, basic information
2. Focus on groups at risk
3. Prospective studies

Causal Factors (stressors/resources)

1. Positive mental health and disorders
2. Individual, family, community culture, and society levels
3. Intergroup and intragroup differences

Implementation

1. Funding
2. Political process
3. Public policy
4. Utilization and dissemination of findings

Solutions

1. Individual
2. Systems
3. Prevention

Status

In the stage of the status of ethnic minorities we need an increase in the quantity and quality of research studies. Because of methodological, conceptual, and practical problems in ethnic research (to be discussed later), we are still at the elementary steps in having systematic and accurate information on various ethnic minority groups. That is why many researchers are attempting to conduct needs assessment of ethnic groups; that is why researchers are constantly frustrated. Basic and essential information is lacking. For example, we still do not know exactly how many Asians are in the United States. Estimates vary from official sources to community leaders. The same situation exists for Hispanic Americans. There continues to be a great deal of controversy over the rates and extent of mental disorders, drug abuse, and alcoholism among ethnic group individuals. Our *first suggestion* is that basic demographic data and epidemiological information be systematically collected on various ethnic groups and subgroups. Without such essential information, policies and programs cannot be effectively planned or developed.

Our *second suggestion* is that subgroups of ethnic minorities who are at particular risk or who have special mental health needs should be identified and should receive high priority in future research efforts. The mental health field has moved in a direction in which groups at risk (i.e., individuals who have a diathesis for mental disorders, who experience substantial stress, and/or who lack resources) are given special attention (President's Commission on Mental Health, 1978). For example, children of schizophrenic parents, divorcees, or children of divorced parents are often considered as high risk groups. Among ethnic minorities, there are also groups that are under particular stress or that have inadequate resources to deal with their needs. These groups may include immigrants, the poor, and the elderly. As shown by Hinkle (1974), immigrants are exposed to tremendous life changes that require a great deal of readjustment. Because of these life changes, the incidences of physical and psychological problems increase. Poverty and lower socioeconomic class conditions are related to psychopathology for all Americans (Dohrenwend and Dohrenwend, 1974). For many ethnic minorities, a race by social class interaction may further accentuate mental health problems that cannot be generated by isolating race or social class alone. The same may be true for elderly members of minority groups who encounter problems of aging as well as those associated with being members of ethnic minorities. Our main point is that research efforts should be prioritized so that identified high risk ethnic minority groups can receive increased attention.

Our *third suggestion* is that needs assessment be planned so that we can project for the future. Changes are rapidly occurring, so that what is true today may not be true tomorrow. For example, Padilla (1977) indicates that Hispanics comprise the fastest growing minority group and that by the year 2000 it will be the largest. In the state of California, nonwhite ethnic groups will in the near future outnumber white Americans. The Asian population in the United States is likely to have doubled between 1970 and 1980 (Owan, 1975); Native Americans are increasingly becoming an urban group (Trimble, 1976).

All of these projections indicate the necessity to address our efforts not only for today but also for tomorrow. A good example of future-oriented research is reported by Kramer and Zane (1980), who were interested in predicting the mental health status of nonwhite minority groups in 1985. By finding out (1) how certain demographic characteristics were associated with psychiatric admissions and with the incidence of schizophrenia and (2) the proportions of whites and nonwhites who would probably have these characteristics by 1985, they were able to make projections. They predicted that if current trends hold, there would be a 45 percent increase in psychiatric admissions for nonwhites (20 percent for whites) and a 43 percent increase in the incidence of schizophrenia for nonwhites (21 percent for whites)! The findings are obviously disturbing. In terms of our discussion of research, studies of this kind are strongly needed so that programs and policies can be proactive rather than reactive in nature.

Etiology

More research should be devoted to causal factors in mental health and mental disturbance. In this regard, a distinction should be made between health and disturbance. Health is not simply the absence of disturbance. Individuals may not be "mentally ill" but, rather, have low positive mental health—e.g., low self-esteem, anger, feelings of powerlessness, etc.—in the same way that one can be free of disease but have poor physical health. We do not wish to carry this analogy too far since medical model concepts are limiting. Nevertheless, the distinction between health and illness is a good one, and the *fourth suggestion* is that attention on causal factors be expanded to include positive mental health as well as what has traditionally been considered disturbed behavior (i.e., psychiatric disorders including drug and alcohol abuse). Development of self-esteem, feelings of personal control, mastery, achievement, self-identify, happiness, etc. would all fall under the rubric of positive mental health. Focusing solely upon the etiology of mental disorders among ethnic minorities, while important, ignores the positive mental health attributes that are of concern to all human beings. Moreover, insight can be gained into how competencies and adaptive capacities develop and how personal, familial, cultural, and societal variables affect well-being.

Another issue in the search for causal factors in mental disturbance is the tendency to dwell on stressors. Culture conflict, culture shock, stereotypes, discrimination, poverty, etc. presumably influence mental health. However, not all persons who encounter stresses in daily life succumb. Some persons deteriorate; others adjust and become strengthened. What determines these differential reactions to stress? As indicated by Caplan (1972) and Kelly (1977), resources and support systems have substantial impact upon mental health. In an investigation of the effects of environmental supports on post-hospital adjustment of short-term psychiatric patients, Lyon and Zucker (1974) found that stability of home life and the presence of friends and neighbors in the former patient's environment was inversely related to the level of disturbance in the patient. The findings suggest that well-being may be associated with the availability of resources. Exclusive focus on the problems encountered by ethnic minority groups perpetuates a deficit model orientation and ignores the familial or cultural resources that ethnic minority groups persons may have. The *fifth suggestion* is that resources and their means of preventing or intervening on behalf of mental health be studied. Note that specific factors can be conceived as having potential as a stressor or resource. Thus, our *sixth suggestion* is that the individual, family, community, culture, and society be studied as stressors *and* resources.

The notion that, depending upon the context, a stimulus or situation may act as a stressor or as a resource is hardly new. A situation may simultaneously have positive and negative elements that affect mental health. Research has typically examined ethnic minority groups from a one-sided perspective. For example, as indicated earlier, the black family was initially viewed as deficient in stability and as a "tangle of pathology"—a view that was subsequently attacked by many black psychologists (Thomas and Sillen, 1972). On the other hand, Chinese- and Japanese-American families have been popularly seen as extraordinarily intact and harmonious. Such characterizations need balance. While it is true that many Chinese families inculcate values involving kinship ties, filial piety, and harmonious relation, it is equally true that conformity and restrictions on individual freedom are fostered (Hsu, 1971). One can easily see how families can act as resources (e.g., kinship support, sense of belongness, etc.) or as stressors (e.g., excessive demands for conformity and obedience) depending upon the circumstances. DeVos (1978) also notes that the Japanese-American family structure has both positive and negative elements for family members. He feels that the family has well-defined and structured roles. Consequently, while family members such as the father may encounter racial prejudice or discrimination outside of the family, they are able to return to a stable setting and to assume well-structured roles and identities. The Japanese tradition, he argues, subordinates concern with the self to role expectation. For example, the traditional Japanese father sees "sincerity" as a matter of acting in accordance with what might be expected in the exercise of a role rather than personal feelings. DeVos points out that the Japanese family structure acts as a buffer to certain stressors; nevertheless, he also believes that such structure introduces a certain degree of emotional distance and tension, particularly between father and children. These examples regarding black and Asian-American families illustrate the value in looking at positive and negative aspects of resources.

At this point, we would like to offer the *seventh suggestion,* which is that intraethnic group variations be studied. Not all members of the same ethnic group share the same values or circumstances. Social class differences, immigrant status, urban-rural residence, residence in integrated-segregated communities, exposure to ethnic culture, etc. constitute important variables to investigate. Empirical investigations, especially those designed to compare mainstream white Americans with ethnic minority groups, frequently hide the tremendous variations within ethnic groups. The concepts of American Indians, Asian Americans, blacks, and Hispanics include persons of different tribes, of different national origins, and so on. These differences must be fully appreciated if stereotypes and overgeneralizations are to be avoided.

Toward Solutions

The search for solutions is crucial. We know that the mental health needs of minority groups are very serious. There is evidence that minority group clients are not preferred by therapists; that even when these clients are in psychotherapy, rapport and a good working relationship between client and therapist are difficult to achieve; and that the mental health delivery system is unresponsive. For example, in one study (Sue, 1977), it was found that approximately half of all Asian American, black, Chicano, and Native American clients failed to return for treatment after one session in community mental health centers, compared to a much lower failure-to-return rate for whites.

We have three recommendations dealing with solutions at the level of (1) individuals, (2) systems, and (3) time of intervention. With respect to the individual level, more research is needed that defines the factors that facilitate positive outcomes in treatment *(suggestion eight)*. It has been frequently stated that treatment needs to be culturally responsive, that similarity in culture between therapist and client is important, that therapists must be open, flexible, and free of stereotypes, and so on. Nevertheless, questions remain and must be researched. For example, what specific therapist attributes are necessary for effective treatment with minority group clients? How can we better train students and paraprofessionals to work with minority clients? The question of therapist attributes and effective treatment is one that faces the entire mental health field. For ethnic minorities, the question has posed a much larger problem because of a lack of resources to examine the issues and because ethnic issues have not received adequate emphasis in the mental health field.

In recent years, there has been an increase of studies into the process of psychotherapy for ethnic minorities. For example, Atkinson, Maruyama, and Matsui (1978) were interested in Japanese-American perceptions of different styles of psychotherapy. They found that the Japanese Americans in their study tended to prefer a more directive style of counseling (i.e., the therapist controlled the flow of discussion and pointed out the clients' problems) than a nondirective approach (i.e., the clients controlled flow of conversation). Acosta and Sheehan (1976) examined the preferences of Mexican and Anglo Americans. By experimentally varying the ethnicity (Mexican American versus Anglo) of the therapist and the status (professional versus nonprofessional) of the therapist, they generated some interesting results. First, Mexican Americans were less trustful of a professional therapist of their own ethnicity than was the case for Anglo Americans. Second, they were less trustful of a therapist labeled as a professional rather than as a nonprofessional. Anglos showed the opposite pattern, indicating more trust in a professional than a nonprofessional. Third, in response to a question on the utility of psychotherapy, Mexican Americans were more likely than Anglo Americans to agree with a statement concerning the helpfulness of psychotherapy. The findings were interpreted by Acosta and Sheehan as perhaps reflecting the few professional Mexican-American therapists available and the lack of public credibility achieved by them. Why Mexican-American subjects rated the nonprofessional over the professional therapist is unclear, but it may indicate a greater ease in sometimes relating to a person of the same status (i.e., nonprofessional therapist). Equally interesting is the positive attitude of Mexican Americans toward psychotherapy. Since they have these positive attitudes and yet tend to underutilize mental health services, other variables, such as the stigma and shame relating to mental health problems, language barriers, or the existence of alternative resources, may be important in utilization patterns.

These studies illustrate the interesting and important research that is being conducted. They also indicate the need for more systematic efforts in studying the process of treatment for ethnic minorities.

At a higher level than the individual one, we need to focus on systems and community processes *(suggestion nine)*. Research into systems can be divided into ethnic and mainstream solutions. Ethnic solutions are those cultural-community means of resolving emotional disturbances. Medicine men, curanderas, third party intermediaries, herbalists, and even ethnic churches often play a vital role in treatment. Their impact and value in ethnic communities have been assumed. For example, the President's Commission on Mental Health (1978) strongly recommended that a major effort be developed for cultural-community support systems as mental health resources. While we believe that these support systems are vitally important, little is actually known about the variety and range of these systems and the conditions under which they are effective. Greater research must be conducted to investigate their effectiveness so that these resources can be better utilized and applied more broadly.

Mainstream solutions are those that are in widespread use today. Community mental health centers, hospitals, clinics, and other facilities form the major part of our mental health care system. What kinds of changes should occur in our system to better respond to minority group needs? In enhancing the mental health of minority groups, the development and assessment of our system should proceed in three directions. First, evaluation should be made of existing services and programs to meet the needs of ethnic groups. For example, many community mental health centers have hired ethnic specialists, utilized nonprofessionals, and engaged in outreach services or client advocacy programs. Have these been effective? Second, independent (free from existing programs) but parallel (i.e., similar to existing services) programs have been established for ethnic groups. That is, many services or agencies have been created to serve minority groups. An important research issue is to determine their effectiveness and to find out what aspects are particularly responsive so that others can initiate or modify programs to better meet the needs of minority groups. Third, new, nonparallel services should be developed and evaluated. New therapies, approaches, agencies, or institutions aimed at ethnic groups are important. Ruiz and Padilla (1977) suggest that for Hispanics or Latinos new and expanded services be offered in promoting mental health. A "business model" approach that aggressively pursues clients for services is advocated. Involving the community in the planning of mental health services, multimedia approaches in English and Spanish to advertise the services, written and oral language translation assistance for clients and government agencies, skills training in obtaining employment and securing promotions, and teaching rights and responsibilities in the politico-legal system are some of their recommendations. These services are usually not found in traditional mental health settings, but they indicate Ruiz and Padilla's desire to (1) create innovative services and (2) define mental health issues in a broad manner that addresses the quality of life (employment, language skills, political participation, etc.) for Hispanics.

Time of intervention is also important to consider in moving toward solutions. *Suggestion ten* is that primary prevention programs in mental health, drug abuse, and alcoholism be given high priority. The reduction of the incidence of disorders through elimination of causal factors or through improved personal and community resources must be investigated. Charles Willie (1980), a member of the President's Commission on Mental Health, acknowledges the key role of prevention. He states that in the past, effective treatment for various disorders including mental disorders have been made available first to the affluent and members of the majority. Prevention, however, benefits both the majority and minority, the affluent as well as the disadvantaged. Minorities, therefore, may help the majority as well as their own members by insisting that preventive efforts pertaining to mental disorders not be delayed.

We are not naive in recommending research on primary prevention: (1) priority is often given to urgent and acute problems needing treatment, (2) the fruits of prevention programs take years to demonstrate, (3) past prevention efforts (such as in early education programs, headstart, etc.)

have frequently lacked sound methodology, and (4) some researchers have doubted whether we know enough to begin massive primary prevention programs. However, if we are to truly respond to ethnic minority groups, reduction in the incidence, not merely in the prevalence, of disorders must occur. Research proposals on prevention should be encouraged and supported. But what kinds of primary prevention programs should be initiated? What are some promising directions for research in this area? While research into the elimination of etiological factors in mental disorders is important, we believe that a more fruitful line of inquiry is in the search for effective competency-based programs of prevention that match or fit individuals' cultural life styles.

Treatment or intervention approaches that do not respond to clients' life styles may result in poor utilization, premature termination of services, poor outcomes, or little transfer of treatment effects (Sue, 1977). This was well recognized by Hobbs (1962), who in his classic article on sources of gain in psychotherapy indicated that persons have to have a "cognitive house" to protect themselves from the incomprehensibilities of existence as well as to provide some architecture for daily experiencing. Certain cognitive houses or personal cosmologies fit with certain forms of treatment better than others. Again, the fit between belief systems and treatment is crucial. If this is the case, then it seems highly likely that prevention-oriented competency programs that do not adequately fit a particular target population's culture will also result in decreased participation, resistance, and poor outcome. But there is also another major factor that must be considered—namely, that cultures and communities may already have "natural" or historical means of dealing with problems. As indicated by Mechanic (1974), the individual's coping abilities also depend upon the availability and effectiveness of solutions provided by one's culture. Cultural solutions are, in fact, much broader than those provided by the mental health professions. An often-cited study by Gurin, Veroff, and Feld (1960) revealed that the vast majority of persons who sought professional help for personal problems did not contact a mental health professional. Rather, a wide variety of others (e.g., clergymen and physicians) were utilized. If nonprofessionals (e.g., relatives, friends, neighbors, herbalists, and other third party intermediaries) are added as caregivers, then natural and accustomed resources are probably used much more widely than professional mental health services. This statement is not meant to disparage the mental health profession or mental health professionals. Instead, it is intended to emphasize realistic limitations as well as to stress how crucial existing natural resources are. Competency programs should therefore consider the cultural context.

Sundberg, Snowden, and Reynolds (1978) define competence as being personal characteristics such as knowledge, skills, and attitudes that lead to achievements having adaptive payoffs. Note that in primary prevention the assumption is that enhancement of competence occurs early, so incidence rates of disorders, emotional problems, etc. are reduced. Most of the work with primary prevention competency programs is aimed at increasing personal or community resources to facilitate coping mechanisms.

What kinds of programs have developed? Good reviews of the area are available (see Cowen, 1977; Kelly, Snowden, and Muñoz, 1977). Some of the most exciting programs include Heber's (1976) work in enhancing the intellectual performance of high risk children by intensive and prolonged early intervention. Other education programs such as compensatory education to develop intellectual and adjustment skills have also been initiated (see Kessler and Albee, 1975). Also included would be the rapidly growing uses of stress inoculation and anxiety management techniques (Meichenbaum, 1977) as prevention oriented competency programs to the extent that they allow increased skills in handling crises or emotional problems in situations subsequent to training. Learning to relax, to cognitively restructure events in a positive manner, and to exhibit self-control rather than helplessness facilitates one's ability to resolve personal stressors and can be used in a variety of different situations and problem areas. It should be mentioned that in competency programs the assumptions are that (1) certain skills can be identified that enhance one's coping and (2) these skills can be acquired. In specifying important skills, we must be careful not to assume that the identified skills are so universal that cultural context can be ignored. The ease with which skills are acquired and utilized also depends to some extent upon culture.

In order to devise competency-based prevention programs, psychologists must first conduct research on (1) what techniques are used in dealing with problems, (2) how much variability there is in using resources across situations, (3) what the cultural and demographic correlates are of the utilization of natural resources, and (4) how effective these techniques are. The first task would be to ask people what methods they use and what makes them feel better in certain situations.

In addition to finding out what resources are used, another task is to determine how to best enhance these resources. One way is to help develop already existing community programs that are prevention oriented, as advocated by Rappaport (1977). A second way is to help individuals become more effective in utilizing techniques. Many individuals do not evaluate the effectiveness of their resources, plan for possible crises or problems, and practice or rehearse resource utilization. In other words, an important process is for individuals to develop an explicit, systematic plan or strategy and to feel a degree of self-control in handling life situations. The advantages of such a process are that (1) already existing resources are used, (2) the techniques are matched to the culture or life style of individuals and to their cognitive houses, and (3) the techniques will be used more effectively. The research process is crucial in all of these tasks.

Implementation

Thus far, the importance of research in determining the status of minority groups, the causal factors in psychological well-being, and the possible directions for solutions have been discussed. The fourth and final step *(suggestion eleven)* in research is to implement strategies and solutions. Funds are needed for mental health research in general and minority group mental health in particular. In addition, there must be means of implementing the possible solutions suggested by research findings. Here the task is to increase funding, to have influence in the political process, to affect public programs and policies, and to make others aware of needs and problems. We have no simple answers as to how this immense task can be achieved. Our point is that implementation is a logical and necessary step in enhancing psychological well-being. Padilla (1979) has argued that research energies be invested into the study of the early phases of the policy process. That is, to implement strategies and plans, it is necessary to know the relationship between psychological research and the development of political influence, legislation, political decision making, etc. This relationship can be ascertained through research.

One model for research into the implementation of solutions can be found in the experimental social innovation approach of Fairweather, Sanders, and Tornatzky (1974). Fairweather and his colleagues were convinced through their own research that chronic mental patients in hospitals should be given more autonomy and live more independently. That is, rather than confining patients in a restricted hospital environment, Fairweather felt that patients living more autonomously would achieve greater productivity and be able to function in the community. In addition, their treatment would cost less than traditional hospitalization programs. He essentially had a "solution" that was based upon research findings. The problem was that it was difficult to implement—to convince hospitals that such a program should be adopted. Consequently, Fairweather's team investigated how to best present the program to hospitals in order to affect decisions and what factors in hospitals were associated with the decision to adopt the proposed program. Research of this kind provides insight into how new programs can be actualized.

In summary, four areas of research involving basic information of the status of ethnic minorities, the stressors and resources that affect mental health, the effective means for enhancing psychological well-being, and the implementation of policies and programs are important.

ISSUES IN THE RESEARCH PROCESS

Value of Research

Research has frequently been attacked as having no applied value, as being too abstract and esoteric, and as perpetuating stereotypic, biased, or even inaccurate views of minority groups. Because of the urgent and pressing needs of minority groups, *suggestion twelve* is that priority be given to research that has the potential of significantly contributing to the betterment and well-being of the minority groups in the short or long term. In the previous section, we have tried to indicate what we believe to be important content areas for research (i.e., the status of minority groups, causal factors in mental disturbance, solutions for problems, and implementation strategies). If mental health needs are to be addressed, then these four areas should receive high priority. The issue is not basic versus applied research. Basic research often has applied value and applied research has many times failed to produce meaningful findings and practical implications. Moreover, results from research frequently require years of work so that implications may not be immediately apparent. The central issue is over the potential impact that research will have in promoting mental health. It would be presumptious to suggest precise kinds of research that should have high priority, other than to indicate the importance of general areas (as we have). Two processes are important: (1) the demonstration of the potential short or long term value of research projects and (2) integration of research projects into systematic programs. Research proposals for funding should be explicit in delineating their impact and significance. Very few, if any, instances can be found where a single piece of research has resulted in social change, social action, public policies, etc. Rather, the systematic, rigorous, and multidimensional approach to attacking a problem or issue has probably been of greatest benefit. Seen in this light, research can serve as documenting needs to the public and to policy makers, as pointing to the underlying roots of problems, and as suggesting possible means of intervention. Research can have tremendous value if properly targeted at problems, systematically conducted, and initiated with adequate research strategies and tools.

Researchers and Those Researched

Since early ethnic research was for the most part conducted by white researchers, and, since minority groups often see research findings as being biased and inaccurate, the essential question of who should conduct research on what populations must be addressed. Some feel that only members of a particular groups should conduct research on that group. Ethnicity of the researcher would be a necessary (but not sufficient) condition. Others believe that regardless of race or ethnicity, qualifications and ethnic sensitivity are sufficient factors for ethnic research. However, the issue is further complicated by the possibility that factors such as qualifications and sensitivity may be related to ethnicity. For example, Brazziel (1973) states that "Today's white researchers are perhaps counterproductive in black communities not because they are white, but because they are poorly trained" (p. 41). Brazziel goes on to argue that white researchers (1) have less credibility than black researchers in black communities and (2) are affected by their own training and have inadequacies in perceiving racism. In this view, ethnicity of researcher and ethnic background are important factors to consider.

It is unwise and impractical to try to limit ethnic research to researchers who have ethnic similarity to the group being studied. There are a number of reasons why this is true. First, there is still a manpower shortage of ethnic researchers. Second, various white researchers (or ethnic researchers who study ethnic groups different from their own) have made valuable contributions. Third, race relations, racism, mental health, etc. must be issues and problems addressed by all Americans, not just ethnic minorities. Fourth, it is simply impossible to limit research on ethnic groups according to race of the researcher. Qualifications, sensitivity, and credibility should dictate who does research on what populations. However, since these characteristics may be related to ethnicity and since ethnic perspectives have been lacking in ethnic research, *suggestion thirteen* is that well qualified researchers with proposals of merit should conduct ethnic research; nevertheless, since researchers of the same ethnicity as their minority group often have special insights, credibility, and sensitivity and are just now beginning to have an impact on ethnic research, these investigators should have increased support and encouragement. The assumption is that ethnic researchers for one reason or another have only recently had influence on research. Another assumption is that researchers who differ ethnically from the group being studied must develop sensitivity, insight, and credibility with that group and must seek assistance and advice from group members.

Methodology and Conceptual Issues

One persistent problem in minority group research is the use of proper conceptual and methodological tools. This problem in ethnic research includes (1) use of culturally biased measures, (2) inadequate consideration of ethnic response sets, (3) faulty interpretations of minority group behaviors, (4) lack of norms in evaluating ethnic responses, and (5) effects of the experimenter's race or ethnicity upon subjects. Many researchers have pointed to conceptual and methodological research issues in areas such as intelligence (Jorgensen, 1973; Williams, 1974), personality and ethnic identity (Banks, 1976; Brand, Ruiz, and Padilla, 1974; Nobles, 1973), mental health (Sue, Sue, and Sue, 1975; Thomas and Sillen, 1972), and family structure (Gordon, 1973; Trimble, 1976). These investigators have been critical of many research findings on minority groups. Strict adherence to traditional concepts and methodological tools has made it difficult to explore the use of more innovative concepts and methodologies that might be applied more appropriately to minority groups.

The problems are not so much over the precise research approach, that is, whether the research is correlational, experimental, single-subject, field, laboratory, or participant-observer; rather, they are in its application. Perhaps a couple of examples can illustrate some of the difficulties.

Many personality or intelligence tests that are administered to whites and racial minorities yield different group scores according to race. How are these differences in scores found on psychological tests to be interpreted? The answer is not a simple one, and cross-cultural researchers as well as investigators on ethnic minority groups have had to confront the problem. What is clear is that racial differences in tests scores must be carefully interpreted. Knowledge of the cultures of the groups being tested, of possible response sets, of the test's limitations, and of the conditions under which the test is administered is critical. As an illustration, let us examine some research conducted by Dohrenwend and Dohrenwend (1969), who were interested in finding out if certain ethnic groups differed in psychopathology. After administering the Midtown 22-item symptom questionnaire, they indeed found ethnic differences: Puerto Ricans scored higher in psychological disturbance than did Jewish, Irish, or black respondents in New York City. One interpretation of the findings is that Puerto Ricans are more disturbed than other groups; another is that Puerto Ricans may simply have a greater tendency, independent of emotional disturbance, to endorse symptoms. To test whether the higher score among Puerto Ricans indicates higher actual rates of disorders, patients matched in types of psychiatric disorders from each ethnic group were administered the same questionnaire. Since patients were matched on type and presumably severity of disorders, one would expect no differences on symptom scores. However, Puerto Ricans again scored higher. Dohrenwend and Dohrenwend conclude that the higher scores for Puerto Ricans probably reflect a response set or a cultural means of expressing distress rather than higher actual rates of disturbance. This study illustrates that in cross-cultural comparisons, test differences in performances should not be interpreted in a simple manner.

Interpretations of research findings on ethnic minority groups represent only one area where difficulties have occurred. There are many others. For example, Korchin (1978) in his APA convention address upon receiving the Division 12 award for distinguished contribution to the science and profession of clinical psychology, related an interesting experience. He was collaborating with a colleague on some research regarding competency among blacks. A paper from the study, submitted for publication, was rejected because a reviewer felt that the study should have included a white control group. Why should the study include a white control group when the primary interest was in black Americans? Are studies of white Americans required to include black control groups? The issues raised by Korchin are meaningful. The main point is that biases have often occurred whereby (1) methodologies, research instruments, and interpretations have been misapplied to minority groups and (2) evaluations of the adequacy of ethnic research are frequently inappropriate. Thus, our *fourteenth suggestion* is that support be given to ethnic research that is carefully thought out (so that biases and inadequacies can be controlled) and that is innovative in strategy and approach.

Implicit in this suggestion is the necessity for more ethnic researchers who can appropriately evaluate the adequacy of research. Although researchers in the area of ethnic minority mental health may not be members of ethnic minorities and many researchers from ethnic minority groups do not conduct research on minority groups, it is interesting to note the tremendous underrepresentation of ethnic minorities on editorial boards of APA journals. The central office of the American Psychological Association has indicated the following proportions of ethnic minorities: 0 percent (0 out of 18) editors, 0 percent (0 out of 48) associate editors, and 2 percent (12 out of 597) consulting editors. No reliable estimates existed for minority representation among journal reviewers.

Community Relations

Within the last decade, many minority group individuals have grown increasingly suspicious of the motives of the researcher and of the outcome of research (Sue and Sue, 1972). Ethnic communities often feel that research is irrelevant or inaccurate. They feel exploited as subjects of research and distrustful of researchers. Indeed, funding for research (ethnic and nonethnic) has come under greater scrutiny by the public and by decision makers. Some of the problems are due to public misunderstandings of the research endeavor. But to a large extent, difficulties have also arisen because communities have not been called upon as collaborators in research. Research, especially that dealing with social issues, societal problems, and ethnic minority groups, requires broad participation. Gordon (1973) advises that "...all parties share in guiding the total research endeavor, including decisions about research conceptualization, design methodology, and the dissemination of the utilization of data. We must recognize that such data are used to influence public policy; they generate political consequences which must be to the benefit of the community involved." (p. 94). *Suggestion fifteen* is that researchers and ethnic communities collaborate and share in research endeavors.

Padilla (1979) has pointed to the conflicts between researchers, practitioners, and the community at large. Different perspectives, needs, and interests make collaboration difficult. He suggests that a first step in collaboration is to enable researchers to be trained in the working of service agencies where contact with clients, practitioners, administrators, etc. can be enhanced. Similarly, practitioners and administrators should require research and evaluation in their service agencies and be knowledgeable in research procedures.

Funding for Research

It is very clear that funding has a profound impact in the direction, nature, quality, quantity, etc. of research. What is also clear is that while a compelling case can be made for the necessity of substantial funds for research in general, ethnic research must receive high priority. Issues of minority group mental health, drug and alcohol use, and racism are urgent ones that have been inadequately addressed. All funding agencies in the mental health arena must systematically and substantially support ethnic minority research *(suggestion sixteen)*. The problems and issues concerning minority group mental health are not limited simply to ethnic minority groups. Aside from the moral or human rights issue, racism continues to affect not only minority groups but also all Americans. Issues concerning integration, busing, poverty, and well-being impact us all. Funding for mental health research should reflect the magnitude of the issue or problem. It is through research that needs, problems, issues, and solutions can be presented to the public, decision makers, scientific and professional communities, research granting agencies, etc.

CONCLUSIONS

In such a brief analysis, it is difficult to examine the issues of minority groups research in much depth. The 16 suggestions are not intended to be specific or definitive. For example, we have not specified whether research on, say, ethnic families is more important than research on cultural values. In view of the need for research in all areas (e.g., needs assessment and epidemiology, stressors and resources, solutions, and implementation), our plea is for *more* research, greater *systematic* efforts, use of *proper* conceptual and methodological tools, involvement of *qualified* and sensitive researchers, increased *collaboration* between researchers and the community, the *enhancement* of mental health, and more research *funds*. Access to policy makers and funding sources should be facilitated. Furthermore, if we are truly to respond to research needs of ethnic minorities, the current trend to include more minority group persons on research review groups, in administrative positions, and as decision makers must be expanded. These suggestions and recommendations are for the most part not new. But they bear repeating in light of the unmet needs and issues regarding minority group mental health.

REFERENCES

Acosta, F., and Sheehan, J. Preferences toward Mexican American and Anglo American psychotherapist. *Journal of Consulting and Clinical Psychology* 44 (1976):272-79.

Allport, G.W. *The Nature of Prejudice.* Reading, Mass.: Addison-Wesley, 1954.

Atkinson, D., Maruyama, M., and Matsui, S. Effects of Counselor race and counseling style on Asian American's perceptions of counselor credibility and utility. *Journal of Counseling Psychology* 25 (1978):76-83.

Banks, W.C. White preference in blacks: A paradigm in search of a phenomenon. *Psychological Bulletin* 83 (1976):1179-186.

Brand, E., Ruiz, R., and Padilla, A. Ethnic identification and preference: A review. *Psychological Bulletin* 81 (1974):860-90.

Brazziel, W.F. White research in Black communities: When solutions become a part of the problem. *Journal of Social Issues* 29 (1973):41-44.

Caplan, G. Support systems. Keynote address to the Conference of Department of Psychiatry. Rutgers Medical School and the New Jersey Mental Health Association, Newark, N.J., 1972.

Cowen, E.L. Baby-steps toward primary prevention. *American Journal of Community Psychology* 5 (1977):1-22.

DeVos, G. Selective permeability and reference group sanctioning: Psychological continuities in role degradation. Paper presented at comparative studies in Ethnicity and Nationality Seminar. University of Washington, Seattle, April. 1978.

Dohrenwend, B.P., and Dohrenwend, B.S. *Social Status and Psychological Disorder.* John Wiley & Sons, 1969.

————. Social and cultural influences on psychopathology. *Annual Review of Psychology* 25 (1974):417-52.

Fairweather, G., Sanders, D., and Tornatzky, L. *Creating Change in Mental Health Organizations.* New York: Pergamon, 1974.

Fischer, J. Negroes, whites and rates of mental illness: Reconsideration of a myth. *Psychiatry* 32 (1969):428-46.

Gordon, T. Notes on white and black psychology. *Journal of Social Issues* 29 (1973):87-96.

Gurin, G., Veroff, J., and Feld, S. *Americans View their Mental Health: A Nationwide Survey.* New York: Basic Books, 1960.

Heber, R. Research in prevention of socio-cultural mental retardation. Paper presented at the 2nd Vermont Conference on the Primary Prevention of Psychopathology. Burlington, VT, 1976.

Hinkle, L.E. The effect of exposure to culture change, social change, and changes in interpersonal relationships on health. In *Stressful Life Events: Their Nature and Effects,* edited by B.S. Dohrenwend and B.P. Dohrenwend. New York: John Wiley & Sons, 1974.

Hobbs, N. Sources of gain in psychotherapy. *American Psychologist* 17 (1962):741-47.

Hsu, F.L., K. Psychosocial homeostasis and jen: Conceptual tools for advancing psychological anthropology. *American Psychologist* 73 (1971):23-44.

Jones, J.M. *Prejudice and Racism.* Reading, Mass.: Addison-Wesley, 1972.

Jorgensen, C.C. IQ tests and their educational supporters. *Journal of Social Issues* 29 (1973):33-40.

Kelley, J.G. The ecology of social support systems: Footnotes to a theory. Paper presented at the American Psychological Association Convention. San Francisco, August, 1977.

Kelly, J.G., Snowden, L.R., and Muñoz, R.F. Social and community interventions. *Annual Review of Psychology* 28 (1977):323-61.

Kessler, M. and Albee, G.W. Primary prevention. *Annual Review of Psychology* 26 (1975):557-91.

Kitano, H.H. *Race Relations*. Englewood Cliffs, N.J.: Prentice-Hall, 1974.

Korchin, S.J. Clinical psychology and minority problems. Paper presented at the American Psychological Association Convention. Toronto, September, 1978.

Kramer, M., Rosen, B.M., and Willis, E.M. Definitions and distributions of mental disorders in a racist society. In *Racism and Mental Health,* edited by C.V. Willie, B.M. Kramer, and B.S. Brown. Pittsburgh: University of Pittsburgh Press, 1973.

Kramer, M. and Zane, N. Projected needs for mental health services. In *Community Mental Health in a Pluralistic Society,* edited by S. Sue and T. Moore. New York: Human Sciences Press, 1980.

Lyon, K. and Zucker, R. Environmental supports and post-hospital adjustment. *Journal of Clinical Psychology* 30 (1974):460-65.

Mechanic, D. Social structure and personal adaptation: Some neglected dimensions. In *Coping and Adaptation,* edited by G.V. Coelho, D.A. Hamburg, and J.E. Adams. New York: Basic Books, 1974.

Meichenbaum, D. *Cognitive-behavior Modification: An Integrative Approach.* New York: Plenum Press, 1977.

Nobles, W.W. Psychological research and the black self-concept: A critical review. *Journal of Social Issues* 29 (1973):11-32.

Owan, T. Asian Americans: A case of benighted neglect. Paper presented at the National Conference of Social Welfare. San Francisco, 1975.

Padilla, A.M. Researching the Spanish-speaking community: Issues in the human service research enterprise. *Research Bulletin* 4 (1979):1-4, 8.

Padilla, A.M. and Ruiz, R.A. *Latino Mental Health: A Review of the Literature.* DHEW Publication No. (HSM) 73-9143. Washington, D.C.: U.S. Government Printing Office. 1973.

Pettigrew. T.F. Racism and mental health of white Americans: A social psychological view. In *Racism and Mental Health,* edited by C.V. Willie, B.M. Kramer, and B.S. Brown. Pittsburgh: University of Pittsburgh Press, 1973.

President's Commission on Mental Health. *Report to the President.* Washington, D.C.: U.S. Government Printing Office, 1978.

Rappaport, J. *Community Psychology: Values, Research, Action.* New York: Holt, Rinehart and Winston, 1977.

Ruiz, R. and Padilla, A. Counseling Latinos. *Personnel and Guidance Journal* 55 (1977):401-8.

Sue, D.W. and Sue, S. Ethnic minorities: Resistance to being researched. *Professional Psychology* 3 (1972):11-17.

Sue, S. Community mental health services to minority groups: Some optimism, some pessimism. *American Psychologist* 32 (1977):616-24.

Sue, S., Sue, D.W., and Sue, D. Asian Americans as a minority group. *American Psychologist* 30 (1975):906-10.

Sundberg, N.D., Snowden, L.R. and Reynolds, W.M. Toward assessment of interpersonal competence and incompetence in life situations. *Annual Review of*

Psychology 29 (1978):179-221.

Thomas, A. and Sillen, S. *Racism and Psychiatry.* Secaucus, N.J.: Citadel Press, 1972.

Trimble, J.E. Value differences among American Indians: Concerns for the concerned counselor. In *Counseling Across Cultures,* edited by P. Pedersen, W.J. Lonner, and J.G. Draguns. Honolulu: The University Press of Hawaii, 1976.

Williams, R.L. Scientific Racism and IQ—The silent mugging of the black community. *Psychology Today* 7 (1974):32, 34, 37-38, 41, 101.

Willie, C.V. Ethnicity and mental health. In *Community Mental Health in a Pluralistic Society,* edited by S. Sue and T. Moore. New York: Human Sciences Press, 1980.

3 Deconstructive Falsification: Foundations of Critical Method in Black Psychology*

W. Curtis Banks

When the state of the art in a discipline is overturned, the ensuing crisis inevitably finds most of its practitioners napping. This is in part because the state of the art is normally quite advanced before its failures accumulate sufficiently to compel its decline. By that time its conventional modes of practive have become so commonplace that its adherents hardly pay attention anymore; and if they are caught unaware by its overthrow, it is as much because the old conventions are so boring as because their demise is so sudden.

One way of characterizing this kind of development is in terms of scientific paradigms and their eventual decline through intellectual revolution (Kuhn, 1970). According to that now-popular view of the history of science, it might be expected that the gradual failure of a conventional theory or methodology to account for factual evidence, or to accommodate advances in the technology of inquiry, could lead to a shift in the mental health sciences of the major approaches to the study of any specific phenomenon. However, that failure in the field of psychology, with respect to Black populations, has been far less gradual in its occurrence than in its notice. In fact, what is most distressing about the field of psychology is that its rather conclusive failures in this regard have gone so long unremarked upon, although in most cases they reflect a failure dating from the very establishment of one or another construct or method to reveal the nature of psychological functioning in Blacks.

*Portions of this manuscript were presented to the New Jersey Association of Black Psychologists (October, 1978), the Delaware Valley Association of Black Psychologists and Virginia State University (April, 1979), Rutgers University (October, 1979), and the University of California at Berkeley (November, 1979).

These observations are offered as a preface to the otherwise rather stark pronouncement of a paradigm shift, one that marks the point of departure for the field now referred to as Black Psychology. Precisely when the paradigm shifted is not really important. In any case, it becomes patently obvious that previous approaches to inquiry and the tacit assumptions that underlie them are no longer either sufficient or necessary. Whether new paradigms are the explicit cause or the effect of such a shift, however, is an important (albeit purely philosophical) question. If experience is to be relied upon, our tentative answer for the field of Black Psychology is "both." New conceptions preceded even the coining of the name Black Psychology, even though their formulations were at best vague and incomplete. Nonetheless, it is apparent that much of the theory building and methodological groundwork for this new mode of inquiry is yet to be done.

At the same time, much credit is to be given a different kind of effort, that of criticism. Criticism and refutation play a role in paradigm shifts equal to that of innovative conceptions (Lakatos, 1970). There is some difference of opinion on how that role is played, however. Kuhn argues that criticism is virtually nonexistent during calm periods of normal science. And, indeed, this has been a critical deficit of conventional psychology in the domain of Black populations. But he further argues that the eventual disenchantment with the conventional paradigm is more sociological than logical and that revolutionary shifts often occur in such a way that, far from critical interchanges, the new and the old paradigms hardly have grounds even for communication (see also Feyerabend, 1970).

Popper (1959) has advanced the idea that criticism overthrows the status quo by exposing it to empirical falsification. Old theories are those that fail the test, or at least more severely than available new ones. This, of course, suggests that a new one must exist to be compared with. Popper argues that this is so even when the inquirer is unaware of it. But much of our experience suggests that we scientists are often hard pressed enough to present the theories we think we have without being encouraged to believe we have those that we think we do not.

After all, it happens at least occasionally that the dominant mode of inquiry is so full of faults that its refutation is an inevitable event in its own right. Even so, criticism, such as it was, tended to be, as Kuhn might have predicted, more sociological in character than logical in the early period of Black Psychology. That is, the primary theme of criticism revolved around an emerging community of scientists who rejected the conventionally accepted paradigms and discoveries as germane to an understanding of Black people. In this respect, it was the failure of certain conventional wisdoms to retain their validity in the widening sociological context of both white and Black psychologists that gave rise initially to the decline of the traditional paradigms (see Masterman, 1970). Nonetheless, it is apparent that a thorough-going and systematic logical-empirical criticism is the Lockean rubbish-clearing[1] precursor to new paradigms. And it is largely in the light of this recognition that much of the current work in Black Psychology is proceeding.

In consequence of these facts, it is imperative to acknowledge that the theoretical state of our art is near zero. It is apparent, for instance, that the foundational work in the field of intelligence, which undergirded the dominant conceptions of intellectual functioning in Blacks, is in disarray. Kamin's (1974) exhaustive critique of the empirical literature has revealed far more than even the most cynical forecaster would ever have expected in regard to that paradigm. In the more general subdiscipline of personality, the situation is effectively the same. Of the four major constructs that form the foundation of conventional conceptions of personality and social behavior in Blacks, none stands the test of empirical falsification. Research has demonstrated neither the inferiority of Blacks in intrinsic motivation, nor the ability of instruments devised to measure it to distinguish individual differences among Blacks.

In the early development of such measures as the need for achievement, validation research that established individual differences within white populations was extended to comparative investigations into the global differences across racial groups. Yet, quite without either logical or empirical merit the further assumption that such measures discriminate individual differences within Black populations was advanced, only to find itself in need of revision (Banks, McQuater, and Hubbard, 1978). Similarly, external locus of control, or a sense of powerlessness in Blacks, has been demonstrated in only 10 percent of the empirical studies aimed at its validation within the psychological literature (Banks, Ward, McQuater, and DeBritto, 1980). The inability of Blacks to delay gratification is without empirical foundation, as is the great majority of evidence demonstrating a virtual indifference toward alternatives of immediate or delayed gratification (Banks, McQuater, Ward, and Ross, 1980). And the white preference behavior upon which four decades of theorizing about Black self-hate has been built is quite without evidential support (Banks, 1976; Banks, McQuater, and Ross, 1979). In every case, the sociological status of conventional paradigms (Masterman, 1970) first came under severe systematic criticism within the community of scientists represented by Black Psychologists. And in that regard, criticism has at once formed the foundation of Black Psychology and the methodological perspective that guides its research practices.

HISTORICAL OVERVIEW

The brief statement of the organizational history of the Association of Black Psychologists,[2] which appeared in every issue of *The Journal of Black*

Psychology up to volume 5, cited aspects of the unifying theme of that body. First and foremost was a desire and commitment to serve the needs of the Black community. Second was a commitment to increasing the opportunities for Blacks in the professional field of psychology. From the very beginning the focus of concern for Black Psychology has not been the dispassionate pursuit of knowledge about the lawful nature of human behavior. Neither has the growth of Black Psychology been marked by any consistent appeal to a unified conception of knowledge or by a confidence that the characteristics of human experience occur in a lawful manner.

It is no accident, therefore, that a consistent criticism of Black Psychology has been that it contains too little serious scholarship and rigorous research. The very aims that formed the foundation of the Association did not explicitly emphasize these endeavors. To be sure, Black Psychology has from the very beginning stood only precariously on the periphery of what is commonly accepted as conventional science. Or at least this is a charge implicit in much of the criticism, the questions, and the misgivings that are expressed by colleagues both within and outside the field of psychology.

However, it would be argued here that we should be struck, first of all, by the degree of coherence that exists in the foundations of the Association as they relate to the aims of research, theory, and the advancement of understanding. If that is not apparent, it is only because we have not thought about it clearly. It is in no way inconsistent to have founded a field of inquiry upon a concern for serving the needs of an identifiable community of people and yet simultaneously to have founded a field aimed at theory building and knowledge.

The concerns and needs of the Black community, particularly those psychological in nature, revolved around a dilemma that has plagued psychology for years. This is an epistemological confrontation between mentalism and operationism. From a mentalistic point of view the important factors that determine the experience and behavior of the individual are features of his unobservable mind, his consciousness, his private-subjective reality. From this perspective all that is critical in defining the experience of the individual is out of view, it is intangible and unobservable by objective analysis. This extreme dispositionalism in psychology, of course, is in one respect a liberalizing influence. It is liberalizing because it permits a wide range of inferences and conjectures about the nature of the experience of people and the meaning of behavior. When it is combined with the complex dynamics of theories such as Freudian psychoanalysis it even throws overboard the assumption that the person or people themselves have special insight into their experience and the substance of their reality. "Black people who have high aspirations for success are exhibiting reaction formation toward goals they actually lack the motivation to pursue." "Those who believe they are comfortable with and confident of their identity indulge in a denial of the inherent negative qualities of Blackness in this culture." The result, therefore, is a liberalization that results in psychological conjectures that can be entertained as readily by others as by self. In that sense, what is strictly private because of its covert character is open to inference and speculation. A strict mentalism opens to conjecture what it closes to observation. What then determines the ultimate status of knowledge claims regarding Black people is the status of power of those who would speculate.

In marked contrast to that orientation is the strictly operationist point of view and its emphasis upon the concrete operations by which psychological concepts are measured and manipulated. In its most radical form, of course, it holds that a psychological property is identical with the operations by which it is elicited and measured. Operationism, in this sense, is a counter-liberalizing influence in the definition of psychological reality. It denies the validity of any experience or behavior that orthodox psychological technology does not measure. Therefore, the problem with "soul" was that it was epistemologically meaningless, there being no conventional operations by which agreed measurements could be made. Intelligence, however, and mental aptitude were eminently meaningful; the psychometric operations by which they were assessed not only revealed their substance, but were themselves the adjudged substance against which no appeal was permissible.

When the small caucus of Black Psychologists assembled in 1968 at the convention of the American Psychological Association to express its concerns about the condition of the Black community and its relation to psychology (see Williams, 1974), it was this double bind that it confronted. Perhaps most significantly, it confronted the new operationism by which an emerging technological establishment in education seemed systematically to be denying access for Black children to mainstream and college-bound, presecondary education. The action of the Bay Area Association of Black Psychologists and others in California to redress this injustice clearly was a rallying point for the new field and its aims (1972). Neither were the larger methodological and philosophy of science implications of that contestment lost on the field of Black Psychology. And I would characterize those net implications as falling on the side of an antioperationist and antiempiricist sentiment.

First let us consider that this early position was a passionate one, for reasons that are apparent. That a system of technology and human service should be devised that both restricts access to resources and denies the freedom of defining reality would be beyond tolerance. Were it not for this felt opposition to policies of curriculum tracking in education, it is possible that a frontal attack against empirical method (and operationism more particularly) would never have been mounted. There was, of course, the psychological literature concerning negative self-concepts, impulsivity, lack of motivation, and low intelligence quite in advance of the onslaught of the new educational technology vis-à-vis Black children, but it had never been sufficient to raise the consciousness of Black researchers to a level necessary to incite a full-scale assault on science.

But the answer to the question shouldn't Black Psychology throw out altogether "the baby with the bath water" (Boykin, 1978)[3] is contained in the fact that empirical research and operationist methods have only been used very incompletely and in many ways improperly. If Black Psychology cannot be confident of a form of knowledge supported by objective evidence, which accumulates toward certain universal laws, it may be because these very notions themselves are invalid. Such a view is not so radical as it may sound.[4] Even though X(Clark), et al. (1975) expressed this criticism in their article "Voodoo or I.Q.," Popper had done the same in his *The Logic of Scientific Discovery* (1959).

In that earlier work in logical empiricism, Popper anticipated, quite unintentionally no doubt, the course of orthodox psychology and the basis of its confrontation with Black Psychology. Popper pointed out that a strict adherence to the canons of logic yields the conclusion that certain statements cannot be proven by fact. In particular, statements that constitute universal claims regarding any entity or event cannot by any finite accumulation of evidence ever be confirmed. This contention is self-evident in the case of certain prototypical statements such as "all men eat bread" or "people work for rewards." Aside from the specific truth value of such propositions it must be noticed that such universal claims stand logically always at risk of refutation by any single item of counter evidence. No matter how many finite units of material evidence we can amass in support of such propositions, it is their logical character that such other evidence is conceivably available that would falsify them altogether.

Clearly this condition depends on the extremity of the claims. But it is precisely this extremity that marks the character of theoretical propositions in the natural sciences—propositions that, according to Aristotle and virtually all of his Western descendents, are properly the aim of science only insofar as they grasp for universals. Moreover, Popper argues that the net implication of his observation is that the role of evidence is one of falsification. The empirical content of theoretical claims is directly proportional to the body of evidence by which they may be falsified.

Yet, in the context of Black populations conventional psychology has found a peculiar and subtle way out of this paradox. For it must be noticed that an essential element of universal claims is their reliance upon material referents that are grammatically common in noun and adjective form (Pears, 1950). Claims regarding *men* are universal in their logical character, while claims regarding *Mr. Jones* are not. Likewise, claims regarding *people* are universal, while those regarding *Negroes* are not. The essential difference, of course, is the delimitation of the domain in question within the universe of possible entities or events. Claims regarding people pertain to all conceivable entities within the universe, while claims regarding Negroes pertain to a conventionally recognizable subset of that universe of entities.

This way out for psychology is illustrated by Popper's observation that claims regarding entities identified by proper grammatical reference are existential in logical character, pertaining to a sharply delimited domain. Claiming, therefore, that Negroes as compared with whites tend to have negative self-concepts is tantamount to articulating "some people" propositions, propositions that by their logical character cannot be refuted by evidence (Popper, 1959).[5]

The implication is profound. Within a comparative paradigm where claims are put forth regarding specified domains of entities defined by proper referent, the role of empirical evidence is limited to that of confirmation. In light of this fact the tendency of many Black Psychologists and other professionals to lament that empirical evidence, and thus research, is by nature bound to support the pernicious theoretical claims of orthodox social science reflects more than political cynicism; it is an observation of a logical reality. Perhaps equally significant is the fact that in contrast to the irrefutable character of its own claims regarding Black populations, conventional psychology has been adamant in its relegation of all propositions of modern Black Psychology to a logical status of unprovability. During the period before the rise of Black political awareness the accepted mode of reference within scientific publications to Black populations was via the proper noun or adjective descriptor Negro. With the emergence, however, of Black Psychology the convention has shifted not only to "Black" but to common grammatical form as well, so that scientific journals now specify the use of lowercase "black" only in conventional usage.

By the same token, Black Psychology, then, is faced with two avenues by which it may pursue knowledge through an empirical strategy that does not violate its intellectual sensitivities or those of the Black community. It may assert its claims regarding the character of Black experiences and behavior in terms of propositions whose logical status permits evidence only to verify and confirm. This status of the theoretical propositions of Black Psychology would most enhance the condition of theory proliferation that some (e.g., Feyerabend, 1970) would regard as the only means by which science can escape dogma. But it is equally inescapable that such a strategy would evoke charges of metaphysical speculation from those whose aim might be to suppress such proliferation and its threat of a new and autonomous paradigm.

Alternately, Black Psychologists might answer the condemnation of an appeal strictly to existential propositions by reclaiming entire classes of previously comparative propositions and recasting them in a universal form. By so doing, we might open them to the threat of falsification by empirical evidence. And this appeal to evidence through research is precisely the role of a properly critical science and skeptical philosophy of knowledge. For this purpose, the major theoretical propositions of past comparative research have been formulated in their extreme universal form, and the rigors of an evidential criterion applied in the falsification of such propositions and the theories from which they derive.

EXAMPLE OF WHITE PREFERENCE

Some of our own recent work has been directed toward falsification, and it illustrates in a potentially illuminating way the nature of the confrontation under examination. This work was conducted in the area of Black self-concept and white-preference behavior. Let us first try to characterize what the state of the issue of white preference had been, what the logical characterization of its claims was, and the manner in which we attempted to rectify those claims and their empirical status. Then we should consider the reaction of orthodox psychology and its attempt to retrench against that attack.

For roughly 30 or 40 years the study of personality in Black populations had revolved around the construct of self-concept, and the analysis of Black self-concept had centered on the paradigm of white preference. In this regard, the proposition entertained was that Blacks hated themselves and that they would tend to express self-identification and evaluative preference for human characteristics that are Caucasian.

Since the role of empirical evidence is to test theoretical conjectures, the null hypothesis that corresponded to that proposition had to be defined and subjected to evidential examination. The comparative null hypothesis was, of course, the nondifference between own-race preferences for Black and for white populations. And, in fact, in a majority of cases empirical research did yield evidence that rejected that null hypothesis with respect to a number of stimulus objects (dolls, puppets, line drawings, photographs) representing white and Black racial characteristics; Blacks had been found to express evaluative choices that researchers interpreted as indicative of preference.

Our assertion against this line of research and its underlying claims was twofold. First, the logical nature of the comparative proposition concerning Black preference results in a weak empirical claim. Since the virtually unanimous behavior of whites was own-race preference, only a small portion of Blacks needed to exhibit other-race preference in order to reject the null hypothesis. This is tantamount to posing an existential (or "some people") claim, which is confirmed by even minimal evidence.

Second, we asserted that in keeping with the principles of demarcation (Popper, 1959) between metaphysical and empirically meaningful statements, such propositions must be adjudged as having no empirical content unless they are set forth in terms of universalistic reference—in this case unless the proposition that Blacks prefer white is posed as a claim concerning all people. For this purpose, Blacks must constitute the entire universe in question, and the null hypothesis to be tested by evidence is strictly nonpreference in Blacks.

This move is tantamount to reformulating the proposition as "All (Black) people prefer white all of the time." Such a statement, of course, cannot logically be conclusively proven, a fact not contrary to our objective. But the principles of probability that dominate empirical hypothesis testing in modern science do permit partial confirmation at an appropriate error level. So we selected the .05 level of error and applied the evidence to the test of the null hypothesis of nonpreference in Blacks.

In a review of the 25 most prominent investigations of white preference in Blacks, we found 94 percent of the studies to have failed to reject the null hypothesis in support of the proposition. Twenty-five percent of studies had in fact demonstrated support of the opposite fact, namely Black preference among Blacks. But the overwhelming majority of studies (69 percent) had failed altogether to reject the null hypothesis at all. What is more, the 6 percent of studies that had succeeded in supporting the proposition of white preference is virtually identical to the rate at which empirical research could be expected by chance alone to do so.

The strategy of retrenchment was predictable. Williams and Morland (1979) argued that the proposition we set forth and tested was unduly strict: "All Blacks cannot be expected to prefer white all of the time." We would agree. But this criticism left them only three possible propositions to work with:

1. "Some Blacks prefer white some of the time." This claim, of course, is so weak that no conceivable evidence could ever refute it; therefore, it is devoid of any empirical content at all.

2. "All Blacks prefer white some of the time." But this was the claim in which our attack had resulted; that is, our critical analysis showed that nonpreference (or choosing white some of the time and choosing Black some of the time) was indeed the predominant pattern of Black behavior. This is the claim with which Williams and Morland disagreed.

3. "Some Blacks prefer white all of the time." In other words, the occasional preference for white stimuli represents a characteristic peculiar to some Blacks, which relates to a uniform rejection of themselves and their racial characteristics.

Clearly, on the face of it the evidence would not reject this last claim. What we had found was that roughly half of Black choices were of white stimuli, which meant either that all Blacks were choosing white some of the time or that some Blacks were choosing white all of the time.

In their reply to our earlier attack on white preference, Williams and Morland published the substance of this latter interpretation of the above claim. It was their contention that such a proposition is equally plausible as that which we advanced to explain the evidence and that our claim must therefore be considered as premature. An editorial communication in the context of the debate went even further, referring to this apparent standoff as an inevitable (possibly irresolvable) difference of opinion! Our contention, however, was that no such claims within the domain of science can reside ultimately with a mere matter of taste and that the confrontation itself between these opposing claims must be resolvable by evidence (Banks, McQuater, and Ross, 1979).

In this regard, we appealed to the framework of validation (Cronback and Meehl, 1955) to establish the truth of Williams and Morland's counterclaim. The proposition that "Some Black people prefer white all of the time," and that such a phenomenon is "important" (Williams and Morland, 1979, p. 29), is identical to the assertion that white preference is a behavior in Blacks that concurs with or predicts some meaningful experience or behavioral event. Clearly, the assertion had been that such behavior is related to self-esteem, to social behavior in the context of peer and friendship choices, and so on. Whether evidence stands in support of the validity of white preference in this respect is an empirical question. Williams and Morland presented three cases of evidence whose status they claimed was precisely that of support (Williams, et al., 1975; Spencer and Horowitz, 1973; McAdoo, 1970).

Our analysis, however, revealed that they were in error. The evidence reported in the study by Williams, et al. (1975), contrary to the contention of Williams and Morland, supported rather than rejected the null hypothesis of nonpreference in Blacks. That they had been led to believe that it did otherwise was the result of a misanalysis of the data that violated the statistical assumption of the nonparametric test they had used. Williams and his associates had administered a 24-item Preschool Racial Attitude Measure Scale, in which children were required to choose between Black and white stimulus alternatives on 24 separate evaluative queries. They reported a binomial test of probability for the within-subjects frequencies of white-stimulus choices across the 24 replicated items of their Preschool Racial Attitude Measure II (PRAM) instrument. Moreover, they reported that 60 percent of the white subjects selected the white-representative stimuli more often than would be expected by chance across the 24 within-subjects replications, as did 39 percent of the Black children. However, their contention of the significance of the choice behavior of 39 percent Blacks who chose the white stimuli on 17 or more of the items, while intuitively compelling, is statistically inappropriate, due to the nonindependence (within-subjects derivation) of those frequency observations. While this within-subjects replication of preference choices may have yielded a more reliable categorization of respondents into white preference and other classifications than did the various one-response procedures of past research, it is these between-subjects category frequencies that are appropriately testable by binomial and related analyses. In this regard, fully 72 percent of white children chose the white stimuli at within-subjects rates, which led Williams, et al. (1975) to label them as indicating "definite" or "probable" bias. While 52 percent of Black subjects fell within these two categories, fully 58 percent would have been expected to do so by chance alone.

A study by Spencer and Horowitz (1973), which Williams and Morland cited as supportive of their argument, was one in which a test of the relevant data had not been performed at all. Mere intuitive conjecture had led Williams and Morland to conclude that Spencer and Horowitz's data supported the proposition of white preference in Blacks, because no statistical analysis of that data rejected the null hypothesis (see Banks, McQuater, and Ross, 1979, p. 34). The choices of the control-group Blacks to which Williams and Morland referred as having displayed white preference were reported only in terms of the mean percentage of white choices (approximately 70 percent). Within a sample of eight, this magnitude of frequencies between subjects would not reject the null hypothesis, since a percentage of roughly 85 would be required at the .05 level. However, since the data were reported as mean percent of choices within subjects, we might instead attempt to assess its significance by a t-test comparison against 50 percent. Using the error term from the analysis of variance reported by Spencer and Horowitz (1973), this test would yield a t-value of approximately 1.31, hardly approaching significance even at the .05 level.

Finally, in the dissertation study of McAdoo (1970), Williams and Morland found evidence of actual white preference in some Black children. However, that same investigation offered important evidence of the concurrent invalidity of such behavior when it does occur in Blacks. Black children from the North and the South were measured concurrently for self-concepts and for racial preferences. In this instance, the Williams, et al. (1975) PRAM measure of racial preference, in fact, was found to be unrelated to northern Black children's self-concepts. And contrary to the assumptions of concurrent-criterion validity that might derive from that instrument, measured white preference among southern Black youngsters was directly related not to negative self-concepts but to positive self-concepts.

The overwhelming majority of all the validation evidence, in fact, shows that white preference even when it does occur in some of the people fails to concur with, predict, or constitute a logical point of convergence for any set of experiences or behaviors that, theoretically, it should. Still, at quite a different level, the validation of white preference in Blacks as representing the construct, for instance, of negative self-concept could proceed via systematic observations of positive correlations between it and logically convergent behavioral phenomena and negative correlations between its occurrence and that of logically divergent phenomena among Blacks. In this regard, one might expect that Blacks would with reasonable consistency express a conception of their own qualities and abilities for successful functioning as lower than those of white persons; one might expect, as well, to find that success in such domains as school would relate profoundly to such racially influenced self-assessments among Blacks. Certain empirical evidence stands in opposition to both the former (see, e.g., Wylie, 1963; Wylie and Hutchins, 1967) and the latter (Coleman, et al., 1966; Guggenheim, 1969; Hunt and Hardt, 1969; Wolkon, 1971) notion. Similarly, within a population whose qualities of racial identification and valuation are supposed to work so destructively against a sense of personal optimism and worth, one would hardly expect aspirations toward intellectual/academic excellence and occupational/socioeconomic ascendance to obtain. Yet they do and most often in measure equal to or beyond that of persons whose sense of racial identity ought to place them in a relatively superior position. (See Boyd, 1952; Brook, 1974; Ducette and Wolk, 1973; Gist and Bennett, 1963; Phillips, 1972).

So the difference in our claim and that of Williams and Morland is not a matter of opinion; rather, it is a matter of fact. And the facts reject their counterclaim.

SUMMARY

In sum, then, it should be clear that of the several tasks to which empirical evidence may be put, only one has been explored by the conventional science of psychology. That is the entertainment of existential propositions concerning the experience and behavior of Black people. In this regard, the domain of inquiry has always been precisely delineated both by reference by proper grammatical form and through a comparative paradigmatic frame that delimits that population relative to whites. The resultant irrefutability of its theoretical claims has been an inescapable source for Black Psychology of cynicism and disenchantment with the methods of empirical science. But the nonconfirmable universalism to which orthodox science would relegate the empirical endeavors of Black Psychology is equally unhopeful if that strategy is applied to the development of our own theoretical frameworks. Therefore it should not be. Where propositions of a universal logical character are entertained it should be in the context of redressing and refuting the previously existential claims of orthodox psychology. For this purpose, the major theoretical propositions of past comparative research should be formulated in their extreme universal form, and the rigors of evidential criteria applied in the falsification of such propositions and the theories from which they derive.

For our own purposes an appeal to propositions whose form contains the existential qualifier of proper "Black" appropriately delimits the domain of our theories. The rigors of evidence may thus be applied toward the confirmation of such theories and claims and advance the needed proliferation of knowledge regarding so diverse a people as is the *Afrikan diaspora*.

What clearly is needed, perhaps, is a more precise delineation between these alternative roles of empirical inquiry for falsification and for confirmation. At the same time, there is a need also for a more systematic effort to criticize the proliferating claims that Black Psychologists wish to advance. So we should not call for an unrestrained anarchism of knowledge (Feyerabend, 1975). Even so, it might be argued that my appeal to the use of certain empirical strategies for falsification of the claims of orthodox psychology and for the use of certain other empirical strategies for the confirmation of the claims of contemporary Black Psychology represents a perversion of scientific method. Perhaps it is so. But philosophers of science have already observed that scientific method is nothing but "an ornament that makes us forget that a position of anything goes has already been adopted" (Feyerabend, 1970). To recognize that Black Psychology is equal to that anarchism is, I believe, an important role for Black scientists. And in that context we should not hesitate to recognize that the foundation of Black Psychology and its aims in accomplishments promote at once the welfare of the Black community and the critical growth of knowledge.

NOTES

1. It is worth recalling here that in his *Essay Concerning Human Understanding* Locke set forth the principles of what he considered a critical program of empirical methods aimed (modestly) at merely clearing the way toward knowledge. Similarly, the appeal to empirical principles suggested here is intended primarily as a strategy for clearing theoretical misconstructions from the domain of research on Black populations.

2. A complete survey of the history of the Association of Black Psychologists can be found in Williams, R., "History of the Association of Black Psychologists: Early Formation and Development," *Journal of Black Psychologists* 1 (1974):9-24, or in King, R.E.G., "Highlights in the Development of ABPsi," *Journal of Black Psychology* 4 (1977-78):9-24.

3. Boykin offers an illuminating discussion of the arguments for and against the abandonment of empirical research strategies within the field of Black Psychology.

4. The whole of postmodern philosophy of knowledge has left the Cartesian-Kantian idols of objectivity, universality, and certainty in "shambles" (cf. C. West's

"Introduction," *Union Seminary Quarterly Review* 34 (1979):67-68.

5. For example, the claim that "some people eat bread" cannot be refuted by any finite accumulation of evidence to the contrary, since it may always be asserted that there may exist someone (somewhere) who fulfills the claim. This assymetry between the evidence that may confirm and the evidence that may refute a claim is a central concept in Popper's analysis of the logical structure of scientific propositions. Existential claims (e.g., "some people") can be confirmed by a single case and yet cannot be refuted by several. Universal claims (e.g., "all people") can be refuted by a single case and yet cannot be confirmed by several.

REFERENCES

Banks, W.C. White preference in Blacks: A paradigm in search of a phenomenon. *Psychological Bulletin* 83 (1976):1179-186.

Banks, W.C., McQuater, G.U., and Hubbard, J.L. Toward a reconceptualization of the social-cognitive bases of achievement orientations in Blacks. *Review of Educational Research* 48 (1978):381-97.

Banks, W.C., McQuater, G.V., and Ross, J.A. On the importance of white preference and the comparative difference of Blacks and others: Reply to Williams and Morland. *Psychological Bulletin* 86 (1979):33-36.

Banks, W.C., McQuater, G.V., Ward, W., and Ross, J.A. Delayed gratification in Blacks: A critical review. Unpublished manuscript. Princeton, N.J.: Educational Testing Service, 1980.

Banks, W.C., Ward, W., McQuater, G.V., and DeBritto, A.M. Locus of control. Unpublished manuscript. Princeton, N.J.: Educational Testing Service, 1980.

Bay Area Association of Black Psychologists. Position statement on use of I.Q. and ability tests. In *Black Psychology,* edited by R.L. Jones. New York: Harper & Row, 1972.

Boyd, G. The levels of aspiration of white and Negro children in a nonsegregated elementary school. *Journal of Social Psychology,* 1952, 36, 191-196.

Boykin, A.W. Black Psychology and the research process: Keeping the baby but throwing out the bath water. *Journal of Black Psychology* 4 (1978):43-64.

Brook, J. Aspiration levels of and for children: Age, sex, race, and socioeconomic status correlates. *Journal of Genetic Psychology,* 1974, 124, 3-16.

Coleman, J.S., Campbell, E.Q., Hobson, C.J., McPartland, J., Mood, A.M., Weinfield, F.D., and York, R.L. *Equality of Educational Opportunity.* (U.S. Department of Health, Education, and Welfare, OE-38001) Washington, D.C.: Government Printing Office, 1966.

Cronbach, L.J. and Meehl, P.E. Construct validity in psychological tests. *Psychological Bulletin* 52 (1955):281-302.

Ducette, J., and Wolk, S. Locus of control and levels of aspiration in black and white children. *Review of Educational Research.* 1973, 42, 40-48.

Feyerabend, P.K. Consolations for the specialist. In *Criticism and the Growth of*

Knowledge, edited by I. Lakatos and A. Musgrave. London: Cambridge University Press, 1970.

———. *Against Method*. London: Verso, 1975.

Gist, N., and Bennett, W. Aspirations of Negro and white students. *Social Forces*, 1963, 42, 40-48.

Guggenheim, F. Self-esteem achievement expectations for white and Negro children. *Journal of Projective Techniques and Personality Assessment*, 1969, 33, 63-69.

Hunt, D., and Hardt, R. The effect of upward bound programs of attitudes, motivation and academic achievement of Negro students. *Journal of Social Issues*, 1969, 25, 117-129.

Kamin, L.J. *The Science and Politics of I.Q.* Potomac, Md.: Lawrence Earlbaum Associates, 1974.

Kuhn, T.S. *Structure of Scientific Revolutions*, 2nd ed. Chicago: University of Chicago Press, 1970.

Lakatos, I. Falsification and the methodology of scientific research programs. In *Criticism and the Growth of Knowledge*, edited by I. Lakatos and A. Musgrave. London: Cambridge University Press, 1970.

Lakatos, I. and Musgrave, A.E., eds. *Criticism and the Growth of Knowledge*. London: Cambridge University Press, 1970.

Masterman, M. The nature of a paradigm. In *Criticism and the Growth of Knowledge*, edited by I. Lakatos and A. Musgrave. London: Cambridge University Press, 1970.

McAdoo, H.P. Racial attitudes and self-concepts of Black school children. Ph.D. dissertation. University of Michigan, 1970.

Pears, D.F. Universals. *The Philosophical Quarterly* 1 (1950-51):218-27.

Phillips, B. School-related aspirations of children with different sociocultural backgrounds. *Journal of Negro Education*, 1972, 42, 48-52.

Popper, K.R. *The Logic of Scientific Discovery*. Harper & Row, 1959.

Spencer, M.B. and Horowitz, F.D. Effects of systematic social and token reinforcement on the modification of racial and color concept attitudes in Black and white preschool children. *Developmental Psychology* 9 (1973):246-54.

Williams, J.E., Best, D.L., Boswell, D.A., Mattsen, L.A., and Graves, D.J. Preschool racial attitude measure II. *Educational and Psychological Measurement* 35 (1975):3-18.

Williams, J.E. and Morland, J.K. Comment on Banks' White preference in Blacks: A paradigm in search of a phenomenon. *Psychological Bulletin* 86 (1979):28-32.

Williams, R. History of the association of Black psychologists: Early formation and development. *Journal of Black Psychology* 1 (1974):9-24.

Wolkon, G. African identity of the Negro American and achievement. *Journal of Social Issues*, 1971, 27, 199-211.

Wylie, R. Children's estimates of their schoolwork ability as a function of sex, race, and self-esteem level. *Journal of Personality*, 1963, 31, 204-224.

Wylie. R., and Hutchins, E. Schoolwork ability estimates and aspirations as a function of socioeconomic level, race and sex. *Psychological Reports*, 1967, 21, 781-808.

X(Clark), C., McGhee, D.P., Nobles, W., and X(Weems), L. Voodoo or I.Q.: An introduction to African psychology. *Journal of Black Psychology* 1 (1975):9-29.

4   Adaptive Strategies in U.S. Minorities

George A. DeVos

The social scientist observing the multiethnic nature of U.S. society, including racial diversity and its stratification into social classes, is motivated to use systematic observation and measurement in order to understand the types of adaptation made by the various groups comprising the United States. Anyone who is more than a casual observer is aware that there have been varying patterns of adaptation among these groups. "Adaptation" is usually measured by Americans in terms of occupational and social mobility. Since most women in the past did not have careers of their own, they were usually judged by whether they made an advantageous marriage and maintained a successful family life. Women were therefore sometimes judged by the relative "success" of their children. Since U.S. society sees itself as future oriented, today anyone who breaks from the traditions of the past and seeks out individual accomplishment is seen as adapting well. Poor adaptation is measured very often by some indication of alienation, withdrawal, deviant or delinquent behavior, marital failure, alcoholism, or symptoms of emotional or mental "breakdown."

We find in the earlier social science literature a dialectic of interpretation between those seeking out social determinants in explaining differences among groups and those searching for psychological or even hereditary factors to explain the variety of adaptive patterns manifest in social behavior. It has been implicitly assumed that all individuals operating within U.S. society are seeking to improve their social position by the acquisition of wealth, power, or prestige by some recognized forms of social accomplishment. Hence, individual differences in achieving these ends are either implicitly or explicitly related to social factors, on the one hand, or personal capacities, on the other.

Those who espoused early theoretical presumptions about hereditary differences in the ability of groups have by and large given way to those who devote their attention to how the individual is "socialized" by growing up in particular families, by being taught in particular schools, and by being influenced by particular communities.

One finds, first, in the development of the sociological study of the U.S. city, assumptions that newcomers would eventually adapt into an already present "Anglo-Saxon" pattern of life. These assumptions were replaced by a "melting pot" concept, which has, in turn, more recently been replaced by concepts of continuing cultural pluralism. The earlier theories concerning assimilation have given way to the present recognition that U.S. society, for the next few generations at least, will remain multiethnic in composition.

One must point out that many past sociological studies, whatever their agreement or disagreement with alternative psychological approaches, assumed sociological determinants without considering possible differences in adaptation that might have been due to *culture patterns* per se. On the other hand, the developmental psychologist or the social psychologist as well as the personality theorist in the past has seldom extended research activities to comparative cultural sampling to verify generalizations. By now, however, the necessity to consider the effects of culture on behavior has become recognized, but systematic examination of the interrelationship between social, psychological, *and* cultural determinants in adaptive or maladaptive behavior is still in the early formative stage. The founding of the *Journal of Cross-Cultural Psychology* in 1971 has been encouraging. There is now a forum for discussion for those seeking to develop better theoretical models of an interdisciplinary nature, with periodic reviews of research, which permit comparison of results cross-culturally.

In examining "adaptive strategies" I cannot presume to review or react in detail to the vast body of literature so far produced in sociology and psychology as well as the more recent studies of contemporary U.S. society by anthropologists. What I propose to do instead is to utilize the conclusions reached in my own earlier minority groups research with Japanese Americans, and my more recent work with the Korean minority and the former pariah caste in Japan, in order to approach some of the more controversial questions about differences in adaptation found in U.S. society. In so doing I shall be commenting on some long-standing issues raised in U.S. social science on which there is as yet no final consensus. I propose to organize my comments around a few contentions. First, all social groups have some implicit image of what it is to be a successful adult; these images of adulthood revolve around basic "instrumental" and "expressive" concerns of a positive or a negative nature (DeVos, 1973). These concerns are inextricably involved with definitions of self and self-assessment, the interaction of self and society generally, or the interaction of self directly with others in primary relationships. This interaction approach is an intermediate one, it does not deal directly with any structural analysis or personality variables per se, nor is it a form of social structural analysis.

ADAPTATION AND ADJUSTMENT

Elsewhere I have contended that there is a basic difference between "adaptation" and "adjustment" (DeVos, 1974, 1976, 1978). For the most part, in the literature of psychology as well as anthropology and sociology, the concepts of "adjustment" and "adaptation" are loosely used in a roughly equivalent manner. They indiscriminately refer both to the internal structures that we assume under the concept of personality or, in many instances, to mutually adaptive human processes of communication and interaction that occur in social role relationships. More generally, they are used indiscriminately as concepts referring to man's response to his environment. I contend that some essential distinction is necessary.

The term "adjustment," as I use it, is not culturally or situationally relative; it assumes an ideal progression of psychosocial *maturation* that is a biological potential for all human beings. The realization of ideal maturation, however, may be fostered or deformed. "Coping" mechanisms may become "defense" mechanisms in a developing personality structure. The converse concept of "maladjustment" refers to rigidification, to some deficiency, to structural lack, and to a resultant incapacity for adaptive response in an individual.

"Adaptation," as I use the term, refers directly to observable social behavior, not to personality dynamics. "Maladaptation," more simply, refers to some form of response that is itself inadequate for social purposes. It is most helpful theoretically to maintain a clear distinction between the *internal structuring of personality, related to the concept of adjustment* or maladjustment, and *social-behavioral responses that are interpreted as socially adaptive* or maladaptive for the individual within his social nexus. The first term, "adjustment," refers to constructs about psychological structure; the second, "social adaptation," may or may not involve fixed psychological structures.

I shall address myself in this chapter to two questions that appear related to social adaptation: (1) Is it valid to consider some subgroups of our complex society as living in a "culture of poverty"? and (2) How are patterns of learning or nonlearning in the U.S. school system related to cultural differences or to social status differences? By addressing myself to these two issues I hope to help delineate how "culture" is or is not involved in social behavior of an adaptive or nonadaptive nature. How socially adaptive or maladaptive patterns are related to underlying adjustive patterns, i.e., to internal personality structure, is examined briefly in reference to research on field dependence-independence and the concept of internalization or superego development.

A CAVEAT ON USING THE CONCEPT OF "CULTURE"

At the present time "culture" as a concept has become an important consideration in the psychological literature and, to a lesser extent, in the sociological literature, but as I shall presently point out some uses of the concept of culture have been questionable from an anthropological perspective. It is very common, for example, to talk in terms of "cultural deprivation." There is also a somewhat loosely considered assertion that certain subgroups such as black Americans are a "separate culture" and therefore cannot be assessed in terms applicable to U.S. society in general.

I would contend that the usage "cultural deprivation" depends on an incomplete understanding of the anthropological use of culture as a concept. Whatever the patterns exhibited by people, one cannot logically consider that they are "deprived" of a culture pattern. It is more meaningful to think of a cultural heritage as emphasizing alternative patterns of adaptation. As used in an anthropological context, the word "deprivation" has no logical meaning.

The second point of view—that there is a separate black American culture—sometimes assumes that living within an ethnic minority is directly comparable to living within a totally independent, self-contained society. It is an essential characteristic of an ethnic minority that it is *part of* a larger society. Hence, the values, judgments, perceptions of adult relationsips, and the like of such a minority cannot be examined apart from the influences, direct and indirect, of the dominant culture or the system of social stratification in which the group is embedded. It is a quite different matter to grow up in an independent culture that is more or less self-contained and can therefore be maintained without considering strong alternative pressures from other segments of a multiethnic society. The definitions of successful adaptation maintained by any minority group become inextricable interwoven with that of the dominant society and are, hence, directly influenced by the knowledge that one is a part of a minority within the dominant society that may or may not be limited to some specified levels in the social hierarchy. Perhaps the use of the term "subculture" for minority groups would clarify this distinction.

These two contrasting extensions of the concept of culture as used in anthropology are also part of an ongoing conflict of theory between those who are problem oriented and concerned with psychopathology or social pathology versus those who would use the concept of culture in a totally affirmative manner. Those examining social problems, by the very nature of their approach, tend to deal with certain negative features found with high incidence in a particular group. Their attention is focused, therefore, on relative indices of social *maladaptation*—rates of delinquency, poor school performance in childhood or adulthood, problems of marital instability, alcoholism, emotional instability, or mental illness. On the other hand, those taking an affirmative approach sometimes lose their objectivity by deemphasizing manifest internal aspects of personal and group social problems and espousing solely externally directed programs of economic, political, or social advancement (cf. Korchin, 1980). They tend to see group patterns only in positive terms and ascribe signs of maladaptation solely to external influences. They decry any approach that suggests that maladjustment may be involved.

IS THERE A CULTURE OF POVERTY?

Oscar Lewis' work in Mexico and among minority Puerto Ricans in New York City (1961, 1966, 1969) has raised a great deal of controversy. Lewis attempted to summarize what he perceived to be a debased minority pattern passed from one generation to the next. He called this pattern the "culture of poverty," a form of maladaptation to marginal roles within a highly stratified society emphasizing individual endeavor. Basically this concept is a description of social alienation. What Lewis calls a culture of poverty should be called a "subculture" because it does not exist independently but within an overall pattern in which some part of a complex society is accorded a relatively degraded social status. Moreover, it may characterize a segment of an ethnic group—not the whole ethnic group. This "subculture of poverty" is a patterned social response to an internal sense of hopelessness and despair passed on from one generation to the next in a disparaged and economically destitute segment of a society.

Lewis contended that this sense of hopelessness develops from a realization of the improbability of change, the improbability of being able to achieve the goals and values of the larger society in which the individual and his family have been accorded disadvantaged roles. Lewis suggests, at least in the two subcultures—peasant migrants to Mexico City and Puerto Ricans in New York—in which he did his own field work, that there is, in some special segments of these ethnic communities at least, compared with the higher-status segments of the same urban populations, early intiation into sex, a relatively high incidence of abandonment of wives and children, and a trend toward matrifocal families, countered by a strong disposition for defensive authoritarianism on the part of adult males. While there are expressed ideals of family solidarity, there is, in actuality, constant internal dissention and competition for limited goods with the dominant culture or the higher classes.

There are strong feelings of marginality and helplessness, dependency and inferiority. Lewis sees in such a transmitted "culture of poverty" the frequent appearance not only of material deprivation but the earlier maternal deprivation of individuals, leading to relatively weak egos. There is in some a lack of impulse control and difficulty in gratification. In effect, he argues from a psychological level that a "culture of poverty" is characterized by a high incidence of various forms of mental maladjustment and interpersonal difficulty as well as observable maladaptive behavior. But his most important contention was that this pattern was a "culture" because it was perpetuated through the socialization experiences of children. Therefore, he did not see it simply as an immediate reaction to social or economic degradation but as a consequent longer-term self-perpetuating syndrome. As he saw it, individuals, in their early socialization, became locked in and found it difficult to alter self-defeating patterns in order to become more adaptive in actualizing what they themselves see as desirable goals. There was a sense of helplessness and frustation. Individuals caught in the "culture of poverty" were not, in his view, simply in an alternative cultural pattern with its own goals, values, and objectives that could be reached with satisfaction by continuing a traditional pattern with its own forms. While agreeing with Lewis' specific observations I would suggest that his point could have been better made about generational continuity by distinguishing between a "culture" and a "subculture" or social groups who are in effect in a specific minority status position within a larger society.

Whatever the terminology used, Lewis' writings are related to the equally strong controversy as to how to explain the very high rates of mental illness and the high rate of delinquency among some segments of black Americans. One of the earliest attempts to explain these problems in terms of adjustive or psychological factors of socialization was the work of Kardiner and Ovesey (1951). Using intensive depth therapy on an admittedly small number of cases, the authors demonstrated that forms of social debilitation were related to damaged self-esteem. They also used Rorschach test data as an adjunct, showing that severe intrapsychic problems of a sadomasochistic nature were related to what they termed the "mark of oppression."

Thomas Pettigrew (1964), in summarizing a great deal of research on black Americans to that date, also stressed the maladjustive effects of oppression over several generations as a key to the high indices of observable deviant and maladaptive behavior. But others have argued that much observable behavior has been an adaptive role taken as a means of survival to avoid severe, aggressive sanctioning by dominant whites. Showing deference or playing dumb was part of the castelike atmosphere in which many blacks were constrained to live. Nevertheless, Pettigrew also argued for the maladjustive nature of a lowered self-esteem and confusion over self-identity experienced from early childhood on within the degraded position to which many blacks have been relegated in U.S. society.

These approaches have been criticized as overusing a deficiency hypothesis. They are the somewhat one-sided approaches of outsiders to American black communities. However, writing about the personal debilitation suffered by U.S. blacks was not done only from the outside by whites. Such experiences have also been recorded by black social scientists. For example, Horace Cayton (1951) published at the same time as the Kardiner and Ovesey volume a description of the general inner feeling of social helplessness as well as the widespread expectation of mistreatment among blacks, leading to a sense of constant oppression, which debilitated many black Americans during the period before the 1950s. Cayton wrote about these matters from his own personal anguish. A potentially brilliant academic career in sociology was vitiated by his own problems over black identity; throughout the latter part of his life, he struggled with severe alcoholism.

In summary, Pettigrew interpreted the problems of many black youth in terms very similar to Lewis' description of the culture of poverty among Puerto Ricans. The socialization that occurred within the dilapidated housing, crowded living conditions, in disorganized neighborhoods, single-parent households is, for Pettigrew, at least a partial explanation for the relatively poor school performance of black youth. He cited specific psychological studies revealing how eight- or nine-year-old children with absent fathers are more likely to seek immediate gratification and are more intolerant of frustration. The alien demands of the classroom are beyond endurance. He stated that, regardless of race, children manifesting such traits tend to be less accurate at judging time, less socially responsible, less oriented toward achievement, and more prone toward delinquency (Pettigrew, 1964, pp. 17ff.). Pettigrew considered single-parent families a manifestation of social disorganization and contended that many individuals whose childhood socialization occurs within a broken home in ghetto conditions become "psychologically vulnerable" and therefore are more likely to show mental illness or to become involved in drug addiction or crime. It is an already psychologically vulnerable youth who faces discrimination in adolescence and who subsequently becomes socially maladaptive as an adult. These influences are particularly devastating on males, though women also show manifest difficulties.

A number of others have made understanding of family interaction a partial key to the subsequent maladaptive patterns manifest in many lower-class black children, youths, and adults (e.g., Antonovsky and Lerner, 1959). This somewhat "clinical" view has been countered by a number of writers, stating that these conclusions perhaps give a one-sided emphasis on social problems and that if one used a more detached cultural perspective one could find positive features in the social interactions of many U.S. lower-class blacks. In the late 1960s there began to appear more affirmative analyses and interpretations by black social scientists, such as those of Charles Keil (1966) and Andrew Billingsley (1968), who wrote a reevaluation of the strengths found in many black families and described how blacks reared in more cohesive families were indeed able to survive the ordeal of discrimination without personal debilitation. Today there has been more reexploration of how fragments of an African heritage have been integrated into some segments of the black subculture, which has positive features as well as inheritance of social degradation. This more ethnographic, less problem-focused approach suggests that some of the sociological as well as psychological literature presented a somewhat oversimplified negative view of the complexities and variations of contemporary black social life. (Cayton and Drake's study of Chicago (1962) is an exceptional early example of a more holistic ethnographic reporting.)

Recent studies suggest that there has been some continuing and identifiable Afro-American subcultural features that help structure family life and behavioral patterns. Here one must understand family life in its broader context of kinship-interrelationship-friendship patterns and other supportive forms of face-to-face interpersonal relationship (Stack, 1974). There are some positive, constructive, adaptive reactions to the social position of blacks in U.S. society on the lower strata as well as in those families that have totally accepted U.S middle-class values. Black writers, past and present, such as Richard Wright (1945), Ralph Ellison (1964), and Maya Angelou (1969), have presented searching and sensitive descriptions of growing up in different class strata of black subcultures within U.S. society. Alex Haley, in his very perceptive work with Malcolm X (1965), as well as his fictionalized account of his own antecedents (1976), has presented patterns of black life to a general U.S. audience in a way that allows for greater comprehension of the strengths as well as the ordeals of life as a black American, past and contemporary. What is quite obvious is that many blacks did not grow up in a "culture of poverty"—but some did and survived.

That there are continually changing subcultures of black Americans has been demonstrated. The question is, does it therefore argue that the relative amount of maladjustment implied in earlier comparative studies is decreasing? I think not. While affirmative patterns within the black communities are changing the self-image of U.S. blacks, there is still evidence that a higher proportion of black Americans than white are having psychological problems related to social degradation. (Conversely many white Americans of given ethnic backgrounds may have psychological problems related to middle-class social status and mobility of a somewhat different nature—a topic we do not have time to explore here.) No one can argue seriously that a contemporary urban black ghetto such as that of Chicago is simply an independent "subculture." Whatever the concept, "culture of poverty" or some other terminology, as social scientists we must face the fact that psychological problems persist from one generation to the next. Alleviation of these problems involves *both* sociological and psychological considerations.

There is "psychological lag" that persists despite legal changes and contemporary changes in economic and social discrimination. There are persistences on a psychological level inherited from the economic and social difficulties experienced in the past. The concept of a "culture of poverty" emphasizes the continuity of a disparaged status in a socially stratified society. *Those emphasizing a "separate culture" seek to avoid considering, to some degree at least, the persistent psychological effects of past as well as present relative social degradation on specifically vulnerable ethnic traditions.* Whether parents wish it or not, they sometimes pass on the burdens of the past as they socialize their children. Their socialization practices underlie some of the maladaptive responses of their children.

Suffice it to say, when examining the adaptive strategies of blacks and various ethnic minorities from a problem orientation point of view, one is constrained to consider maladjustment and maladaptation, to some degree at least, from the standpoint of how an individual responds to or is influenced by the major values of the dominant society. Approached within this framework, some ethnic groups manifestly do better, some more poorly, in adapting to formal learning situations imposed in childhood, which are supposed to prepare the individual for adult occupational adaptations. What are the adjustive processes at work on a personality level? What are the cultural as well as the sociological and psychological factors contributing to patterns considered unsuccessful, whether in "learning" or in later adult roles? How are these determinants of behavior interrelated? Let me start by examining the complex interrelation between internal personal adjustment and social adaptation patterns manifested by Japanese Americans.

ACHIEVEMENT, CULTURE, AND PERSONALITY: THE CASE OF THE JAPANESE AMERICANS

The long history of discrimination against the Japanese came to a climax with World War II. United States citizens of Japanese ancestry, as well as their immigrant great grandparents who had long been denied naturalization, were in 1942 mass deported from their homes on the West Coast and detained for the duration of the war in so-called relocation centers, most located in western desert areas of the United States. At war's end, Japanese Americans were finally permitted to resettle, and by 1947 over 17,000 had chosen to resettle in the Chicago area. There were several of us in sociology, anthropology, and psychology at the University of Chicago who were interested in what was presumed to be problems of social adaptation faced by both the Issei immigrants and their U.S.-born Nisei children coming into a new urban environment after what we presumed was a traumatic disruption of their previous lives. Instead of finding among the Japanese Americans various symptoms of social and personal dislocation, we found, by and large, a quick, seemingly positive adaptation by them and a surprising degree of social acceptance by midwestern Americans, given the previous wartime climate. The Japanese Americans were able to find new jobs and an interest in continuing educational advancement despite their previous lack of job opportunities in California and other states where discrimination against Asians had been very severe.

Visiting them in their new homes in the marginal ghetto areas of Chicago, "zones of transition" so well studied by a previous generation of sociologists at the University of Chicago, we found that the Japanese Americans were not conforming to previous patterns established by migrant waves moving into the Chicago slums. It became quickly obvious that sociological generalizations about the effects of slum conditions were not sufficient to explain the particular nature of Japanese-American adaptation.

As our work progressed, William Caudill and I, who were specifically responsible for working with psychological tests, found that both the immigrant generation and their children, on the level of psychological adjustment, manifested very strong patterns of need achievement (Caudill, 1952). Personality patterns that I obtained on the Rorschach test (DeVos, 1954) showed a characteristic Japanese pattern, the Issei generation more so than their Nisei children. The Nisei sample in many respects resembled the norms of the U.S. control sample used by Beck and his colleagues in their research with the Rorschach (Beck et al., 1950). The Japanese records as a whole, both Nisei and Issei, showed a very strong concern with intellectual striving.

At that time I made an examination of the extant psychological literature on Japanese Americans. I found that there had been a number of psychological studies of Nisei children from the late 1920s on in the California public schools (e.g., Darsie, 1926; Clark, 1927; Bell, 1933; Kubo, 1934). As a whole, Japanese children showed no significant difference from other U.S. children on total IQ scores, but there were obvious patterned discrepancies in their lower verbal and high performance subtests. The Japanese Americans did significantly better than average in performance subtests, especially those on block design. They did relatively poorly on the verbal subscales.

E.K. Strong (1934) had summarized much of the earlier material, asking the question: How shall we explain the fact that the Japanese people of Los Angeles have the same IQ as the average pupil, and score about the same on educational tests and obtain strikingly better grades? It may be that they possess to a greater degree than whites, the qualities which endear pupils to a teacher; that they are most docile, occasion less disciplinary trouble, and given the appearance of being busy, striving to do their best. Another explanation would be that "they come from poor homes, and early realize that they must make their own way in the world; in consequence, they are better motivated to do their best" (Caudill and DeVos, 1956, p. 1103).

I noted at that time that Strong, in summarizing all the evidence of psychological materials, made no mention of the concept of culture or the effect of cultural traditions or cultural variables on the patterns of school adaptation or the patterns of socialization probably experienced by these Nisei pupils. Indeed, that was the major contention proposed by Caudill and myself, namely, that one could not understand the behavior of Japanese children in California schools or the subsequent pattern of occupational achievement of Japanese Americans without taking into consideration their cultural background and how it patterned their IQ scores, or their motivation and how their adjustive patterns would be manifested in social adaptation.

Subsequently, I spent two years in Japan with a large group of Japanese social scientists using survey techniques, with an overall sample of 2,400 subjects in both urban and rural settings. From our basic sample we also gathered overlapping samples of a large number of intensive interviews, as well as normative samples of over 800 each of Rorschach tests, Thematic Apperception Test (TAT) protocols, and a modified version of a problem situation test (DeVos, 1973, pp. 61-130).

In the course of my writings of Japan, I have discussed in great detail the nature of achievement motivation in Japanese culture. The continual preoccupation with adequacy and continual doubts about personal capacity are resolved by continual hard work. A need to achieve is internalized with a strong sense of potential guilt because of the form of disciplinary socialization used by Japanese mothers (DeVos, 1973, pp. 131-70). Neither parent used physical punishment but disciplined by demonstrating to a child how irresponsible behavior leads to the suffering of parents and family members generally. Japanese develop, as a consequence, a very highly internalized concern with obligation and responsibility. They remain docile and conforming to authority. They are accustomed to cooperative group interaction, and they play down individual competition, emphasizing collective endeavors. This type of instrumental, goal-oriented pattern is conducive to both individual accomplishments and collective group efforts.

As part of their patterned emotional expression there is continual preoccupation with group harmony and the suppression of overt aggression by patterns of self-effacement and politeness. There is a sacrifice of closeness and intimacy within the family but a greater emphasis on mutual inter-dependency than found in U.S. culture. From the standpoint of their cultural tradition, expressive concerns with family harmony and mutual nurturance are as important to Japanese as are instrumental concerns with individualistic ambition. As a matter of fact, Japanese do not phrase their desire for accomplishment in individualistic terms, but as members of a family or occupational unit. Therefore we do not see any conflict between affiliation and nurturance as major expressive considerations and a strong internalization of social directive toward achievement. There is within Japanese culture a great deal of competition between groups. However, the emphasis is more on within-group cooperation.

There is an ever-present sensitivity to social approval or disapproval. This sensitivity to "shame" is, however, in my judgment overemphasized by some observers such as Ruth Benedict (1946), who in writing about group conformity overlooked the high degree of personal internalization involved in achievement behavior (DeVos, 1973, pp. 144-70). Overall, the chief Japanese virtues are endurance and perserverance, which may be carried to the point where one may say that some Japanese are capable of making a virtue of suffering.

Working with Japanese culture, one is struck by the fact that Japanese are highly internalized and very strongly motivated to various forms of accomplishment. They are prone to guilt as much as any north European Calvinist in their work orientation. At the same time they are family and group oriented to a degree that makes the casual Western observer sometimes misconstrue their culture as "shame" oriented. Indeed, Japanese are susceptible to peer-group and community sanctioning, but one must also note the peer group or community is *not* antagonistic to the values and goals espoused by the primary family. The peer group is in most instances in harmony with, and a reinforcement of, the values held by the family. There is relatively little generational revolt. Hierarchy in Japan is age graded. One expects to remain dependent on those who precede. There is an openness or permeability to learning from those older than oneself.

The results demonstrating a higher national average on the Koh's block tests as part of the standardization of the Wechsler Intelligence Scale in Japan (the Japanese average is significantly higher than that reported in the U.S. standardization) would argue that on a structural psychological or cognitive level the Japanese are field independent (see p. 89), whereas *socially* they are hierarchical and remain dependent on others in their social adaptation. These results correspond to the supposed incongruity that on the TAT they demonstrate *both* high achievement motivation and a high concern with affiliation and nurturance as well as family responsibility, subordination to authority, and concern with family harmony.

In understanding these present-day features of Japanese psychological organization as they relate to manifest patterns of social adaptation, we must look back at Japanese cultural traditions in both family and community. Class definitions of status were important, but a line demarcating psychological self-acceptance from social disparagement was drawn between a proper people and outcast pariah groups. Among proper folk within what was the traditional merchant-artisan class, and the farming class as well as the samurai, upward striving and achievement motives were realized within one's group, though movement from one class to another was almost impossible.

Today, differences between these former classes have disappeared, but, contrary to the experience of European society, they have not been replaced by a sense of strong cleavage between a working class and a commercial-industrial-managerial group. Also, what remains as more typically Japanese is an age-grading system, which subordinates peer-group affinities to a basically hierarchical structure. In effect, what is more apparent than class cleavage in contemporary Japanese culture is the overall age grading, which occurs within organizations as well as within traditional sibling relationships within the family. Patterns of mentorship obviate any intense focus on the immediate age peer group as a source of emotional satisfaction. The pattern of age grading between older and younger brothers and between parents and children is transmuted into other social networks, including the occupational realm, in which younger members are treated "paternalistically" by older individuals. There is no hiatus or lack of communication between older or younger in this structure. In effect, expressive satisfactions are to be gained across age grades as well as from one's peers. However, there are also peer-group relationships in Japanese culture that can operate together for mutual benefit. There are also older rural traditions that do not depend on hierarchy but are based on cooperation. In summary, one finds continuing in Japanese culture today vertical as well as horizontal relationships that mutually reinforce the role positions of individuals rather than placing emphasis on individualistically conceived concepts of self. Attention to individualistic goals is seen as socially disruptive and is discouraged, both implicitly and explicitly, in Japanese career patterns. The fact that individualistic goals are discouraged and competition muted does not mean that Japanese are not highly internalized nor that many Japanese do not develop a field-independent mode of cognitive orientation. Nor is peer interaction at odds with family functioning.

This hierarchical pattern was transposed by Japanese immigrants to the United States. It should not be surprising, therefore, to find that the goals and successes of individual Japanese within the U.S. school system were perfectly consonant with docile acceptance of learning from older authority figures, long emphasized in the traditional culture pattern. As we pointed out (Caudill, 1952; Caudill and DeVos, 1956), it is on the basis of this type of pattern, given the maintenance of family cohesion within Japanese-American communities, that one can explain the extraordinary adaptation of this minority group relative to others within U.S. society. It was not that the Japanese duplicated the U.S. middle-class pattern; it was that their own pattern of adaptation was totally consonant with U.S. normative expectations.

Koreans in Japan: Derogation and Alienation

In contrast, let us turn to the experience of the Koreans in Japan and their different history. First of all, it must be noted that 85 percent of the Japanese coming to the United States were of farm background and were, for the most part, from financially destitute areas. However, when one looks at the educational statistics on the Issei immigrant men and women, one finds they averaged over an eighth-grade education. At the time of their immigration from Japan, there had been established universal education for boys and girls that made six years of schooling compulsory. The immigrant population, therefore, showed a tendency toward more education than that required by law. The farmers coming to the United States were, by and large, literate and brought with them a strong sense of using education as a means for increasing social success.

By contrast, the Koreans who after their colonization by Japan in 1910 moved from destitute farming regions to find employment in Japan brought with them no such educational experience. They were illiterate and came from a society in which the farming group, although in the Confucian class ideology theoretically of proper status, had come to have little sense of themselves as a worthy class. Korean society had long been governed from a distant capital by a disinterested nobility. The status of Korean farmers could in some aspects at least be more readily compared with that of Polish peasants or Mexican peons than with their contemporary Japanese counterparts.

After Korea was formally annexed as a Japanese colony in 1910, there was an increasing flow of Koreans to the Japanese mainland, but only a few of them came from the professional and commercial classes. The final large wave of Koreans came to Japan after 1939 to supply the ever-increasing need for unskilled conscript labor to replace Japanese drafted into the armed services during the Pacific war. In effect, for most Koreans, whether in Korea itself or in Japan, the first educational experiences were those of a subordinate minority within the Japanese imperial system, which granted them no equal social dignity with the dominant Japanese. All schooling was in Japanese, and Korean culture was accorded no appreciation. In every respect Koreans were subject to a system of severe social disparagement. It is not surprising, therefore, that our research found them manifesting the stigmata of minority groups disparaged elsewhere, namely, high rates of delinquency, crime, family disorganization, and above all a general lack of positive experience within the Japanese school system (Lee and DeVos, 1981). What is hard to document statistically but is observable in case history records is the relative lack of family cohesion, the social vulnerability of Korean youth, and the direct effects of mutual parental disparagement within the family.

When I make these remarks I am talking about a proportion of cases, not implying that social and mutual parental disparagement is a norm for the Korean family in Japan. It is simply that a relatively large number of Koreans face problems of this nature compared with ordinary Japanese. Some, in effect, are considered to be living in ghettoes similar to those described by

Lewis for Puerto Ricans in New York. The overall incidence of delinquency is seven times higher for Korean youth in Japan that it is for majority Japanese (DeVos, 1973, p. 387). As I shall subsequently discuss, the minority status of Koreans results in the inculcation of a negative or defensive social identity in a larger proportion of Korean children than in majority Japanese. What is quite apparent in the case histories is that in many Korean families the disparaged social status of unemployed or underemployed fathers becomes reflected in family tensions and the expression of mutually derogatory attitudes between parents. It is lack of family cohesion that we deem to be a significant variable in the appearance of delinquency in Korean youth. The evidence of this as a major factor is found in our other studies in Japan and Italy.

In our study of lower-status Japanese themselves in the early 1960s, where the overall rate of delinquency compared with European or U.S. norms remains relatively low, we nevertheless found significantly more delinquents coming from homes in which we found diparagement directed toward a husband by a wife. Elsewhere in other research with Italians the same relationship between patterns of parental disparagement and appearance of delinquency in a child are equally demonstrable (DeVos 1980C). I shall return to this contention later in my discussion.

For Koreans in Korea itself something entirely different is occurring. As an example, the Koreans are split politically by international as well as internal dissensions. But in South Korea where they are practicing a relatively free economy, 3.5 million Koreans are competing successfully with the Japanese in the Asian market and elsewhere. They are among the world's first 20 industrial societies, with a rising standard of living and a declining birth rate.

In the area of education they have reached an intensity of concern that has produced high levels of scholarly and professional competence. We are now also witnessing a selective immigration to the United States of relatively well-trained Koreans, who with their families constitute the third highest rate of contemporary immigration. Recent statistics suggest that within the 12-year span between 1968 and 1980 close to 400,000 Koreans entered the United States. Preliminary observation suggests the children of these immigrants are doing relatively well in U.S. schools.

Let me now turn to the research findings of others on issues related to learning and nonlearning and the effects of minority status in the United States. I shall make some interpretations of my own on yet to be resolved issues from a comparative perspective. I do not presume to demonstrate any acceptable proof for what I shall contend. What I am doing is looking at areas of dynamic interrelationship that are in need of further systematic research. I shall try to suggest that there is an insufficient understanding of how childhood socialization within the family influences cognitive development. I shall contend that in studying cognitive development one cannot leave aside a study of the internalization of social directives and attitudes toward authority. A study of the internalization process must also examine both the context of a contemporary peer group and social climate and a past cultural tradition being transmitted more or less effectively in a primary parent-child relationship.

U.S. MINORITIES IN THE CLASSROOM: SOME PSYCHOCULTURAL CONSIDERATIONS

The above brief considerations of my continuing research and theoretical orientation should indicate that I have taken a "problem approach" in my own psychocultural research. As a social scientist I cannot conceive of studying any human behavior without a single frame of reference; that is to say, one must be equally cognizant of cultural traditions, contemporary social forces, and psychological features influencing human behavior, since all these are involved in any behavioral response or human thought. Only by developing controlled methods of analysis for given specific issues can we explore separately either socially patterned behavior, on the one hand, or psychological structure, on the other.

As a psychological anthropologist I am compelled to look not only at the normative patterns that comprise a culture but also at forms of deviant behavior that are an inherent part of any culture pattern. It is impossible to understand any society or segment thereof as an ideal pattern. For example, I have too often seen descriptions of Japan without any indication that there were social problems related to caste status, to crime and delinquency, to suicide, or to other forms of personal alienation. I am impatient with a description of any society as some ideal or idealized organization. As a social scientist I have been aware of ethnocentric interpretations of their psychological findings by members of the American majority culture. These have been often used to the implicit disadvantage of given minorities. Happily, there is now increased direct participation in the social sciences by members of previously submerged groups. Unhappily, this participation has not always led to greater objectivity in the interpretation of results or the detached explanation of cause and effect in social problem areas. What is very apparent at this moment, whether it be in sociology, anthropology, or psychology, is a great deal of counter-ethnocentrism that does not transcend the former inadequacies of interpretation.

I hope we can eventually reach a stage in which there can be a more scientifically objective assessment of social and personal problems. We must aim toward effective interdisciplinary approaches by researchers from disparate cultural traditions.

Minority Status and Classroom Competence

The field of cross-cultural psychology in the United States has been developing as a partial response to the crisis that occurred concerning the relatively poor showing of ethnic minorities in the schools and the validity or advisability of using culturally biased psychological test measurements in the classroom in a multiethnic society.

IQ tests, as they were used in the past, demonstrated relatively poor scores for certain ethnic minorities. I shall not enter into this controversy here. Others have well pointed out the lack of consideration of cultural background and social status variables as well as the problems of psychological defenses related to the maintenance of self-image, which I have briefly considered elsewhere (DeVos, 1980b).

In Japan we have noted (DeVos and Wagatsuma, 1966, pp. 258-72) that there are quite apparent relationships between minority status, poor IQ scores, poor school performance, lack of family cohesion, and high rates of delinquency. These interrelationships are complex. For example, delinquency and IQ have no significant relationship, but in Japan, as in the United states, delinquency is significantly high in broken families. We also have demonstrated in both Japan and Italy that male delinquency occurs in families with little internal cohesion, poor supervision, inconsistent discipline, and lack of affection afforded a son (DeVos, 1980C). Delinquency is significantly higher among truants and poor performers in school, and yet in no minority group we have dealt with intensively can we report any lack of respect for schooling or any devaluing of formal education. I would contend that social values are not that different for U.S. minority groups. What differs is the priority of other social concerns and the methods of discipline used by parents to encourage internalization of social expectations on the part of their children.

One must consider the possibility, however, that for some minorities the "problem" concept of "school dropout" itself may be an ethnocentric evaluation on the part of the majority society. There may be children of certain ethnic minorities in the United States that do relatively poorly in school but do not become singled out as objects of concern.

There evidently remain some ethnic minorities in which one does not find a primary interest in a pattern of accomplishment through formal education. Some of these minorities call no special attention to themselves of either a positive or a negative nature. There are, for example, within the state of California over 550,000 Portuguese Americans. This is a relatively invisible ethnic group, since they are noted neither for outstanding educational accomplishment nor for the manifestation of social problems. They, therefore, do not come to public attention and are ignored by social scientists generally.

To my knowledge there has been no attention paid by psychologists to this relatively large minority. There is no outside concern with Portuguese social adaptation at present. One does not find concern expressed that the members of this minority should do better in school or that they are "dropouts" relatively disinterested in scholastic careers. They live, for the most part, in relatively self-contained rural communities in the central valley of California. As reported to me by one anthropology graduate student, they tend to maintain an integrated subculture with cohesive family units. Generally speaking, their culture pattern does not emphasize formal education for their youth nor the seeking out of professional careers. I would not wish to predict how individuals in this subculture would respond on the tests of "cognitive style" I am about to discuss. They might or might not manifest patterns of a "field-dependent" nature. What is apparent is that they do not presently show patterns of social difficulty as a "problem minority."

Differences in Cognitive Style Related to School Performance

Psychologists today in increasing numbers recognize the necessity for comparative studies of groups in understanding patterns of cognitive development as a response to the total cultural environment, including ecological and nutritional determinants as well as patterns of child rearing and peer-group interaction. Psychologists are also aware that the U.S. public school as a social institution is in a period of crisis. In many urban classrooms more time is spent in vain attempts to maintain a climate conducive to learning than in the learning process itself.

Research on "cognitive style" attempts to overcome the criticism of the earlier approach to cognition through IQ tests. It combines cross-cultural research in perceptual, cognitive, and social development (Witkin and Berry, 1975; Berry, 1976; Goodenough and Witkin, 1977; Witkin and Goodenough, 1977; Kagan and Buriel, 1977). Witkin and his colleagues developed the concept of cognitive style and related it to what they term "psychological differentiation." They see in children a progression and maturation of thinking from less differentiated to more differentiated concepts. Conceptually greater differentiation allows for the parts of a context to be experienced discretely. Witkin believes that greater differentiation shows up in the cognitive domain as well as in perceptual discrimination. What has been most exciting in this research are experiments that suggest there is an interrelationship between a maturation of perceptual processes, cognitive styles, and other dimensions of personality. This is to say, a cognitive style is involved in self-concepts and in the management of social relationships. The more global, less differentiated perceptual approach that Witkin has called "field dependent" appears to be consistent with a social interaction style in which the individual appears to be more sensitive to both positive and negative social cues. In contrast, a more differentiated "field-independent" conceptual mode is found in individuals who are more independent in decision making and more competitive in social interaction. U.S. children, at least those who have greater field independence, seem to have experienced a type of childhood socialization encouraging separation from parents and individualized internalization and regulation of impulses.

Witkin and others have conducted studies with U.S. subgroups of blacks, Irish, Italians, and Jews, showing the differences among boys whose fathers were present from those whose fathers were absent (Witkin, 1969). Black youths were more field dependent generally than white youths. Witkin (1967) demonstrates that field-independent children, when interviewed, report that they have had a high level of companionship almost on equal footing with their parents. They perceive themselves to be subject to a reasonable amount of discipline. There is very little in the form of physical punishment from the father. Studies of Eskimo youth by MacArthur (1973, 1974) and of Mexican youth by Mebane and Johnson (1970) agree with Witkin in finding that greater field independence in children occurs in socialization situations in which parents encourage initiative and separation from the family. Common to reports on field-dependent children is their subjective perception of severe socialization pressures. Werner (1979), summarizing the evidence, says that cross-cultural studies suggest that a relatively field-dependent cognitive style is likely to prevail in social settings characterized by tight social organization, insistence on adherence to authority, and the use of strict or even harsh practices to enforce social conformity by otherwise weak or ineffectual fathers. The family structure most often linked to field dependence or less differentiated functioning in children is an extended family or a father-absent family. These situations have a characteristic in common: strong male role models are relatively absent or lacking. In contrast, societies that foster the development of field independence are loose in their organization and place less stress on conformity in the social, political, and religious areas (cf. Werner, 1979, p. 182).

In reviewing this research literature as a whole I find that it blurs possible adaptive differences in regard to the specific effects of a given minority status and social self-identity on issues of cognitive and emotional development within given subcultural settings. Cognitive development must be judged differently in respect to social adaptation in an intact culture as compared, for example, with a situation of rapid change involving migration of people into new environments in which they are likely to be judged rather negatively or pejoratively. The adaptive value of cognitive development that takes place in children in such a situation is not strictly comparable with that occurring in a native setting. Part of the new social self-identity occurring in some minorities is the possible partial internalization of some of the negative attributions coming from the majority culture. A minority identity may foster particular defensive coping mechanisms resulting in selective permeability or "non-learning" in an attempt to ward off these attributions. Moreover, negative attributions from the outside give rise to resentments and increasing manifestations of deviant behavior, with further negative social consequences.

This point can be illustrated by an examination of recent studies involving interdisciplinary research by psychologists and anthropologists into problems of formal education experienced in two subcultural settings, that of Mexican Americans (Madsen, 1967; Kagan and Madsen, 1971, 1972a, 1972b; Madsen and Shapira, 1973; Kagan, 1974; Ramirez and Price-Williams, 1974) and native Hawaiians.

There have been numerous studies in the past that amply demonstrate that Mexican-American children, on the average, when tested with traditional IQ and achievement tests, do poorly in American schools. There are even some studies reporting that the average IQ goes down year by year. While these results were in keeping with observed school performance, the early studies made no attempt to explicate these results within the cultural or social context of Mexican-American children. Madsen has taken a new approach that considers the interpersonal attitude of traditional Mexican culture as well as cognitive performance in assessing what is operating in these minority children. It becomes obvious that emphasis on individual competition, which is characteristic of the U.S. schools, creates a difficulty for many of these children. Individual teacher-pupil interaction is the implicit U.S. method of learning, each child being expected to internalize a desire to perform well and meet the expectations of the teacher. Kagan and Madsen (1972b) found that Mexican-American children were consistently less rivalrous and avoided conflict more than Anglo-American children. These differences tended to increase with age, in contrast to the special emphasis on rivalry, especially among Anglo-American boys. The psychological use of the peer group is evidently part of a pattern of field dependence found in Mexican children; moreover, there is an avoidance of confrontation among Mexican-American children as a consequence of the sanctioning against such behavior by Mexican parents.

The studies of Madsen and those stimulated by him emphasize the fact that Anglo-American children tend to manifest competitive attitudes in interaction with their peers, whereas Mexican-American children are much less likely to do so. In contrast, both Mexican-American and some lower-class urban Anglo children are more apt to be concerned with cooperative interaction with their peers than with their teachers.

In comparing the behavior of mothers in six different cultures, Minturn and Lambert (1964) report that Mexican-American and Anglo-American mothers were at the opposite extremes regarding peer-group competition of an aggressive nature. The Mexican mothers severely discouraged aggressive behavior between peers.

From the standpoint of isolating the social or familial context shared by many Mexican-American youth, I find these research reports somewhat lacking in any attempt to relate them directly to real-life or case history situations. There are two issues that must be related. First, how is the field-dependent cognitive pattern and sensitivity to the peer group in the

Mexican children related more generally, psychodynamically to the internalization of social norms in given families and to tensions between family expectations about school and peer-group antagonism to school authorities? Second, how does the field-dependent pattern relate to observable patterns of delinquency among Mexican youth that occur in some communities but not in others? That is, how do family and community sanctions operate or fail to operate in respect to delinquent group behavior or peer-group antagonism to school participation? I find almost total neglect of systematic anthropological observation of the evident linkage of peer-group reinforcement and resistance to learning.

While working as a psychological consultant in a prison for young adults, I had seen reports of how the collective peer-group attitudes to which Mexican-American youth were subjected were influential not only in involving youths in the activities that led to their incarceration, but how Mexican peer groups in school heavily sanctioned against individual attempts at learning. It seems evident that those who are good students have to resist strong group pressure.

It is crucial to learn more about how the group may be involved in either learning or nonlearning in ethnic groups characterized by field dependency. One finds this issue more directly addressed in the studies of classroom competition and cooperation made by Ron Gallimore and Allen Howard (Gallimore, Boggs, and Jordan, 1974; Howard and associates, 1971, 1974), who examined the learning difficulties of "culturally Hawaiian" children in U.S. schools. Although the category "Hawaiian" includes all individuals with some trace of native Hawaiian ancestry, those who are considered culturally Hawaiian are not actually racially different from those who have become more assimilated to the dominant American cultural traditions. It is the children who remain culturally Hawaiian who show the greatest difficulty in formal school settings.

Howard found that with such children language and other institutional aspects of Hawaiian culture had disappeared, but they had been socialized in ways that deemphasized individual competitive behavior and stressed the positive social virtues of peer-group affiliation. This affiliative pattern of interrelationship among Hawaiians was pervasive. Howard discusses how early parental interaction, especially between mother and child, is relatively nonverbal compared with U.S. middle-class patterns. Both adults and children are more peer-group oriented. Commitments to work-mate or childhood peers often supersede commitments to one's spouse or one's children. Howard points out cogently how investment of material or emotional resources has been directed toward a loose social network rather than toward members of one's primary family. In a sense, one accumulated the goodwill of one's peers rather than material objects. Relationships today generally tend to be nonhierarchical. This finding about nonhierarchy in the Hawaiian and Samoan family and community conflicts with some other reported generalizations (Werner, 1979). (One must note, however, hierarchical differences between *Alii* or nobles and the commoners in the old Hawaiian traditions.)

Howard and Gallimore applied these ethnographic considerations to an understanding of the lack of learning taking place in the formal school environment. By interrelating ethnographic and formal psychological research methods they were able to make a rather cogent explanation of why the teacher-pupil relationship did not produce positive learning behavior. In effect, the Hawaiian culture-oriented children bring to the school a relatively nonverbal pattern of communication as well as implicit orientation toward expressive affiliation with peers rather than an internalized, instrumental need achievement in which the child gains his primary satisfaction through his own goal-oriented activities.

The Hawaiian affiliative pattern is not a school problem until it becomes defined as such by a dominant society that expects Hawaiian children to *learn individually* and to take on the competitive pattern. Hawaiian society no longer exists in isolation; Hawaiians have become a minority group in their own islands.

Culturally, from the standpoint of the dominant U.S. society, Hawaiian children are described as intellectually unmotivated and present oriented. There is some continuing argument whether these observed patterns are part of the traditional Hawaiian culture or whether what is perceived as socially maladaptive behavior is due to the inundation of the old culture by present-day U.S. industrial society.

Very recently Hawaiian youth have become overrepresented in every category of "social problem" (Liliuokalani Trust, 1978), with a progressive increase in delinquent behavior. Their present-day behavior is described by some observers as a reaction to new definitions of success in which the easier life style of the Hawaiians is now contrastively perceived as unsuccessful. Hawaiians who were content in the past with a simple nonmaterial life style are perceived now as living in some relative degree of poverty, even by themselves.

When we look at what has been happening recently with the Hawaiians in Hawaii, we find that there has been increasing concern in the majority society with the fact that some Hawaiians remain embedded within their traditional culture and are therefore not "integrated" with the middle-class goals of the dominant society.

Adaptation has to be judged both "emically" from within the minority itself and "etically" from the outside in terms of objective behavioral indices observable by the social scientist. (The social judgments by the dominant society at large are also "etic" and may differ from those of the social scientist). There may arise a general concern that a group "should" integrate, as in the case of the Hawaiians. This general social concern may help cause problems by changing the perception of the group itself from one that is "different" to one that is "inadequate."

As in the case of Hawaiians, the "adaptation" of any minority group must be examined longitudinally through time. As I have briefly suggested, the actual adaptation of native Hawaiians to the dominant U.S. culture has been changing with social circumstances. In the past there were even terrible periods of almost physical annihilation due to the effect of unfamiliar diseases on the Hawaiian population. There have been subsequent periods of increased or decreased social tension. Now, one notes that some Hawaiian youth manifest both an increased sense of personal alienation as well as hostility toward members of other groups.

Thus, there has been a greater amount of delinquent behavior, more recently turning into overt violence, than there was a generation ago. It is not simply that the ethnic interaction patterns have become more difficult with the greater overall population density with the influx of mainland Americans, it is also that, whatever the previous Hawaiian culture, the youth now growing up feel a sense of anger and antagonism that the previous generation did not feel with the same intensity toward outsiders now made manifest in destructive behavior. The economic well-being of the Hawaiian group has not changed as much as their sense of relative deprivation (cf. Aberle, 1966) vis-à-vis the majority U.S. society.

From a psychodynamic viewpoint, there remains also the essential issue of the interrelation between instrumental adaptive functions and the pattern of internalization of norms prevalent in a group. Alternatives between the opposing patterns, described by David Reisman (in Reisman, Denny, and Glazer, 1955) as "other-directed," on the one hand, and "inner-directed," on the other, are complex when examined within the context of specific cultures. It becomes apparent that one must distinguish between cross-cultural and cross-national studies per se and the so-called subcultural studies of ethnic minorities. In some recent reviews of comparative studies, insufficient attention has been paid to these different social circumstances. A number of the reviews do not distinguish sufficiently between growing up in an ethnic minority situation and growing up in a traditional culture, be it preindustrial, preliterate, or "tribal." Granted, differences in culture backgrounds produce differences in cognitive patterns of social institutions and learning. These patterns have a different meaning in situations of cultural isolation than they do in situations in which the individual is being socialized in a traditional pattern *as part of a minority subculture*. While it is quite apparent that psychologists in the past have not taken sufficient consideration of sub-cultural variations in social status, it remains apparent today that there is some neglect of the fact that in a multiethnic society the development of cognitive patterns often takes place within an atmosphere of social degradation or social depreciation, especially in contexts where racial, caste, or class discrimination has been practiced for several generations by the dominant majority (DeVos, 1978b).

PEER GROUP VS. FAMILY AS A REFERENCE GROUP

An important issue in discussing subcultural modes of adaptation related to any minority situation is under what conditions do youth become antagonistic not only to the majority society but to their own parental generation. Compared to the frequent conflict perceived between the peer group, the parents, and the school found among black and Mexican-American children, what one sees in contemporary Japan as well as in many Japanese-American children in the United States is a peer-group orientation that mutually reinforces an intense emotional commitment to the formal learning processes of the school.

However, the fact that harmony of peer-group and family directive did not hold up in all circumstances in Japanese Americans is well illustrated if one compares the striking record of the U.S.-born Nisei within the regular U.S. school system with the very poor results obtained in teaching Japanese in the Japanese-language schools established in the 1920s and 1930s by Japanese parents. Parents wanted their children to preserve the language and culture of their homeland. However, the special Japanese-language schools to which children were sent after regular school hours did not "take." There was great implicit as well as explicit resistance to learning the Japanese language among Nisei. In this instance the peer group reinforced the more general social attitudes found among the children of other immigrant groups who resisted learning the parental language. Such resistance has been a characteristic of the social self-identity of U.S. immigrants rather generally and was also adopted by the first sizable generation of U.S.-born Japanese.

In regular schools, however, the social attitudes shared by the Japanese community and by Japanese families were reinforced by the collective activity of the Nisei peer group. In this respect, behavior of Japanese in the ordinary public schools resembled that of U.S. middle-class children rather than lower-class children. The automatic U.S. social self-identify taken on by the Nisei child resembled, therefore, the assimilative patterns taken on by waves of European immigrants in U.S. cities. That is to say, the automatic language of the Japanese child, as happened with European children in Chicago and New York schools at the turn of the century, became the lingua franca, English. Any attempt to maintain at least a bilingual heritage in Japanese, as in most immigrant ethnic minorities, was defeated by peer-group resistance. Spontaneously, English became the "natural language" of most American-born children of immigrants.

Such an acculturative peer-group pattern contrasts very directly with alternative patterns more frequently found among some groups: blacks and Mexican Americans as well as Hawaiians. Symbolically, separate modes of speech—"black English," "Latina," "pidgin"—are reinforced in dissident peer groups as part of the continuity of a different identity. One must note that in these extreme cases the peer group also goes counter to any assimilative type of school interaction. It is noticeable now that Mexican-American and black peers tend to create a contrastive interaction with other members of a school population as well as with their own parental generation, which in good part hopes that their children will do well in school.

Whereas in some of the earlier immigrant situations separate gangs of youth would form, the general language of the peer group usually became English. This is not to overlook other cultural and class differences in the use of the school by the children of immigrants as an adaptive instrument for social and educational advancement. It was not accidental that immigrant eastern European Jews with a tradition of scholarship did relatively well in the schools and children of immigrant Poles of peasant background did relatively poorly. Again, to reiterate, one has to look back to specific cultural traditions in the use of cognitive styles within the family, including verbal communication between parents and children from early childhood. Moreover, it is very important to consider differences in the methods of childhood discipline used to foster internalization of modes of cognitive functioning. Patterns of parental discipline contribute to U.S. subcultural patterns of peer group interaction that become established in the schools. There are also subcultural variations in the type of interaction established between the family and the peer group as primary reference groups. These interactive processes continually contribute to the development of social self-identity in the children of migrants or minorities. Of crucial issue in the development of field independence in respect to adaptive patterns among the children of migrants to U.S. cities is how parents discipline, whether deliberately or inadvertently, to cause forms of internalization that emphasize particular coping mechanisms. One must then ask, how do characteristic forms of internalization fostered in a group relate to the use of the peer group as a further formative influence in the final development of an ethnic identity? These important questions have not as yet, to my knowledge, been subjected to sufficient systematic inquiry.

IS OCCUPATIONAL ADAPTATION NECESSARILY IN CONFLICT WITH SOCIAL SENSITIVITY?

From a comparative anthropological perspective, some of the presently available comparative studies of achievement motivation seek to point up indirectly the somewhat ethnocentric preoccupation in middle-class U.S.

culture, with analytic thought and individualistic achievement motivation as the main priority. This pattern is the implicit one advocated by McClelland and others as a necessary universal for personal economic advancement (1953, 1958, 1961). They see expressive affiliative needs as counterposed to instrumentally-oriented need achievement. From the vantage point of the Japanese and Japanese-American cultures with which I have been dealing (DeVos, 1973, pp. 170-200), I find it questionable whether this theory of successful achievement motivation can be applied cross-culturally without serious modification. An invariant opposition of "expressive" need affiliation and emphasis on "instrumental" individualistic achievement suggested by McClelland does not hold up, for example, when one examines the internalized interpersonal attitudes operative within an economically success-ful Japanese society. I would contend that the indirect evidence to date suggests that Japanese are cognitively field independent when compared with the Mexican-American and Hawaiian groups just described. However, while they remain much more concerned with internalized directives inculcated by parents without the use of physical punishment, at the same time they are socialized to remain subject to reference group pressures from their peers. While adjustively, internalization emphasizes cognitive field independence, they are taught, socially, to adapt by being interdependent with others. Moreover, they continue to conform to the authority of elders because they expect nurture and care from superiors. Authority implied the bestowing of care as well as making demands and holding expectations of others (DeVos, 1975). Instrumental concerns with need achievement are interwoven with fantasies of aging into an authority position, not to be free of the influence of others but to arrive at a mentoring role, in turn bestowing knowledge or care on younger individuals. Instrumental goals are conceptualized in a paternal-istic framework in which those in authority are supposed to gain expressive satisfaction from their nurturing as well as controlling roles. The young peer group, generally speaking, supports authority rather than conflicting with it.

In Mexican-American culture the concept of paternal authority can sometimes be idealized in the role of a "don," a detached fatherly gentleman, but seldom are ordinary government officials or other authorities conceptual-ized as benevolent dons. More characteristically officials and even family heads are distrusted. Authority is often perceived as exercised for personal benefit, not for benevolence. Sometimes the Catholic priest as "father" is allocated a type of mentoring or guiding role, but he is so conceived because he has given up competitively defined, materially oriented ambition. He is also not perceived as a "macho" authority figure.

There is also a certain impasse in contemporary Mexican-American minority culture between material success and remaining a peer-oriented person not seeking special economic advantage. A person who pushes himself forward is quickly considered self-seeking and without virtue.

One can distinguish in the writings of Kagan and Madsen (1972a, 1972b) some differentiation between positive "competition" as a means of self-fulfillment and the negative attributes of "rivalry" in which rivalrous behavior is intended to maximize one's own gain. One notes in their writings, however, that in their analysis of cooperation there is no counterpart between positive cooperation, which emphasizes joint effort and mutuality in the reaching of goals, and certain negative concomitants inherent in the less differentiated cognitive style examined in Witkin's theory of differences between "field-dependent" and "field-independent" cognitive approaches. That is to say, emphasis on cooperation without some concomitant development of internalized directives may inhibit certain forms of intellectual development and, indeed, lead to forms of social subordination and diffidence that ultimately incapacitate members of the group from reaching positively considered goals. In my judgment, there is an implicit bias in some of this literature toward viewing as positive all forms of cooperation or cognitive patterning leading to cooperation, and, contrariwise, in the writings of others, toward viewing them as implicitly negative. Hence, the present controversy over the implications of Witkin's theory. There is in effect an implicit confusion between psychological adjustment (cognitive differentiation) and adaptation (social cooperation).

Kagan and Kogan (1970), Kagan (1974), and Kagan and Buriel (1977) suggest that there is a dilemma of values represented in Witkin's research. They state that field independence is correlated with learning and achievement in U.S. schools and, hence, necessarily linked to patterns of social adaptation emphasizing competition. In contrast, field-dependent individuals are considered to be adaptively more alert to social stimuli, capable of achieving consensus in less time than field-independent groups, and therefore probably more skilled in the art of interpersonal accommodation. The Japanese case, however, demonstrates that cognitively independent youngsters can also be trained to be alert to social stimuli.

I would contend, therefore, that field-independent persons may be better able to resist the influences of others in give-and-take democratic discussions but at the same time may also be trained to be socially sensitive in their concern for the viewpoint of others, whereas field-dependent youngsters are less able to become objective or detached in assessing the merits of a decision. One could therefore make a quick counter argument that field-dependent individuals are less capable of carrying out democratic discussions that demand individual integrity. The type of accommodation that occurs among field-dependent individuals in actually observable situations is often a subordination of self in an authoritarian structure. A field-dependent approach does not equip individuals for making objective decisions in a modern, nontraditional, changing social setting either as administrators or as public servants seeking to resolve conflicts among others. Adaptation within modern industrial and postindustrial societies necessitates differentiated cognitive approaches. The fact that field-dependent individuals have had adaptive values in previous forms of social organization does not argue for equivalence any more than concrete thinking in a Piagetian form can be seen as ultimately adaptive in a variety of situations requiring abstract deductive thought. The fact, is, psychology as a science, through methods such as those used by Piaget and others (Piaget and Inhelder, 1969), is affirming the fact that psychophysiological maturation occurs in a given sequence and that one does not go back to previous forms of maturation as a defensive maneuver except in emotionally disruptive situations (Dasen, 1972).

A type of cross-cultural cognitive relativism is too quickly argued by individuals attempting to take a nonevaluative anthropological approach. The fact of the matter is that there are maturational sequences in human psychology. Different cultures in their socialization practices may influence individuals to take a shorter or longer time to achieve certain points of maturation, depending upon cultural facilitation or inhibition. Nowhere has there been discovered a different progressive sequence in regard to maturation in the cognitive or emotional realm. Ultimately, greater cognitive differentiation is more adaptive in more varied circumstances; it is related in many instances, if not all, to less rigidified forms of personality orientation. In those cases where certain features of cognitive differentiation are consonant with forms of emotional rigidification, it is sometimes too quickly, and erroneously, assumed that it is the cognitive pattern that is at issue, whereas rigidification can be in the emotional realm as well as the cognitive realm. Finding individuals in some cultures emotionally rigidified but with highly differentiated cognitive abilities does not argue against the greater occupational adaptability of cognitive differentiation itself.

A cultural emphasis on *analytic thought* as part of personality structure may also be more "adaptive" in a U.S. classroom organized to maximize a competitive form of social adaptibility. This is independent of the fact that, *adjustively,* analytic thought is more differentiated. That is, it is part of a progressive maturational development beyond a global field-dependent cognitive pattern that appears at an earlier stage in a psychophysiological sequence. Given a particular culture pattern, analytic thought can, of course, be part of an imbalanced personality pattern that selectively emphasizes defensive cognitive coping at the expense of a concomitant progressive maturation of social rapport. But social sensitivity per se is not a necessarily alternative pattern to cognitive differentiation. *Social* and *cognitive* maturation can become selectively rigidified in socially emphasized defensive maneuvers that, on the one hand, inhibit cognitive maturation or, on the other hand, inhibit sensitivity to the feelings of others.

It is interesting to note that contrary to the easy supposition that field-dependent teachers would do better with field-dependent pupils, research evidence (Kagan and Buriel, 1977) points to the fact that teachers rated high on field independence actually do better *both* with field-dependent and field-independent pupils. Again, the social sensitivity of some teachers and field independence are not necessary psychological alternatives. What is more generally lacking in "Anglo culture" in comparison with the Mexican minority subculture is characteristic socialization that also emphasizes some emphatic development of a concern with the feelings of others. The internalization of social directives and emphasis on self-control do not, however, preclude a parallel maturation of other coping mechanisms related to social sensitivity.

"CULTURE" IN A COMPLEX SOCIETY:
SOCIAL DEGRADATION AND MINORITY ADAPTATION

As both a psychologist and an anthropologist working with Japanese culture and minority groups in the United States and Japan itself, I had to attempt some resolution of these issues of minority status and subcultural continuities in my own work. Let me therefore restate the conclusions I have reached on this question of whether one can use a concept, the "culture" or "subculture" of poverty, for at least some segments of given minority groups. We must begin by recognizing some theoretical insufficiencies in the alternative basic sociological approaches often applied. There is often the contention that the different values held by different groups offer some explanation of the relative incidence of various forms of deviant and socially maladapted behavior, given the social definition of success and achievement within U.S. culture. In opposition to some sociologists and anthropologists, I would argue against any absolute relativism about different social values as explaining differences in the effectiveness of social adaptation of members of a subgroup. Nor can some forms of maladaptive behavior be explained solely as a direct reaction to experiences of discrimination. In such a relativist position there is little attention or even recognition of personality variables or any concept of problems than can distort more optimal psychological maturation. In addition, there is no recognition that there can be adjustive as well as adaptive conflict and incompatability between positively perceived goals. That is to say, one can note that incompatible definitions of commonly held values in any society result in varying degrees of internal conflict or discord. Difficulties experienced on a personality level may result in evident forms of self-defeating behavior. Moreover, one can find difficulties within societies, related to a chronic lack or realization from one generation to the next of patterns generally considered positive by the society itself.

There is some consensus in every group, simple or complex, about the meaning of social success, and the meaning is shared generally even by those in disadvantaged positions in the society. There are also, in all societies, certain deviant modes of attaining what is defined as power, prestige, economic well-being, or actualization of the sacred values of the culture in terms of artistic expression, holiness, and other achievements. Societies, from the very simple to the most complex, have developed forms of status stratification within political, economic, lineage, and sacred definitions of social functioning. No segment of such a stratified society is without some broadly shared evaluation of how an individual ideally achieves status as an adult, whether man or woman.

Is culturally pluralistic societies the further complication therefore arises that most of the subordinate ethnic or social class minorities are *not* totally independent from those in dominant positions in their own evaluation of status. There is an interpenetration of values from the dominant segments influencing even those living in relatively incapsulated minority status.

Problems of actualizing a satisfactory adult role are passed on to the children of a minority subculture because the young members of the subculture cannot easily remain free of accepting to some degree the values and expectations espoused by the dominant segment of the society. True, the individual within a minority group is interacting basically with his own group, but such minority ethnic enclaves are seldom independent cultures that are totally free from alternative considerations. What one has to assess, therefore, is the relative degree and in what manner values originating in the dominant society penetrate a given subgroup. Second, adaptation is influenced by how the socialization pattern of any given group coincides or comes in conflict with that of the dominant society. Third, one must consider how this conflict is resolved both adjustively in certain defense mechanisms and adaptively in manifest behavior. Further defensive incapsulation does not usually result in the development of more integrated minority reference groups that can maintain opposition to the dominant society as a whole. Let me again illustrate concretely.

Oscar Lewis' concept of the "culture of poverty" is one that expressly includes the notion that some individuals from one generation to the next live in relative social degradation vis-à-vis others. In some instances, social degradation is related to class or caste (race). In others, social degradation is related to ethnic minority status.

On the other hand, in some cultures hierarchy of itself does not imply social or personal disorganization or degradation of lower-status segments of a population. One must, for example, distinguish between (1) a socially cohesive working-class culture, such as those that developed in France and England, where there are more stable antagonistic relationships with middle-class segments of the society, and (2) a disorganized ghetto that is usually also termed "lower class." Marxist theory, for example, does distinguish the urban lower class generally from what is described as a disorganized "lumpen proletariat." In Marxist terminology, therefore, the "culture of poverty" does not include all individuals of working-class or lower-class status within a society. It is specific to certain segments of a lower class and can often be compounded with a traditionally disparaged ethnic minority status. Caste-racial differences must also be examined as somewhat different from class or ethnic considerations.

In the volume *Japan's Invisible Race* (DeVos and Wagatsuma, 1966) both Berreman (pp. 277-324) and I (pp. 325-86) have argued from somewhat different perspectives that U.S. society has "caste" characteristics that overlap its class and ethnic divisions. My contention in examining caste in Japan has been that the forms of exploitation characteristic of a caste society can become more heavily weighted in terms of expressive or psychological problems than in terms of material or economic ones. Indeed, caste feelings are engendered in the early socialization of revulsion and are therefore not easily changed in given individuals (DeVos and Wagatsuma, 1966, pp. 376-86). These feelings also depend on negative psychological projections that derogate a despised, segregated group in the population. This group is scapegoated to represent what is unacceptable to "proper" people. Since these pariahs are "contaminated" on an hereditary basis, intermarriage contaminates offspring. The resultant problem is that some percentage of the derogated group becomes susceptible to a damaged self-regard because of partial internalization of a negative self-image.

There is in some degraded groups a special functioning of a mechanism of selective permeability that leads to nonlearning in formal education (DeVos, 1978b). This is collectively strengthened in such groups by peer reference group participation. Such psychocultural processes can be institutionalized readily when there are physical differences in racial ancestry in a population. But as Wagatsuma and I have demonstrated for Japan, processes involved in caste or "race" derogation can occur even in situations of no actual physiological or ancestral differences—a myth of supposed differences can become the basis of a belief system that has the same effects as racism on those derogated by the majority society.

In U.S. society class stratification is compounded by ethnic and racial minority status. It is in such circumstances that we find complex indices of some forms of social and personal breakdown. Malfunctioning, whether it be judged simply in terms of social adaptation or by psychological measurements that pick up behavioral or attitudinal manifestations of inner maladjustment, appear in relatively greater numbers among given segments of a population. In countries such as the United States, which are multiethnic, one finds some ethnic minorities represented in higher proportion in such social indices as crime, delinquency, alcoholism, mental illness, addiction, etc. This is particularly true when racial differences create personal visibility (Plog and Edgerton, 1969, pp. 285-479).

A second consideration runs throughout a great deal of psychological literature. By using psychological tests as well as intensive observation one can note that there are differences between those who manifest social indices of acting out behavior such as delinquency and crime, on the one hand, and those who evince forms of personal maladjustment such as neurosis or mental illness, on the other. A good bit of clinical and abnormal psychology is concerned with attempts to differentiate among individuals or among families in respect to the genesis of social deviancy or internal maladjustment. Let us return, therefore, to see how Japanese culture and contemporary Japanese society affords us some perspective on these issues.

The Effects of Social Degradation in Japan

As indicated in the introduction, the Japanese Americans in Chicago after World War II did not conform to sociological predictions in regard to the maladaptive effect of discrimination on a racial minority group. Yet, in Japan itself there are two minorities with notable degrees of manifest maladaptation. The first is the former outcast group of over two million whose premodern status was based on considerations of ritual impurity to the point of untouchability not unlike that found in the Indian caste system. The second is the Korean minority of 750,000, many of them working as unskilled laborers. These groups both manifest many of the stigmata of social and personal disparagement reported for such U.S. minorities as Native Americans, blacks, Mexican Americans, and Puerto Ricans. The historical reasons for social disparagement in the United States and Japan are somewhat different. In both instances, however, one can analyze comparabilities in respect to economic exploitation. The derogation of Koreans took place within a framework of the forceful colonization of Korea by the Japanese. A traditionalist, economically backward society was quickly taken over by an expanding, modernizing Japan. The almost total illiteracy of the rural Korean folk allowed for their easy derogation as uncouth, stupid, and innately inferior to the Japanese. Public education introduced into Korea was conducted in Japanese, not Korean. The attitudes that Japanese directed toward Koreans were not too dissimilar from those that permitted the institutionalization of slavery in U.S. society, or the use of Slavic serfs by the Teutonic Knights who set up the kingdom of Prussia on the border of eastern Europe (DeVos and Wagatsuma, 1966, p. 378).

In our own volume (1966), Wagatsuma and I have described in great detail how the former untouchables of Japan were in effect subject to "racial" discrimination, since the Japanese with no historical validity, considered them of different biological origin than ordinary Japanese. Although they are now supposedly integrated into full Japanese citizenship, castelike feelings persist. I have long contended (ibid., pp. 325-86) that one must deal with a psychological dimension in understanding caste interaction, or what I term the psychological exploitation of a debased minority. It is this type of debasement that is particularly strong and that has particularly persistent effects over a period of generations on the socialization of the young. There is no doubt in my mind that a major determinant of problem behavior in minorities is the manner in which a negative or resigned self-identity has become established and the manner in which this image is passed on from one generation to the next through family mediation. In a previously debased group the primary family itself sometimes comes to lack cohesiveness. The peer group becomes a dissident group resisting not only parental authority but other forms of authority exercised by the dominant majority. Within a given minority, reinforcement of negative patterns is highly influential in defining the individual's acceptance or rejection of expected role behavior.

I have long been making intensive case history studies of Japanese families in Japan. More recently I have obtained a great deal of observational evidence as well as some psychological tests from minority Koreans. Two considerations related to self-identity that are continually manifest in case history data are the disturbed cohesiveness within the family and indications of a degraded self-concept as part of a minority heritage.

Americans consider the ideal personal relationship to include considerable capacity for the individuals to relate directly to one another in intimate nonhierarchical contact. This contact occurs between "selves" rather than between role-playing individuals relating to one another in accordance with status expectations. We have described elsewhere (DeVos and Wagatsuma, 1970, pp. 334-70) how in the Japanese tradition, in contrast to the U.S. tradition, family relationships emphasize role playing. The role emphasis works well expressively in supplying nurturance and, to a considerable degree, appreciative evaluations. There is an emphasis on harmony, well-being, and a gratification of dependence. There is not, however, the same emphasis as in the U.S. ideal on personal intimacy, on seeking to resolve affiliative needs.

One finds that role behavior and its expectations still characterize the Nisei family in the United States (Connor, 1977). The experience that the father remains distant from the children is a frequent complaint of Japanese Americans. Yet, one must also recognize that the mother maintains the father's status as head of the family and that this social distance has been used integratively. Even when the wife does not like the husband she does not denigrate his role as father. Ultimately, one would not describe Japanese families as lacking cohesion. On the contrary, very solid bonds bind family members together and preclude deviant behavior. In going to Japan itself to study the appearance of delinquency in a relatively high-delinquency area of Tokyo we decided to conduct an intensive family study that would operate in the field for over five years. I took on the issue of deviant behavior to test out why delinquent behavior appeared in some individuals and not in others. Admittedly, the overall rate of delinquency in Japan is very low compared with any other industrial state, and, most noteworthy, this rate of delinquency has not appreciably grown over the past 30 years but, on the contrary, has remained fairly stable with minor fluctuations.

Conducting intensive interviews and observations as well as psychological tests with 50 families, 30 with a delinquent child and 20 with nondelinquent children as a matching control group from the same schools and neighborhoods, we found that there were very easily distinguishable patterns in respect to social cohesion, discipline, and supervision contrasting the two groups (DeVos and Wagatsuma, 1972). One of the most notable findings was that in the families of delinquents the mothers tended not to "role play" the father. That is to say, the father was not treated with the ritual deference accorded the family head but was reacted to directly in terms of his insufficiencies. The Japanese family head, as much as an army officer, expects respect regardless of his personal characteristics. The mothers in the delinquent families expressed attitudes in front of children that conveyed their sense of dissatisfaction with an inadequate father. The father's manifest social and personal inadequacy was more hidden from the children in the nondelinquent families. Whatever his personal and economic failure, the father was still accorded deference and support by his wife in the role of mother. And the mother saw to it that her children observed a proper attitude toward the head of the family in their day-by-day behavior. The Japanese child, male or female, internalizes both cognitively and socially by the time he or she reaches school age.

In the normative patterns most frequently seen in Japanese families, whether in Japan or the United States, the father is placed within a role definition that is protective of him. The observing child, girl or boy, witnesses a patterned role deference regardless of the chronic or temporary feelings of the parents toward one another. In some cases there develops a deep bond of affection between husband and wife, which is not demonstrated openly in front of others, whereas in other instances the mother has a sense of dissatisfaction, which she never displays in the presence of her children. The curt behavior toward the mother by some Japanese men may cause some resentment in children, but the mother does not encourage such feelings in her children in manifest behavior. The prevalence of such a patterned role play contrasts with what is more frequently reported for Mexican-American families, for black American families, and for some middle-class white or "Anglo" families in more recent years.

The overt expression of mutual dissatisfaction within the family is apparent to many U.S. children. Single-parent families have been a frequent result among lower-class blacks, and more recently middle-class families, white and black, in the United States have also shown a notable trend toward single-parent families. There is as well an increase of manifest social resentment and deviant behavior among middle-class youth. Note well that the single-parent family does not occur as an ideal "culture pattern."

But the fact of the matter remains in many instances that the idealized concept of mutual respect and love that is supposed to occur is also manifestly lacking and that what the children actually witness is open expression of animosity and sometimes contempt. This latter case was very apparent also in some families of minority Koreans in Japan. In the Confucianist tradition of Korea there is supposedly respect for the position of the father in the family, which is supposedly reinforced by total cultural values. In actuality, however, in the minority status situation of Koreans in Japan, the father very often is not only socially debased externally by Japanese attitudes toward Koreans, but he is seen in very pejorative terms by the mother, whose dissatisfaction is freely expressed.

There are recent attempts by U.S. anthropologists (e.g., Carol Stack, *All Our Kin,* 1974) to contend that single-parent families or matrifocal families are, in effect, an alternative cultural tradition and that such patterns find caretaker support for children in extended networks that, in effect, function as informal kin-type networks. Such arguments view matrifocal family arrangements as a not-too-dysfunctional alternative to a traditional authoritarian male-dominant family. What is overlooked in these studies of matrifocality is that such families do not in actuality occur independently, in social isolation, but that they have in the past occurred principally only within communities whose social status is relatively low, in minority ethnic or lower-class communities that are part of a larger social structure in which the father of the family is generally the respected breadwinner. Moreover, such communities have been subject to focused social disparagement from the dominant segments of the social system in which they are found. They are, therefore, not actually as separate in thought or values as implied in these studies. In effect, the men in these communities are not simply disparaged by the society, but they are often disparaged as failures within their own group, in antagonistic heterosexual relationships wherein they are accorded little respect or affection. The idea of a "successful" man to women in lower-status groups is often the distant, occupationally successful male of some dominant segment of the society; the men with whom the women of a matrifocal society have direct contact are disparaged. In some instances, however, where the lower-status male maintains dominance the women are coerced at least temporarily into a subservient role wherein it is the woman who is disparaged and degraded.

This is a complex topic. Suffice it to say that such patterns also manifest attitudes of mutual disparagement between the sexes that start in early family experiences in which children witness much mutual antagonism between the parents. The increase of divorce and the manifest antagonistic relationships in middle-class segments of U.S. society is recent and as yet little studied in respect to its effects on youth.

A socially debased matrifocal segment of a society is an obverse of the dominant male status in other higher-status groups. It is not a democratic-egalitarian alternative. Equal status between men and women is not forthcoming from matrifocal situations. Arrangements of equivalent status cannot arise out of situations where there is manifest antagonism between the sexes and in which maneuvering for dominance is more characteristic than the working out of increasing closeness and intimacy. Matrifocal arrangements are usually marked by a lack of affiliative closeness between the sexes. It must, therefore, be considered somewhat Pollyannish to describe the actual relationships as simply satisfactory alternative living patterns to those found in the reigning U.S. middle class.

There are a relatively large number of single-parent families among Koreans in Japan, but no one argues that matrifocality or lack of parental cohesiveness is the traditional culture pattern of Koreans. When one goes to contemporary Korea itself, one finds Confucianist values still idealized. Among the family of the contemporary farmers one sees reinforcement of the status position of the father. The Korean minority in Japan came from a patriarchal tradition in which the values were not different from those of the Japanese. They were therefore more vulnerable to the social disparagement inflicted on them. They saw the Japanese practicing a system in which they too believed but, given their vulnerable background of illiteracy and lack of supportive status as downtrodden peasants, they saw themselves as less capable of realizing their ideals. The Korean farmer coming to Japan did not think of himself as worthy of asserting middle-class status.

In contrast, the impoverished farmer from Japan entering the United States brought with him a much firmer, confident concept of proper social status that was not easily negated by U.S. anti-Asian discriminatory practices or attitudes. The Korean farmer in Japan was susceptible to Japanese pejorative attitudes, whereas the Japanese immigrant in the United States continued to believe in his culturally different background and the status accorded him in its traditional context.

In Japan, Korean children growing up in an impoverished ghetto could witness not only the externally inflicted social degradation but also parental disparagement within the family. Conversely the Japanese Americans who came to the United States by and large brought with them no pattern of previous social degradation such as that experienced by impoverished, illiterate Korean farmers. Instead they brought with them an intense pride in their culture and in their past status, despite the poverty experienced in the rural regions of Japan at the time of their immigration. This traditional sense of social status was roughly comparable to that held by middle-class Americans in the United States. It was this sense of status that was conveyed in the interpersonal dynamics operating within the family. Also, Japanese communities sprang up in which knowledge of past status was transmitted as part of community relationships. For example, the actual occupation of an immigrant Japanese in the United States had nothing to do with his relative status within the Japanese minority community. He was not defined by any external occupational criteria but by a criteria derived from the formal family status of landowning farmers in Japan, as well as from the assumption of responsible roles in voluntary organizations within the community and the like. A sense of self buttressed by community attitudes made the person relatively invulnerable to whatever the outside white majority might think about Japanese in general.

Strong attempts by whites to limit the occupational choice of Japanese on the West Coast—strictures on land ownership or the suppositions that Nisei would grow up to be good houseboys or gardeners—had little effect on the attitudes of the Nisei themselves because they were socialized within a Japanese family and community ambience. Wherever they lived in the United States, including the traditional ghettos of Chicago, they remained immune to what prevailingly occurred to other individuals subject to the circumstances of a ghetto neighborhood life. Shaw and McKay (1942) themselves pointed out that not all ghetto families produce delinquent, deviant, or mentally ill inhabitants.

There is an affirmative culture even in what is seemingly, from the outside, the most squalid ghetto. Nevertheless, in some circumstances, conditions are such that the lack of cohesiveness within a given family or lack of mutual regard between adult men and women witnessed by a growing child will make a dissident peer group attractive as a compensatory source of emotional gratification. It can become the primary reference group for such children. It is precisely this compensatory use of the peer group that has to be studied as it relates to the nature of prior internalizations within the family. Like the type of coping mechanisms emphasized in family interaction, the school performance reflects both the past family traditions of given groups and the inexorable pressures of present social circumstances. The trend toward other-directed behavior in the middle class, suggested in the writings of Reisman, Denny, and Glazer (1955) and by Miller and Swanson (1958) in the late 1950s may well be reflected in signs that achievement motivation in the U.S. middle class has been changing. Is there also a change toward field dependency that might show up in restudies of previously studied groups or communities as well as individuals? We need such longitudinal follow-ups in a changing society.

ADAPTIVE STRATEGIES: CONCLUSIONS

In discussing the various controversies related to adaptation in minority Americans, it should become apparent that no single line of approach is sufficient to explain differences between ethnic minorities. What I am espousing is a full consideration of cultural factors, but not at the expense of looking at intrafamily socialization, on the one hand, or sociological conditions within U.S. society generally, on the other. I have tried to indicate that the historical circumstances of when and how a particular minority group entered and became part of a pluralistic society must be interpreted in cultural as well as sociological terms.

To recapitulate, cultural explanations do not necessarily negate psychological or sociological ones. However, under certain circumstances they may help explain group differences in the incidence of maladjustment or maladaptation as well as patterns of relative success in economic or social terms.

Working with Japanese Americans has made me critical of some overarching psychological theories of achievement motivation or relativistic theories of subcultural adaptation. Particular forms of psychological adaptation cannot be seen independent of a total social pattern. From this standpoint I have argued in the past against the approach of McClelland, Atkinson, and Lowelle (1953) and others to achievement motivation and against theories considering delinquency or deviancy only in terms of sociological factors operative in the U.S. city. I am equally against more recent anthropological theories that see differences in such groups as Mexican Americans or Hawaiians as due simply to cultural considerations, ignoring the fact that these ethnic minorities are in some instances living in a derogated status position within the larger society.

In looking at minority adaptation, one must attend to changes from one generation to the next. This longitudinal shift in adaptation we noted in respect to what is happening with Hawaiian youth. This generation manifests more self-consciously hostile and antagonistic behavior toward outsiders than did past generations. In effect, may we be seeing in some enclaves of Hawaiians the development of those characteristics of a "subculture of poverty" because of changes in self-concept vis-à-vis the majority society? The relationship of the growing individual to his peer group may differ with such changing relationships. As Howard (1971, 1974) points out, it was traditional for the Hawaiian to be oriented to the peer group as his primary reference group. However, the relationship of the peer group to the outside culture may change with changing social attitudes. Whereas in the past the youthful peer group was not antagonistic to the adult society or to outsiders, one may be witnessing the development of a youthful peer reference group that is developing an antagonism toward the older generation as well as toward what they perceive as an encroaching white society that affords them neither understanding nor respect and patronizes them as entertainers for gaping waves of tourists interested in "native" behavior.

The role of the peer reference group in the development of one's social self-identity and its relationship to the process of internalization of certain norms is very complex. It differs from group to group and it differs with the degree to which the family itself has been unsatisfactory as the locus for emotional support or satisfaction. There is a great difference between the compensatory use of the peer group as a refuge from unsatisfactory family relationships and the adaptive use of the peer group for acquiring a different social identity from one's parents. The degree to which there is family cohesion will be an important factor in what type of group is sought out.

It is obvious that psychodynamic theory has paid insufficient attention to the interaction of family and peer group as a dynamic tension in all psychosexual development, including relative emphasis on the defensive utilization of given coping mechanisms. In some cultures, particular classes, or social segments, it is quite obvious that peer-group relationships become almost totally dominant and the family, for some period of time at least, has very little influence over the individual's pattern of maturation. In other cultures, as in the case of the Japanese, which I have illustrated, the peer group and the family mutually reinforce the acquisition of learning within the school as a formative institution.

The evidence is strong that in many situations the Mexican-American peer group in the U.S. city is at odds with the school as a learning institution. This is also true for lower-class peer groups among U.S. blacks. It is also true for an increasing portion of the U.S. middle class.

Middle-class socialization has in the past tended to be more toward the acquisition of more rigidified or internalized superegos. The peer group, therefore, has had less influence over the individual (see Reisman, Denny, and Glazer, 1955, or Miller and Swanson, 1958). The present generation of middle-class children has, by some appearances at least, become more group-oriented than their more individualistically oriented parents. Priority given to a peer-group orientation tends to emphasize cooperation and socially sensitive attitudes. Such a pattern is sometimes inconsistent with individual competition. It deemphasizes differences in ability or judgment. Individuals emphasizing this type of social orientation, as has been pointed out, may or may not tend to remain more "field dependent," or more vulnerable to the opinions of associates and in some ways, as in the present situation, more resistive to authority figures seen as older or different from themselves. Conversely, the field-independent person remains more attuned to his own standards but can also be directed toward social sensitivity, as in the case for many Japanese.

Our Japanese evidence would point up that there are, in effect, two forms of dependence: one social, one cognitive. The family as reference group seems to have priority to the peer group in some circumstances. But Japanese dependence emphasizes conformity to, or regard for, authority and hierarchy. The Japanese and Japanese Americans in the United States by and large seem to be able to combine some form of perceptual field independence with culturally emphasized submission and emphasis on cooperative behavior. Instrumentally, they demonstrate a highly internalized achievement motivation. They have also a highly internalized sense of social as well as family responsibility. They remain preoccupied by worries over the development of their capacities for mastery.

In their expressive concerns not only are they mutually interdependent but they also seek out hierarchical dependent relationships with promises of nurture and mentorship. They are selectively permeable to individuals perceived as authority figures. They are not resistive to "taking in" from such mentors. They are more likely than those in some other societies to endure suffering and momentary displeasure for ultimate realization of a social goal. These traits are somewhat opposite to those listed as field independent in Witkin's formulations. A sense of "separate identity" as perceived by Witkin (1967) is inherent in field independence, and yet the Japanese seem cognitively capable of field independence in psychological tests. According to Doi (1973) and others, many Japanese are self-consciously aware of suffering from a lack of realization of an independent social self. There is a price to be paid by many socialized in a stringently conformist Japanese culture, and yet cognitive field independence continues to be found in many Japanese.

In U.S. society we know that some minority youth groups become extremely antagonistic to any perceived authority and are susceptible or vulnerable to sanctioning only from their immediate peers. The teacher in the school becomes perceived as alien and as requiring of them deportment out of key with their previous experience.

While the writings of Howard (1971, 1974), Madsen and Shapira (1973), and others are useful to warn about the implicitly pejorative attitudes taken by Westerners toward traditionally cooperative peer-oriented societies, they fail to relate their studies to the manifest problems of contemporary social deviancy and debased minority status. The fact that a cooperative peer-oriented tradition exists in a particular minority does not at the same time negate evidence that some psychological uses of the peer reference group can be compensatory in situations in which family cohesion has become weakened or broken. The child thereupon moves out to the peer group to escape domestic disharmony and discord. It is to address situations of this nature that I suggest that one must differentiate between a culture pattern that exists independently and a "subcultural" pattern that exists within a pluralistic society in which traditional family patterns are disrupted. There are peer-group patterns that reflect antagonism to constituted authority because exercised authority is seen by group members as alien and distant.

Some of my contentions I recognize as hypothetical, in that they as yet lack adequate demonstration. More research is necessary about how patterns of internalization occur in different social contexts by groups maintaining family cohesion, in contrast to those lacking cohesion wherein a social or ethnic identity has been more influenced by patterns of social degradation.

Only by further understanding the underlying psychological or maladjustive patterns that may influence some forms of manifest social maladaptation can we hope to overcome and ameliorate the effects of past social history influencing the next generation. It is appropriate that different ethnic groups maintain their cultural heritages. I would affirm, however, that such continuities can occur without necessarily assuming all the past burdens of social disparagement from one generation to the next.

REFERENCES

Aberle, D. *The Peyote Religion Among the Navajo.* Chicago: Aldine, 1966.

Angelou, M. *I Know Why the Caged Bird Sings.* New York: Random House, 1969.

Antonovsky, A., and Lerner, M. Occupational aspirations of the lower-class Negro and white youths. *Social Problems* 7 (1959):132-38.

Beck, S., Rabin, A., Thiesen, W., Molish, H., and Thetford, W. The normal personality as projected in the Rorschach test. *Journal of Psychology* 30 (1950):241-98.

Bell, R. A study of effects of segregation upon Japanese children in American schools. Ph.D. dissertation, Stanford University Library, 1933.

Benedict, R. *The Chrysanthemum and the Sword.* Boston: Houghton Mifflin, 1946.

Berry, J. *Human Ecology and Cognitive Style: Comparative Studies in Cultural and Psychological Adaptation.* New York: John Wiley & Sons, 1976.

Billingsley, A. *Black Families in White America.* Englewood Cliffs, N.J.: Prentice-Hall, 1968.

Brislin, R.W., Lonner, W.J., and Thorndike, R.M. *Cross-Cultural Research Methods.* New York: John Wiley & Sons, 1966.

Caudill, W. Japanese-American personality and acculturation. *Genetic Psychological Monograph* 45 (1952):3-102.

Caudill, W. and DeVos, G. Achievement, culture, and personality: the use of Japanese-Americans. *American Anthropologist* 58 (1956):102-126.

Cayton, H.R. The psychological approach to race relations. *Reed College Bulletin* 25 (November 1946):5-27.

————. The psychology of the Negro under discrimination. In *Race, Prejudice, and Discrimination,* edited by A. Rose, New York: Knopf, 1951.

Cayton, H.R., and Drake, S. *Black Metropolis.* New York: Harper & Row, 1962.

Clark, K., and Potkin, L. A review of the issues and literature of cultural deprivation theory. In *The Educationally Deprived.* New York: Metropolitan Applied Research Center, 1972.

Clark, W. Differences in accomplishment in schools of varying average intelligence quotient. *Los Angeles Educational Research Bulletin* 6 (1927):13-16.

Connor, J. *Tradition and Change in Three Generations of Japanese-Americans.* New York: Thomas Nelson, 1977.

Darsie, M.L. The mental capacity of American-born Japanese children. *Comparative Psychological Monographs* 3 (1926):15.

Dasen, P. Cross-cultural Piagetian research: A summary. *Journal of Cross-Cultural Psychology,* 1972, 3:23-29a.

DeVos, G.A. A comparison of the personality differences in two generations of Japanese-Americans by means of the Rorschach test. *Nagoya Journal of Medical Science* 17 (1954):3.

————., ed. *Socialization for Achievement*. Berkeley, Calif.: University of California Press, 1973.

————. Cross-cultural studies of mental disorder: An anthropological perspective. In *American Handbook of Psychiatry*, edited by Gerald Caplan. vol. 2., New York: Basic Books, 1974.

————. Apprenticeship and paternalism: Psychocultural continuities underlying Japanese social organization. In *Modern Japanese Organization and Decision-Making*, edited by Ezra Vogel. Berkeley, Calif.: University of California Press, 1975.

————. The interrelationship of social and psychological structures in transcultural psychiatry. In *Culture-Bound Syndromes, Ethnopsychiatry, and Alternate Therapies*, edited by William Lebra. Honolulu: University of Hawaii Press, 1976.

————. Adaptation and adjustment: Cross-cultural perspectives on mental health. *Colloquia in Anthropology*, vol. 2. Southern Methodist University: Dallas, 1978a, pp. 21-46.

————. Selective permeability and reference group sanctioning: Psychocultural continuities in role degradation. In *Major Social Issues*, edited by Milton Yinger and Stephen Cutler. New York: Free Press, 1978b.

————. Afterward. In *The Quiet Therapies*, edited by D. Reynolds. Honolulu: University of Hawaii Press, 1980a.

————. Ethnic adaptation and minority status. *Journal of Cross-Cultural Psychology* (1980b):101-25.

————. Family, deviancy and minority status: A psychocultural perspective on social indices of deviant behavior. In *Crime and Deviancy: A Comparative Perspective*, edited by Graeme Newman, ch. 6. Beverly Hills: Sage, 1980c.

DeVos, G.A. and Wagatsuma, H. *Japan's Invisible Race: Caste in Culture and Personality*. Berkeley, Calif.: University of California Press, 1966.

————. Status and role behavior in changing Japan. In *Sex Roles in Changing Society*, edited by Georgene Seward and Robert Williams. New York: Random House, 1970.

————. Family life and delinquency: Some perspective from Japanese research. *Transcultural Research in Mental Health*, edited by William P. Lebra, pp. 59-87. Honolulu: University of Hawaii Press, 1972.

Doi, T. *The Anatomy of Dependency*. Tokyo: Kodansha, 1973.

Ellison, R. *Shadow and Act*. New York: Random House, 1964.

Gallimore, R., Boggs, J., and Jordan, C. *Culture, Behavior and Education: A Study of Hawaiian-Americans*. Beverly Hills, Calif.: Sage, 1974.

Goodenough, D.R. and Witkin, H.A. *Origins of the Field-Dependent and Field-Independent Cognitive Styles*. Princeton, N.J.: Educational Testing Service, 1977.

Haley, A. *Roots*. Garden City, N.Y.: Doubleday, 1976.

Haley, A. (assistant to Malcolm Little) *The Autobiography of Malcolm X*. New York: Grove Press, 1965.

Howard, A. *Ain't No Big Thing*. Honolulu: University of Hawaii Press, 1974.

Howard, A. and associates. Households, families and friends in a Hawaiian-American community. Working Paper 19. East-West Population Institute, Honolulu, 1971.

Kagan, S. Field independence and conformity of rural Mexican and urban Anglo-American Children. *Child Development* 45 (1974):765-71.

Kagan, S., and Buriel, R. Field dependence-independence and Mexican-American culture and education. In J. Martinez, *Chicano Psychology*. New York: Academic Press, 1977.

Kagan, S. and Kogan, J. Individual variations in cognitive processes. In *Carmichael's Manual of Child Psychology,* 3rd ed., edited by Paul Mussen. New York: John Wiley & Sons, 1970.

Kagan, S. and Madsen, M. Cooperation and competition of Mexican, Mexican-American, and Anglo-American children of two ages under four instructional sets. *Developmental Psychology* 5 (1971):32-39.

_____. Experimental analyses of cooperation and competition of Anglo-American and Mexican-American children. *Developmental Psychology* 6 (1972a):49-59.

_____. Rivalry in Anglo-American and Mexican children of two ages. *Journal of Personality and Social Psychology* 24 (1972b):214-20.

Kardiner, A. and Ovesey, L. *The Mark of Oppression.* New York: W.W. Norton, 1951.

Keil, C. *Urban Blues.* Chicago: University of Chicago Press, 1966.

Korchin, S.J. Clinical psychology and minority problems. *American Psychologist* 35 (1980):262-69.

Kubo, R. The revised and extended Binet-Simon tests applied to the Japanese children. *Pedagogical Seminary* 29 (1934):187-94.

Lee, C. and DeVos, G.A. *Koreans in Japan: Cultural Continuities and Minority Status.* Berkeley: University of California Press, 1981.

Levine, R. Cross-cultural study in child psychology. In *Carmichael's Manual of Child Psychology,* 3rd ed., edited by Paul Mussen. New York: John Wiley & Sons, 1970.

Lewis, O. *Children of Sanchez.* New York: Random House, 1961.

_____. *La Vida.* New York: Random House, 1966.

_____. Review of Valentine, C. *Culture and Poverty: A Critique and Counter-Proposal. Current Anthropology* 10 (1969):189-92.

Liliuokalani Trust. *A Survey of the Socio-Economic Status of the Hawaiian People Today.* Honolulu, 1978.

MacArthur, R.S. Cognitive Strengths of Central Canadian and Northwest Greenland Eskimo Adolescents. Paper presented at the Western Psychological Association meeting. Anaheim, Calif., April 1973.

_____. Differential Ability Patterns: Inuit, Nsenga, and Canadian White. Paper presented at the Second International Conference of the International Association for Cross-Cultural Psychology. Kingston, Jamaica, August 1974.

McClelland, D. *The Achieving Society.* Princeton, N.J.: Van Nostrand, 1961.

McClelland, D.C., Atkinson, J.W., Clark, R.H., and Lowelle, E.L. *The Achievement Motive.* New York: Appleton-Century-Crofts, 1953.

McClelland, D.C., Baldwin, A.L., Bronfenbrenner, U., and Strodtbeck, F.L. *Talent and Society: New Perspectives in the Identification of Talent.* Princeton, N.J.: Van Nostrand, 1958.

Madsen, M. Cooperative and competitive motivation of children in three Mexican subcultures. *Psychological Reports* 20 (1967):1307-20.

Madsen, M. and Shapira, A. Cooperative and competitive behavior of urban Afro-American, Anglo-American and Mexican village children. *Developmental Psychology.* 9 (1973):16-20.

Martinez, J. *Chicano Psychology.* New York: Academic Press, 1977.

Mebane, D. and Johnson, D.L.A. Comparison of the performance of Mexican boys and girls on Witkin's cognitive tasks. *Inter-American Journal of Psychology* 4 (1970):227-39.

Miller, D. and Swanson, G.E. *The Changing American Parent.* New York: John Wiley & Sons, 1958.

Minturn, L. and Lambert, W.W. *Mothers of Six Cultures: Antecedents of Child Rearing.* New York: John Wiley & Sons, 1964.

Pettigrew. T. *Profile of the Negro American.* Princeton, N.J.: Van Nostrand, 1964.

Piaget, J. and Inhelder, B. *The Psychology of the Child.* New York: Basic Books, 1969.

Plog, S. and Edgerton, R. *Changing Perspectives in Mental Illness.* Holt, Rinehart and Winston, 1969.

Price-Williams, D. *Explorations in Cross-Cultural Psychology.* San Francisco: Chandler & Sharp, 1975.

Ramirez, M. and Price-Williams, D. Cognitive styles of children of three ethnic groups in the United States. *Journal of Cross-Cultural Psychology* 5 (1974): 212-19.

Reisman, D., Denny, R., and Glazer, N. *The Lonely Crowd: A Study of the Changing American Character.* New Haven, Conn.: Yale University Press, 1955.

Shaw, C.N. and McKay, N.D. *Juvenile Delinquency in Urban Areas.* Chicago: University of Chicago Press, 1942.

Stack, C. *All Our Kin.* New York: Harper & Row, 1974.

Strong, E.K. *The Second-Generation Japanese Problem.* Stanford, Calif.: Stanford University Press, 1934.

Werner, E.E. *Cross-Cultural Child Development.* Monterey. Calif.: Brooks/Cole, 1979.

Witkin, H.A. Cognitive styles across cultures. *International Journal of Psychology* 2 (1967):233-50.

_____. Social influences in the development of cognitive style. In *Handbook of Socialization Theory and Research,* edited by D.A. Goslin. New York: Rand McNally, 1969.

Witkin, H.A., and Berry, J.W. Psychological differentiation in cross-cultural perspective. *Journal of Cross-Cultural Psychology* 6 (1975):4-87.

Witkin, H.A. and Goodenough, D. Field dependence and interpersonal behavior. *Psychological Bulletin* 84 (1977):661-89.

Witkin, H.A., Price-Williams, D., Bertini, M., Christiansen, B., Oltman, P.K., Ramirez, M., and Van Meel, J. Social conformity and psychological differentiation. *International Journal of Psychology* 9 (1974):11-29.

Wright, R. *Black Boy.* New York: Harper, 1945.

5 Stress, Ethnicity, and Social Class: A Model for Research with Black Populations*

Hector F. Myers

INTRODUCTION

This chapter presents a theoretical model for research on stress in minority populations that is consistent with a holistic perspective. While the proposed model was developed with black populations in the United States specifically in mind, the basic issues addressed and the proposed relationships between the variables discussed are assumed to be generic to the study of stress generally. The model is based on the available black, as well as nonminority, literature in the field. The model is designed, therefore, not so much to be applicable to minority populations only; but rather as a generic model that includes and permits the meaningful analysis of the experiences of stress among blacks. This is accomplished mainly by including the variables of race and social class in the analysis, both as individual factors and as aggregate-historical factors.

Before we proceed with the elaboration of our model, further attention should be given to the role that social and political factors play in the state of health and illness of individuals and groups within our society. Many have argued that illness and health are social and political entities. McKinley (1975), in discussing the factors underlying the pattern of occurrence of cardiovascular disorder in modern industrial societies, notes that our cultural

*The preparation of this chapter was supported by NIMH research grant No. 5-R01-MH-25580 and NIH research grant No. 1-R23-HL-235-22. The author is appreciative of the helpful comments of Lewis King, Vernon Dixon, Michael Goldstein, Charles Nakamura, Constance Hammen, the editors, and the Staff of the Fanon Research and Development Center.

118

values and practices reinforce at-risk behaviors such as smoking and drinking and a hard-driving, achievement-oriented, high stress life style. All of these factors have been consistently demonstrated as having etiological significance in coronary heart disease. Similarly, Kosa, Antonovsky, and Zola (1969) argue that poverty is a psychological, social, and economic condition that is created and maintained as a necessary by-product of our industrial economic system. By nature, poverty is an illness-inducing state because of the excessive and continuous pressures the person faces, because of the long-term consequences of the continuous exposure to pathogens and to endemic stressors (i.e., high vulnerability), and because of the chronic scarcity of services, resources, and assets.

L. King (1978a, b), H. Myers (1979b), and H. Myers and L. King (in press) further elaborate on this theme and argue for a model of minority mental health that is based on the notion of a negative self-society dialectic. They argue that the health of minority groups is intimately connected to the social structures and policies that reinforce and perpetuate social discrimination and class exploitation. These structures and practices create crisis states within the individual and society (i.e., a high stress state).

The argument in favor of stress as a primary villain in the politics of health and illness among ethnic minorities and the poor is heuristically very appealing. The idea that being poor and being discriminated against makes life more stressful and increases the risks for disease and instability is well documented in both the scientific and popular literature. However, efforts to systematically define the pattern of effect and the mechanism of operation of stress in the dynamics of health and illness in these groups have often failed to live up to expectations. Several important reasons for these failures can be identified. Primary among these is that the research evidence linking stress and health generally has often been inconsistent and contradictory. This is due principally to the difficulties involved in consistently and reliably defining and measuring the construct of stress. Second, the conceptualization and measurement of the stress-disease relationship has generally been too simplistic. Many studies define and measure stress as a status phenomena rather than as a dynamic process; or they seek to identify individual, episodic stressors as the principal causes of health or illness; or they restrict their focus of attention to the physiological or psychological byproducts of stress exposure as if they were distinct and unrelated phenomena. Third, measurement strategies have generally been discrete and univariate, rather than complex and multivariate. Fourth, sociopsychological factors such as ethnicity and social class are usually conceptualized as external sources of stress affecting mainly objective stress exposure. Such views stop short of fully exploring the complex dialectical nature of the contributions of race and class, which include both external and internal dynamics and which affect the entire stress, coping, and health relationship.

This chapter conceptualizes stress as a complex and dynamic process affected at the outset by a host of internal and external antecedent and mediating factors. The model presented here accounts for differences in coping and adaptation over time, a process that is viewed as affecting both the experience and the consequences of stress, as well as contributing to the elaboration of a stress-vulnerable or stress-resistant life style. This stress model is based on a comprehensive review and integration of the generic literature in the field (i.e., research in both majority and minority populations). Again, it is conceptualized as generic to the hypothesized relationship between stress and health in the population as a whole. The utility and applicability of the model to black populations will be illustrated by our analysis of the role of ethnicity and social class as status-related sources and mediators of stress.

The final section of the chapter addresses the methodological issues and problems posed by such a complex conceptual model. Current work on stress and essential hypertension in black populations will be briefly presented to illustrate the practical research application of the model.

GENERIC MODEL OF STRESS

The effort to study and to elaborate conceptually elegant yet programmatic and useful models has been hampered by problems of definition, conceptualization, and measurement. These issues are discussed in detail in several excellent views and critiques, such as those by Basowitz, et al. (1955), Korchin (1965), Appley and Trumbull (1967), Janis (1958), McGrath (1970), Dohrenwend and Dohrenwend (1974), Selye (1950, 1959), and Lazarus (1966, 1974). A central theme in these reviews is that investigators have generally failed to arrive at a consensus on the meaning and appropriate use of the term stress. Stress has been used variously to refer to a stimulus, a response, an organismic state, and an adaptational process (Appley and Trumbull, 1967). Similarly, the term has been defined as synonymous with anxiety, discomfort, pressure, arousal, tension, and other similar descriptors of strong emotional states.

Conceptually, stress has been generally regarded as an organismic condition that is characterized by the disruption of the system's homeostasis resulting in consequences that range from mild attentional and performance disturbances to severe physical and emotional disorders. Empirical studies of the effects of stress have shown, however, that stress can result in either of several outcomes: (1) stress can produce no immediate, discernable effect, or 2) it can disrupt functioning and threaten one's health and well-being, or 3) it can stimulate performance and may in fact be essential for growth and development (Lazarus, 1978). Such contradictory findings have stimulated a serious reevaluation of the field to determine the common functional meaning of stress as suggested by the evidence to date and generated conceptual models that propose to integrate the variety of stress effects reported.

Korchin (1965), Selye (1959), Lazarus (1978), and others have suggested that functionally speaking the construct stress should be used to refer to the complex, integrated, total organismic response to stimulus demands that are appraised as likely to exceed the organism's adaptive capabilities and resources and to disrupt its equanimity (i.e., threat or challenge).

Several important external and internal antecedents and mediating factors are identified as affecting which stimuli are appraised as stressors, what degree of threat or challenge will be perceived, and how much potential disruption in the organism's equanimity is likely to result from a particular stressor or class of stressors. In addition, it has been suggested that the resultant state of disrupted equanimity (i.e., tension) triggers a complex adaptational process, the outcome of which locates an individual somewhere along the ease-disease and the health-illness continua. The direction, the pattern of development, the unique characteristics, and ultimately the effectiveness of the adaptational process is in itself affected by many of the same antecedent and mediating factors that affect stress resistance and reactivity. It is this complex, interacting process over time that is conceptualized as resulting in the range of behavioral, health, and illness outcomes that have been attributed to the effects of stress.

STRESS AS A FACTOR IN PATHOGENESIS

Most studies have attempted to relate stress directly as a pathogen in the etiology of specific disorders. These studies tend to restrictively emphasize the experience of *distress,* i.e., negative, disrupting stress (Selye, 1974). Further, most of these studies attempt to identify direct causal relationships between the experience of distress and specific disorder outcomes in a simplistic, find-pro-quo, dose-effects model. Whether stress is measured in terms of discrete life-disrupting events (Holmes and Rahe, 1967), or as endogenous to daily activities (Ilfeld, 1977), the empirical evidence clearly suggests that stress (i.e., distress) influences the degree of risk or vulnerability to disease and disorder generally, rather than predicting any specific disease outcome (Cassel, 1974). What specific disorder an individual under stress is likely to experience, then, is not predictable simply from knowing what stresses he or she is currently under. Rather, a more complete understanding is needed of the amount, kind, and duration of the stress exposure, what coping strategies are used and their relative effectiveness in reducing stress, what affective, cognitive, and behavioral responses are elicited, and what disease-specific vulnerabilities are present (Akiskal and McKinney, 1975).

As a consequence, therefore, Janis (1958), Korchin (1965), and Lazarus (1966, 1977, 1978) suggest complex conceptual and research paradigms based on an exploration of the stress adaptation process as a precursor to disease and system malfunction. These models affirm that the most productive direction for research on stress-related diseases should emphasize: (1) the multilevel, simultaneous measurement of stress (i.e., environmental, political, psychological, social, affective, and behavioral), (2) a combined state and process conceptualization of stress, (3) the measurement of both chronic and endogenous stress experiences (i.e., life events), and (4) naturalistic stress experiences rather than laboratory induced stress.

Collectively, this literature suggests that central to the pathogenic model of stress (i.e., distress-illness) is the identification of generalized and specific vulnerability factors, which interact at at specific point in time and space in a person's life to increase their risk for disease generally, as well as to specific disorders.

At the psychological level, these vulnerability factors may evolve over time and as a product of one's experiential history into a *sense of personal disjunction*[1]—i.e. a sense of limited personal control, a reduced sense of coherence and integration, and a limited sense of resistance, resiliency, and hardiness. This subjective sense of vulnerability, in a dynamic retrogressive loop, affects the range of stimuli viewed as potentially threatening, the intensity of the distress response likely to be triggered, and the degree of severity of the resultant disordered functioning and/or illness outcomes.

STRESS AS A FACTOR IN SALUTOGENESIS

In a limited number of studies, we see increasing attention paid to the facilitating, health and growth-enhancing role that stress is also likely to play. Selye (1974) suggested the term *lustress* to characterize this positive effect of stress and began exploring the issues and factors that increase the likelihood that daily stress may be transformed to energizing, life-enhancing lustress.

More recently, Antonovsky (1979) elaborated a rather elegant model of stress and health based on the mediation of the effects of potential endogenic and exogenic stressors through the presence of genetic, psychosocial *generalized and specific resistance resources* and psychological *sense of coherence*. This model proposes that health results not from the absence of stress,[2] but rather through the development of generalized and specific resistance resources that interact with consistent, predictable, and controllable life experiences to produce a strong sense of coherence. The latter, in turn, serves to mediate the appraisal and impact of potential stressors and to facilitate successful tension reduction.

Despite the apparent differences in emphasis and in the specification of pivotal factors in the various stress-health models, these appear to be consistent, generic core formulation of stress. Collectively, these conceptual models identify a generic stress research paradigm consisting of six basic components: (1) *exogenic and endogenic antecedents* (precursors) that define the state of the individual, his experiential and genetic history, and the sociopolitical context in which he develops and functions, (2) the set of *internal and external mediators* that alter (i.e., increase or decrease) the experience and impact of the stressor(s) on the individual, (3) the *eliciting stressor(s)*—the objective stressful psychosocial or physical stimuli that trigger adaptation or change in the usual level and pattern of functioning, (4) the *stress state*—the generalized reaction to tension created by the disruption of the pattern of usual functioning that varies from relative ease to considerable disease, (5) the *coping and adaptation process*—the complex physiological, cognitive-affective, and behavioral stress-response process that includes primary and secondary appraisal, coping efforts, and the reappraisal of outcomes, and finally, (6) the *health outcome,* resultant from the stress and coping process. Underlying this process is the factor of time, which underscores the dynamic, developmental nature of this process.

Short-term reactions to episodic stresses are affected by the person's state of being at the time of onset. These episodic periods of tension, in turn, modify the usual, basal level of stress under which the person functions. A simplified depiction of this paradigm is diagramed in Figure 5.1.

Figure 5.1.   Simplified conceptual and research paradigm depicting the role of stress in health and illness.

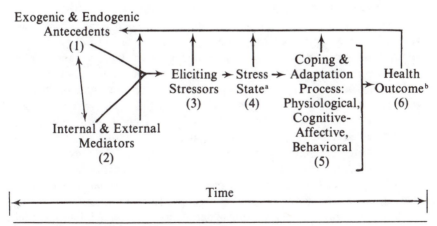

[a]Point along lustress—distress continuum.
[b]Represents both the point along the health (+)—illness (–) continuum as well as the specific disorder(s) that may result.

STRESS AND BLACK MENTAL HEALTH

In applying this proposed model of stress to the analysis of mental health generally, and more specifically to the mental health of black populations, several assumptions are made. First, it is assumed that a person's or group's general health can be meaningfully understood from knowledge of their race, social class, sex and age related stress dynamics (H. Myers, 1976; Bardwick, 1971; H. Myers and L. King, in press; Lazarus and Cohen, 1976a, b). Second, it is further assumed that our understanding of the amount, pattern, type, and level of impact of stresses on an individual could be greatly enhanced by including factors of race, social class, sex, and age in our analysis, when those factors are applicable and appropriate (Dohrenwend, 1967; Dohrenwend and Dohrenwend, 1967, 1969, 1970; Gersten, et al., 1977). Third, the relative impact and meaning of any stresses, as well as the pattern of responses elicited, are influenced by the person's social class, ethnicity, and culture, in addition to the effects that individual biological and psychological mediating processes might have on these appraisals and responses (Dohrenwend and Dohrenwend, 1969, 1970; Askenasy, Dohrenwend, and Dohrenwend, 1977; L. King, 1978a; Paulley, 1975; Miller, et al., 1974; Wyatt, 1977). Fourth, consistent with the empirical evidence on life-events stress, we assume the greater the amount, intensity, undesirableness, uncontrollability, and duration of the stress experienced, the greater the risk for severe disorder outcomes (Holmes and Rahe, 1967; Dohrenwend and Dohrenwend, 1974; J.K. Myers, Lindenthal, and Pepper, 1974; Brown, Bhrolchain, and Harris, 1975; Mueller, Edwards, and Yarvis, 1977; Gersten, et al., 1977).

The available literature on black mental health strongly suggests that blacks generally, and especially poor blacks, experience comparatively more stress, may experience a wider range of events as stressful, experience more undesirable stressful events, and are more often required to cope with stresses over an extended period of time than a comparable group of whites and members of the middle classes (Dohrenwend and Dohrenwend, 1970; Dohrenwend, 1973a, 1973b; Askenasy, Dohrenwend, and Dohrenwend, 1977). As a group, blacks also show a pattern of higher stress vulnerability, as evidenced by higher casualty rates for a number of learning, behavioral, physical, and emotional disorders. Therefore, stress as an index of oppression can be expected to be more evident among blacks than whites and among the poor than among the middle and upper classes. These differences should be viewed as both quantitative and qualitative and should parallel the ethnic and social-class differences in the incidence of physical illnesses and psychopathology. The evidence and logical reasoning in support of these hypotheses can best be illustrated by elaborating in detail our proposed six-factor model of stress and by briefly discussing how it might be used to address issues of health and illness in black populations.

EXOGENIC AND ENDOGENIC ANTECEDENTS

This first set of factors serve as precursors of health and illness that influence from the outset what experiences are likely to be deemed stressful, how stressful they are likely to be, what coping strategies are available and likely to be triggered by these experiences, what if any individual and group vulnerabilities are present and likely to be elicited, and what outcomes are most likely to result. These factors can be parsimoniously grouped into two major categories: the exogenic or sociocultural antecedents and the endogenic or individual predisposing antecedent factors. The former are believed to affect the relative stress vulnerability and stress resistance of individuals and groups by determining the objective social, economic, and political context in which they exist (i.e., the social niche). The latter acknowledges the critical role that genetic endowment and developmental history play in additionally predicting individual stress vulnerability and stress resistance. This formulation is consistent with the basic theoretical position that behavioral and health outcomes can be most meaningfully understood as products of the dialectic between person (group) and social context at some point along a historical, developmental continuum.

Included among the antecedent factor, but in no way assumed to be an exhaustive list, are such factors as unique ethnicity and social class status and dynamics as the principal exogenic antecedents. Among the major endogenic antecedents are genetic and constitutional endowments and individual developmental history.

Exogenic Antecedents

In a series of articles, H. Myers (1976, 1977, 1979a, b) and Myers and King (in press) suggest that a cross-generational pattern of higher basal stress and a conditioned physiological reactivity and psychological vigilance for a wide range of "threats" may very well underlie the pattern of stress-related disorders among blacks, other ethnic groups, and the poor reported in the epidemiological literature. This higher basal stress hypothesis is derived from the objective realities of race and class prejudices that create greater stress exposure and that institutionalize obstacles that block effective access to resources and coping options. This combination of factors is believed to increase the risk for disorders and to reduce the likelihood of a competent and healthy existence for many low-income blacks. There is some empirical evidence to support the contention that blacks face greater stress demands (J.K. Myers, Lindenthal, and Pepper, 1974), are exposed to more insidious status, class, and race related sources of stress (Dohrenwend and Dohrenwend, 1970), have earlier experiences of stressful life events (Gersten, Langner, and Orycek, 1974; Gersten, et al., 1977), often perceive events as more stressful than whites (Wyatt, 1977), and are exposed more frequently than whites to undesirable and uncontrollable events in their lives (Mueller, Edwards, and Yarvis, 1977).

These race and class dynamics, however, must also be seen as potential sources of strengths and resources. The negative experiences of discrimination and restricted access to material goods and services has also been shown to result in the development of personal and group resistance resources in the form of a strong collective identity, an extended family network, creative and flexible coping strategies, a sense of personal and collective resilience, and even physiological and genetic resistances to disease (R. King, 1978; Stack, 1974; Hill, 1972; Jackson, et al., 1979; Pollard, 1979; Boykin, 1979).

If we were to extend this line of reasoning further and include the factors of sex role and age-related social status into our analysis we would obtain an even more complex pattern of antecedents affecting group risks and resistances. The available evidence on employment, education, social mobility, and health provides no clear picture of whether black males or females are under greater stress or possess greater resources. In the area of employment, employed black men generally command higher salaries and have higher-status jobs. In the area of education, black women are more likely than black men to complete high school and college, but black men have greater access to the professions and receive higher salaries at comparable educational levels. (National Urban League, 1977).

This suggests, then, that while blacks as a group appear to carry a heavier stress load and to run greater stress risks than whites, important differences among blacks are, nevertheless, evident due to the complex interaction of SES and age.

Endogenic Antecedents

The objective social policies and practices postulated herein are proposed as factors that account for group differences in stress vulnerability and risk or resistance to disease as a function of the major sociodemographic factors noted. However, we must also acknowledge that not all blacks, ethnic minorities, women, or poor individuals experience equal amounts of stress or are equally vulnerable to stress-related disorders. Individual differences across groups in general vulnerability and resistance to disorders such as depression and essential hypertension, have been shown to be affected by such factors as genetic heritage (Akiskal and McKinney, 1973, 1975; Saunders and Williams, 1975), developmental histories (Brown, Bhrolchain, and Harris, 1975; Brown and Harris, 1978), and idiosynchratic stress appraisal and coping styles (Janis, 1958, 1962; Lazarus, 1966, 1967; Seligman, 1975).

Hypotheses about genetic contributions to susceptibility or resistance to disease have always generated considerable debate and controversy. This is perhaps due to the serious political and treatment implications that such hypotheses suggest. Individual differences in general vulnerability (i.e., hardiness and resistance), as well as patterns of vulnerability and resistance to specific disorders, however, are clearly affected by one's genetic heritage (Akiskal and McKinney, 1975). This is especially evident in the case of genetically transmitted immunities (e.g., resistance to malaria in Africans) and, to a significantly lesser degree, the biochemically based susceptibility and risks for schizophrenia and depression.

While the evidence specifying the role and mechanism of operation of genetic and constitutional factors in stress-related diseases remains tenuous and suggestive, we cannot entirely discount this source of individual variation. Within-group differences among blacks exist that cannot be fully attributed to social class, to past experiences, or to personality differences. Similarly, the recent and growing interest in research on melanin and the pineal gland in the metabolism of dopamine and other neurotransmitters is suggestive of genetic differences between ethnic groups in degree of sensitivity and reactive potential to external noxious stimuli, as well as resistance to cancer and to the deteriorative effects of aging of the skin (McGee, 1976; R. King, in press).

Secondarily, individual and even group differences in vulnerability to stress may be due to differences in developmental histories. There is ample research in the social sciences documenting the relationship between early development experiences and the later development of a variety of diseases and disorders. Brown et al. (1975) noted that one of the factors that significantly differentiated men and women diagnosed as clinically depressed was parental separation prior to age 11 in the women studied. Similarly, the work by Schachter, et al. (1974) noting the higher basal heart rates of low-income blacks neonates compared to white cohorts has been suggested to reflect very early signs of greater stress sensitivity and cardiovascular reactivity in the former group, which puts the groups in the risk for hypertensive disease.

The reasoning of the developmentalist is that individuals who experience early traumatic and stressful events develop deficiencies either behaviorally and/or psychologically that restrict the range and effectiveness of their subsequent coping repertoire. Thus, when exposed to later traumatic events, and in the absence of compensating and buffering supports from significant others, there is a conditioned greater risk of becoming overwhelmed and of suffering physical and/or psychiatric breakdowns (Brown, Bhrolchain, and Harris, 1975; Brown and Harris, 1978).

The experiences of many black and other minority children and youth include exposure to many early traumas that can be attributed mainly to the dynamics of class and race oppression (Dohrenwend and Dohrenwend, 1970; H. Myers, 1977, 1979b; H. Myers and L. King, in press). There is reason to suspect that many stresses on blacks and other minorities begin their insidious influence even in-utero in mothers who must cope with the vicissitudes of poverty (i.e., poor nutrition, inadequate health care, inadequate financial, emotional and psychological support, etc.). Considerable empirical evidence exists to partially substantiate this assertion (Powell, Morales and Yamamoto, in press). Additionally, this pattern of early deprivation continues through life experiences that are characterized by instability and unpredictability and where the individual and family perceive their fate as controlled by factors that are outside of their influence and control (e.g., unemployment due to cutbacks, changes in policies governing such programs as welfare, job training, and health care, etc.).

In summary, how an individual or group defines what is stressful and how they respond to it is influenced by a host of genetic, constitutional, developmental, political, cultural, and behavioral precursors. These antecedent factors set the stage that influences the pattern and direction of the subsequent stress-health relationships. For many blacks, particularly those that are poor, the critical antecedents appear to be the higher basal stress level and the state of high stress vigilance at which normative functioning often occurs. This "stress-primed" state of existence is believed to be conditioned by the historical and structural politics of race and class oppression and to be reinforced by the early and chronic exposure to the wide variety of stressors that are present in highly variable, unpredictable, and crisis-ridden social conditions. Individual constitutional, personality, and behavioral differences further exacerbate this heightened state and increase the probability of illness generally, as well as increase the risk for specific disorders such as learning disabilities, depression, and hypertension.

For others, the politics of race and class—in conjunction with stable and relatively safe developmental histories, the absence of major constitutional or genetic vulnerabilities, and in the presence of strong social supports (e.g., family and community)—combine to produce healthy stress-resistance resources that protect against stress-related disorders.

INTERNAL AND EXTERNAL MEDIATORS

The importance of sociopolitical and personal antecedents in influencing relative risk or resistance to stress-related disorders cannot be denied. However, these factors cannot by themselves account for the quality and intensity of stress likely to be experienced, nor do they predict the stress-related outcomes of those experiences. Many blacks exist in similarly oppressing conditions, with many of the same antecedent factors operative. Yet, there are significant individual differences among blacks in the pervasiveness of stress in their lives and in its negative consequences. Some become casualties of the education, legal/penal, economic, social, and health systems, while others seem to thrive despite the pressures and obstacles faced.

The empirical evidence to date suggests that the critical determiners of relative stress risk or stress resistance is due to the complex array of factors, both external and internal, that mediate the effect of stressors on any given individual or group. These mediators serve as screens that reduce or as prisms that concentrate the impact of stressful experiences. For purposes of clarity, we have divided this second set of factors into external mediators (i.e., factors outside of the person's control) and internal mediators (i.e., factors within the person).

External Mediators

Many of the factors previously discussed as antecedent factors also contribute in the present as external mediators of the stress potential of current events. Particularly significant in this regard are: (1) the present social and economic conditions, (2) the operating race and social class dynamics that influence both stress exposure and the contingencies governing stress-coping options, and (3) the availability and accessibility of resources and supports.

The present state of the economy is an important factor predicting both stress exposure and stress impact for blacks. On it rests the direction of social policies that serve as a mechanism through which race and social class dynamics are operative. In relatively prosperous economic times (i.e., what economists call positive-sum economic conditions), social policies are likely to be more liberal because the healthy economy allows all segments of society to make progress. The poor benefit directly by gaining access to a greater share of pie (i.e., economic gains can be distributed more equitably). Thus, programs such as job training, increases in social support payments, and affirmative action programs in education and industry are all more likely to be implemented.

However, when economic downturns occur (i.e., zero-sum gain economic conditions), there is a general trend towards conservative social policy and a preoccupation with selfish and nonhumanitarian concerns. Under these conditions, the gains of individuals and groups must come at the expense of others. One group's progress means another's retrogression. What resources exist are distributed in accordance with the distribution of power. The least economically vulnerable are the most likely to reap material benefits, while the most economically dependent are likely to be sacrificed.

Race often serves as the sorter of the struggle. During good economic times blacks are sometimes allowed to achieve social gains. During economic recessions, however, whatever gains were achieved are now redressed, and greater social economic and political stresses are faced. Race as a source of stress, then, is mediated by the complex dynamics of economics and social conditions that determine relative group status and power and that manipulate the options and contingencies governing coping behavior.

Similarly, another important external stress mediator is the availability and quality of social resources and supports. Nuckolls, Cassel, and Kaplan (1972), Cassel (1974), and Cobb (1976) note that the relative detrimental effect that major stresses such as unemployment, unwanted pregnancy, or death in the family may have is significantly influenced by whether or not individuals have available to them the necessary social supports and resources. Individuals under high stress who also have requisite social supports tend to experience significantly fewer health problems than their high stress, low support peers.

Research on the effects of prolonged unemployment and high-stress occupational histories, realities that are far too common for many blacks, shows that the greatest negative consequences were experiences by those who were living alone, who were single (either from divorce, separation, or death), who had fewer contacts with friends or relatives, and who had fewer significant and meaningful ties to their communities (Liem and Liem, 1978; Gore, 1978; Dean and Lin, 1977; J. Myers, Lindenthal, and Pepper, 1971, 1975).

The concept of social supports as a mediator of stress is especially critical in a research paradigm of stress in ethnic minorities and the poor. Traditionally, blacks have relied on close families and communities as buffers against the vicissitudes of life. Families, churches, and entire communities came to the aid of those in need to provide instrumental, emotional, and spiritual guidance during trying times (Stack, 1974; Aschenbrenner, 1975). With urbanization and the struggles for upward mobility, we now find many black families and communities increasingly becoming more isolated and vulnerable. This is sometimes a source of difficulty for the black middle classes, who as part of their continued striving for upward mobility and economic betterment, reduce their contact with extended family systems, often without effective replacements. Thus, these isolated individuals, despite greater personal resources, run a greater risk that the increasing stresses of corporate and professional life will exceed their individual capacity to adapt. And, in the absence of reliable and effective support systems we find increasing incidence of divorce, alcoholism, ulcers, heart disease, depression, and other stress-related disfunctions among the vulnerable members of the black middle class (Frazier, 1957; Kronus, 1970; Steele, 1978).

In essence then, current economic conditions affect the degree to which the factors of race and social class will be sources of high or low stress for blacks. Individual blacks who currently live under conditions of material and personal stability are likely to experience relatively low levels of stress and to run a relatively low risk of stress-related disorders, irrespective of past history. This is especially the case during economically prosperous times.

Their present reality should serve to mitigate the potentially-deleterious consequences of a rocky history and to increase their overall stress-resistance (Antonovsky, 1979). If, on the other hand, the black individual possesses a stress-risk history, is also living under conditions of poverty with recession-induced high stresses, and possesses limited social supports, then additional stressors should have a magnifying effect since they are impacting on an already overtaxed system. Past history and existing vulnerabilities will combine to further limit the person's coping effectiveness, to increase the subjective stress load, and to increase the risk of illness.

Internal Mediators

The impact that a given level of exposure to stress (i.e., external mediator) will also be influenced significantly by the host of internal factors that give subjective meaning and importance to those events and experiences. Primary among the internal mediating factors of stress are: (1) individual temperaments and dispositions (i.e., the tendency to overreact or to underreact in response to stress), (2) developed skills and competencies, especially problem-solving styles and skills (Dreger and Miller, 1968; Watts, 1974; Sewell and Severson, 1975), (3) past experiences with success or failure in coping both in general as well as specific to the stresses faced (Scott and Howard, 1970; Lazarus, 1966, 1967), (4) the accuracy and sophistication of analytic skills (i.e., the ability to analyze situations accurately and determine the best course of action), (5) the perception of oneself as effective at manipulating and controlling the occurance and outcome one's life experiences (Dohrenwend and Dohrenwend, 1970; Baron, et al., 1974; Guttentag and Klein, 1976; DeCharms, 1968), and finally, (6) a developed and integrated sense of self and the consciousness of the group (McAdoo, 1973, 1976; Sue, 1978; L. King, 1978a; Nobles, 1976; Cross, 1978; Akbar, 1974).

Individual temperaments are important mediators of stress at the biological (i.e., physiological, hormonal), psychological (i.e., subjective sense of arousal and discomfort), and interpersonal levels (i.e., perceived by others either as stress resistant and hardy or as easily excited and disturbed). Similarly, stress reactivity is also intimately related to the availability or absence of the requisite coping skills and competencies (H. Myers, 1974; Scott and Howard, 1970). As noted previously in our definition of stress, the experience of stress is related to the discrepancy between demands imposed and coping resources available. Individuals who lack the requisite skills and resources are more likely to experience new demands as stressful (i.e., a threat) than those for whom the demand is perceived as a challenge that is within their capacity to master given time, effort, and new learning (DeCharms, 1968; Kobasa, 1979).

The presence or absence of the needed skills and competencies is tied to past experiences of success or failure with previous coping efforts. The latter, in turn, contribute to creating a sense of personal competency that is characterized by either impotence and helplessness or by effectance and competence. Those individuals who have experienced considerable failure in previous coping efforts are more likely to find a wider range of stimuli as stressful and to question their ability to meaningfully remove or control adverse events in their lives. To the extent that they perceive these experiences as consistent in their lives, and attribute them to personal inadequacies, the more likely they are to suffer a loss of self-esteem and to become "helplessness prone"[3] (Gurin, et al., 1969; Sue, 1978; Abramson, Seligman, and Teasdale, 1978; Kasl and Cobb, 1967; Averill, 1973; Wortman, et al., 1976; Weiner, Russell, and Lerman, 1978).

On the other hand, persons who have experienced considerable success develop a strong sense of personal competency and reduced stress risk. Similarly, for those who have experienced failures, but accurately distinguish failure for which they are personally responsible from those that were due to external factors, the amount of stress experienced is less, and little or no reduction in self-esteem occurs (Gurin, et al., 1969; Sue, 1978; Wortman, et al., 1976). This is a particularly significant observation for blacks and the poor, who may experience frequent failures and frustrations. To the extent that they are able to accurately distinguish when the failures are externally controlled, they can successfully reduce the amount of subjective stress experienced and avoid the sense of failure and of worthlessness that follow self-attributed failure (i.e., psychological absolution). It is worthy of note here, however, that external attributions are only partially effective pallatives. If overused, they become convenient excuses, which ultimately interfere with the development of necessary instrumental coping skills.

In summary, I have noted that external and internal factors play an imporant role in mediating (i.e., increasing or decreasing) the subjective experience of stress. And, as such, they mediate the risk of stress-related disorders. In interaction with antecedent events, these mediators determine the state of vulnerability and risk of the individual at the point of exposure to potential stressors. To the extent that these factors interact in potentially debilitating ways (i.e., sense of dysfunction), they create a state of high stress vulnerability and trigger a stress coping process that is mediative of increased risk for disorders, disease, and general system malfunctions. To the degree that they are present, however, and operate as positive, resistance resources (i.e., sense of coherence) they increase stress resistance and overall health status.

THE ELICITING STRESSORS

We have been focusing our attention thus far on the factors that influence the response ability of the person prior to the onset of the threat. In the section that follows, we will discuss specifically the nature of the potential stressors and the process of coping and adaptation likely to be elicited.

Research on stress as a contributor in the pathogenesis of disease and disorder generally falls into two major categories: (1) those studies that demonstrate a strong association between episodic life changes and disease outcomes, and (2) those studies that contend that disease is more likely to be the result of the accumulation of insidious, day to day stresses rather than determined by discrete events.

In the present model, I propose that both chronic, basal stress level (i.e., accumulated, chronic stress), and episodic stressful events must be taken into account in evaluating relative stress risk in resistance and in predicting general health. The set of antecedent and mediating factors previously discussed influence the state of prepared need or of vulnerability of the individual at the time of the onset of specific stressor(s). The charactistic of the stressor, in turn, further contributes to determining the degree, level, and pattern of generalized and specific reactions elicited, the type and effectiveness of the resultant adaptation and coping effort, and the implications for future functioning and health.

The basic hypothesis proposed here is that the higher the basal stress level, the greater the risk that the onset of future episodic life-disrupting events will be overwhelming and trigger a pathogenic process that will result over time in some disorder or disability. Empirical support for this proposition is obtained from the literature on risk for accidents and fractures (Rahe, 1968, 1972), with the risk of myocardial infarctions and second coronaries (Theorell, Lind, and Floredusi, 1975), with the risk for psychiatric disorders, generally (Srole, et al., 1962; J.K. Myers, Lindenthal, and Pepper, 1971, 1974, 1975; Dohrenwend and Dohrenwend, 1969, 1970, 1974; Gersten, et al., 1977; Mueller, Edwards, and Yarvis, 1977), and with the experience of depression (Brown, Bhrolchain, and Harris, 1975; Brown and Harris, 1978; Ilfeld, 1976a, 1976b, 1977).

Additionally, attention must be paid to the nature of the stressor(s) in order to determine their pathogenic potential. Generally speaking, the most potentially pathogenic stressors are those that are negative, that involve losses, that are uncontrollable, unexpected, and long lasting, that are of high personal and group meaning, and that have either too few or too many coping options from which to choose (Cochrane and Robertson, 1973; Vinokur and Selzer, 1975; Wortman, et al., 1976).

In earlier formulations of this stress model (H. Myers, 1976, 1977, 1979a), I have contended that for many blacks and low-income individuals, a high basal stress level is normative. Episodic crises, which are also somewhat more often experienced by these groups, have different meanings and impact as a result of this higher basal stress level. The higher the basal stress level, the more damaging and disruptive each discrete life event becomes. Thus, for example, the death of a spouse or relative, the loss of a job due to economic downturns is likely to be more psychologically and economically devastating to the person who is struggling to find enough money to eat, to pay the rent, and to support three or four children than it would be to someone without those basic day to day concerns. In two recent studies testing this hypothesis, Askenasy, Dohrenwend, and Dohrenwend (1977) and Wyatt (1977) found that low income blacks experienced greater losses and rated their life crisis events as subjectively more distressing than the normative sample of whites reported by Holmes and Rahe (1967). Individual differences in stress-risk and incidence of disorders I suggest, then, reflects differences in level of basal stress among blacks and differences in exposure to high-threat life crises. Healthy blacks, all other things being equal, are those with greater resistance resources, those with lower chronic stress levels under which they function normally, and those that experience fewer negative and uncontrollable losses and crises in their lives.

THE STRESS STATE

The stress state represents the state of relative tension or distress resulting from exposure to stressors. The intensity of the reaction experienced places the person at some point along the ease-disease continuum. Further, depending on the presence of either pathogenic or salutogenic antecedents and mediators, which determine the basal stress state at the time of onset of the eliciting stressor, the person is located at some point along the health-illness continuums.

THE COPING AND ADAPTATION PROCESS

The fifth variable in the model is the coping and adaptation process that is both characteristic of the person (i.e., coping style) as well as that elicited by particular stressful events. Can we on the basis of the available empirical data and our own experiences and observations suggest that all blacks or persons of low income backgrounds experience similar levels of stress or run the same risk for psychiatric or other disorders? Probably not. Realistically, there is considerable within-group variability in actual subjective experience of stress and in disease risk even among the poorest segments of these populations. What then accounts for these differences given shared high stress environments and living conditions?

In a recent article, Kobasa (1979) reported differences in rates of disease among employed males under similarly high stress conditions, which she attributes to a psychological profile of "hardenss or resilience." This hardiness included such factors as "vigorousness toward the environment" (i.e., perceive changes as challenges rather than as threats), "a sense of meaningfulness" (i.e., feelings of commitment to various life activities), and "an internal locus of control" (i.e., greater decisional control, cognitive control, and coping skills in the face of life demands). The hardier subjects differed from their more disease-susceptible peers in their appraisal of the stressful occupational situations faced and in their coping.

These findings are consistent with the cognitive model of stress coping and adaptation proposed by Lazarus and his colleagues (Lazarus, 1966, 1977, 1978; Lazarus and Launier, in press; Lazarus and Cohen, 1976a, b; and Lazarus, et al., 1962, 1974) and with the notions of cognitive control (Seligman, 1975), commitment (Antonovsky, 1974), and challenge (Maddi, 1967) as effective stress mediators.

Basically, these concepts and models differentiate a three-stage coping and adaptation process that includes the appraisal of stimulus, the coping efforts, and the reappraisal or feedback. These stages are viewed as interconnected: behaviors at step one—stimulus appraisal—affect behaviors at the other two steps, and vice versa. Further, all of the previous factors (i.e., the precursors and the internal and external mediators) interact to influence the appraisal and coping process. Therefore, all other factors being equal, individual differences in the experience of stress, in response to it, and in the consequences of stress exposure can be attributed to differences in the coping and adaptation process.

At the appraisal phase, the nature of the particular event is evaluated for its potential stressfulness. This occurs, as Lazarus and his colleagues suggest, as a conscious warning process, which results in a decision about the stress potential of the stimulus (i.e., neutral, positive, or negative stimulus), the level of risk involved (i.e., harm/loss, threat, or challenge), and the ability of the respondent to cope with it (Lazarus, 1978).

However, for many stressful experiences there appears to be an immediate reaction without any formal appraisal. Events such as having a near accident, being stopped late at night by a policeman, or running into one's spouse while in the company of a friend of the opposite sex are experiences that elicit automatic reactions of anxiety and fear. These stressors are conditioned either through direct or unconscious experiences and trigger automatic reactions.

The concepts of appraisal and of automatic reactions to stress are particularly meaningful in research efforts with blacks and other ethnic minorities. Far too often researchers make structural observations (e.g., marital status, SES, employment, etc.) and erroneously attribute to them general meaning. For example, the absence of a father in the home means that the family is automatically an inadequate or high-risk family, or that living in a low income community automatically means that the family must have experienced the ravages of poverty and deprivation. The meanings and impact of these conditions on the lives of the individual black families may vary widely, even when the objective conditions appear to be the same. Thus, the assumptions of common consequences given common stressors is an erroneous one.

Similarly, we may expect group differences in appraisal and automatic reactions given group differences in experiential histories. For instance, many blacks may, in fact, perceive a wider range of events as threatening rather than as challenging or neutral; they may perceive each event as having greater threat potential than whites and/or members of the middle classes (Wyatt, 1977; Askenasy, Dohrenwend, and Dohrenwend, 1977). Brenner's (1973) classic study on the economy and mental illness demonstrated that, while there was a general relationship between economic downturns and the rate of psychiatric hospitalization, differences in the impact of economic downturns were related to ethnicity and SES. Low income blacks found these experiences to be more threatening, as evidenced by higher psychiatric hospitalization rates, than did middle- and upper-income nonethnic whites.

Further, we may also expect differences across groups in the types of stimuli that elicit automatic reactions. Blacks as a group tend to be more "sensitive" to social situations and symbols perceived as having racial connotations (i.e., generally involving whites or representatives of "the system"). Thus, while many people experience some degree of anxiety when seeking employment, for many low-income blacks, going for a job means facing a white employer who will probably either ignore you, or be condescending and demeaning, or simply reject you outright. Failures in previous job searches reinforce this fear and may result in an almost phobic refusal to engage in this unpredictable and painful process.

The second step in the stress response and adjustment process is the coping process, which is designed to both remove the source of stress and to control the accompanying emotional distress. Coping is itself a continuous and dynamic process that is affected by several factors, including the appraisal of the stress stimulus, the focus of the appraisal, the time orientation, the function of coping, and the mode of coping (Lazarus, 1978). Together these factors determine what behaviors in the individual's response repertoire will be used with what stressors under what set of circumstances and what the ultimate outcome will be.

Empirical studies of coping styles suggest that the most effective copers are those who possess the requisite skills and who use a rational/intuitive and flexible approach to coping (Goldstein, 1973; H. Myers, 1974; Kobasa, 1979; Antonovsky, 1979). Recent interest in cognitive social psychology and in information processing and the implications for stress coping and health have begun to elucidate many of the issues involved in how individuals and groups process social information in developing their attitudes and behaviors (Abelson, 1976; Taylor and Crocker, 1979; Hamilton and Warburton, 1979).

Unfortunately, very little of this research addresses the issues of stress coping among blacks (e.g., urban, low-income blacks, southern blacks, rural blacks, black youth, professional blacks, etc.). It is possible that different groups of blacks socialize distinct coping patterns among the members of these groups. For example, among many low-income, urban black youngsters, cappin, rappin, conning, and fighting constitute primary stress-coping strategies required for survival on the streets. For others, the ability to remain calm, cool, and collected in the face of a crisis is a primary coping strategy. These may represent scripted behaviors that are elicited in response to a wide range of stress stimuli rather than coping efforts selectively used in response to and as appropriate to specific stressors (Abelson, 1976). Others may turn to drugs and alcohol, or to religion, or to some flexible combination of all of the above in dealing with the response of stressors they face. The absence of careful empirical research in this area severely limits our ability to fully understand the black stress experience and to prescribe supportive or corrective action when needed.

THE HEALTH OUTCOME

The final factor in this stress model is the health outcome. The specification of outcomes from the specific combination of the factors discussed is an exciting yet elusive and error-filled enterprise. Ideally, at this point in the presentation, it should be possible to articulate a set of relationships and sequences of related variables and to specify contingency rules and gates that define the stress path leading to some specific outcomes or a class of outcomes. Unfortunately, the state of the field is such as to preclude such specificity. Nevertheless, we have enough information to be able to make some general conclusions about the rule of stress in health and illness generally, as well as in certain disorders (e.g., essential hypertension).

In general, we can say that health results not so much from the absence of stress, as from the presence of economic, social, and psychological resistance resources; from life experiences that are stable, consistent, and in which the individual can play an active part in determining their outcome; from a sense of integration and coherence—all of which combine to maintain a relatively low basal stress level and to allow for the effective coping with episodic stressors. Since few people are composed entirely of genetic vulnerabilities or of psychological weaknesses, the state of health will vary as the quality and effectiveness of the resistance resources vary in the face of demands. Illness risk increases significantly as vulnerabilities, both biological and psychosocial, increase; as life experiences are increasingly more unpredictable and uncontrollable; as resources are limited and unaccessible; and as appraisal and coping styles are scripted, stereotypical, and ineffective.

Minority Mental Health

For blacks as a group, the stress-related illness risks appear to be higher than the norm. This is due, I suspect, to the higher normative basal stress level at which a substantial number must function and the frequent impingement of life crises outside of the person's control. To the extent that ethnic cultural identity can be developed and stably integrated into the personality structure, to the extent that skills and competencies necessary to meet the varied demands can be obtained, to the extent that flexible, contingent response strategies can be developed, and to the extent that support systems can be maintained and strengthened, then resistances can be developed that will enhance stress tolerance and reduce individual and collective risk for disorders and disabilities.

As an illustrative application of this stress model to the study of a specific disorder outcome, we will briefly review what we know about essential hypertension, a psychosomatic disease of high prevalence among blacks across all socioeconomic conditions.

A MULTITRAIT, MULTIMETHOD APPROACH TO THE STUDY OF ESSENTIAL HYPERTENSION IN BLACKS

Essential hypertension has been shown to be disproportionately prevalent among blacks, women, the poor, and urban populations. Approximately 20 percent of the U.S. black population, or approximately six million black people, suffer from this disorder (Saunders and Williams, 1975). Current thinking on the factors that affect blood pressure suggests a complex etiological pattern (i.e., the mosaic theory), consisting of such primary variables as physiological malfunctioning, heredity, psychosocial factors such as stress, and a host of intervening variables such as diet, obesity, smoking, and exercise (Saunders and Williams, 1975). To date, the strongest evidence seems to favor the hereditary predisposition-physiological malfunction explanation. Psychosocial factors such as stress and health habits such as smoking, diet, and exercise are generally viewed as intervening to create the pathogenic conditions that actualize the genetic predisposition for cardiovascular malfunction.

The evidence in support of health habits as risk factors in hypertension is rather substantial (Harrell, 1980). However, the evidence specifying the etiological role of stress in this disease is rather tenuous at best. In a program of research designed to explore the stress-hypertension relationship in blacks, this investigator and his colleagues have utilized a multitrait, multimethod approach that is consistent with the research model presented here. This program of research hypothesizes that essential hypertension is a clinical outcome of a chronic stress induction process that includes (1) a genetic "weak-link" (i.e., family history of the disease), (2) a high stress-chronic life that is subjectively experienced as such (i.e., objective and subjective stress appraisal), (3) multiple symptoms, (4) a tendency to react to stress somatically with a cardiovascular response pattern, (5) a characteristic tendency to be highly anxious and to experience conflicts in the expression of anger, (6) a predominately avoidant coping style, and (7) inadequate access to effective support systems (H. Myers, 1976).

Early studies comparing black hypertensives and normotensives showed that black hypertensives were older, were more likely to have hypertensive parents and grandparents, experienced higher life stress, were generally more symptomatic and less hardy, and were more anxious and likely to be cardiovascular somatizers than were black normatives (H. Myers, 1979a; H. Myers and R. Miles, 1979).

The results of the most recent study (Myers, 1980) showed that in a relatively young and healthy sample of black college students, none of the various measures of psychosocial stresses were directly correlated with blood pressure. Only cardiovascular symptoms by themselves were related to blood pressure variability. However, in testing for the best predictors of blood pressure it was found that subjective stress; total somatic reactivity; cardiovascular, renal, and cognitive disorder symptoms; and cognitive disorganization as a somatic stress response accounted collectively for approximately 16.6 percent of the variance on systolic blood pressure. For diastolic blood pressure, the best predictors were total symptoms and, more specifically, cardiovascular, renal, and anxiety/stress symptoms. They accounted for approximately 17 percent of the variance.

Comparing the results for males and females separately showed that stress appears to have a differential impact as a function of sex and that different stress indicators predict systolic and diastolic variability for males and females. For females, 19.3 percent of their systolic variability was accounted for by two life-stress measures—subjectively weighted life change and total negative life change, along with cardiovascular cognitive disorder and other symptoms. On the other hand, 27.5 percent of their diastolic variability was accounted for by total subjective stress and cardiovascular, cognitive disorder, and anxiety/stress symptoms.

For males, 16.17 percent of their systolic blood pressure was accounted for by the proportion of positive to negative life-change events, by cardiovascular symptoms, and by sympathetic reactions. In contrast, 28.28 percent of diastolic blood pressure variability in males was predicted by total subjective stress, subjective ratio life-change stress, and anxiety/stress and other physical symptoms (H. Myers, 1980).

These results suggest that psychosocial stress appears to contribute indirectly and in conjunction with other factors (namely, physical health) to blood pressure variability. Further, that for black males and females different measures of life stress are found to be implicated in systolic and diastolic variability.

SUMMARY AND CONCLUSIONS

In this chapter I have presented a conceptual model for research on stress that is both generic and applicable to the study of health and illness in black populations. An extensive body of research has been reviewed and conceptualized as the basis for the model, and empirical data on ongoing research on stress and hypertension have been presented to demonstrate the concrete applicability of the model.

In essence, the model conceptualizes stress as generic to human existence but differentially prevalent and potentially pathogenic in the life of individuals and groups (e.g., blacks, the poor, etc.) as a function of the complex interaction of the groups of major factors. Antecedent factors, both internal and external, (such as the dynamics of race and class and individual genetic and developmental histories) operate to influence overall stress exposure and relative vulnerability or resistance. Mediational factors (such as present economic and social conditions and the quality of life) and the individual factors (such as temperament, skills and competencies, coping history, effectiveness of analytic skills, and the stability and integrity of one's personal and ethnic ego identity) serve to either enhance or to mitigate the impact of life stresses. The combination of these factors over time, resulting in the development of resistance resources and a strong sense of coherence, even in the presence of objectively stress-chronic environments (e.g., ghettos), will mitigate against the pathogenic impact of exposure to stress. If, on the other hand, these factors combine to produce a sense of personal disfunction and a pattern of vulnerability, then the risk for the pathogenic impact of life stresses is increased.

The model further notes the importance of assessing the characteristics of the eliciting stressors and the resultant appraisal and coping process, which interact with the current physiological and psychological person to predict the true state of risk or resistance to disfunctions and illnesses.

For blacks this generic stress-health paradigm is affected at all levels by the structural dynamics of race and social class oppression. These factors are viewed as influencing the amount of stress exposure, the access to coping options, the history of stress-coping successes and failures, the availability and effectiveness of social supports, stress appraisal tendencies, the attribution of control and responsibility for coping outcomes, the choice of coping strategies used, the success or failure of these efforts, and, finally, the personal price paid. I propose on the basis of this model that, collectively, blacks and the poor run a greater risk for stress-related disorders and disabilities than nonminorities and the more affluent. However, important within-group differences in risk are also evident as a function of individual differences in the degree of impact and vulnerability to oppression, of differences in the presence and availability of resistance resources, and differences in the degree to which the critical necessary factors in the model are operative in their lives. Considerable empirical research is needed with a model such as this to specify more clearly the specific contributions of the factors noted in predicting health and illness outcomes among blacks.

NOTES

1. This is conceptualized as the opposite to Antonovsky's (1979) *sense of coherence* as the key factor in a salutogenic model of stress and health.
2. A stress-free existence would be stressful since all living organisms seem to need some optimum amount of stress (i.e., challenge) in order to develop and grow.
3. I prefer the alternative construct "manufactured incompetence" as a substitute for "learned helplessness" when applying this paradigm to the analysis of the behavior of oppressed people. This alternative better captures the critical role that existing societal structures and processes play in creating obstacles and restricting coping options to produce feelings of helplessness and vulnerability in the less resilient members of minority groups and the poor.

REFERENCES

Abelson, R.P. Script processing in attitude formation and decision-making. In *Cognitive and Social Behaviors,* edited by J.S. Carroll and J.W. Payne, pp. 33-41. Hilldale, N.J.: Lawrence Erlbaum Associates, 1976.

Abramson. L., Seligman, M., and Teasdale, J. Learned helplessness in humans: Critique and reformation. *Journal of Abnormal Psychology* 88 (1978):49-74.

Advance Data from Vital and Health Statistics of the National Center for Health Statistics, U.S. Department of Health, Education, and Welfare, No. 2, November 8, 1976.

Akbar, N.L. Awareness: The key to black mental health. *Journal of Black Psychology* 1 (1974):30-37.

Akiskal, H.S. and McKinney, W.J. Depressive disorders: Toward a unified hypothesis. *Science* 182 (1973):20-29.

————. Overview of recent research in depression. *Archives of General Psychiatry* 32 (1975):285-305.

Antonovsky, A. Conceptual and methodological problems in the study of resistance resources and stressful life events. In *Stressful Life Events: Their Nature and Effects,* edited by B.S. Dohrenwend and B.P. Dohrenwend. New York: John Wiley & Sons, 1974.

_____. *Health, Stress and Coping.* San Francisco: Jossey-Bass, 1979.

Appley, M.H. and Trumbull, R., eds. *Psychological Stress.* New York: Appleton-Century-Crofts, 1967.

Aschenbrenner, J. *Lifelines: Black Families in Chicago.* New York: Holt, Rhinehart and Winston, 1975.

Askenasy, A.R., Dohrenwend, B.P., and Dohrenwend, B.S. Some effects of social class and ethnic group membership on judgements of the magnitude of stressful life events: A research note. *Journal of Health and Social Behavior* 18 (1977):432-39.

Averill, J.R. Personal control over oversize stimuli and its relationship to stress. *Psychological Bulletin* 80 (1973):286-303.

Baker, M., Dorzab, J., Winokur, G., and Cadoret, R. Depressive disease: Evidence favoring polygenic inheritance based on an analysis of ancestral cases. *Archives of General Psychiatry* 27 (1972):320-27.

Bardwick, J. *Psychology of Women: A Study of Biocultural Conflicts.* New York: Harper & Row, 1971.

Baron, R.M., Cowan, G., Ganz, R.L., and McDonald, M. Interaction of locus of control and type of performance feedback: Considerations of external validity. *Journal of Personality and Social Psychology* 30 (1974):285-92.

Basowitz, H., Persky, H., Korchin, S.J., and Grinker, R.R. *Anxiety and Stress.* New York: McGraw-Hill, 1955.

Boykin, A.W. Psychological/behavioral verve: Some theoretical explorations and empirical manifestations. In *Research Directions of Black Psychologists,* edited by A.W. Boykin, A.J. Franklin, and J.F. Yates, pp. 351-67. New York: Russell Sage Foundation, 1979.

Brenner, H. *Mental Illness and the Economy.* Cambridge, Mass.: Harvard University Press, 1973.

Brown, G.W., Bhrolchain, M.H., and Harris, T. Social class and psychiatric disturbance among women in an urban population. *Sociology* 9 (1975): 225-54.

Brown, G.W. and Harris, T. *Social Origins of Depression.* New York: The Free Press, 1978.

Cassel, J. Psychosocial processes and stress: Theoretical formulation, epidemiology and methods. *International Journal of Health Sciences* 4 (1974):471-82.

Cobb, S. Social support as a moderator of life stress. *Psychosomatic Medicine* 38 (1976):300-14.

Cochrane, R. and Robertson, A. The Life Events Inventory: A measure of the relative severity of psychosocial stressors. *Journal of Psychosomatic Research* 17 (1973):135-39.

Cross, W.E. Negro-to-Black conversion experience: Toward a psychology of Black liberation. *Black World* 20 (1971):13-27.

_____. The Thomas and Cross Models of psychological nigrescence: A review. *Journal of Black Psychology* 5 (1978):13-31.

Dean, A. and Lin, N. The stress-buffering role of social support. *Journal of Nervous and Mental Disease* 165 (1977):403-17.

DeCharms, R. *Personal Causation: The Internal Affective Determinants of Behavior.* New York: Academic Press, 1968.

Dohrenwend, B.P. Social status, stress and psychological symptoms. *American Journal of Public Health* 57 (1967):625-32.

Dohrenwend, B.P. and Dohrenwend, B.S. *Social Status and Psychological Disorders: A Causal Inquiry.* New York: John Wiley & Sons, 1969.

————. *Stressful Life Events: Their Nature and Effects.* New York: John Wiley & Sons, 1974.

Dohrenwend, B.S. Life events as stressors: A methodological inquiry, *Journal of Health and Social Behavior* 14 (1973a):167-75.

————. Social status and stressful life events. *Journal of Personality and Social Psychology* 28 (1973b):225-35.

Dohrenwend, B.S. and Dohrenwend, B.P. Field studies of social factors in relation to three types of psychological disorders. *Journal of Abnormal Psychology* 72 (1967):369-78.

————. Class and race as status-related sources of stress. In *Social Stress,* edited by S. Levine and N.A. Scotch, pp. 111-40. Chicago: Aldine, 1970.

————. Future research in stress related disorder. Paper presented at the annual meeting of the American Sociological Association. New York, 1976.

Dreger, R. and Miller, S. Comparative psychological studies of Negroes and whites in the United States: 1958-1965. *Psychological Bulletin Monograph Supplement* 70 (1968): part 2.

Frazier, E.F. *Black Bourgeoisie.* New York: The Free Press, 1957.

Gersten, J.C., Langner, T.S., Eisenberg, J.G., and Sincha-Fagan, O. An evaluation of the etiologic role of stressful life-change events in psychological disorders. *Journal of Health and Social Behavior* 18 (1977):228-44.

Gersten, J.C., Langner, T.S., and Orycek, L. Child behavior and life events: Undesirable change or change per se? In *Stressful Life Events: Their Nature and Effects,* edited by B.P. Dohrenwend and B.S. Dohrenwend, pp. 159-70. New York: John Wiley & Sons, 1974.

Goldstein, M.J. Individual differences in response to stress. *American Journal of Community Psychology* 1 (1973):113-37.

Gore, S. The effect of social support in moderating the health consequences of the unemployed. *Journal of Health and Social Behavior* 19 (1978):157-65.

Gurin, P., Gurin, G., Lao, R.C., and Beattie, M. Internal-external control in the motivational dynamics of Negro youth. *Journal of Social Issues* 25 (1969):29-53.

Guttentag, M. and Klein, T. The relationship between inner vs outer locus of control and achievement in Black middle school children. *Educational and Psychological Measurement* 36 (1976):1101-109.

Hall, W.S., Cross, W.E., and Freedle, R. Stages in the development of Black awareness: An exploratory investigation. In *Black Psychology,* edited by R. Jones. New York: Harper & Row, 1972.

Hamilton, V. and Warburton, D.M., eds. *Human Stress and Cognition: An Information Processing Approach.* New York: John Wiley & Sons, 1979.

Harrell, J.P. Psychological factors and hypertension: A status report. *Psychological Bulletin* 87 (1980):482-501.

Hill, R.B. *The Strengths of Black Families.* Urban League Report, 1972.

Holmes, T.H. and Rahe, R.H. The social readjustment rating scale, *Journal of Psychosomatic Research* 11 (1967):213-18.

Ilfeld, F.W. Characteristics of current social stressors. *Psychological Reports* 39 (1976a):1231-247.

———. Methodological issues in relating psychiatric symptoms to social stressors. *Psychological Reports* 39 (1976b):1251-258.

———. Current social stressors and symptoms of depression. *American Journal of Psychiatry* 134 (1977):161-66.

Jackson, J.S., Bacon, J.D., and Peterson, J. Correlates of adjustment in urban black aged. In *Research Directions of Black Psychologists,* edited by A.W. Boykin, A.J. Franklin, and J.F. Yates, pp. 131-45. New York: Russell Sage Foundation, 1979.

Janis, I.L. *Psychological Stress.* New York: John Wiley & Sons, 1958.

———. Psychological effects of worrying. In *Man and Society in Disaster,* edited by M.C.W. Baker and D.W. Chapment. New York: Basic Books, 1962.

Jenkins, C.D. Recent evidence supporting psychologic and social risk factors for coronary disease (First of two parts). *The New England Journal of Medicine* 294 (1976a):987-94.

———. Recent evidence supporting psychologic and social risk factors in coronary disease (Second of two parts). *The New England Journal of Medicine* 294 (1976b):1033-38.

Kasl, S.V. and Cobb, S. The effects of parental status incongruence and discrepancy on the physical and mental health of adult offspring. *Journal of Personality and Social Psychology Monograph* 7 (1967):1-15.

King, L.M. Social and cultural influences on psychopathology. *Annual Review of Psychology* 29 (1978a):405-33.

———. Transformation of the wretched of the earth: Towards a political psychology. Paper presented at the 3rd International Research Conference of the Fanon Research and Development Center. Trinidad, February 1978b.

King, R. *Pineal Gland Review, 1945-1974.* Los Angeles: Fanon Center Publication, 1978.

———. Pineal calcification in Blacks. *Journal of National Medicine Association,* in press.

Kobasa, S.C. Stressful life events, personality, and health: An inquiry into hardiness. *Journal of personality and Social Psychology* 37 (1979):1-11.

Korchin, S.J. Some psychological determinants of stress behavior. In *The Quest for Self-Control,* edited by S.Z. Klausner, pp. 247-66. New York: The Free Press, 1965.

Kosa, J., Antonovsky, A. and Zola, I.K. *Poverty and Health: A Sociological Analysis.* Cambridge, Mass.: Harvard University Press, 1969.

Krate, R., Leventhal, G., and Silverstein, B. Self-perceived transformation of Negro-to-Black identity. *Psychological Reports* 35 (1974):1071-75.

Kronus, S. *The Black Middle Class.* Columbus, Ohio: Charles E. Murill, 1970.

Lazarus, R.S. *Psychological Stress and the Coping Process.* New York: McGraw-Hill, 1966.

———. Cognitive and personality factors underlying threat and coping. In *Psychological Stress: Issues and Research,* edited by M.H. Apply and R. Trumbull, pp. 151-81. New York: Appleton-Century-Crofts, 1967.

———. The concepts of stress and disease. In *Society, Stress and Disease Vol. I.:*

The Psychosocial Environment and Psychosomatic Diseases, edited by L. Levi, pp. 53-58. New York: Oxford University Press, 1971.

————. Psychological stress and coping in adaptation and illness. *International Journal of Psychiatry* 5 (1974).

————. Psychological stress and coping in adaptation and illness. In *Psychosomatic Medicine: Current Trends and Clinical Applications,* edited by Z.J. Lipowski, D.R. Lipsitt, and P.C. Whybrow, pp. 14-26. New York: Oxford University Press, 1977.

————. The stress and coping paradigm. Paper presented at the Critical Evaluation of Behavioral Paradigms of Psychiatric Science Conference. Oregon, November 3-6, 1978.

Lazarus, R.S., Averill, J.R., and Opton, E.M. The psychology of coping: Issues of research and assessment In *Coping and Adaptation,* edited by G.V. Colhol, D.A. Hamburg, and J.E. Adams. New York: Basic Books, 1974.

Lazarus, R.S. and Cohen, J.B. Theory and method in the study of stress and coping in aging individuals. Paper presented at the 5th World Health Organization Conference on Society, Stress and Disease: Aging and Old Age. Stockholm, Sweden, June 14-19, 1976a.

————. Environmental Stress. In *Human Behavior and Environment: Advances in Theory and Research, Vol. I,* edited by I. Altman and J.F. Wohlwill, 1976b.

Lazarus, R.S. and Launier, R. Stress-related transactions between person and environment. In *Internal and External Determinants of Behavior,* edited by L.A. Pervin and M. Lewis. New York: Plenum Press, in press.

Lazarus, R.S., Speisman, J.C., Wordkoff, A.M. and Davison, L.A. A laboratory study of psychological stress produced by a motion picture film. *Psychological Monographs,* 1962, *76,* whole No. 553.

Liem, R.T. and Liem, J. Social class and mental illness reconsidered: The role of economic stress and social support. *Journal of Health and Social Behavior* 19 (1978):139-56.

Maddi, S.R. The existential neurosis. *Journal of Abnormal Psychology* 72 (1967): 311-25.

McAdoo, H.P. An assessment of racial attitudes and self-concepts in urban black children: Final report. Washington, D.C.: Children's Bureau, Department of Health, Education, and Welfare, 1973.

————. A re-examination of the relationship between self-concept and race attitudes of young black children. Paper presented at the conference on Demythologizing the Inner City Black Child. Atlanta, March 25, 1976.

McGee, D.P. Psychology: Melanin, the physiological basis for oneness. In *African Philosophy: Assumptions and Paradigms for Research on Black Persons,* edited by L.M. King, V.J. Dixon, and W.W. Nobles, pp. 215-22. Los Angeles: Fanon Research and Development Center, 1976.

McGrath, J.E. *Social and Psychological Factors in Stress.* New York: Holt, Rhinehart and Winston, 1970.

McKinlay, J.B. A case for refocusing upstream—The political economy of illness. In *Applying Behavioral Science to Cardiovascular Risk: Proceedings of a Conference, Seattle, Washington, June 17-19, 1974,* edited by A.T. Enelow and J.B. Henderson. American Heart Assoc., Inc., 1975.

Miller, F.T., Bentz, U.X., Aponte, J.F., and Brogen, D.R. Perception of life crisis events. In *Conference on Stressful Life Events: Their Nature and Effects.* edited by B.P. Dohrenwend and B.S. Dohrenwend, pp. 259-73. New York: John Wiley & Sons, 1974.

Mueller, D.P., Edwards, D.W., and Yarvis, R.M. Stressful life events and psyciatric symptomatology: Change vs undesirability? *Journal of Health and Social Behavior* 18 (1977):307-17.

Myers, H.F. Cognitive appraisal and competence as determinants of behavioral responses to stress. Ph.D. Dissertation, 1974.

————. Holistic definition and measurements of states of nonhealth. In *African Philosophy: Assumptions and Paradigms of Research on Black Persons,* edited by L. King, V. Dixon, and W. Nobles, pp. 139-53. Los Angeles: Fanon Research Center, 1976.

————. Cognitive appraisal, stress coping and Black mental health: The politics of options and contingencies. Paper presented at the National Association of Black Psychologists Convention. Los Angeles: August, 1977.

————. Life change stress and somatization in hypertension. National Heart, Lung and Blood Institute, Technological Grant Report, 1979a.

————. Mental health and the Black child: The manufacture of incompetence. *Young Children.* 1979b *34* (4) 25-31.

————. Life stress, somatization and blood pressure variability in Black college students. Technical Research Grant Report, Institute of American Cultures, Center for Afro-American Studies, UCLA, 1980.

Myers, H.F. and King, L.M. Mental health issues in the development of the Black American child. In *The Psychosocial Development of Minority Group Children,* edited by G.J. Powell, A. Morales, and J. Yamamoto. New York: Brunner/ Mazel, in press.

Myers, H.F. and Miles, R. Life change stress, subjective appraisal and somatization in hypertension: A pilot study. Paper presented at the 4th Annual Empirical Conferene in Black Psychology. La Jolla, California, January 1979.

Myers, J.K., Lindenthal, J.J., and Pepper, M.P. Life events and psychiatric impairment. *Journal of Nervous and Mental Disease* 152 (1971):149-57.

————. Social class, life events and psychiatric symptoms: A longitudinal study. In *Stressful Life Events: Their Nature and Effects,* edited by B.P. Dohrenwend and B.S. Dohrenwend, pp. 191-206. New York: John Wiley & Sons, Inc. 1974.

————. Life events, social integration and psychiatric symptomatology. *Journal of Health and Social Behavior* 16 (1975):421-29.

Nobles, W.W. African science: The consciousness of self. In *African Philosophy: Assumption and Paradigms for Research on Black Persons,* edited by L. King, V.J. Dixon, and W.W. Nobles, pp. 163-74. Los Angeles: Fanon Research Center, 1976.

National Urban League. *The State of Black America.* 1977.

Nuckolls, C.B., Cassel, J., and Kaplan, B.H. Psycho-social assets, life crisis and the prognosis of pregnancy. *American Journal of Epidemiology* 95 (1972):431-41.

Paulley, J.W. Cultural influences on the incidence and pattern of disease. *Psychotherapy Psychosomatic* 26 (1975): 2-11.

Pollard, D.S. Patterns of coping in Black school children. In *Research Directions of*

Black Psychologists, edited by A.W. Boykin, A.J. Franklin, and J. Frank Yates, pp. 188-209. New York: Russell Sage Foundation, 1979.

Powell, G.J., Morales, A., and Yamamoto, J., eds. *The Psychosocial Development of Minority Group Children.* New York: Brunner/Mazel, in press.

Psychiatric services and the changing institutional scene, 1950-1985. NIMH Report, Series B., No. 12, 1977.

Rahe, R.H., Life-change measurement as a prediction of illness. *Proceedings of the Royal Society of Medicine* 61 (1968):44-46.

Rahe, R.H., Subjects recent life changes and their near-future illness susceptibility. In *Advances in Psychosomatic Medicine,* edited by F. Reichsman. New York: S. Karger, 1972.

Saunders, E. and Williams, R.A. Hypertension. In *Textbook of Black Related Diseases,* edited by R.A. William, pp. 333-57. New York: McGraw-Hill, 1975.

Schachter, J., Kerr, J.L., Wimberly, F.C., and Lachin, J..M. Heart rate levels of black and white newborns. *Psychosomatic Medicine* 35 (1974):513-24.

Schar, M., Reeder, L.G., and Dirken, J.M. Stress and cardiovascular health: An international cooperative study-II: The male population of a factory at Zurich. *Social Science and Medicine* 1 (1973):585-603.

Scott, R. and Howard, A. Models of stress. In *Social Stress,* edited by S. Levine and N.A. Scotch. Chicago: Aldine, 1970.

Seligman, M.E.P. *Helplessness: On Depression, Development & Death.* San Francisco: W.H. Freeman, 1975.

Selye, H. *The Physiology and Pathology of Exposure to Stress.* Montreal: Acta, 1950.

———. Perspectives in stress research. *Perspectica Biologica Medica,* 1959, 2, 408-16.

———. *Stress Without Distress.* Philadelphia: J.B. Lippincott, 1974.

Sewell, T.E. and Severson, R.A. Intelligence and achievement in first grade black children. *Journal of Consulting and Clinical Psychology* 43 (1975):112.

Srole, L., Langner, T.S., Michael, S.T., Opler, M.K., and Rennie, T.A.C. *Mental Health in the Metropolis.* New York: McGraw-Hill, 1962.

Stack, C.B. *All Our Kin: Strategies for Survival in a Black Community.* New York: Harper & Row, 1974.

Stamler, J., Stamler, R., and Pullman, T.N. *The Epidemiology of Hypertension.* New York: Gruen & Stratton, 1967.

Steele, R.E. Relationship of race, sex, social class, and social mobility to depression in normal adults. *Journal of Social Psychology* 104 (1978):37-47.

Sue, D.W. Eliminating cultural oppression in counseling: Toward a general theory. *Journal of Counseling Psychology* 25 (1978):419-28.

Taylor, S.E. and Crocker, J. Schematic basis of social information processing. In *The Outline Symposium on Personality and Social Psychology,* edited by E.T. Higgins, P. Hermann, and M.P. Zanwa, pp. ? Hilldale, N.J.: Lawrence Erlbaum Associates, 1979.

Theorell, T., Lind, E., and Floredusi, B. The relationship of disturbing life-changes and emotions to the early development of myocardial infarction and other serious illness. *International Journal of Epidemiology* 4 (1975):281-93.

Theorell, T. and Rahe, R.H. Life changes in relation to onset of myocardial infarction. In *Psychosocial Factors in Relation to the Onset of Myocardial Infarction and to Some Metabolic Variables—A Pilot Study,* edited by T. Theorell. Stockholm:

Department of Medicine, Seraphimer Hospital, Karolinska Institute, 1970, II-1-20.

Thomas, C. Different strokes for different folks. *Psychology Today* 4 (1970):48-53, 78-80.

———. *Boys No More*. Beverly Hills, Calif.: Glencoe Press, 1971.

Vinokur, A. and Selzer, M. Desirable vs undesirable life events: Their relationship to stress and mental distress. *Journal of Personality and Social Psychology* 32 (1975):329-37.

Watts, G. New evidence in the argument about race and intelligence: How about Jensen? *World Medicine* 9 (1974):77.

Weiner, B., Russell, D., and Lerman, D. Affective consequences of causal ascriptions. In *New Directions in Attribution Research. Vol. 2,* edited by J.H. Harvey, W.J. Ickes, and R.F. Kidd. Hillsdale, N.J.: Lawrence Erlbaum Associates, 1978.

Williams, I.J. An investigation of the developmental stages of Black consciousness. Ph.d. Dissertation, University of Cincinnati, 1975.

Wortman, C.C., Panciera, L., Shusterman, L., and Hibscher, J. Attributions of casuality and reactions to uncontrollable outcomes. *Journal of Experimental Social Psychology* 12 (1976):301-16.

Wyatt, G. A comparison of the scaling of Afro-American life-change events. *Journal of Human Stress* 3 (1977):13-18.

6   Mental Health in the Japanese-American Community

Harry H. Kitano

The purpose of this chapter is to analyze the state of mental health among Japanese Americans. There are a number of definitions of mental health, ranging from a narrow view emphasizing a lack of mental illness to a broad one relating to a sense of fulfillment through achieving one's maximum potential. Although we prefer the broader definitions, we recognize the variety and will therefore present multiperspectives on Japanese-American mental health. One of the problems in dealing with cultures other than the majority, is that their definitions of what constitutes mental health may be at variance with white professional norms, which in turn may be at the root of their nonuse of professional services and their application of priorities to areas such as employment and economic satisfaction, over psychological and emotional needs.

In this chapter we will focus on (1) Japanese-American mental illness, (2) their use or nonuse of professional mental health services, and (3) a model of ethnic identity that will address the problem of how the ethnic variable affects role performance in a pluralistic society. These topics will help to illustrate the wide range of areas that can be subsumed under "mental health" and how these varying perceptions influence the availability and use of mental health services.

BACKGROUND OF THE JAPANESE

The major immigration to the United States took place between 1890 and 1924, so by the 1920 census there were a reported 111,010 Japanese on the mainland. An additional 109,274 were reported in the territory of Hawaii, thus bringing the total population in 1920 to 220,284. By 1970, the Japanese population was 588,324, of which 217,175 resided in Hawaii and 213,277 in California.

The initial immigrants, called the Issei or first generation, "were generally homogeneous in terms of age (young), education (four to six years of schooling), sex (male), and general background, having originated in what may be thought of as rural Japan" (Kitano, 1976, p. 8). They were joined by Japanese females, sometimes referred to as "picture brides" since, for many, the only prior contact was through the exchange of photographs.

Most found employment as agricultural laborers, in small businesses, and in the service professions such as gardening, cooking, and house cleaning. There was a general tendency towards self-employment and of interdependence within the ethnic community.

Most Issei held modest expectations for themselves in terms of economic and social mobility: they did not know the country, the language, or the culture; they were minimally trained; and they did not possess the capital for large-scale enterprises. Rather, a large part of their expectations and hopes were placed on their U.S.-born children, the Nisei or second generation, in the spirit of self sacrifice, or as Ogawa (1978) writes, "kodoms no tame ni" ("for the sake of the children").

At the present time the surviving Issei are in their twilight years, and they will disappear in another decade. It would be difficult to assess the mental health of this generation except to note that they had low crime, delinquency, mental illness, and divorce rates (as measured by official statistics) and were a hard working "low profile" group.

The Nisei were born between 1900 and 1940, so they represent the bulk of the current adult population. The period before World War II was an especially difficult one for them since they were caught between the expectations and demands of their Japanese-reared parents and U.S. ways. The situation was compounded by other realities such as the Great Depression, racism, prejudice, and discrimination. Although many possessed a college education, economic opportunities were limited and the possibility of equal-status interaction with members of the mainstream was nonexistent. In 1929 concern for the lack of employment opportunities for Japanese Americans was the focus of a Carnegie Corporation grant to Stanford University. The study found that the Nisei were victims of employment discrimination and that their future was one of insecurity and painful choices. Some Nisei talked of their future in terms of Japan, Manchuria, or South America; others were reconciled to finding low level jobs in the United States. Other data revealed that Japanese Americans were equal to Caucasians as measured by IQ tests, that their rates of crime and delinquency were low, and that, as a group, they showed a record of strong school achievement (Strong, 1934). The study concluded that race prejudice was the fundamental cause of the Nisei's employment problems.

West Coast Japanese, numbering over 110,000, were incarcerated during World War II. They were accused of being traitors and seen as potential enemies, even though the majority were U.S.-born citizens with little interest or identification with Japan. Many lost their life savings; most temporarily lost their faith in U.S. democracy. Camp life meant camp norms and complete isolation from the mainstream of U.S. society. It weakened family life since the federal government took over the role of provider and forced Japanese Americans to look at their ethnic identity ("If you think you're white, what are you doing in camp?") in realistic terms.

Part of the damaging effects of the incarceration were mitigated by a program of resettlement; by 1943 an estimated 35,000 Japanese were released in order to resettle in areas in the East and Midwest. Others volunteered for the United States Armed Forces; thus, a sizeable number of Japanese experienced life away from their previously restricted ethnic communities. However, the dispersal of the Japanese throughout the United States proved to be temporary; by the 1970s the vast majority were back on the West Coast and Hawaii.

There were instances of terrorism, of riots, of beatings and of rebellion in the camps. However, the general adaptation was that of passive acceptance and a fate orientation (shikata ga nai, or "it can't be helped"), with the understanding that powers greater than the group itself were in charge of the major decisions. Daily rituals became important—standing in line for meals, for taking a shower, and for almost every other need demanded patience, while the communal bathrooms and housing arrangements precluded privacy. There are a wide number of books and articles that describe this unique event (Daniels, 1971; Kitano, 1976; Weglyn, 1976). The effects of this experience on the Japanese Americans remains difficult to evaluate. Many former evacuees still prefer not to talk about the camps, and factors such as time and intervening experiences have also complicated any assessment. However, the Japanese American Citizen's League in 1978 passed a resolution calling for the United States Congress to provide redress for the evacuation, so the incident remains alive.

The camps were closed in 1945, and the Japanese Americans were able to participate much more competitively in the postwar "boom." College graduates were in demand, and younger Nisei took advantage of the GI Bill to attend universities in large numbers. A summary picture of the Japanese American drawn from the 1970 U.S. census is as follows: 86 percent of the families were intact, which was the same as for the country as a whole. Their family size was slightly above the national average (3.7 to 3.5), as was the number of extended families (16 percent compared to 12 percent). Mean family income was $13,511, which was among the highest of all ethnic groups, while 7.5 percent were in the poverty category (compared to 11 percent for others), with the preponderance of low income in the 65 year or older category.

One other fact should be mentioned in the background material. In 1972 Japanese rates of outmarriage were in the 50 percent category (Kikumura and Kitano, 1973), which is one indication that Japanese Americans were assimulating into the U.S. mainstream.

MENTAL ILLNESS

One definition of mental health is related to the lack of mental illness. It is presumed that groups with low rates of mental illness are groups with good mental health, although such a relationship has yet to be validated. However, it is important to know how many Japanese Americans break down to the point of hospitalization, who defines the behavior as "crazy," and how the patient is brought to the attention of the authorities.

For this information, we draw on a study of mental illness in the Japanese community (Kitano, 1969) and some recent data from the California State Mental Hospital system (Okano, 1979).

First, the "official rates" of mental illness for the group, defined as the number who appear at the California State Hospital system for admission and hospitalization, is very low. For example, the rates for admission of the Japanese, per 100,000, in 1965 was 60, compared to 180 for Caucasians, 40 for Mexican Americans, 180 for Indians, 90 for Chinese, and 280 for blacks (Kitano, 1969).

Admissions to Hawaii State Hospital during the same era showed 88 Japanese per 100,000, as compared to Caucasian rates of 99. Therefore, in the two states that comprise the bulk of the Japanese population in the United States,[1] their admissions for mental breakdown were low in comparison to other groups.

Data on admissions for 1976-77 are available from Metropolitan State Hospital, located in a suburb of Los Angeles. Japanese admissions were very low: 39 (from a total of 11,890 admissions) in 1976 or .3 percent, 45 (from a total of 10,410 admissions) in 1977 or .4 percent. Since Japanese Americans comprised 1.1 percent of Californians in 1970, they are underrepresented in terms of these figures. Other comparisons for 1977 include admissions for whites 52 percent, total in population 89 percent; blacks 27 percent, total in population 7 percent; Indians .2 percent, total in population .5 percent; and Chinese .15 percent, total in population .9 percent.

Hospitalization figures present another picture. In 1964 California State Mental Hospital statistics indicated 198 Japanese per 100,000 as residents of the system. Caucasian rates were 213, Mexican American 74, Indians 174, Chinese 361, and blacks 296. Japanese rates of hospitalization in California were therefore among the lowest of all comparison groups. An analysis by age indicated that the majority of the Japanese-American hospitalized population was in the 55 years and older category (Kitano, 1969).

Therefore, as in the case of admissions, the Japanese contribute less than their proportionate representation to the hospitalized "mentally ill" population and are among the lowest of all ethnic groups. However, once hospitalized, they were apt to remain under care for a very long time. It is plausible to hypothesize that only the most severely disturbed Japanese end up at the hospital, so that once there, they tend to remain.

More recent data on hospitalization is available from the California State Department of Mental Health for 1978. In June of that year, there was a total of 91 hospitalized Japanese-American patients in the state hospitals from a total of 14,292 or .6 percent, which is below their proportion in the 1970 census of 1.1 percent.

Okano (1979) reports on Asian-American hospitalized patients at Metropolitan State Hospital and emphasizes their small numbers. For example, in August 1978 there was a reported total of 20 Asian patients at the hospital: six Japanese; four each of Chinese, Filipino, and Korean patients; one Cambodian; one Vietnamese. The Japanese percentage is again slightly over .6 percent. Okano reports that most of the Japanese patients were single and somewhat younger than those reported in previous studies on Japanese Americans. Because of the low numbers, generalizations are limited. The overall drop in the total figures for all groups reflects a philosophy that discourages hospitalization in large mental institutions. An unanswered question concerns those who would have been hospitalized in a previous era but who are now at large in the community.

Another study on hospitalized mentally ill Japanese patients (Kitano, 1970) was conducted in Los Angeles, Hawaii, Tokyo, and Okinawa. The purpose of the study was to compare the "paths" leading to hospitalization for Japanese in each of the four sites. One generalization was that hospitalized Japanese Americans were similar on a number of variables, no matter where the site. For example, the patients were characteristically males who had lived lonely, isolated lives within lonely, isolated families. The isolation was often of a long-term nature, so that the onset of "crazy" or "kichi-gai" behavior was not the primary cause of isolation.

The pattern leading to hospitalization was similar. The outbreak of "kichi-gai" behavior led to heightened conflict in already weak family relationships. The families resorted to the use of arguments, discipline, appeals to shame, and cajoling as techniques to attempt to change the behavior. Many reported that the harder they tried, the less effective the results, with the stricken individual eventually turning against the family. Because of the lack of results, the family turned to outside sources for assistance, such as neighbors, extended family, friends, police, and professionals, including ministers, social workers, psychologists, the family doctor, and psychiatrists. However, it should be noted that most of these families did not have a rich network of extended kinship ties and were likely to be isolated. All samples were characterized by their generally low use of professional assistance.

The most salient variable for detecting difficulties was in the area of work. All of the respondents placed a high value on work; therefore, demotions, firings, and walking off the job were the first symptoms of distress. The interviewees complained that the afflicted member was getting "lazy" and attributed the loss to a weakness of character. Very few families saw the behavior as a possible sign of mental illness, rather they saw the behavior in terms of malingering and the lack of motivation. Work is a critical factor among Japanese Americans, especially among the older generations, and is linked to their mental health. Unemployment and lack of things to do can be devastating, and one of the main complaints among Japanese Americans during their incarceration during World War II was the boredom and the enforced idleness that was a part of camp life. One problem related to this orientation is that of those who overwork, or the "workaholics." There is a high probability that such individuals will continue to be rewarded for their behavior, thereby exacerbating the problem.

Another factor leading to the decision to hospitalize was the disruption of family life. The patients were reported as going through a period of negativism and of creating a difficult family situation. Thus, the combination of problems of employment, of creating conflict in the family, and the lack of effective means for coping led to the decision to hospitalize. The issue is brought more sharply into focus when violent behavior was reported, since hospitalization was much more rapid for individuals who fell into this category.

Voluntary commitments were more frequent in Los Angeles and Hawaii, whereas family commitments were more typical of the Japanese sites. The patients facing the greatest problems after hospitalization were in Los Angeles, especially those less familiar with English and the "American culture," since hospitalization meant isolation in "non-Japanese" surroundings. There was also a greater tendency in the U.S. settings to adopt a "we've done all we can" attitude, so that families would ignore the afflicted member once hospitalized. This is in contrast to continued close ties between the family and hospitalized individual in the Japanese settings.

One other factor is important in dealing with Japanese Americans and deviant behavior. There is a high sense of shame and a desire to protect the family name, which is often translated into "hiding" or denying any public acknowledgment of deviant individuals. Therefore the social control exerted by families to limit deviance has been a strong part of the ethnic community and is another hypothesis explaining the lack of use of social and counseling services. The lack of public awareness of problems of the group may show up in various ways, such as Japanese-American families doing without rather than applying for public welfare, or hiding a mentally disturbed individual rather than committing the person to a public institution. However, the weakening of extended family, kinship, and ethnic community ties should be followed by a rise of Japanese Americans' applying for public services.

In summary, data on admissions and hospitalization for the Japanese reveal low rates for both. The combination of problems in employment and family disruption was likely to lead to outside calls for assistance, and, if the problems continued, the mental hospital became a resource. It should be noted that one of the cultural characteristics among Japanese, whether in the United States or Japan, is that of work. We have heard many stories of individual Japanese who sound "crazy" (e.g., hearing and responding to voices; irrational, childlike behavior) but who still maintain the work orientation. It is our observation that as long as these individuals work and support their families, tolerance for their "unusual ways" will continue. Nevertheless, there is a recognition that under certain conditions individuals may have gone beyond the family and community's definition of mental health, and it is under these conditions that public resources are used. There also remains a strong feeling of shame concerning public disclosure of family deviance, which tends to inhibit the use of outside resources.

ATTITUDES TOWARDS MENTAL HEALTH

Another important area for discussion is that of the attitudes of Japanese Americans towards mental health. Okano (1977) conducted a mental health survey among 235 Japanese Americans in Los Angeles and his most important findings were as follows:

1. Japanese Americans did not perceive forms of obviously disturbed behavior differently from other populations. The sample was asked to respond to a number of vignettes and to check whether they saw them as mental health problems. It should be noted that the sample attributed significantly fewer mental health problems to Japanese Americans.

2. There was a general low awareness of ethnic community social service resources. For example, of the nine Asian-American social service agencies listed (i.e., Asian American Drug Abuse Program, Asian Rehabilitation Services, Oriental Service Center), only a minority knew about these agencies. The best known services were those for Asian-American aged.

3. Racism was viewed as a problem. A majority (70 percent) agreed that Japanese Americans still faced prejudice and discrimination. Fifty-six percent of the sample agreed that there was discrimination in housing. Younger Japanese Americans felt more strongly about this issue than the older.

4. The majority of the sample responded that Japanese Americans were faced with problems of juvenile delinquency, divorce, drug abuse, crime, alcoholism, low self-esteem, depression, identity confusion, and culture conflict.

5. In response to the question, "compared to the general population, how many mental health problems do you believe there are among Japanese Americans?" (p. 21), 13 percent answered "more," 42 percent answered "less," and 45 percent answered "about the same."

6. The majority of respondents saw themselves as "mentally healthy," with a minimum of emotional or physical problems. Of personal problems, health was the most often mentioned, while marital and sexual problems were the least often cited.

7. Ministers were mentioned as the primary resource for emotional problems. Relatives, friends, and the family doctor were mentioned more frequently than professional counselors. Finally, over one-half of the sample indicated that they would work out emotional problems on their own.

Okano's study shows a group that at present does not give high priority to emotional or psychological problems and is therefore less apt to use professional counseling resources. However, the process of acculturation, the continued fragmentation of the Japanese family and community, and the increasing sophistication of the younger Japanese American in terms of social-psychological insights will probably lead to a greater awareness of the importance of mental health services.

THE USE OF MENTAL HEALTH SERVICES

Another measure related to mental health is that of the use of mental health services. However, it is a complicated relationship because of cultural differences in needs and definitions and the "fit" between the potential consumer and the provider. There is also the issue of how to interpret use or nonuse; for example, is a group presumed to be healthy if it uses mental health resources or can such use be interpreted as a measure of its vulnerability?

Kitano (1969) found that in Los Angeles the Japanese Americans seldom went to mental health services such as family service agencies, child guidance and psychiatric clinics, and other counseling resources. A survey of these agencies showed almost no Japanese-American clients, although a social service agency set up by the Japanese Chamber of Commerce with a Japanese-speaking worker had a steady clientele.

However, the lack of use of these services cannot be used as evidence for a population without mental health problems. A survey of mental health workers (Kitano, 1969) showed a high consensus concerning the need for mental health services in the community. Most respondents cited parent-child difficulties, marital problems, intergenerational stresses, and problems of ethnic identity as central concerns that were not being met through professional resources. A combination of the strength of the Japanese family and community to control and to "hide" problem behavior, the cultural styles of expressing problems, the inappropriateness of current therapeutic organizations, and the lack of relevant connections to the therapeutic community were hypothesized as reasons behind the lack of use of larger community resources. Current information indicates no significant change in the pattern.

Miranda and Kitano (1976) hypothesize that many Third World populations do not use mental health services because of problems of service delivery. The *fragmentation* of services is one problem, wherein professional experts are prone to refer a client from one worker to another, leading to a lack of a central person, which can be confusing for culturally different clients. Language and differing cultural perspectives further strain the relationship. Another problem is that of *discontinuity,* whereby the professional therapist and the ethnic client operate on different life realities.

For example, the ability to ventilate and to let one's feelings "all hang out" may be appropriate to the life style of the therapist, but it may be incongruous and less relevant for a client whose major interactions will be in less verbal, less feeling oriented systems. Therefore, what is continuous and rational for the professional may be unrealistic and discontinuous for the Japanese American.

The third problem is that of *inaccessibility,* both in terms of physical and psychological distance between professional services and the world of the client. The fourth is that of *unaccountability,* whereby the professional services are more accountable to fellow professionals than to the client or the ethnic community. Finally, it may be that the "culture" of the ethnic group, such as the Japanese, does not include the background for using mental health resources in the most effective manner. There may be unrealistic expectations, or there may be a wide number of procedures that professionals take for granted that may jar the sensibilities of Japanese Americans.

The lack of the use of available services may be interpreted in a variety of ways. I prefer the explanation that views the lack as related to deprivation— that the inability to use community resources is a symptom of a group that remains apart from the mainstream and is relatively disadvantaged and deprived of what the community has to offer.

PROBLEMS OF IDENTITY

Another area related to mental health is that of identity and self-concept. Mental health, in this context, can be equated with an individual's feeling of worth within the context of the total cultural and social system, and also within the identifiable groups to which he or she belongs. For the Japanese it would include the perceptions and treatment from both of the majority community and the ethnic community.

For individuals belonging to the dominant group, ethnic identity may be voluntary and transient; for nonwhites it is much less voluntary. Although each person carries a number of identities and there is a degree of voluntary choice from among them, physically visible minorities are given an ethnic identification that may override all other issues and that, therefore, can be termed a "master identity." The inability to resolve some of the problems caused by the master identity is hypothesized as one of the factors that hinders the develoment of good mental health.

The critical element in an identity for the Japanese American is that of ethnicity or race. As long as there is racial visibility, and as long as racial signs are used by the dominant group as a means of categorization and differential treatment, the meaning of an ethnic identity remains central to Japanese Americans. At one extreme, one may completely deny the ethnic background and assume a total identification with the dominant group; on the other hand, there may be a total rejection of dominant group definitions and a decision to remain totally Japanese. A model by Newman (1976) distinguishes among the identities and their affect on ethnic group identification. We have adapted this model to analyze the Japanese American.

The model (see Table 6.1) visualizes multiple roles and multiple choices in a pluralistic society. The challenge is to create a social environment whereby groups and individuals may voluntarily choose their identities and find reasonable satisfaction among the choices. But it is also critical to note that negative images and stereotypes from the dominant majority (choices 2 and 4, in the table) force a minority member into a number of roles, situations, and adaptations that have an effect on "mental health."

Choice 1 (positive, positive)

This choice corresponds to an "ideal" situation for the Japanese American. Although the meanings and role requirements of being a Japanese may differ between the dominant and ethnic communities, the individual may enjoy and accept both definitions of his ethnicity.

For example, being a Japanese may mean a strong and proud self-concept, a means to higher education, an aid towards desirable employment, and a degree of status in the majority community. The individual may also derive enjoyment and self-esteem in the religions, the culture, and the organizational activities of the ethnic community.

Table 6.1
Role Choices and Identities for Japanese Americans

Choice	Response to Majority Group Definitions and Stereotypes of Japanese	Response to Japanese Community Definitions of Japanese	Role Situation	Role Techniques
1.	positive	positive	multiple role compatability	multiple role compliance
2.	negative	positive	role conflict	role distance, role change
3.	positive	negative	role conflict	role distance, role change
4.	negative	negative	multiple role conflict	multiple role rejection and role change

Source: Adapted from Newman, W. Multiple realities: The effects of social pluralism on identity. In *Ethnic Identity in Society,* edited by Arnold Dashefsky, pp. 39-47. Chicago: Rand McNally, 1976.

This category illustrates a position of minimal basic conflict in being a Japanese in U.S. society. The response to both the majority role definitions and the minority role definitions is positive; there is compliance to both roles with a minimum of difficulty. The individual is free to develop up to his or her maximum level. In terms of mental health, there are no role discrepancies or conflicts. Early writers were referring to this situation when advocating the ideal of a culturally pluralistic society.

In historical terms, there was seldom any period where the majority group definitions of the Japanese had any positive elements. The stereotypes were vicious and consistent, prejudices were rampant, and discriminatory laws were the norm. It is only in recent times that majority group definitions have approached the positive, so the idea of maximizing one's potential may be a realistic one.

Choice 2 (negative, positive)

Under choice 2 there is role conflict. The Japanese American may reject the role and the definitions placed upon him or her from the dominant society and feel more comfortable within the ethnic community. This adaptation was most common among the Issei, or the immigrant generation of Japanese, who faced prejudice and discrimination, were the victims of stereotyping, and who were forced to find a meaningful life within their ethnic enclaves. Most settled for modest enjoyment within the ethnic community; those who found jobs on the outside were primarily in the service trades as cooks, chauffeurs, gardeners, and housekeepers. Because the ethnic communities were not large enough to provide for all of their needs (except in areas such as Hawaii), there was a degree of interaction with the dominant community. Role conflict was often resolved through what Newman terms "role distance," that is, an adaptive style that maintains a perceptual distance between the individual's view of self and the social roles that are forced upon the self. For example, role distance for the Japanese servant meant bowing and acting humble, ignorant, and dependent, even though the individual did not see this deferential being as the real self.

Terms like "playing up to whitey" and, in Hawaii, "putting up with the dumb Haole" refer to the dual identities and the use of role distance to perform expected tasks when dealing with the dominant community.

People in this category may eventually wall themselves off from all but the most minimal interactions with the white world and, instead, find primary need satisfaction in the ethnic community. The existence of a cohesive Japanese community is an important consideration; goals such as self-fulfillment can not be reached in the dominant community but are possible in the ethnic structures.

Nevertheless, the adaptation of the Issei using this category raises interesting questions regarding mental health. On the one hand, many were employed in positions much below their capacities (i.e., gardeners, service workers, small business); few had the education and training to achieve up to their maximum potential; most had to practice "role distance" in order to survive—and one common orientation was to "sacrifice" their own lives for the sake of their children. Even in modern day Japan the feeling of sacrifice remains, for as Nakane writes, "because I could not go to college or university and I ended up at the bottom of the barrel, I wish to have my children succeed" (1970, p. 111).

But on the other hand, the Issei had low rates of mental illness and did not perceive the need for mental health services. The Issei were also low in rates of behavior often considered as signs of disorganization, such as crime, delinquency, divorce, and dependence on the welfare system (Kitano, 1976). Most worked hard, brought home regular paychecks, maintained decent homes, and were good citizens. So, on one level, it could be argued that they could never be mentally healthy, while, on another, they behaved in conformity to the realities of an unequal stratification system.

Choice 3 (positive, negative)

Under choice 3, the Japanese American seeks an identity with the dominant community (no matter how discriminatory) and a rejection of the ethnic definition. This has been the experience of many European groups who have acculturated to dominant community norms and have viewed the ethnic culture as a hindrance to Americanization.

The Nisei, or second Japanese generation (the children of the Issei), fit into this model, especially during their formative years in the 1930s and early 1940s. There was a desire to be "100 percent American" and to deny their Japanese heritage. Preferred language, values, communication patterns, and life styles became "typically American," but their physical features remained Japanese. Terms currently in use to cover this adaptation have a pejorative quality: the banana (yellow on the outside, white on the inside) for the Asian, the Oreo for the black, and the coconut and apple for other ethnic groups. The meaning is essentially the same: the individual may look ethnic (the outside), but his or her identification is with the white world (the inside).

It was the Japanese choosing this model who probably faced the most difficult time during World War II since their belief in the United States and their loyalty was sorely tested because of the wartime evacuation. Many could not believe that they were to be treated the same as Japanese aliens and others who were more closely identified with Japan. Many were shocked, most were disillusioned, and some began to lose their faith and their strong identification with the country. This situation points to a fundamental problem with denying a visible ethnic identity: there may come a time when the issue reaches a crisis, and those who have repressed this reality may be less able to cope with the new situation.

Choice 4 (negative, negative)

The final situation is where the Japanese American denies both the majority and minority master definitions of his or her social role. There are a number of ways of adapting to this situation, which is characterized by multiple role conflict.

One adaptation is to withdraw completely from the role conflict by finding another residence, society, or culture that is perceived as providing different and, one hopes, better role definitions for being Japanese. The Nisei who went back to Japan prior to World War II would be an example of this adaptation, although many Japanese Americans who have gone back to the old country report how different they are from the natives and how they are treated more like Americans than Japanese. Examples of others who have taken this route include black jazz musicians who have settled down in European countries and others who attempt to find a new life with new roles in the South Sea Islands.

Another possibility for individuals who find little identification with either culture, and are therefore less committed to the norms and social control mechanisms of either, is to engage in "deviant" behavior.

Because neither of the reference groups command any degree of identification, the individual may seek alternative reference groups who are more apt to violate the norms and social definitions of both the majority and ethnic communities. The individual may think, "a plague on both your houses," and may join counter culture groups, mystics, gangs, and the like. The ability of the Japanese family and community to provide a sense of identification and loyalty and to exert social control is hypothesized as one critical element in controlling deviant behavior (Kitano, 1976). Perhaps the most drastic form of withdrawal from essentially negative alternatives includes suicides, drugs, alcoholism, and mental illness.

Another way of challenging the negative definitions is to call for different definitions of ethnicity and color. Ethnic militants and revolutionaries may challenge both the majority and minority perceptions and call for a new order. Symbols of previous pariah status may be changed so the "black is beautiful" and "yellow is mellow." There is an attempt to provide positive self definitions from previous negative prescriptions.

The model emphasizes the difficulty in achieving a healthy self-identity for the Japanese under three of the choices and indicated that the potential for fulfillment is theoretically possible only under choice 1. Yet, our evidence indicates that Japanese Americans have also lived "mentally healthy" lives under choices 2 and 3. Thus, that the existence of a cohesive ethnic community may provide a reasonable alternative for achieving an identity (choice 2) just as a strong degree of identification with the majority community (choice 3) may also be possible under conditions of accessibility to that system. However, there is always the possibility that visible ethnics may remain vulnerable to changes in their treatment by the dominant group, such as occurred with the Japanese Americans during World War II.

The challenge for mental health professionals lies in their ability to provide healthy "master" identities to those who look "different" and whose plural identities include essentially negative images.

ANALYSIS AND SUMMARY

We have presented various ways of assessing mental health in the Japanese community and analyzed their implications for mental health professionals. We reviewed one perspective that sees mental health as a "lack of mental illness" and points to the very low number of Japanese who end up in mental hospitals. We described definitions of "craziness" and the resources and procedures used to reach the afflicted individual. Although many of the processes were (and are) influenced by culture, there was a degree of similarity among hospitalized Japanese patients, whether in Tokyo, Okinawa, Honolulu, or Los Angeles. Most showed problems at work and in the home, and it is this combination that leads to the hospital. Or for the patient without a family, the path may be as follows:

Mr. H., owner of a small hotel in the "Little Tokyo" area of Los Angeles begins to notice gradual deterioration of Mr. Watanabe (fictitious name). Mr. Watanabe had moved into the hotel with 2 other bachelor Issei— although information was difficult to obtain, all three had come from the same ken (state) and had worked as fruit pickers the majority of their lives. Now they were too old to continue, so they came to Los Angeles for retirement. The low rates at the hotel (average rent = $45 month) and a communal kitchen helped to stretch the dollar. The nearby Japanese community, the recreation rooms at the Chamber of Commerce Buliding ("go," "shogi," "hana"—all Japanese games) filled up some space, but lack of money precluded gambling, a once favorite pasttime. Savings were meager.

With the death of his two friends last year, Mr. Watanabe withdrew further and further from the outside world. He soon failed to get up from bed—problems of going to the bathroom, of getting up to eat and of cleanliness mounted. Eventually Mr. H. contacted the Japanese social worker who in turn brought Mr. Watanabe to the County Hospital. Diagnosis was schizophrenia and Mr. Watanabe was sent to a State Hospital. There were no known relatives in the U.S. (Kitano, 1969)

The same story, with minor variations, describes much of the "mentally ill" caseload. One variation includes an elderly, widowed Issei living with his married children—high conflict and lack of communication finally leads to his moving out to a cheap hotel. Eventually, he experiences the loneliness, the absence of friends, the feeling that "no one cares," and symptoms similar to ones felt by Mr. Watanabe. Finally, he is referred to the Japanese social worker.

Common behaviors indicating "mental illness" include "hearing voices" (of dead friends in Japanese), emotional crying, heightened irritability, loss of toilet control, and withdrawal.

The Japanese in this category (the usual diagnosis is schizophrenia) represent the "severest" forms of psychological disorder. Those who end up in the mental hospitals are those who have run out of community and family resources. It is our judgment that there are still many Japanese whose behavior is as "crazy" as those in the hospital, but they have been able to survive through the care of the family and the extended family network. This would be especially true if these individuals were able to retain some semblance of gainful employment.

Another view of mental health places priority on functional requisites necessary to survive in a society. The Japanese American may equate mental health with working hard, supporting the family, and providing adequate food, clothing, and shelter. Issues that may be of high priority to mental health professionals such as quality of life, open relationships, sharing of feelings, and psychological insights may be given a lesser order of importance. This discrepency may be one factor behind the low use of counseling agencies by the Japanese American. Either the group must redefine mental health to more closely fit the perceptions of the clinical agencies or the professionals must redefine mental health to more closely fit the ethnic definitions. Or perhaps the most reasonable alternative is to educate both of the groups, so that some meeting of minds and needs can be accomplished.

The last and broadest definition of mental health is related to the problems of identity in a pluralistic society, wherein a large number of messages from the dominant community are essentially negative. It is important to recognize the role conflict and the possible maladaptive adaptations for groups such as the Japanese Americans. This view of mental health points up the broad issues in a society where prejudice, discrimination, stereotypes, and racism exist and emphasizes that people and groups have to function under these conditions. Helping one achieve one's maximum potential and lead a fulfilling life under such conditions is the challenge to the mental health profession.

REFERENCES

Daniels, R. *Concentration Camps USA.* New York: Holt, Rinehart and Winston, 1971.

Kikumura, A. and Kitano, H. Interracial marriage: A picture of the Japanese Americans. *Journal of Social Issues* 29 (1973):67-81.

Kitano, H. Japanese-American mental illness, In *Changing Perspectives on Mental Illness,* edited by S. Plog and R. Edgerton, pp. 256-84. New York: Holt, Rinehart and Winston, 1969.

————. Mental illness in four cultures. *The Journal of Social Psychology* 80 (1970):112-34.

————. *Japanese Americans: The Evolution of a Subculture,* revised ed., Engelwood Cliffs, N.J.: Prentice-Hall, 1976.

Miranda, M. and Kitano, H. Barriers to mental health: A Japanese and Mexican dilemma. In *Chicanos: Social and Psychological Perspectives,* 2nd ed., edited by C. Hernandez, N. Wagner and M. Haug. St. Louis: C.V. Mosby, 1976.

Nakane, C. *Japanese Society.* Berkeley: University of California Press, 1970.

Newman, W. Multiple realities: The effects of social pluralism on identity. In *Ethnic Identity in Society,* edited by Arnold Dashefsky, pp. 39-47. Chicago: Rand McNally, 1976.

Ogawa, D. *Kodomo No Tame Ni.* Honolulu: University Press of Hawaii, 1978.

Okano, Y. *Japanese Americans and Mental Health.* Los Angeles: Coalition for Asian Mental Health, 1977. Pamphlet.

————. Survey of Asian/Pacific patients at Metropolitan State Hospital. Unpublished paper. Norwalk, California: Metropolitan State Hospital, 1979.

Strong, E., Jr. *The Second Generation Japanese Problem.* Stanford, Calif.: Stanford University Press, 1934.

Weglyn, M. *Years of Infamy.* New York: William Morrow, 1976.

7   Mental Health Attitudes and Opinions of Chinese

Roger G. Lum

INTRODUCTION

Within the past 20 years, numerous investigators have studied attitudes and beliefs about mental illness. In one of the early studies of mental health attitudes, Nunnally (1957, 1961) contrasted the beliefs of the average layman with those of mental health experts. Later, Cohen and Struening (1962) investigated the beliefs of hospital employees at various levels of responsibility, and several other researchers (Manis, Houts, and Blake, 1963; Giovannoni and Ullman, 1963) studied the beliefs of psychiatric patients. However, it was the scarcity of studies on the mental health attitudes and opinions of minorities, and on those of minority mental patients in particular, that led to this study of the mental health attitudes of Chinese patients and "normals" and of whether the experience of patienthood alters beliefs in a characteristic, systematic fashion.

Some of the specific questions in mind were: Do the kinds of emotional problems a person has lead to definite beliefs and opinions regarding mental illness? Does the amount of time under professional treatment, or clinical diagnosis, significantly account for differences in beliefs among patients? Do patients prefer to be treated at home or in the community rather than in state mental hospitals? What effects do education and social class have upon mental health beliefs and attitudes?

Since minority psychologists have insistently called attention to the need for knowing the mental health attitudes of *minority* communities as a basis for social planning (e.g., Pierce, 1972), an additional purpose of this study was to provide information that could be used as a basis for improving mental health services to the Chinese-American community.

BACKGROUND

Relevant Studies of U.S. Mental Patient Beliefs and Attitudes

A selective review of the relevant literature reveals that U.S. mental patients' attitudes (here "mental patients" are hospitalized patients) are generally like those of nonpatients of comparable age, education, and social class and that the condition of patienthood does not significantly alter beliefs and judgments. In a study of 35 hospitalized male psychiatric patients from five different wards of a Veterans Administration hospital, Giovannoni and Ullman (1963) found that patients were not better informed about mental illness than nonpatients and that their attitudes toward the mentally ill were as highly negative as those of normals. Both groups gave negative ratings to the concept of "Insane Man," describing such a concept as dirty, bad, cold, dangerous, unpredictable, and worthless. In a related study, hospitalized psychiatric patients and nonhospitalized normals described the mental patient in such unfavorable terms as excitable, foolish, unsuccessful, unusual, slow, untimely, active, cruel, weak, and ugly (Crumpton, et al., 1967). Manis, Houts, and Blake (1963) compared the attitudes of hospitalized psychiatric patients with those of medical patients and mental health professionals and found no significant attitudinal differences between medical and psychiatric patients. However, in both groups, those with more education believed that mental patients are like normals in appearance and that mental illness is curable.

In summary, patient status does not seem to significantly account for differences in mental health attitudes and opinions among the U.S. public. Several studies have shown that patients are generally as negative in their opinions about mental illness and the mentally ill as the general public. When such variables as class and social background are adequately controlled for, patient beliefs resemble those of nonpatients. The studies reported in the literature also pinpoint age and education as more crucial determinants of mental health attitudes and opinions than patienthood.

Traditional Chinese Conceptions of Mental Health and Mental Illness

Psychiatric concepts or mental illness and explanations of deviant behavior have evolved through an historical sequence of supernatural, natural, somatic, and psychological stages. Throughout the prehistoric periods, mental illness was framed in supernatural terms and insanity was often considered the result of meddling by supernatural powers, gods, and devils. Consequently, treatment consisted largely of magical rituals and prayers; petitions, negotiations, or threats were also addressed to the supernatural being in an attempt to remove its interference (Veith, 1963; de Groot, 1892-1910). Veith (1963) captures the essence of these supernatural beliefs in the following passage:

Each aberration had its specific cause, and a curative magic was directed towards the expulsion of the offending agent. Since many of the ceremonies were associated with violence that may have acted somewhat in the nature of shock treatment and all of them involved an intensive preoccupation with the patient, it is likely that the treatment was often effective. Above all, the belief in demonic powers made the patient an innocent victim and placed the sanction of his derangement beyond the influence of rational treatment and into the hands of priests. As a result, no stigma was attached to mental disease, and society was ready to receive the patient on pre-illness terms as soon as his behavior became normal.

It was especially during the period between the Chin Dynasty and the Five Dynasties (265 to 960 A.D.) that illness was thought to be a consequence of natural forces. The observation of change in the natural world, especially culminating from storm, flood, or drought, led to the belief that natural agents were the primary cause of illness. One such popular belief held that various illnesses were brought about by the ill effects of wind (Tseng, 1973; Lee, Ch'eng, and Chang, 1962; Veith, 1949). Ch'ao Yuen-Fang, a famous court physician of sixth century China, published a volume on the classification of these so-called wind diseases. In his *General Treatise on the Causes and Symptoms of Diseases* he lists some 59 such diseases, including apoplexy, hysteria, paralysis, and epilepsy—a wind affliction he studied in depth, listing as its predisposing factors: alcoholism, sudden fright, excessive sexual indulgence, and injury during the fetal stage. Ch'ao Yuen-Fang emphasized that illness could be prevented by avoiding exposure to extraordinary wind, cold, or humidity and by maintaining regularity and harmony.

Focus on the human body as the source of abnormality first took place during the pre-Chin period (2800 to 220 B.C.) and gradually evolved along with other theories in subsequent periods. Various bodily functions, such as the circulation of blood and the breathing of air, received attention at first because these phenomena were readily observable in a living person and because the cessation of either was recognized as a sign of death. In addition, these physiological activities were considered similar to the phenomena of water and air circulation in the natural world.

Developments in anatomical knowledge led to further emphasis on the function of solid organs instead of humor or blood, primarily reflected during the T'ang Dynasty (around 618-907 A.D.), as the key factor in disease. According to this view, life and health depended on the cooperative interaction of visceral organs and living according to the Way of Tao. Immoderate living habits would cause imbalance in the relationship of Yin and Yang, of opposite yet complementary forces or energies, in the bodily organs and disrupt the flow of life energies, or Chi, throughout the body, resulting in disease (Veith, 1949; Wallnofer and Rottauscher, 1972; Lee, Ch'eng, and Chang, 1962). Various methods, such as pulse reading of the body meridians, became indispensable as aids in the diagnosis and treatment of visceral imbalances and diseases.

In continuation of the somatic orientation, the physiological study of the brain, which flourished in the nineteenth century, combined mechanical and biological ideas. But it was not until the end of the nineteenth century that the psychological concept of mental illness with its emphasis on functional disorder took hold.

Once Chinese medicine was separated from superstition and sorcery, it was seldom influenced by it. In contrast, European medical practice in the Middle Ages was so heavily influenced by Christian doctrines that priests declared that psychiatric patients were bewitched and society meted out cruel punishments to the insane. Tseng (1973) reports that historical records indicate that the mentally ill received relatively humane treatment in China throughout its history; however, several investigators contend that treatment was often quite harsh (Kiev, 1968). Ingram (1918) writes that the "disposition to treat them (i.e., patients) cruelly was enhanced by the fear and dislike inspired by the belief that madness is due to possession by evil spirits. Compared with Japan, there can be little doubt that the treatment of the insane in China was very much worse.

Since *The Yellow Emperor's Classic of Internal Medicine* (dating back to the third century B.C.), Chinese medicine has recognized the influence of emotional factors upon physical illness and has emphasized the improvement of the emotional condition as a way to improve ill health, particularly for psychosomatic disorders. However, Chinese medicine itself has always been characterized by its herb-oriented treatment. Therefore, regardless of whether illness was seen as psychological or biological, treatment always involved the prescription of herbal medicines. This orientation has prevailed in contemporary society. Chinese psychiatric patients, even when consulting a psychiatrist, usually expect the doctor to prescribe medication for their (psychiatric) illness, and the psychiatrist frequently does so to meet his patient's expectations and needs (Tseng, 1973; Lum, 1973; Tom and Lum, 1974).

Traditional Chinese medical concepts of the function of visceral organs also continues to influence Chinese medical practice. Many patients describe their problems in terms of an organ, even if the problems are psychiatric in nature. Some commonly used expressions are "injured heart," meaning sadness, or "elevated fire," meaning agitation and tension (Tseng, 1973).

In one of the first major empirical studies on the ideas Chinese and other Asian ethnic groups have about mental illness, Arkoff, Thaver, and Elkind (1966) surveyed the opinions of graduate students of different ethnic backgrounds at the University of Hawaii using Jim Nunnally's mental health information questionnaire (Nunnally, 1961). Participating in this study were Filipinos, Thais, Japanese, Chinese, and Caucasian students who were matched in age (mean of 25.8 years) and educational background. A sixth group of subjects was made up of 20 male counseling and clinical psychologists. General findings indicated that Chinese subjects believed that external causes contribute more to the onset of mental disorders than personality factors, aging, or the avoidance of morbid thoughts. Chinese tended to reject the idea that mentally ill people look and act differently from normal people and that organic factors cause mental illness.

Through their study, Arkoff, Thaver, and Elkind demonstrated that differences in beliefs between Asian groups are not statistically significant; the greatest discrepancy is between Asian and Caucasian students. The most significant differences occur in the Nunnally factors related to willpower and the avoidance of morbid thoughts: Asian students are more prone to believe that exercising willpower and avoiding morbid thoughts help a person to maintain mental health. Another distinction that emerged is that Asians more than Americans think of counseling or psychotherapy as a relatively authoritarian process.

In a related study of immigrant Chinese and U.S.-born Chinese undergraduate students, Lum (1974b) also found that the two factors that most clearly differentiate these two groups are beliefs about (1) the effectiveness of willpower and (2) the avoidance of morbid thoughts. Chinese not born in the United States, being more traditional in their cultural values, are more likely to agree that pleasant thoughts have a positive effect on a person's mental health, whereas Chinese-Americans, more like Arkoff's group of Caucasian students, generally reject these beliefs.

METHOD OF STUDY

Design

A comparison of the mental health opinions of Chinese patients and normals was conducted by administering a modified version of Nunnally's mental health information questionnaire (Nunnally, 1961) in two years, 1975 and 1978. In 1975 the bulk of the data was collected from 30 patients and 39 normals; an additional 30 Chinese patients were studied in 1978 as part of a larger investigation of the impact of mental illness in Chinese families.

The first patient group (1975) was drawn from clinic rosters at an outpatient facility and a day treatment center in San Francisco's Chinatown. To verify term of treatment (only those subjects in treatment for five years or less were placed in a pool for random selection), as well as to obtain additional clinical information, patient records were reviewed and the patient's primary therapist was interviewed. The second patient group (1978), also in the San Francisco Bay area, met the following criteria: (1) unmarried male, (2) between 18-40 years of age, (3) at least one parent living locally, (4) diagnosed as having a functional or psychological disorder, and (5) psychiatric illness developed while living with his parents (Lum, 1979).

Originally, normal subjects were to have been randomly selected from Chinatown, but because of problems encountered in the pilot project (one of the major problems being a low response rate of 20 percent), members of community groups, local Chinatown residents, and college students from a local university were interviewed (N = 39).

Demographic Background of Subjects

Patient Samples. The 1975 and 1978 patient groups differ somewhat in terms of background, especially age and sex. Since most of the analyses are based on the first group of patients and normal subjects, we will need a closer look at these data (Table 7.1).

The 1975 sample is the most representative of the Chinese patient population, in large part because it was randomly selected from a pool of those who had been in treatment five years or fewer. This group is comprised of about two-thirds women (63 percent, which matches the general finding that about 68 percent of all patients utilizing mental health services in San Francisco Chinatown are women (Lum, 1974a). These patients also tend to be older, less well-educated, but with better means of support than the 1978 patient sample. Half of the group is also married, 40 percent are single, and 10 percent are divorced or separated. Two-thirds are immigrants from Hong Kong with a mean stay in the United States of 12.8 years (S.D. = 10.8 years), and most speak English rather poorly. Diagnostically, 47 percent are schizophrenics and 27 percent are neurotic depressives. The third largest number of patients (17 percent) falls into the "all others" category, which includes various personality and neurotic disorders. Most of these patients have been in treatment for under one year (57 percent).

Normal Sample. The percentage of women among our normal subjects (62 percent) is close to that of the 1975 patient sample. Normal subjects range in age from 18 to 60 years, with a mean of 28.3 years (S.D. = 12.2 years). The majority of respondents have a college education or beyond (80 percent). Close to 70 percent are single; only 28 percent are married. A large percentage of these subjects (44 percent are from at least middle-class families (annual income of over $15,000). More than half are native-born citizens, and 41 percent are immigrants with a mean stay in the United States of 12.7 years (S.D. = 7.9 years). Most are bilingual.

In summary, patients are primarily poor, though fairly well educated, and immigrants. Normal subjects are predominantly middle class, very well-educated, native-born Americans and female.

Table 7.1
Demographic Data on Patients (N = 60) and Normals (N = 39)

Characteristics	Patients (1975) N = 30	Patients (1978) N = 30	All Patients N = 60	Normals (1975) N = 39
	..............(percent)...............			
Sex				
Male	37	100	68.5	38.5
Female	63	0	31.5	61.5
Age				
15-24	16.7	30	23.3	61.5
25-34	16.7	50	33.3	7.7
35-44	33.3	20	26.7	7.7
45-54	23.3	0	11.7	17.9
55 and over	10.0	0	5.0	2.6
No data	0	0	0	2.6
Mean age in years	38.9	28.2	33.6	28.3
S.D.	12.2	6.4	9.3	12.2
Years of Education				
None	0	0	0	2.6
Elementary school	30.0	13.3	21.7	17.9
High school	43.3	36.7	40.0	69.2[a]
College	23.3	53.4	38.3	10.3
No data	3.3	0	1.7	0
Mean years of education	10.7	[b]	—	14.2
S.D.	3.7	—	—	2.1
Annual Income				
Under $5,000	73.3	86.7	80.0	10.3
$5,000-$9,999	23.3	6.7	15.0	7.7
$10,000-$14,999	0	3.3	1.7	33.3
$15,000 and over	3.3	0	1.7	43.6
No data	0	3.3	1.7	5.1
Occupation				
Executives and propri- etors of large concerns and major profes- sionals	3.3	3.3	3.3	7.7

Table 7.1, continued
Demographic Data on Patients (N = 60) and Normals (N = 39)

Characteristics	Patients (1975) N = 30	Patients (1978) N = 30	All Patients N = 60	Normals (1975) N = 39
	. . . . (percent)			
Managers and propri- etors of medium- sized businesses and lesser professionals	0	0	0	2.6
Administrative personnel of large concerns, owners of small inde- pendent businesses, and semiprofessionals	6.7	0	3.3	10.3
Owners of small busi- nesses, clerical and sales workers, and technicians	13.3	3.3	8.3	5.1
Skilled workers	3.3	0	1.7	2.6
Semiskilled workers	36.8	6.7	21.7	5.1
Unskilled workers	20.0	13.3	16.7	0
Housewives	13.3	0	6.7	5.1
Students	3.3	13.3	8.3	61.5
No past occupational history (e.g., never employed)	0	60.0	30.0	0

[a]Most subjects had just begun college at the time of the study.
[b]Not coded.

Measures

Mental Health Information Questionnaire. The questionnaire used in this study was modified from Nunnally's 60-item instrument (Nunnally, 1961). By eliciting reactions to hundreds of statements on some aspect of mental illness (with a Likert-type scale of 1 to 7, strongly disagree to strongly agree), Nunnally was able to tap beliefs about the causes, symptoms, and treatment of mental illness. He then subjected the data to factor analysis in order to derive ten major clusters of beliefs (see Table 7.2). Thus, the first 40 items of his 60-item instrument comprise the ten factors (four items per factor).

Table 7.2
Nunnally's Information Factors

Factor	Description
1. Look and act different	The mentally ill are recognizably different in manner and appearance from normal persons.
2. Willpower	Willpower is the basis of personal adjustment. Once adjustment is lost, the psychiatrist exercises his own willpower to bolster the patient's failing will.
3. Sex distinction	Women are more prone to mental disorder than men are.
4. Avoidance of morbid thoughts	Preoccupation with pleasant thoughts is the basis of mental health. Mental disturbances can be avoided by keeping busy, reading books on "peace of mind," and not discussing troublesome topics. The psychiatrist recommends hobbies and other ways for the patient to occupy himself.
5. Guidance and support	Mental health can be maintained by depending on strong persons in the environment. The therapist explains to the patient the origin of his troubles and tells the patient where his ideas are incorrect. The mentally ill are persons who lacked affection in childhood.
6. Hopelessness	There is little that can be done to cure a mental disorder. Psychiatrists cannot tell whether a condition is curable.
7. Immediate external environment vs. personality dynamics	The individual's state of mental health is dependent on the pressures in his immediate environment. A cure can be effected by a vacation or change of scenery. The opposite point of view is that the individual's state of well-being is dependent on his personal history, especially his childhood.
8. Nonseriousness	Emotional difficulties are relatively unimportant problems that cause little damage to the individual. (This factor differs from the hopelessness factor in that hopelessness is concerned with the likelihood of recovery and the value of treatment, regardless of the extent to which the problems are damaging.)

Table 7.2, continued
Nunnally's Information Factors

Factor	Description
9. Age function	Persons become more susceptible to emotional disorders as they grow older—an apparent analogy with increasing susceptibility to some of the "physical" disorders. Children are less affected by frightening experiences.
10. Organic causes	Mental disorder is brought on by organic factors like poor diet and diseases of the nervous system and can be cured by "physical" means.

Source: Adapted from Nunnally, J., Jr. *Popular Conceptions of Mental Health.* New York: Holt, Rinehart and Winston, 1961.

The modification of Nunnally's questionnaire was originally pilot tested on a small group of 22 Chinese normals during the spring of 1974 (Lum, 1974a). This original adaptation consisted of 80 items, with the latter 40 items either drawn directly from Nunnally or new additions. All changes in Nunnally's instrument were effected to make items more culturally appropriate for Chinese, as, for example, Item 55 ("Using the appropriate herbal remedies will help cure an emotionally ill person") and Item 59 ("If a person acts strangely, then he has become possessed by demons or evil spirits for his bad behavior").

In developing the survey instrument, two experienced translators were independently used to create a bilingual measure. There were independent checks of the translations of items before they were integrated into the questionnaire.

Pretesting resulted in a number of important changes. Items not differentiating significantly among groups of respondents were omitted. The final questionnaire consists of 65 items in a bilingual format. In addition to reducing the number of items, the scale range was reduced to 5, under the assumption that neither reliability nor differentiating power between subject groups would be jeopardized.

Patient-profile questionnaire. Additional information on patient characteristics (e.g., clinical diagnosis, length of time in treatment, treatment plan, and person treating the patient) was obtained from a patient-profile questionnaire given to the primary therapists. Therapists were asked to base their diagnoses on standards set forth by the American Psychiatric Association's *Diagnostic and Statistical Manual of Mental Disorders* (DSM-II).

RESULTS

Comparison of Mental Health Opinions of Chinese Patients and Normals

Differences in Nunnally factor scores. A consistent pattern is that patients tend to indicate higher agreement with the Nunnally factors than do normal subjects (Table 7.3). However, the similarity of the overall profiles of the two groups shows that belief patterns differ more in extent of agreement than in a major qualitative dimension (patient data includes samples collected in 1975 and 1978). Only on four of ten factors do patient beliefs differ significantly from those of normals ($p < .05$).

Table 7.3
Factor Means and T-Tests among Chinese Subgroups (N = 99)

Factor	Patients *N = 60*	Normals *N = 39*	*t*
1. Look and act different	2.95	2.56	2.78[a]
2. Willpower	3.00	2.90	.64
3. Sex distinction	2.70	2.82	.89
4. Avoidance of morbid thoughts	3.43	2.81	2.72[a]
5. Guidance and support	3.55	3.19	2.08[b]
6. Hopelessness	2.77	2.78	.14
7. Environment vs. personality	3.54	3.25	1.93[c]
8. Nonseriousness	2.88	2.68	1.44
9. Age function	3.22	3.29	.53
10. Organic causes	2.81	2.34	3.00[a]

[a]Level of significance: $p < .01$.

[b]Level of significance: $p < .05$.

[c]Level of significance: $p < .10$.

1. Look and Act Different (Factor 1). Normal subjects tend to more strongly reject the notion that the mentally ill are behaviorally and physically distinguishable from normals. Patients, on the other hand, tend to neither agree or disagree with this belief.

2. Avoidance of Morbid Thoughts (Factor 4). By far the largest difference between patients and normals occurred on Factor 4. Patients clearly believe that preoccupation with pleasant thoughts and avoidance of morbid ideas are the basis of mental health. Normals are less likely to believe this.

3. Guidance and Support (Factor 5). Patients tend to agree more strongly with the belief that mental health can be maintained by depending on strong persons in the environment and that the task of the therapist is to explain to the patient the origin of his troubles and to tell the patient where his ideas are incorrect.

4. Organic Causes (Factor 10). Another significant difference between patients and normals emerged on Factor 10. Patients as a group neither agree nor disagree with the belief that mental disorder is brought on by organic factors like poor diet or diseases of the nervous system; normals are less likely to disagree strongly with this notion.

There were only three factors that *normals* were more likely to endorse than patients, those involving Sex Distinction, Hopelessness, and Age Function. The greatest mean difference involved normals more strongly endorsing the belief that women are more prone to mental disorder than men; however, this was not statistically significant.

Relationship of Sociodemographic Variables and Beliefs

To ascertain whether patient status could significantly account for variance in factor scores among Chinese, as well as to determine relative effects of other independent variables, the data was examined by multiple regression analysis. Patients from the 1978 sample were not included in this analysis. An important finding is that patienthood is *not* a good predictor of mental health beliefs among Chinese as compared to such variables as formal education and age. Extent of formal education best predicts mental health beliefs among Chinese (especially for Factors 2, 4, 5, 6, 7, and 10) and is comparable to Nunnally's analysis of a nationally representative sample of Americans (see Figure 7.1).

Correlation of Patient Demographic Variables and Beliefs. More detailed correlations are provided by examining each group under study. In general, degree of formal *education* among patients correlates highly with more

Figure 7.1. Nunnally factor means of Chinese patients (N = 60), Chinese normals (N = 39), and Americans (N = 700).

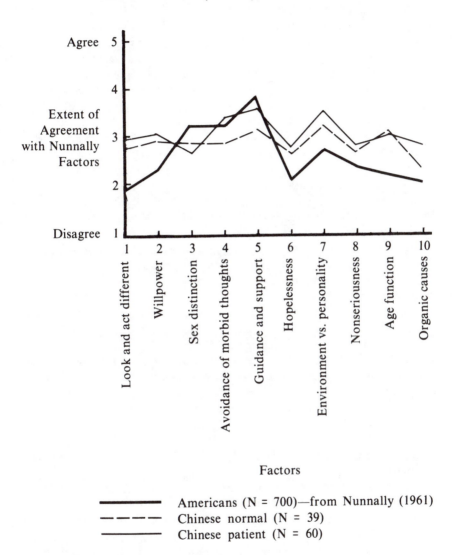

Factors

Americans (N = 700)—from Nunnally (1961)
Chinese normal (N = 39)
Chinese patient (N = 60)

informed views of mental illness. Beliefs strongly rejected by the better-educated patients include: the mentally ill look and act different from normals, and mental health can be maintained by depending on strong persons in one's environment. Better-educated patients also tend to reject the belief that mental illness can be cured.

There is a high positive correlation between *age* and agreement with the factors (very likely confounded by an interaction effect with education; older patients were far less educated than younger patients). Older patients were generally uninformed or misinformed about mental illness and were inclined to endorse superstitious beliefs. The data suggest that they were relatively ignorant of Western or, more specifically, U.S. views of mental illness. An implication of this is that mental health education geared toward mental patients is less likely to succeed with older, more traditional Chinese who probably adhere more strongly to folk beliefs and superstitions about the nature of mental illness. Other variables such as sex, income, and degree of acculturation do not correlate as highly with the Nunnally factors as do either age or education.

Correlation of Normals' Demographic Variables and Beliefs. A consistent finding among Chinese normals is that extent of formal *education* correlates highly with more-informed mental health beliefs. Better-educated normals reject the belief that mental health can be ensured by avoiding morbid thoughts. They also believe that mental health is curable, that mental health does not necessarily result from depending on strong persons in one's environment, and that mental health does not result from exercising willpower.

Though education and age were not fully controlled, it is still worth noting that immigrant normals have beliefs that are roughly distinguishable from their more acculturated counterparts. Relatively unacculturated Chinese tend to believe that mental health results from avoiding morbid thoughts, that mental illness is caused by external or environmental factors rather than by personality disorders, and that mental illness is caused by organic factors. In contrast to immigrant patients, immigrant normals are less likely to endorse superstitious beliefs.

Other Attitudes Toward Mental Illness Among Chinese Patients and Normals

Three non-Nunnally questions were also included in the mental health information questionnaire to assess attitudes towards mental illness (see Table 7.4). Patients are more inclined than normals to believe that it is shameful for a family member to be hospitalized in a mental hospital (although less than 25 percent of patients said "Yes.") Of special significance is the very high percentage of "Don't knows" among both groups. Among normals this may be due to the lack of actual exposure to this possibility, and for the patients it is highly probable that family members simply do not talk about their feelings, especially because of the great sensitivity of the issue.

Greater differences emerge on the second question: 36 percent of normal subjects would tell friends that a family member is mentally ill, whereas

43 percent of patients said they would. Exactly 41 percent of normal subjects would keep quiet, compared to about 13 percent of patients. Patients seemed ambivalent about disclosing their condition to others. Again, the high percentage of "Don't knows" is significant, which may very well point to prevailing feelings of ambivalence regarding disclosure to others.

Table 7.4
Attitude Questions (1975 Sample)

Is it shameful for a member of the family to be hospitalized in a mental hospital?

	N	Yes %	No %	Don't Know %
Chinese-American Normals	39	17.9	23.1	58.9
Chinese-American Patients	30	23.3	16.7	60.0

Suppose a member of your family became mentally ill. Do you think you would tell your friends and acquaintances about it as though he had gastric ulcer or apoplectic stroke, or would you try to keep it as quiet as possible?

	N	Would Tell %	Would Keep Quiet %	Don't Know %
Chinese-American Normals	39	35.9	41.0	23.1
Chinese-American Patients	30	43.3	13.3	43.3

People who have some kind of mental illness are better off being taken care of at home than being hospitalized in a mental hospital.

	N	Yes %	No %	Don't Know %	No Answer %
Chinese-American Normals	39	20.5	28.2	48.7	2.6
Chinese-American Patients	30	43.3	30.0	23.3	3.3

Finally, it is significant that twice as many patients as normals feel that home or community treatment is better than institutional care. However, normals are twice as likely to answer "Don't know," probably because of a lack of familiarity with treatment issues and problems.

Mental Health Beliefs of Chinese and Americans—A Comparison with Nunnally's Sample

To compare Chinese and U.S. attitudes toward mental illness, the U.S. sample was based on the findings reported by Nunnally in 1961. Two obvious methodological problems arising from the use of this sample are: (1) Nunnally's study was conducted over 20 years ago, and the general public's knowledge of mental health issues has improved; and (2) the sample Chinese population was by no means randomly selected, nor was it truly representative of the Chinese population nationally or even locally.

Nevertheless, for heuristic purposes, various comparisons were made with Nunnally's U.S. sample by examining the factor means of Chinese patients (N = 60) and Chinese normals (N = 39). Combining the Chinese patient and normal groups did not pose a problem because multiple regression analysis had demonstrated that patient status does not significantly account for variance in respondents' beliefs. To obtain comparable data for the comparative graphs (see Figure 7.1 on page 000 and Figure 7.2 on following page). Nunnally's 7-point scale was arithmetically reduced to fit the 5-point response range used in this study.

Mental Health Beliefs of Chinese (N = 99) vs. Those of Americans (N = 700).

An analysis of all Chinese subjects and Nunnally's sample of Americans indicates that although *patterns* of mean responses to the factors are somewhat similar for both groups (Figure 7.2), there are significant mean differences in several areas. Americans and Chinese both generally reject the notion that the mentally ill look and act different. On the other hand, Chinese endorse the belief that older people are more prone to mental illness (Age Function) whereas Americans disagree rather strongly with this notion. Finally, Americans strongly reject the belief that mental illness is a hopeless, incurable condition, whereas Chinese are more inclined to endorse it. It is worth noting that Factor 5 (Guidance and Support) is one of the most salient beliefs for both Chinese and Americans.

Overall, U.S. subjects indicated lower agreement with the Nunnally factors than did Chinese normals, but on the three factors they most strongly endorsed the Americans had higher factor means than did Chinese normals. The profiles pictured in Figure 7.1 suggest that despite these differences there is a marked similarity in Americans' and Chinese normals' trends of endorsement; thus, patterns of belief on mental health issues are fairly comparable for the two groups.

Summary of Results

We can summarize the major findings on the mental health opinions of Chinese living in the San Francisco area as follows: (1) Patients and normals hold similar beliefs. Both patients and normals reject notions that the mentally

Figure 7.2. Nunnally factor means of Chinese (N = 99) and Americans (N = 700).

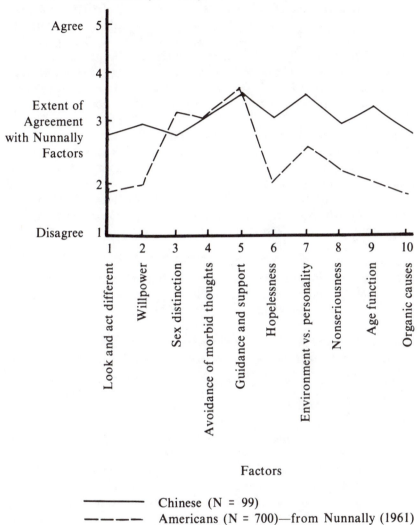

Factors

———————— Chinese (N = 99)

– – – – – Americans (N = 700)—from Nunnally (1961)

ill look and act differently from normals, that women are more prone to mental illness than men, that mental illness is incurable, and that mental illness is not a serious condition. Both groups tend to support the ideas that mental health is dependent upon guidance and support from strong people in one's life, that environmental determinants are more crucial than personality dynamics in the deterioration of mental health, and that older people are more susceptible to mental illness. The Nunnally factors that most clearly distinguish patients from nonpatients (patients endorsed them more strongly) are Avoidance of Morbid Thoughts and Immediate External Causes vs. Personality Dynamics. (2) The age and education of the respondent, rather than patient status, are the best predictors of mental health beliefs. (3) The sense of shame and the denial of mental illness are most pronounced among Chinese normals. (4) The mental health beliefs of most Chinese are not highly structured; however, in a comparison of the attitudes of patients and normals, patient beliefs appear somewhat more crystallized and consistent.

Impact of Mental Illness in Chinese Families

As mentioned earlier, additional data on Chinese attitudes and beliefs about mental illness were gathered in 1978 as part of a study of the impact of mental illness in Chinese families (Lum, 1979). Since some of these data were reported in another section of this chapter, I would like to present other findings of pertinence to our concern with Chinese mental health attitudes.

Before doing so, it would be helpful to review the purpose and design of this particular study. Thirty single Chinese patients, between 18 to 40 years of age and diagnosed as functionally disturbed, were selected for study. Subjects were interviewed along with their parents to determine three general areas of impact: (1) how family members initially identified and subsequently defined manifestations of mental illness, (2) how family members coped with mental illness, and (3) what impact mental illness had on family relationships, expectations, and the issues of shame and stigma. These interviews also explored family reactions to psychiatric services, including recommendations on therapeutic improvements. Separate questionnaires administered to patients included a mental health information survey (i.e., Nunnally) and a brief symptom checklist. Interview schedules and codebooks were adapted from the work of John A. Clausen and associates (personal communication) in their studies on impact of mental illness in families (see Clausen and Yarrow, 1955).

The findings suggest that most Chinese family members, including the patient, had difficulty in initially identifying psychotic-like behaviors in mental illness terms. Such behaviors were generally seen as indications of character weakness or behavioral deviance. Only when behaviors became increasingly difficult to understand or explain did family members come to accept some psychiatric explanation or to acknowledge the presence of a psychiatric problem.

When professional help was finally sought, most family members initially turned to physicans and not to mental health clinics or psychiatrists, even though the problem was clearly psychiatric in nature. Although many Chinese subjects denied feeling ashamed about seeking help and having a mentally ill member in the family, various interview responses suggested otherwise. Evaluations of psychiatric services, however, were fairly positive. Specific recommendations about therapeutic improvements included suggestions that therapists become more structured, authoritarian, or directive.

These findings have important implications for psychotherapy and for therapeutic styles that would be more acceptable to or preferred by Chinese patients. Furthermore, the evidence suggests that greater outreach and educational programs on early identification and treatment of mental illness are presently needed in the Chinese community.

GENERAL DISCUSSION AND CONCLUSIONS

The sociopsychological implications of these findings have a direct bearing on such issues as psychotherapy for Chinese, the understanding of personality dynamics, mental health education in the Chinese community, and the reconstruction of definitive attitudes toward mental health and mental illness among Chinese.

Definition of Mental Health and Mental Illness

Our data enable us to describe popular definitions of mental health and mental illness among Chinese—as derived from the Nunnally factors. However, there are limitations to defining beliefs on this empirical basis since the very nature of the factors imposes constraints on the universe of beliefs included in the definitions. Extrapolations from ten structured factors necessarily exclude whole dimensions of belief. With this in mind, we can speculate that the average Chinese considers mental illness to be the loss of willpower and self-discipline, a preoccupation with morbid thoughts, the sense of insecurity brought on by a lack of social support, emotional distress precipitated by negative environmental (i.e., external) factors, and an affliction found particularly among older people.

Conversely, mental health is interpreted as the capacity for self-discipline and the willpower to resist conducting oneself or thinking in ways that are not socially or culturally sanctioned; a sense of security and self-assurance stemming from support and guidance from significant others; relative freedom from unpleasant, morbid thoughts, emotional conflicts, and personality disorders; and the absence of organic dysfunctions, such as epilepsy or other neurological disorders.

Patienthood and Mental Health Beliefs

A basic assumption of most psychotherapists is that through greater exposure to mental health concepts and ideas, particularly in treatment settings, mental patients acquire more correct information about mental illness and health. One study that lends support to this assumption found that the ideas held by mental patients became more similar to those of hospital staff as a result of treatment (Manis, Houts, and Blake, 1963). Though their research design differed from the present study (namely, they administered the Nunnally both before and after treatment), we found that the information possessed by Chinese patients who were in varying stages of treatment at the time of the interviews was not any more correct than, nor significantly different from, the information held by Chinese not undergoing treatment. Several implications of these findings concern the relationship between psychotherapy and mental health beliefs.

It is probably that psychotherapy influences a person's whole universe of beliefs in a manner inadequately measured by Nunnally's opinion questionnaire. Furthermore, patient attitudes might shift without detection by questionnaire items. Nevertheless, I question whether most treatment presently given Chinese patients is really geared towards insight (in traditional psychodynamic terms). The treatment received by most patients we surveyed consisted of activities therapy, rap groups, individual and group counseling led primarily by nonprofessionals, and infrequent, brief sojourns to psychiatrists for routine consultation. Most of these modalities are not geared towards insight-oriented, depth psychotherapy, and as such the mental health beliefs of consumers are not significantly altered. On the surface, it would appear that Chinese patients do not acquire more correct and sophisticated notions about mental health and mental illness in the course of their treatment.

The findings support earlier studies showing that patienthood does not significantly alter beliefs about mental illness (Giovannoni and Ullman, 1963; Manis, Houts, and Blake, 1963; Crumptom, et al., 1967; Bentinck, 1967). All of these studies indicate that patient status is relatively unimportant in determining beliefs compared to other variables such as age and education. Available research also suggests that Chinese and U.S. psychiatric patients hold similar views about mental illness (see Manis, Houts, and Blake 1966 for data on U.S. psychiatric patients). Both groups of mental patients do *not* believe that the mentally ill look or act different from normals, that women are more susceptible to mental disorder than men, that mental illness is hopeless and incurable, or that mental illness is a relatively harmless condition. Both Americans and Chinese *do* believe that mental health can be maintained by depending on strong persons in one's environment.

Chinese Patients and Psychotherapy

Chinese patients generally prefer a clinician who is authoritarian and directive in style. They tend to believe that a good psychiatrist recommends hobbies and other means of occupying the mind and that he strives to be like a father to them. They do not, as some people think, want their psychiatrist to limit his role to the prescription of medication. However, younger, better-educated patients (as well as Chinese normals) prefer a therapist who is less authoritarian and directive in his approach (therapy that is less structured and more insight oriented may be preferred). Prevailing practices in San Francisco's Chinatown mirror these preferences.

In the Chinatown catchment area, older, less-well educated patients often receive directive guidance treatment, which includes the administration of drugs, whereas younger patients are generally placed in psychosocial treatment models such as group or individual therapy (Lum, 1974b). In interpreting these findings, it is important to bear in mind that older patients are usually more chronically ill, more traditional, and not as psychologically minded as their younger counterparts; consequently, treatment modalities for the different generations would necessarily differ. Research on psychotherapy and social class (e.g., Jones, 1974; Hollingshead and Redlich, 1958) parallels my findings about the San Francisco Chinese community: older, less-well educated patients of lower social class, regardless of race, receive more drug-oriented, custodial, and authoritarian types of therapies.

Personality Dynamics of Chinese

What clearly emerges from this study, as well as that of Arkoff, Thaver, and Elkind (1966), is that Chinese tend to externalize blame for mental illness and that they would rather avoid confronting the emotions and thoughts that trouble them. Their high endorsement of beliefs related to environmental etiology of mental illness and their professed conviction that the insane lack adequate support and guidance from significant others throughout their lives, particularly during childhood, lends support to this notion of externalization. Chinese patients and the older normal subjects also believe that one must learn to inhibit and control one's emotions. In effect, more traditional Chinese emphasize control of strong emotions as a prerequisite for maintaining mental health and as an indication of maturity and wisdom. Therapists must acknowledge the cultural value and function of emotional inhibition and moderation of expression and not rigidly confront these qualities as indications of transference or treatment resistance.

A related point is that more traditional Chinese, both normals and patients, believe that mental health can be maintained by avoiding unpleasant thoughts and by keeping preoccupied and busy, which raises a number of questions. Would Chinese define mental illness as a state of mind in which one is preoccupied with morbid thoughts and hampered by lack of willpower? How does the belief about suppressing unpleasant thoughts and emotions fit into our understanding of Chinese personality or, more specifically, of Chinese defensive styles? Cultural anthropologist Francis Hsu (1949) suggested that Chinese are more inclined to rely on suppression as a defense mechanism, whereas Westerners are more reliant on repression. The reason, he argued, is that Chinese culture emphasizes the control of emotions and strict self-discipline as signs of personal fortitude and maturity. If we take this argument further and examine suppression as a defense mechanism, we can conclude that a person must rely on volition, or willpower, to implement such a defense. The defense is obsessional because to use it effectively a person has to rationalize, justify away, or otherwise intellectually denude the unpleasant trappings of anxiety. In effect, these cultural values encourage the development of obsessive-compulsive qualities in the Chinese personality and are evident in a person who is overly conscientious, neat and meticulous, acquiescent yet stubborn; in a person who is at times cognitively, emotionally, or phsycially rigid; or in someone who prefers thinking to emoting. There is no intention to stereotype Chinese with such traits nor imply that psychopathology is their inevitable concomitant, but the results suggest that Chinese beliefs about mental health are determined by certain traditional values and traits, such as control of emotions, rationality, and reserve.

Mental Health Education

Mental health education programs aimed at the Chinese community have to take into account the crucial role of stigma and shame associated with mental illness. Such shame may lead to denying the seriousness and prevalence of mental health problems in the community. Chinese patients particularly feel ashamed and ambivalent about their illness or difficulties and express this uncertainty in their reluctance to tell others about their emotional problems as they would tell them about a physical illness. This study supports other findings documenting shame in disclosure and in being labeled mentally ill (Sue and Sue, 1972; Tom and Lum, 1974). Most investigators have suggested that the low utilization rates of mental health facilities by Chinese may be partly due to an underlying sense of shame and fear of stigmatizaiton, as well as to the lack of bilingual and bicultural treatment facilities and resources.

To effectively address this issue, it is absolutely important that mental health professionals intervene at the individual, group, and institutional-community levels. Mental health educators must begin by working in institutional and community settings, developing programs with schools and other community centers, and establishing regular meetings (preferably in the hub of the community) where an exchange of information and a sharing of perspectives can take place. The use of mental health information questionnaires can help provide additional information on a community's attitudes and beliefs and would be useful to service providers in tailoring mental health education programs to meet individual, group, or institutional needs.

Conducting Social Surveys in the Chinese Community:
Some Methodological Considerations

Efforts to locate subjects for the survey were difficult and discouraging. Only 20 percent of those contacted responded. Many residents refused to participate on grounds of ignorance, inconvenience, and difficulty in communicating. Some offered no reason. Most of those who refused did not bother to open their doors, but instead talked from behind their doors.

Let me speculate on the reasons behind the high rate of refusal. First of all, the age of the interviewer probably figured prominently in how contacts responded. All of the interviewers were female Chinese college students, and most of them were bilingual. Although they had received basic training in interviewing techniques, the fact that they were young, inexperienced, and apprehensive probably caused many respondents to be concerned about the interviewer's motives and objectives. To minimize interviewee anxiety and thus improve response rates, it might be wise in the future to send out older (and hence more respected), more experienced interviewers who are long-time residents of the community. Second, suspicion about our survey might also be due to historical and cultural factors. In old China and Hong Kong, the only people who came around asking "nosy" questions were government and other public officials inquiring about such matters as taxes, fugitives, criminal activity, or census information. In the United States, many older residents of Chinatown have unpleasant memories of the 1950s (the McCarthy era) when U.S. government authorities harassed immigrants over illegal entry or possible subversive activity (Tom and Lum, 1974) and caused many Chinese to develop a deep mistrust of outsiders. Whatever their reasons, many Chinese refuse to participate in social surveys because they are suspicious of the interviewer's intentions and motives, and, on a more fundamental level, because they often do not understand why the study is done and how the results will benefit them.

In conclusion, there is a pressing need to study not only the popular mental health beliefs of Chinese but those of other racial and ethnic minorities as well. The study of the popular beliefs of these groups would help public agencies plan comprehensive health care for minority and poor communities. Toward this end, several crucial questions must be raised and, one hopes, answered. To what extent and in what manner does the experience of poverty lead to a deemphasis of personality dynamics in the etiology of mental illness? What social implications does this relationship have for general health care planning in a poverty-stricken or minority community? If we find clear-cut racial differences in beliefs about the etiology and treatment of mental illness, what implications do these have for mental health catchment areas serving ethnic and racial minorities? Would knowledge about community preferences and needs put sufficient pressure on mental health professionals to discard "assembly-line treatment" in favor of beginning the difficult task of creating more differentiated direct and indirect services to meet the multiracial, multicultural needs of minority communities? Admittedly, it will be difficult to find adequate answers to these complex questions, and it will be even more demanding to find ways of implementing solutions to mental health care problems. Nevertheless, the use of mental health attitude and opinion surveys will be of great value to mental health professionals in their planning and delivery of comprehensive community mental health services.

REFERENCES

Arkoff, A., Thaver, F., and Elkind, L. Mental health and counseling ideas of Asian and American students. *Journal of Counseling Psychology* 13 (1966):219-23.

Bentinck, C. Opinions about mental illness held by patients and relatives. *Family Process* 6 (1967):193-207.

Ch'ao Yuen-fang. *General Treatise on the Causes and Symptoms of Diseases,* 610 A.D.

Clausen, J.A. and Yarrow, M.R., eds. The impact of mental illness in families. *Journal of Social Issues* 11 (1955).

Cohen, J. and Struening, E. Opinions about mental illness in the personnel of two large mental hospitals. *Journal of Abnormal Social Psychology* 64 (1962): 349-60.

Crumpton, E., Weinstein, A., Acker, C., and Annis, A. How patients and normals see the mental patient. *Journal of Clinical Psychology* 23 (1967):46-49.

de Groot, J.J.M. *The Religious System of China* (6 vols.). Leyden, 1892-1910.

Giovannoni, J. and Ullman, L. Conceptions of mental health held by psychiatric patients. *Journal of Clinical Psychology* 19 (1963):398-400.

Hollingshead, A.B. and Redlich, F.C. *Social Class and Mental Health: A Community Study.* New York: John Wiley & Sons, 1958.

Hsu, F. Suppression versus repression: A limited psychological interpretation of four cultures. *Psychiatry* 12 (1949):223-42.

Ingram, D. The pitiable condition of the insane in northern China. *China Medical Journal* 32 (1918):153.

Jones, E. Social class and psychotherapy: A critical review of research. *Psychiatry* 37 (1974):307-20.

Kiev, A., ed. *Psychiatry in the Communist World.* New York: Science House, 1968.

Lee, T'ao, Ch'eng, C., and Chang, C. Some early records of nervous and mental diseases in traditional Chinese medicine. *Chinese Medical Journal* 81 (1962): 55-59.

Lum, R. Community mental health in San Franciso Chinatown. Unpublished manuscript, 1973.

————. Characteristics of Chinese patients utilizing mental health services in San Francisco. Unpublished manuscript, 1974a.

————. Issues in the study of Asian-American communities. *Newsletter of the Association of Asian-American Psycholgists* 1 (1974b).

————. Impact of mental illness in Chinese families. Ph.D. Dissertation, University of California, Berkeley, 1979.

Manis, M., Houts, P., and Blake, J. Beliefs about mental illness as a function of psychiatric status and psychiatric hospitalization. *Journal of Abnormal and Social Psychology* 67 (1963):226-33.

Nunnally, J., Jr. The communication of mental health information: A comparison of the opinions of experts and the public with mass media presentations. *Behavioral Scientist* 2 (1957):222-30.

_____. *Popular Conceptions of Mental Health.* New York: Holt, Rinehart and Winston, 1961.

Pierce, W. Comprehensive community mental health planning in the Black community. In *Black Psychology,* edited by R. Jones. New York: Harper & Row, 1972.

Sue, D. and Sue, S. Counseling Chinese-Americans. *Personnel and Guidance Journal* 50 (1972):637-44.

Tom, S. and Lum, R. Mental health in the San Francisco Chinese community: An interview with Dr. Sanford Tom. *Newsletter of the Association of Asian-American Psychologists* 1 (1974):3-10.

Tseng, W. The development of psychiatric concepts in traditional Chinese medicine. *Archives of General Psychiatry* 29 (1973):569-75.

Veith, I. *The Yellow Emperor's Classic of Internal Medicine.* Berkeley: University of California Press, 1949.

_____. The supernatural in Far Eastern concepts of mental disease. *Bulletin of the History of Medicine* 37 (1963):139-55.

Wallnofer, H. and Rottauscher, A. *Chinese Folk Medicine.* New York: Crown, 1972.

PART II
INTERVENTION

8 The Psychological Assessment of Blacks: New and Needed Developments

L. Snowden and P. Todman

INTRODUCTION

In recent decades, the black community has strongly expressed its dissatisfaction with the consequences of psychological testing of its citizens. The strongest resistance to the status quo in testing of blacks has come from black psychologists, educators, and political activists. The major portion of their criticism has focused on two areas: (1) The greater denial of opportunity to blacks than to whites that often results from psychological testing, and (2) the underlying psychometric and clinical judgment issues that account for black-white test differences.

Sparked by the race-IQ controversy, black disenchantment with testing has been heavily influenced by the widespread use of psychological test data in decisions that bar blacks disproportionately from desirable institutional options. In industry, in education, and in the clinic, blacks have been found less capable or more disordered than whites, and they have received less favorable dispositions as a result. Sensitive to this society's long-standing tradition of rejecting blacks, some have wondered whether psychological assessment is a mere rationalization for racism. One may consider this view overstated, yet respond with skepticism and concern to the fact that, in major social institutions, psychological tests often function to place blacks at a relative disadvantage.

To understand the meaning of test results, it is necessary to probe the theoretical, psychometric, and statistical underpinnings of the assessment procedure in question. The central issue is whether test-identified differences between blacks and whites reflect legitimate differences in psychological status or are systematic errors of measurement. The validity and reliability of assessment procedures become the appropriate targets of scrutiny.

193

Assessment specialists have been spurred to examine the technical explanations for poor black test performance. Perhaps the best known of the resulting methodological debates has been over the genetic versus environmental origin of black-white differences in I.Q. A less conspicuous but equally important dialogue has occurred in industry, where psychologists have considered various psychometric definitions of test bias to evaluate the discriminatory effects of various employment tests (Cleary, et al., 1975; Hunter and Schmidt, 1976).

Concern with test bias in the clinical realm has been more scattered and informal. This may be partly because, unlike industrial managers and school superintendents, clinicians have not yet been sued. But there is evidence of possible invalid black-white differences for some tests and suspicion of such differences for other tests. Since a test finding of greater psychological impairment often consigns the testee to less desirable forms of treatment, one may argue that clinical testing presents a disturbing parallel with educational and industrial testing and holds a similar potential for legal action.

Most critics have stopped short of demanding that psychological testing with blacks be altogether abandoned. Rather, they have called for tests that accurately capture the psychological status of blacks. If deficits are found, psychological assessors must be certain that they are truly deficits and not artifacts resulting from the misapplication of inappropriate techniques. Central to this position is the belief that many psychological tests, developed and normed on heavily-white samples of subjects, are of questionable validity for blacks. Some critics have argued that, because of distinctive values, beliefs, and expectations, at least some items and indicators on tests must be interpreted differently for blacks than for whites. To claim such differences as these is to assert that blacks must be considered as a distinguishable culture.

The view that U.S. society is multicultural has increasingly gained credence. From a stance of cultural pluralism, one attempts to understand minority behavior from its own frame of reference. Black families, for example, would be understood within their own tradition of extended parenting and role flexibility and as a viable institution distinct from mainstream U.S. prototypes.

However, the psychosocial implications of cultural pluralism, and their extension to Afro-Americans, are only beginning to be explored. At present, cultural attributes distinguishing blacks cannot be delineated with certainty, nor can a definitive justification for invoking culture be stated. On the other hand, there is indeed reason to believe that at least some black-white differences are best conceived in cultural terms. With respect to language (Baratz and Baratz, 1970), attitudes and values (Jones, 1978; Gynther, 1972b), and socioeconomic assimilation, three empirically emergent dimensions of acculturation cited by Olmedo (1979), blacks have been deputed as in some significant ways similar to each other and different from whites.

Without assuming complete or even primary divergence between blacks and whites, this chapter will argue that cultural pluralism is a useful working hypothesis for efforts to explore the psychology of blacks, and to assure accurate clinical assessment.

The present authors will continue the growing practice of applying a cross-cultural analysis to the behavior of blacks. Like other papers of more recent origin (e.g. Jones and Zoppel, 1979; Olmedo, 1979), this chapter will apply a formal cross-cultural perspective rigorously and direct it to the problem of valid clinical psychological assessment of blacks. The chapter is primarily theoretical in emphasis; practical suggestions to practitioners must await further basic developments of types to be outlined later. The chapter includes four approaches to assessment: (1) objective evaluation of intelligence, (2) objective evaluation of personality, (3) projective evaluation of personality, (4) behavioral evaluation of specific problems. To allow for a deeper consideration of issues, only one representative of each approach of particular importance to clinicians will be reviewed.

First, the position to be taken in the chapter will be placed in a broader perspective of general trends in psychological thought.

GENERALIZABILITY OF PSYCHOLOGICAL RESEARCH

The push for recognition of cultural differences in assessment is by no means an isolated phenomenon. The broader social and political context, featuring vigorous efforts by minority groups to overturn the apparatus of oppression, constitutes one important perspective. Another source of impetus—perhaps less widely recognized—is the mounting skepticism of psychologists toward the assumption that their principles and methods are broadly generalizable. As a potentially illuminating context and source of ideas, these developments are worthy of examination.

Widespread concern about generalizability is leading psychologists to question standard procedures in an area of great professional investment— systematic empirical research. Increasing numbers of psychologists have called for a reappraisal of our ability to produce knowledge that transfers from the narrow research environment to the broader social context. This thrust has called into question particularly the real-world applicability of laboratory analogue research. Expressed in the terms of experimental design, the issue becomes whether excessive concern for precision, or internal validity, has undermined the attainment of generalizability, or external validity.

Gibbs (1979) has analyzed this reawakened perception of the imbalance between internal and external validity. Commenting on its pervasiveness, he asserts: "the most popular reformist plea in contemporary psychological research is the call for ecologically oriented inquiry. In perception and memory, in learning and development, in social influence and attitude change, one hears the same lament of trivial and irrelevant research and the same plea for sensitivity to the contextual continuities and potentialities of human behavior" (p. 127). For those seeking reform, the optimum state of affairs is not to forsake the rigor of more artificial research methods, but rather to pay equal attention to the contextual relevance of resulting findings. Pragmatically, however, internal and external validity seem inversely related. In this dilemma, Gibbs sees an updated version of a classical philosophical tension between the needs for certainty and authenticity about knowledge.

Minority calls for reform of psychology and psychological assessment can be understood as a special case of the ecological critique. Being asked of psychology is precisely "sensitivity to the contextual continuities and potentialities of human behavior." For minority critics, one neglected aspect of human context is the distinctive cultural features of minority communities. Lacking attention to these factors, minority critics join other ecologically oriented critics in feeling skepticism toward what may be "trivial and irrelevant research."

In general, there is an increasing awareness that psychologists must establish the limits of their explanatory principles and methods of study. The previously discussed ecological critique, as well as a revival of the ideographic approach, involving the search for unique patterns of individual behavior (Bem and Allen, 1974), are among the indications of this concern. An issue underlying these developments is the tension between uniformity and variety in human psychology. Without denying the existence of uniformity, critics have asked that psychologists' approaches afford greater opportunity for legitimate variations in concepts and principles to be grasped.

A Cross-Cultural Perspective

The field of cross-cultural psychology is one in which the uniformity-variety issue is confronted directly and a resolution is attempted. The ultimate goal in cross-cultural psychology is no different from the goal of psychology in general: to build theory in personality, cognition, child development, psychopathology, and other realms of human behavior. However, unlike psychology in general, belief in the universal applicability of Western principles and paradigms has been set aside. In its place is the knowledge that social context and culture play a large role in shaping the behaviors and cognitions of any group of people.

Cross-cultural psychologists routinely assume the existence of cultural differences, as well as cross-cultural continuities, and have developed a methodology to assess cultural influences on behavior and cognition. Thus far they have applied this methodology almost entirely to cultural groups that speak different languages and live in different nations. However, the methods do not require such gross distinctions and are equally applicable even under

conditions of considerable cultural overlap. By allowing the possibil
cultural variety, but not demanding it, cross-cultural strategies can docu...
cultural similarities and differences as to both nature extent. Inasmuch as
psychologists increasingly seek to explain black-white differences in the
United States in cultural terms, it is timely to turn to the cross-cultural field
for conceptual and methodological guidance.

As psychologists have attempted cross-cultural work, they have seen ever
more complicated problems reveal themselves in successive layers. it was
recognized early that straightforward application of Western-derived measures to non-Western populations was a false procedure. However, the most
obviously needed adaptation, i.e., allowing for language differences, was
increasingly seen to offer only a partial solution. On the effectiveness of one
proposed strategy, that of using pictures of objects on tests to avoid language
altogether, Price-Williams (1975) quotes a perceptive early critic, Biesheuvel,
"To make the object pictured culturally meaningful is of little avail, if
pictorial presentation itself is unfamiliar, and if it does not invoke the attitude
of interpretation which a European group automatically assumes" (p. 52).
Such difficulties in guaranteeing that test materials are used similarly by
respondents who have had roughly similar prior exposure may be termed
problems of *stimulus familiarity*. As indicated above by Biescheuvel, not only
the actual stimulus, but also the mode and context of presentation, may be
unfamiliar to a particular cultural group, leading to nonequivalences that are
easily overlooked.

Another important category of nonequivalence haunts cross-cultural
research. Rarely are psychologists interested in a test stimulus per se; rather,
they are interested in the stimulus as an indicator of an abstract category or
concept. How can the researcher guarantee that a particular empirical
stimulus refers cross-culturally to equivalent concepts? A less precise but
more familiar way of posing this question is to ask whether a test item means
the same thing outside of the culture where the test was developed. As
highlighted by Berry (1969), this general problem is a classical one in the
history of anthropology. If every culture provides its own distinctive frame of
reference, how does the scientist conduct meaningful cross-cultural comparisons? The available solutions seemed to involve rejecting comparisons
altogether, on grounds that cultural products could only be understood
within their cultural contexts, or conducting apparently fruitful comparisons
without certain knowledge that the basis for comparison was nonethnocentric. This problem has been dubbed the Malinowskian Dilemma (Berry,
1969). The resolution to this dilemma awaited a culturally transcendent
schema for establishing the equivalence of institutions and behaviors.

By shifting attention away from human institutions themselves, and onto
the issues in human existence the institutions address, Goldschmidt (1966)
provided anthropologists with a universal framework for comparison. He

argued that certain human problems are invariant, although the functionally equivalent modes of response to these problems may be quite varied. According to Goldschmidt, common societal functions relate to the fulfillment of biologically rooted needs and to the maintenance of social processes important for collaboration in pursuit of need satisfaction.

Berry (1969) has applied this framework to the realm of psychological conceptualization and measurement: "(1) Aspects of behavior settings may be compared only when they can be shown to be *functionally equivalent,* in the sense that the aspect of behaviour in question is an attempted solution to one of Goldschmidt's recurrent problems. (2) When aspects of behaviour occurring in differing behaviour settings are *functionally equivalent,* a comparative descriptive framework, valid for both behaviour settings can then be generated from an internal description of behaviour within each setting. (3) Only when *both* these conditions are met may one attempt to construct and apply instruments to gauge behaviour in the two settings. This attempt must also satisfy the criterion that the instruments are *conceptually equivalent* to individuals in the two setting" (p. 122).

Brislin (1976) has described another approach to the development of psychological measures that are true cultural analogues. The units of measurement are not behaviors, but items and scales provisionally adopted as indicators of abstract categories or concepts. Equivalence is defined empirically by the pattern of interrelationships obtained between two test items or scales that are specific to different cultures and other indicators of the same concept that have been shown to be culturally invariant. The two culture-specific items need not correlate with each other, since each is irrelevant in the other culture. However, both items must correlate with the culturally invariant indicators to be considered equivalent.

For both items and scales, the underlying logic of this strategy corresponds to that underlying construct validation within a single culture. An accepted procedure for validating an instrument, construct validity involves analyzing the meaning of test scores in terms of interrelationships among constructs and related behavior. "In order to show that a given construct applies to a test, it is necessary to derive hypotheses about test behavior from theory related to the construct, and to verify them experimentally. The theory of 'anxiety' accepted by the tester (attempting to validate an anxiety test) might include such expectations as the following: Anxiety increases when subjects are exposed to a threat of electric shock; neurotics are more anxious than non-neurotics; anxiety is lowered by a certain drug; anxious persons set high goals for themselves. Each of these expectations can be tested by an experiment or statistical study" (Cronbach, 1970, p. 123).

The strategies outlined by Brislin and Berry are distinct approaches to the problem of cross-cultural equivalence. Both attempt to enable psychologists not to be misled by the fact that, cross-culturally, the same response may have different meanings and different responses may have the same meaning. At the heart of Berry's approach lies an analysis of psychological and social tasks and a comparison of whether culture-bound behaviors engage the same or different tasks. Brislin, on the other hand, concentrates on the conceptual reference of behavior: Culture-bound responses are determined to be expressions of the same or different constructs.

Although the concepts of equivalence outlines above are clearly desirable, it is not apparent how they may be attained. One broad strategy attempts to unite two formerly divergent traditions in anthropology into a framework for cross-culturally valid, empirically based theory building—an approach that insists upon understanding every culture on its own terms, the *emic* approach, and a second perspective that directs its attention toward forming general theories about human nature applicable in a number of cultures, the *etic* approach. The terms emic and etic come from a distinction in linguistics between phonemics, the study of the sounds used in a particular language, and phonetics, the development of a general system taking into account all meaningful sounds in all languages. Berry was the first to apply these formerly anthropological principles to psychological research. His distinction between the two approaches is presented in Table 8.1.

Table 8.1
Definition of the Emic and Etic Approaches According to Berry

Emic Approach	Etic Approach
Studies behavior from within the system.	Studies behavior from a position outside the system.
Examines only one culture.	Examines many cultures, comparing them.
Structure discovered by the analyst.	Structure created by the analyst.
Criteria relative to internal characteristics.	Criteria are considered absolute or universal.

In sum, he proposes the following research model:

      1. Aspects of behavior may be compared only when functional equivalence of the behaviors can be demonstrated.

2. Descriptive categories derived from past research, perhaps in only one culture, can then be tentatively applied to the behavior in the other culture (imposed etic).

3. The imposed descriptive categories must be modified so that they become an adequate description from within that culture (emic).

4. Shared categories can then be used to build up new categories valid for both systems (derived etic) and can be expanded until they constitute a universal.

5. New instruments and research techniques can be devised and validated using the derived etic as a conceptual base, and they must be equivalent in meaning to each of the cultures under study. (Berry, 1969; Brislin, Lonner, and Thorndike, 1973).

An example that is concise and specific may illustrate the utility of this model. Consider a researcher interested in the in-group/out-group distinction and the differences in reactions to people who are classified as in-group or out-group members. Having developed certain theoretical consequences of this distinction, the researcher may wonder about the universality of these propositions. He or she might select Greece as a second culture to begin cross-cultural investigation, a choice that would lead to the discovery of cultural differences in this area of interpersonal relations. "In the United States it is well known that an in-group consists of family, close friends, and (if a choice is demanded between other Americans and visitors to the United States) fellow countrymen. In Greece, however, the 'in-group' consists of family, close friends, and visitors, but excludes other Greeks; the latter are part of an individual's out-group" (Brislin, 1976, pp. 217-18). (See Triandis, 1972, for a detailed, empirical consideration of aspects of Greek versus U.S. systems of belief.)

If our psychologist contemplating cross-cultural exploration of in-group/out-group theory were without this knowledge, it would still be possible for him or her to capture the existing cultural variation, by following the outline provided by Berry. First, from interviews with Greek citizens and psychologists, and from various naturalistic accounts of Greek culture, the researcher would demonstrate that Greeks recognize a distinction paralleling that of in-group/out-group as found among Americans. The critical similarity needed would be functional equivalence, that the two concepts served similar psychological needs and purposes. If, for example, Greeks felt closely, psychologically bound to all of humankind, no functional equivalent would exist. Second, the U.S. concept of in-group would then be tried tentatively in preliminary studies as an imposed etic. If done sensitively, this stage of investigation would reveal that fellow countrymen are in-group members and visitors out-group members among Americans, but that the reverse is true among Greeks. A new emic category schema for Greeks would thereby be created from the imposed etic. Third, instruments would be devised accordingly. For example, a test measuring "strength of out-group rejection" would include questions concerning rejection of foreign visitors on the U.S. version. Another requirement at this third step would be conceptual equivalence, involving establishing that the different test items have comparable meanings to Greeks and Americans.

Joining the procedures proposed by Brislin to those of Berry just described, we would require another stage of investigation to establish what we have called theoretical equivalence. At this added stage, the test of "out-group rejection" would be administered in U.S. and Greek forms to samples from both populations. Intercorrelations among items would be computed, and a certain pattern of interrelationships expected. Among the resulting relationships, a set of out-group rejection items should intercorrelate highly in both Greek and U.S. samples. However, the rejection of the "visitors" item should correlate discriminatively, relating to this common core for the Greek sample but not for the U.S. sample.

An alternative strategy for constructing an out-group rejection scale for use with Greeks might also have been followed. A scale developed among Americans, and therefore containing questions concerning rejection of foreign visitors, could simply be translated and administered to a large, representative sample of Greeks. Upon comparing Greek and U.S. group scores, the researcher would observe a discrepancy, giving the appearance of less out-group rejection on the part of Greeks, but resulting actually from Greek nonendorsement of inappropriate items pertaining to what is actually an in-group for them, i.e., foreign visitors.

At this point, there is little basis to detect the cross-cultural invalidity of the improper items. But attempts to insure culture-fair assessment might still proceed. If the plausible assumptions were made that Greeks should be no less out-group rejecting than Americans, and that lower scores by Greeks were a product of reluctance to disclose disapproval of others, or some other response-biasing artifact, the researcher might attempt to control the obtained differences in scores by statistical means. This often involves identifying test items that discriminate between Greeks and Americans and assembling from them a new scale for use in subsequent adjustment of out-group rejection measurements. Eventually, those tested would have their out-group rejection scores raised according to their score on the supplemental Greek-U.S. scale. This procedure modeled after the suppressor variable method of improving test validity (e.g., Wiggins, 1973), gives the appearance of being not only rigorous and fair, but even enlightening in revealing contrasting features of Greek versus U.S. culture. However, it is important to examine whether the scores resulting from this procedure guarantee accurate measurements of out-group rejection. Actual cross-cultural work supplies us with critical information that items concerning rejection of Greeks should have replaced those concerning rejection of foreign visitors. Does the correction scheme outlined above provide information about scores on the missing but appropriate items? It does not; it boosts the scores of Greeks according to how much they respond like most Greeks and, in turn, how much they regard Greeks as out-group members, but not according to how much they reject the out-group. All completely acculturated Greeks would receive the same corrective adjustment; individual differences in the evaluated dimension would be lost and only found if information contained in the appropriate items could be substituted.

An essential shortcoming of this strategy is an assumption that in a second culture for cross-cultural assessment the same concept as in the first culture is being measured, although possibly inaccurately. It does not allow for the alternative possibility of a test having different cross-cultural meaning and measuring the wrong thing. Both before and after correction, the test is an imposed etic. We have explained this method of scale refinement at length because it will appear again, buttressing claims of culturally responsive assessment in two areas: intelligence and personality.

For specific techniques, in applying the emic-etic framework to research and the problems associated with these techniques, Brislin, Lonner, and Thorndike (1973) is an extremely useful guide. Issues of translation and back-translation, decentering survey methods, and statistical methods are discussed in detail. Lonner (1975) in a later publication notes that the methods used in cross-cultural psychology differ from traditional psychology methodology in only three major ways: (1) sampling, (2) establishing equivalence conceptually (constructs across cultures) and linguistically (translation), and (3) synchronizing anthropological material with psychological precedents as a rationale for research. The goal is to eliminate any plausible rival hypotheses to the proposed rationale. It is these three principles that identify cross-cultural research as such and that psychologists must now apply to the assessment of minority groups in the United States.

OBJECTIVE ASSESSMENT OF INTELLIGENCE:
THE SYSTEM OF MULTICULTURAL PLURALISTIC ASSESSMENT

The theoretical and practical objections voiced by minority critics come into stark focus in the area of intelligence testing. At the center of the IQ controversy stands the simple fact that blacks as a group score one standard deviation below whites as a group. Both sides in this controversy, the geneticists (Jensen, 1969; Herrnstein, 1971) and the environmentalists (Kamin, 1974; Block and Dworkin, 1976) possess certain shared assumptions about the meaning of intelligence and about the nature of environmental influences. The cross-cultural perspective highlights these assumptions by comparing them with alternative possibilities that are hidden from a monocultural point of view.

In this section, we will examine the problem of providing culturally-fair assessment in the area of intelligence, a standard domain of clinical concern. Academic and political debate over intelligence testing has carried into the courtroom, where the issues and policy implications have been clearly drawn. One outcome of this legal confrontation has been the development of alternative methods of evaluation that promise culturally-fair results. The System of Multicultural Pluralistic Assessment, the SOMPA, (Mercer and Lewis, 1978) is perhaps the most widely accepted of these new approaches to multicultural evaluation. Because of its explicit foundation in cultural relativity, as well as its ever increasing popularity, the SOMPA will serve as the focus of our discussion. We hope to contrast monocultural and pluralistic paradigms as embodied in actual clinical instruments and, also, to demonstrate that cultural relativity is a matter of degree.

Relatively familiar procedures comprise the SOMPA, belying its innovative character. Both the child being assessed and his or her parent serve as sources of information. In a parent interview, the assessor administers: (1) the Adaptive Behavior Inventory for Children, a measure of performance of social, nonacademic roles (the subscales are: Family, Community, Peer Relations, Nonacademic School Rules, Earner/Consumer, Self-Maintenance), (2) the Socio-Cultural Scales, measures of the socioeconomic circumstances of the child's family (the subscales are: Family Size, Family Structure, Socioeconomic Status, Urban Acculturation), and (3) the Health History Inventories, measures of past and current physical health. In testing sessions with the child, the assessor administers: (1) the WISC-R, a standard measure of IQ, (2) the Bender Visual Motor Gestalt Test, a measure of perceptual motor integrity, (3) physical dexterity tasks, measures of fine and gross motor coordination and balance, (4) a visual acuity test and (5) an auditory acuity test. Weight and height also are taken and combined in a weight by height index of overall physical thriving.

What distinguishes the SOMPA from most conventional psychological tests is a multifaceted, controversial, conceptual framework. To establish the rationale for the SOMPA, Mercer and Lewis (1978) illuminate the ideological matrix of intelligence testing. They identify two underlying models of minority and minority group relations: Anglo Conformity and Cultural Pluralism. The Anglo Conformity model emphasizes the cultural hegemony achieved by early Western European immigrants to the United States, whose institutions, values, customs, and language are asserted to have displaced the cultural forms of other groups. The Cultural Pluralism model emphasizes the enduring cultural integrity of non-Anglo ethnic groups. Related to each model, but distinguishable from it, is a corresponding political ideology. One ideology, that of Anglization, holds that the English language and Anglo culture are superior and should be perpetuated as matters of public policy. An alternating ideology, that of cultural democracy, holds that all languages and cultures are equal and merit support through public policy.

Bridging the gap between social philosophy and assessment technology, Mercer and Lewis delineate four specific consequences of Anglo Conformity ideology on conventional testing practices. The first identified consequence is reliance on the English language and Anglo cultural content to form test items, a legitimate practice only if one assumes that non-Anglo children have had equal exposure and incentive to learn the tested material. The second identified consequence is use of a single, largely Anglo distribution of test scores as the reference group in making normative comparisons of individual performance. The third identified consequence affects psychologists' definitions of several critical terms: validity, fairness, and bias. Their position is somewhat unclear, but Mercer and Lewis seem to be saying that psychometrists' technical definitions of these terms are misleading because they ignore cultural variables, both as determinants of test performance and as value judgments in selecting criteria for test validation. The fourth identified consequence of Anglo Conformity assumptions is to draw an unjustified distinction between intelligence and other tests of aptitude, on the one hand, and tests of achievement, on the other. Mercer and Lewis join ranks with the increasing number of psychologists who maintain that, because they rely on prior experience with the tested skills and knowledge, all tests are achievement tests. The fifth identified consequence of Anglo Conformity is that it leads to confusion of the diagnostic and prognostic functions of assessment information. Whereas a low IQ score is usually used diagnostically, to indicate inferior intellect, it should properly be used prognostically, to indicate future academic problems in school. The latter interpretation suggests only a probable outcome and leaves the matter of explanation open to further inquiry.

How does psychological assessment proceed from a stance of Cultural Pluralism? Mercer and Lewis propose a framework for pluralistic assessment that is the inverse of Anglo Conformity. Their requirements are: (1) multilingual, multicultural test content, (2) multiple norms, (3) test validation using multicultural criteria, (4) treatment of all tests as measures of learned behavior, with the result that the distinction between aptitude tests and achievement tests vanishes, (5) IQ test scores used prognostically and diagnostic inferences resorted to only under specially arranged circumstances.

The SOMPA was designed in full accord with several of these pluralistic assessment principles but only in partial accord with others. To score the Adaptive Behavior Inventory for Children and the WISC-R, multiple norms have been provided. The Socio-Cultural Scales and WISC-R are scored twice, in relation to two sets of norms. First the assessor compares the child's scores with a black, Hispanic, or white distribution of scores, depending on the child's ethnic group memberhsip. His or her scores are then compared with a second set of norms for the majority culture; this comparison indicates where the child will stand in the usual school situation.

With the WISC-R, the first normative comparison, using the standard WISC-R normative distribution, yields the School Functioning Level (SFL), an index of the child's prospects for success in conventional Anglocentric schools. The second comparison is unorthodox; it uses the Socio-Cultural Scales described above to control for environmental differences in children's upbringings. From an assessee's sociocultural scores, his or her IQ is predicted in a multiple regression equation, and the deviation from the predicted level is noted. Whatever deviation occurs is considered an indicator of intellectual functioning that holds environmental differences constant. By means of this statistical control, what is considered typical functioning for a child depends on the functioning of socioculturally-comparable children. Therefore, departures from typical performance are argued to reflect inherent capacity and are considered a valid basis for inferring learning potential. The scores resulting from manipulations are termed Estimated Learning Potential (ELP). Because the ELP and the Socio-Cultural Scales allow for comparisons within more homogeneous normative subgroups, they are identified with a Pluralistic Model for assessment.

Clearly, the SOMPA was designed to be responsive to cultural differences, and we may now turn to consideration of how well it has succeeded. To do this, we must clarify which aspects are considered culturally responsive and why.

By design, several parts of the battery evaluate assessee behavior from the context of the enveloping Anglo culture and its somewhat unavoidable standards. The Adaptive Behavior Scale for Children, and the WISC-R IQ interpreted using standard norms (the ELP), both appear under the Social System Model. Identifying them with this model, instead of with the Socio-Cultural Model, constitutes a disavowal of any cross-cultural justification for their use.

It is the Socio-Cultural Scales that are by expressed intent cross-cultural. In devising them, Mercer and Lewis sought environmental correlates of IQ (e.g., family size, SES) and composed scales from the pool of items that proved effective predictors. That social factors are indeed related to IQ is a long established fact. The contribution of Mercer and Lewis has been to insist that such factors are environmental and not genetic and to calculate IQ by subtracting out their influence as a matter of standard practice.

But what is the role of culture in such a scheme? To bolster their assumption that interethnic IQ discrepancies are rooted in environment and not heredity, Mercer and Lewis have staked out an ideology underscoring general interethnic differences and calling them cultural. To critics from a genetic perspective who challenge their environmental explanation and statistical control of these differences, they attribute an Anglo Conformity set of beliefs. Thus, culture is a major component of an ideological counter-weight. However, it is unclear how integral the factors labeled cultural are, how adequate a description they provide, and indeed whether they are even best characterized as cultural.

Upon closer examination, it appears that the Mercer and Lewis position fails to distinguish between *culture* and *social environment*. One needs only an environmental predilection to support Mercer's view, not a cultural one. Thus, writing on the meaning of IQ scores, David McClelland (1973) mounts a formulation of IQ scores remarkably similar to Mercer and Lewis—without recourse to cultural explanations.

Statistical control for environmental differences is useful because it places on systematic footing a practice that many clinicians now perform intuitively—adjusting their interpretation of measured IQ to allow for socioeconomic background. However, if we consider interethnic differences as truly cultural, in what sense does this modification engender cross-cultural validity? Those whose scores depart from Anglo scores on the Socio-Cultural Scales are, by definition. different from Anglo's in some IQ-related way. But if a group of such persons constitutes a distinguishable culture, the question of analogous measurement remains. Directly put, one issue is: Are the scores obtained from statistical adjustment identical to those that would have been obtained from a test constructed and validated within the culture being corrected for?

Scores produced by this correction and by a truly analogous test may be equivalent but they need not be. As illustrated in our previous presentation of a hypothetical out-group rejection scale, statistical allowance for group differences in test scores was inaccurate and misleading if the test happens to be measuring different things within the groups. The cross-cultural meaning of a test—its conceptual and functional equivalence—is avoided by statistical corrections to allow for the extent of assimilation among those tested.

The approach embodied in the SOMPA may be contrasted with the cross-cultural research methodology presented earlier. Like Mercer and Lewis, cross-cultural psychologists face the paramount challenge of ensuring that assessment results are comparable; they must prove that identical scores will have identical meaning across cultural boundaries. Central to the cross-cultural approach, and distinguishing it from the SOMPA, is an emphasis on conceptual equivalence—the requirement that any concrete event alleged to represent a particular concept show a predictable pattern of interrelationships with other variables. Before a test item or scale is considered equivalent in two cultures, it must be linked to the same concept in empirical research.

Applied to the assessment problem grappled with by Mercer and Lewis, a cross-cultural strategy would have taken a somewhat different course. Investigators would begin by analyzing the concepts being assessed: intelligence, social adjustment, family acculturation, and physical health. Items and tasks as prospective indicators might initially be borrowed from the culture of the investigator and tried out under conditions of varying cultures. Items purportedly indicative of social adjustment, for example, would be included in an initial pool of prospective indicators. Of central importance would be evaluating the cross-cultural conceptual equivalence of these items by intercorrelating them with other items and with outside criteria.

The SOMPA is an important innovation. For the first time, psychological evaluators can formally adjust for differences in children's backgrounds when making judgments about competence. In the past, sensitive assessors have doubtless made such allowances using clinical judgment. But they are now empirically based and a standard feature of the scoring system. Despite these successes, however, the SOMPA has little to say about culture; as a model of cross-cultural assessment it falls short of its promise.

OBJECTIVE ASSESSMENT OF PSYCHOPATHOLOGY: THE MMPI

The second area of assessment to be considered is objective assessment of psychopathology. The Minnesota Multiphasic Personality Inventory (the MMPI) continues to be the most widely used inventory and to generate the largest number of research references since its inception; and we have chosen it as our focus. Because of its popularity, it has inevitably come under fine scrutiny and broad criticism from all directions. Some issues appear to have been satisfactorily resolved in favor of the MMPI, for instance, whether responses to MMPI items are a reaction to the content of the item, or a function of social desirability, or an acquiescence response tendency (Gynther, 1972a). Others continue to be controversial. Rodgers (1972), in a review of the MMPI for Buros: *The Seventh Mental Measurements Yearbook,* comments at length on psychometric considerations that potentially invalidate use of the MMPI in a number of situations. Although the MMPI was conceptually and metrically developed and validated as a psychiatric nosologic categorizing device, it is often used to make judgments about personality. Its scale development focused on the dichotomous discrimination of a pathology group from a normal group, within a white, rural, Midwestern population. There is no real evidence that the scale scores discriminate the degrees along each dimension among normal groups.

There are also problems with the clinical interpretation of the MMPI. Each scale was validated as an independent measure, since the classifications originally were conceived of as mutually exclusive. Yet, in practice, test-takers often have elevated scores on two or more scales simultaneously, in part because of the overlap of items between the scales. Diagnosticians are forced to interpret profiles in ways that were not anticipated by the early developers of the MMPI. Despite these problems, Rodgers and numerous others have concluded that the MMPI in fact works so well that one can afford to overlook its psychometric deficiencies.

The problems of the interpretation of the MMPI with black subjects are not so easily ignored. Jones (1978) notes that the investigation of black-white personality differences have been primarily tied to the MMPI. If this is the case, blacks must especially be concerned about the implications of pathology and maladjustment that are inherent in such comparisons, given that the samples on which the MMPI was normed were exclusively white and that the instrument is designed to measure symptomatology. Concerns of this nature have been legitimized by the fact that blacks from normal and psychiatric or inmate populations have consistently had significantly higher scores on Scales F (Validity), 8 (Schizophrenia), and 9 (Mania) (Gynther, 1972b). Analyses of MMPI items that discriminated between blacks and whites have shown ever more striking results, with up to 39 percent of MMPI items shown to be sensitive to race differences (Harrison and Kass, 1967). These authors conclude that there may be a canceling out process of items within each scale, and they further report that 32 percent of the discriminating items appear on none of the clinical scales, with the implication that they are responsive to cultural differences rather than to the incidence of pathology. A number of more recent studies have confirmed black-white differences on the MMPI, using both scale comparisons and item analyses (Costello, Tiffany, and Gier, 1972; Costello, Fine, and Blau, 1973; Cowan, Watkins, and Davis, 1975; Davis, 1975; Davis and Jones, 1974; Witt and Gynther, 1975).

Gynther (1972b) lists five possibilities that may account for the differences noted above. The first, and most common, is the conclusion that blacks are simply more maladjusted than whites, based on the clinical and actuarial analysis of MMPI profiles. Recently, the argument has been made by implication that blacks deny this possbility out of undue sensitivity or racial pride (Shore, 1976). However, Gynther points out that there are absolutely no external validating criteria to support this conclusion. While peer ratings, professional assessments, Q-sorts, and actuarial schemes have been amassed for validating the diagnoses of whites, no such data has been gathered for blacks. Further, actuarial analyses by Gynther and his associates have shown that a given profile or code type may have different behavioral referrents (as evidenced by item analyses) for blacks and whites (Gynther, Altman, and Warbin, 1973).

Findings such as this are particularly important from a cross-cultural perspective, for they are examining the notion of the functional equivalence of diagnostic categories across cultures and the conceptual equivalences of items used to assign membership in a category. Gynther establishes definitively that conceptual equivalence of MMPI items across groups does not exist and that the conceptual equivalence of diagnostic categories one assumed by the pattern of interrelationships among specific variables cannot be assumed and has yet to be adequately tested. Gynther and Witt (1976) found their highly educated, professional black group to give higher endorsement to Harrison and Kass' "black" items than did their more representative black sample, who were lower on indices of education and occupation in a within-group study of normal blacks.

The evidence, therefore, is mixed, and, as Gynther acknowledges, explanations of cultural differences in values and behaviors are largely post hoc. This is because the MMPI is a monocultural device, which is assumed to be universal, and functions as an assumed rather than a "derived" etic with groups other than its normative sample. The method suggested by cross-cultural researchers, if applied here, would utilize the MMPI as an "imposed etic," a temporarily useful device while the process of cross-validating it in other cultures takes place.

The remaining explanations suggested by Gynther refer explicitly to the concept of conceptual equivalence of specific items rather than the more global cultural values discussed above. These are differences in scale composition, differential social desirability of the items for blacks and whites, and differences in the connotative meanings of key words and phrases. On the issue of scale composiiton, Gynther notes that the F (Validity), 8 (Schizophrenia), 9 (Mania), and 3 (Hysteria) scales are particularly open to question, with blacks endorsing items with much more frequency on all but Scale 3.

Second of Gynther's possible explanations for black-white differences on the MMPI is the notion of cultural differences between blacks and whites reflected in different values, interests, and expectations. The evidence found by Harrison and Kass (1967) that one-third of their race-sensitive items were not on any clinical scale is significant support for this conclusion. In a factor analysis of these items, the major factors were estrangement, impulse-ridden fantasy, self-consciousness, dislike of school, religiosity, romantic interest, and cynicism—factors that seem to reflect attitudes and values rather than psychopathology.

Davis and his associates have addressed this issue from a perspective of the acculturation of the black middle class, finding in their psychiatric patient samples that highly educated blacks (12 years or more) did not score differently from whites, although poorly educated blacks did (Davis and Jones, 1974; Davis, 1975). This conclusion is supported by a second analysis of the Harrison and Kass data (1968), finding that northern black women were halfway between southern black women and northern whites on most personality dimensions. However, Costello, Fine, and Blau (1973) found significant differences between black and white females, although not between males, despite rigorous subject matching of their psychiatric patient and inmate samples on age and SES.

Gynther conducted the only social desirability research available comparing blacks and whites for this review (1972b). He obtained ratings of the 144 most discriminating items and compared these with black-white rates of endorsement from the Harrison and Kass (1967) data. Of these items he found 48 significant differences in the social desirability ratings, 75 percent of which were in the predicted direction.

The possible explanation of differences in connotative meaning of items is taken from cross-cultural research with the Semantic Differential Scale (Snider and Osgood, 1969). Some support for this hypothesis comes from a study by Witt and Gynther (1975), who had black and white subjects rate 13 of the Harrison and Kass race-sensitive items in the Semantic Differential. Ten of the 13 items were rated more favorably on the evaluative (E) dimension of the Semantic Differential by blacks. These had to do with the cynicism, estrangement, and religiosity factors found by Harrison and Kass (1967). Seven of the cynical and estranged factor items were rated more favorably by men than by women. In sum, there is solid support, although not definitive because of insufficient research, for the proposition that items and scales on the MMPI might be conceptually unequivalent for blacks and whites.

Costello (1977) has attempted to deal with this issue through the initial construction of a Black-White Scale of the MMPI, which would parallel use of the K Scale as a correction factor. Compiling 32 items that have shown themselves to be discriminating from the results of six comparative studies, he has carried out preliminary cross validation of the scale on both a psychiatric and a normal sample from the black population. As might be expected from the fact the selection of items was made from studies of psychiatric populations, he has found more efficient classification of race in his psychiatric than in his normal population.

Costello's Black-White Scale is conceptually equivalent to the correction factor (K Scale) and also, if less apparently, to the Socio-Cultural Scales of the SOMPA. This mode of accommodating assessment to racial differences was investigated in the hypothetical Greek-U.S. scale noted earlier and its limitations discussed. At the heart of such corrections lies a critical assumption—that the scale receiving an adjustment has the same meaning and empirical correlates among blacks and whites. Stated more precisely, the underlying premise is one of functional and conceptual equivalence. But these are empirical issues and their presumptive resolution seems unnecessary and, given the above mentioned data suggesting conceptual nonequivalence of MMPI items, hazardous as well.

The Black-White Scale may be useful in the short term for making interpretive adjustments to allow for known differences; however, it must be seen as a stopgap measure. In the long run, it leaves unanswered all the pertinent questions raised by both cross-cultural and environmentalist psychologists alike. We still do not know whether the items that comprise the scale reflect an underlying construct or category that is culturally determined and yet to be defined. We do not know whether the items are conceptually equivalent in measuring some identified construct, and the differences that emerge reflect a cultural difference in the expression of that construct, or whether the items are simply meaningless to blacks. Finally, we do not know whether these differences are due to genuine cultural influences on response patterns, or to differential rates of pathology in the black and white communities. The Costello Black-White Scale does not ask these questions; it merely corrects for them. The logical extension of this scale could very well be the following: If one subtracts a factor of x from the score of a black male, his profile is then "as good" as if it were of a white. One can conclude with confidence that the MMPI has never established its validity as a diagnostic or assessment instrument with blacks.

Adoption of the research methodology proposed by Berry (1969) and Brislin, Lonner, and Thorndike (1973) would require the establishment of base rates for the incidence of Schizophrenia, Mania, and other diagnostic categories in the black population and norms for the validity of personality dimensions also measured by the MMPI in the black population. Gynther's actuarial analyses are an important step in this direction. Gynther (1972a) suggests that new scale development should take place based on the dichotomous discrimination of items of a pathology black group from a normal black group, essentially the same method used in the original development of the MMPI. Based on further research into differences in the connotative meanings of items, the item composition of certain scales might have to be changed to ensure conceptual equivalence across both cultures.

The result would be a step further than Gynther's (1972a) suggestion for the construction of a new MMPI for blacks. He conceives of a black MMPI using the current set of items and scale labels, although combined differently. A genuinely cross-cultural approach to the revision of the MMPI would perhaps involve the techniques of back-translation and decentering for specific items to ensure valid items in both cultures (Brislin, Lonner, and Thorndike, 1973). Only then could one determine whether the personality configuration of blacks is different from whites and the incidence of various categories of psychopathology greater or less than among whites.

Jones' (1978) study of San Francisco Bay area college students is a significant step toward identifying dimensions on which the personality configuration of blacks may be different from whites. However, we still do not know the extent to which the items used in the Coping and Defense Scales (many of which are derived from the MMPI) are conceptually equivalent for both groups. To take one hypothetical example, items under "conventional mores" may have different connotative meanings to both groups. The debate on black-white differences in the personality and psychopathology continues unabated, but the relevant research addressing this issue is practically nonexistent. Use of the cross-cultural method, while undoubtedly lengthy and somewhat cumbersome, would finally put to rest some of these issues.

PROJECTIVE ASSESSMENT OF PERSONALITY: THE TAT

The projective method of personality assessment rests on the assumption that the more unstructured methods of assessment, those that present the individual with highly ambiguous or inherently meaningless stimuli, obtain a qualitatively richer yield of the unique aspects of the individual personality. Careful interpretation of the data presumably allows clinicians to make inferences about the deep rather than surface structure of personality: the individual's needs, fears, conflicts, and ego-defensive mechanisms and other dynamic aspects of personality. In addition to eliciting the qualitative, dynamic aspects of personality, most projective techniques attempt to organize this data into a standardized, quantifiable form, interpretable in systematic, universal ways. Underlying this effort is the basic psychological endeavor, the discovery of universal principles of human behavior.

The projective method attempts to satisfy the need for both clinical and psychometric analyses of personality and is vulnerable to criticism on both fronts. On the clinical side, critics have contended that a projective test record cannot be considered a sufficient sample of behavior from which to make judgments of deep, often unconscious, personality structure; nor can it be assumed that it taps either the same or equivalent psychological determinants across ethnic groups, cultures, or socioeconomic status (Holtzman, 1980).

From a psychometric perspective, the development of standardized projective measurement has proven difficult, if not impossible. Holtzman traces many of the methodological problems to the free response nature of the projective test. Transforming the test protocol into objective scores frequently requires the imposition of arbitrary categories of response type. Validity and reliability over time are not easily established. The examiner, the social context, and other non-test-related stimuli exert a powerful, and often unmeasurable, influence over the response of the individual. And, as further noted by Holtzman, the transformation of the test into an objective instrument often means the loss of those projective qualities that made it unique and valuable to the clinician. These are issues that make any discussion of projective methodologies necessarily limited in scope and open to controversy. With the field of projective assessment vulnerable to the criticisms that, as a methodology, it is unsound and unreliable, and that even its own theoretical rationale is as yet empirically untested, it may seem all the more hazardous to extend an imperfect assessment methodology for cross-cultural use.

Projective techniques have found relatively wide use by anthropologists in their cross-cultural investigation of culture and personality. The Rorschach and the TAT were particularly valued because of their psychoanalytic theoretical foundations and the opportunity to "test" the universality of Freudian concepts. These applications of the projective method have encountered the special problems of cross-cultural research. These include inconsistent definitions of "personality" variables and, therefore, the lack of comparability across experiments; the use of culture-bound stimuli such as pictures or words, leading to difficulties in establishing semantic equivalence; the lack of equivalence in the meaning of the testing situation, the interaction with the examiner, and other factors in the complex administration of projective techniques; and the lack of conceptual equivalence in the imposed scoring categories and quantification of the data, leading often to gross, culture-bound errors in interpretation (Holtzman, 1980).

Despite these recognized drawbacks in both the clinical and cross-cultural use of projective techniques, they have remained attractive instruments for the investigation of personality in both arenas. The remainder of this section on the cross-cultural application of projectives will focus on the TAT, because of the development of a small body of literature on its validity with blacks.

The TAT more than other projective instruments has been recognized as culture bound, and it has been adapted widely for use with different cultures, ages, sexes, occupational groups, etc. Despite this fact, the appearance of a modified TAT for use with blacks (Thompson, 1949) met with something akin to outrage from reviewers (Riess, Schwartz, and Cottingham, 1950; Korchin, Mitchell, and Meltzoff, 1950; Schwartz, Riess, and Cottingham, 1951). Many of their objections were justified on theoretical and psychometric grounds, others seemed to arise out of reticence to consider cultural variability between blacks and whites (Abel, 1973; Korchin Mitchell, and Meltzoff, 1950). Despite the fact that the Thompson TAT was never in general use as an alternative instrument, and the controversy surrounding its publication has long since died down, we will revive it briefly in this section for the sake of discussion of the cross-cultural method.

Thompson developed his modification of the TAT to test a hypothesis that black subjects did not identify with the white stimulus figures of the Murray TAT, assuming that this lack of identification led to an inhibition of self-disclosure manifested in low productivity on the protocols. Thompson substituted black figures in the male series of the Murray TAT (M-TAT), leaving the background situations and instructions for the most part unchanged. Using the criteria of number of words produced per story, he administered both sets of pictures to 26 black male veterans of Dillard

University, varying the order of presentation and the time interval between administrations. He found that all groups were significantly more productive to the Thompson TAT (T-TAT), concluding that these pictures produced more empathy in blacks.

Clearly, Thompson's study falls far short of minimum standards of experimental rigor, and the conclusions he draws are not supported by his data. Yet, in their follow-up and rebuttal studies, Thompson's supporters and critics often regrettably fell prey to using the same experimentally unsound methodologies, both from a psychometric and a cross-cultural perspective. As Korchin, Mitchell, and Meltzoff (1950) correctly point out, Thompson's use of a word count as a measure of productivity and, thereby, as an indirect measure of identification, is invalid. Yet, a number of researchers used the same or similar criteria (Riess, Schwartz, and Cottingham, 1950; Mitchell, 1950; Schwartz, Riess, and Cottingham, 1951; Bailey and Green, 1977). From a design point of view, Thompson makes a number of unsupported assumptions about the relationship between self-disclosure and identification, also repeated by some of the above critics. This inferred relationship is disputed by at least one study, which inferred a trend toward less ego defensiveness (as measured by verbal productivity, vagueness, uncertainty, and the offering of alternatives to the main story) accompanying greater remoteness of identification (Cook, 1953). This study has its own difficulties, in that the "remoteness of identification" measured is one-directional, based on the increased verbal productivity of white subjects to the T-TAT but not a similar response of black subjects to the M-TAT.

These few examples may suffice to demonstrate some of the design and measurement problems that have plagued the study of the T-TAT. Such problems have been sufficient to leave the fundamental question of the validity of the instrument with blacks unanswered.

Recognizing the limitations of this body of literature, we may now go on to discuss the conceptual issues raised by critics in their reviews of Thompson's test.

Three main issues are raised in the critiques of Thompson's test. First is the issue of culture, the question of whether blacks live in a culture that is sufficiently different from mainstream, white, U.S. culture to require a distinct and cross-cultural approach in their psychological assessment. It is the contention of this chapter that black culture is an entity that can and must be addressed empirically. For the most part, this was not done in the early discussion of the Thompson TAT. Some authors attempted to skirt the issue altogether, claiming the existence of purely socioeconomic difference, the effects of racial discrimination, or alternatively identifying white, Western psychological theory as universal paradigms of personality (Abel, 1973; Korchin, Mitchell, and Meltzoff, 1950; Mitchell, 1950). Others, including Thompson, narrowly defined culture as equivalent to race, altering features and color of the stimulus figures (Thompson, 1949; Bailey and Green, 1977; Cowan and Goldberg, 1967; Cowan, 1971), systematically varying the races of administrators and test-takers as well as stimulus figures (Riess, Schwartz, and Cottingham, 1950; Mitchell, 1950; Schwartz, Riess, and Cottingham, 1951), and finding varying degrees of positive and negative effects.

In addition, the units of measurement and therefore the basis of comparison and interpretation used by these authors—word counts, idea counts, and need content scores—are ones that contradict the basic premises of a cross-cultural investigation. These summation scores reveal nothing about dynamic differences based on culture between the two groups. Mussen (1953) and Korchin, Mitchell, and Meltzoff, (1950) both accurately point out this fact; however, Mussen was alone in his attempt to study dynamic differences in the fantasy productions of black and white boys.

An example from the literature may help to illustrate this point. Bailey and Green (1977), in an attempt to indirectly measure the identification of blacks with black and white stimulus materials, scored three groups of black responses to the M-TAT, T-TAT, and a black TAT of their own design for Need Achievement, Need Aggression, Need Sex, and Need Succorance. Their failure to find quantitative differences in these variables across tests may tell us something about the stability of these psychological variables in demographically different groups of blacks, despite exposure to a variety of stimuli. This cultural interpretation of their findings differs from the authors' own racially-derived interpretation. They focused on black identification with a racial stimulus rather than on the integrity of the cultural meaning of these variables to blacks as a group and, therefore, were not able to follow up on the implications of such a finding.

The cultural interpretation is by no means complete, however, because of the failure to establish the conceptual and functional equivalence in meaning of these variables. It can perhaps safely be assumed that needs for aggression, sex, succorance, and achievement are present in some form in most societies. However, one cannot assume that these needs follow the same pattern of interrelationships with other variables or that they manifest themselves in the same forms in other cultures. For example, needs for succorance and achievement might be positively related in cultures that both foster interdependency and reward achievement within the group and negatively related in cultures that stress independence and individual striving. How they are related within black culture is an empirical question that has yet to be answered. Beginning with the data already accumulated by Bailey and Green, an initial step in the process of establishing cross-cultural equivalence of these variables in mainstream U.S. and black culture could now be taken. This would be the development of a black "emic" paradigm, based on a study of the uniform ways in which black respondents talked about need succorance, etc. in their stories. Comparison of the black emic thus constructed and the mainstream emic already in use would lead to the development of a new paradigm, a derived etic valid in both the black and mainstream cultures, for interpreting these psychological variables.

Some indications already exist of the areas in which the conceptual meanings of particular psychological variables may diverge in the black and white populations. Mussen's study, in particular, highlights these divergences and the potential role of the TAT in bringing them to light. Contrary to Megargee's (1966) conclusion that the TAT was relatively insensitive to interracial differences, Mussen found considerable differences in content of responses between black and white boys. These included the perception by black boys of the environment as more hostile to the heroes of their stories. The heroes of the black subjects had fewer friendly relationships and leadership positions and fewer strivings for achievement. In addition, they placed more emphasis on thinking, reflecting, and relaxation, less on the use of extreme forms of aggression, and less on feelings of rejection, particularly from the mother, than did the heroes of the white subjects. These are all differences that Mussen attributes to group membership, including historical, social, and economic forces impinging on the group, and to cultural background.

The next two issues raised by Thompson's critics are related; they are identification with the stimulus and ambiguity of the stimulus. Both reflect problems in the theoretical conceptualization of the thematic apperception technique as a method of assessment, problems that cannot be addressed with the attention they deserve in this chapter. However one aspect of these issues pertinent to the cross-cultural perspective we are proposing here is the concept of stimulus familiarity.

This concept, first raised by Biesheuvel and later Price-Williams (1975), was introduced earlier in this chapter. In a modified form, stimulus familiarity is the issue that underlies the development of the Thompson TAT. The argument is not that pictorial representation is unfamiliar to blacks. Rather, it is that the stimuli should be psychologically more meaningful to the black respondent, thus facilitating the respondent's meaningful participation in the assessment task and producing valid results. The question of stimulus familiarity as part of the cross-cultural paradigm must be separated from theoretical formulations on the design and efficacy of the TAT as a clinical instrument if either problem is to be adequately addressed.

Thompson erred in defining the issue too narrowly. He, like Bailey and Green after him, took a racial rather than a cultural perspective in his critique on the validity of the TAT when he chose skin color as the most important factor in determining stimulus familiarity. His critics accepted this formulation of the problem and responded to it as such, leading to confusing and often contradictory arguments on the racial identity of black Americans. Illustrative of the resulting confusion are the simultaneous implications of a number of authors that blacks would both overidentify with and be unable to identify with a black TAT (see Korchin, Mitchell, and Meltzoff, 1950; Riess, Schwartz, and Cottingham, 1950).

A more broadly cross-cultural approach to stimulus familiarity would consider a number of other issues. Included among these would be cultural norms of story telling, which could be expected to differ for blacks and whites. Blacks as a group and as an African-based culture have a strong oral tradition, which has been documented in social science research over the years. It is reasonable to believe that the norms of communication and story telling found among blacks in a variety of social situations would also apply to the testing situation in which they are asked to tell a story from a TAT card. It is encumbent upon researchers using this methodology to fully explore the issue and identify those norms that are operative in the testing situation and their impact on the interpretation of a response.

Another important issue affecting stimulus familiarity and therefore the cross-cultural validity of the TAT with blacks is that of a culturally variable response to the testing situation itself. One by-product of the research on the black TAT was a repeated finding that blacks in general proved less responsive and more guarded in their participation. Cook (1953) found fewer verbal responses, a greater degree of vagueness and uncertainty, and the offering of more alternatives to the main story regardless of the stimulus and summed this up as ego-defensiveness. Riess, Schwartz, and Cottingham (1950) and Bailey and Green (1977) found a certain degree of reticence about revealing personal, thematically rich material to the TAT stimulus.

This preliminary data suggests a need to examine more closely relevant cultural attitudes that may influence the testing behavior of black subjects. Hypothetically, the common experience of racism in many facets of this society could lead to a culturally-determined guardedness in any testing situation. When combined with cultural norms of story telling, which might also mitigate against the readiness of black subjects to respond in accordance with traditional expectations, these data may eventually lead to the conclusion that the TAT is not appropriate in the global assessment of personality with blacks.

Stimulus familiarity is but one facet of the cross-cultural paradigm in its application to assessment techniques and methodologies. We have devoted some time to its discussion because the TAT controversy raised by Thompson and his critics revolved around this issue. A more complete cross-cultural analysis would have to include some consideration of functional and conceptual equivalences and emic and etic concepts in the interpretation of the TAT.

We will conclude this section on projectives with a brief review of an alternative approach to the use of the TAT from which a more complete analysis of these issues can be undertaken.

In recent years the cross-cultural use of thematic apperception techniques by anthropologists has moved increasingly away from the global assessment of individual personality. These techniques have been revised to reflect specific social situations that are familiar within the culture and functionally equivalent across cultures, leading to the fruitful investigation of attitudes, values, and role behavior as social and cultural rather than individual phenomena (Holtzman, 1980). From the cross-cultural perspective, those thematic apperception studies, which have defined the research question more narrowly and have devised a standard scoring system for the interpretation of results along the prescribed dimensions, show more promise for the study, refinement, and cross-cultural application of particular psychological concepts.

An example of this type of study is the research conducted by McClelland and his associates (McClelland, et al., 1953) on the achievement motive using the thematic apperception technique. TAT pictures designed to specifically elicit the achievement motive are most commonly used, although more recently sentence stems designed to arouse the motive have been substituted for pictures with equal success.

The achievement motive as defined by McClelland is measured in fantasy rather than behavior, reflecting its definition as an internal need state that determines whether instrumental acts are achievement related. Achievement imagery is scored when one of three criteria is present: (1) competition with a standard of excellence, (2) involvement in a unique accomplishment, or (3) long-term involvement in the attainment of an achievement goal. Thus, need achievement is not specifically related to success or failure at any given task; but it is related to goal-directed striving and to the anticipatory and affective response of the subject to failure.

McClelland, Atkinson, and their colleagues have also studied the childhood socialization of the achievement motive and patterns of thought and behavioral correlates. Cross-cultural assessments of need achievement and the development of training programs to raise the levels of achievement motivation in underdeveloped nations, particularly India, were worked out of this basic research and theory development. The cross-cultural validity and rationale for the methods of assessment and training that ensued are difficult to establish, at least partly because of ethical questions on the transposing of Western values to non-Western cultures. Nevertheless, the achievement motive as an empirically supported construct with a standard system of test administration, scoring, and content analysis is relatively open to evaluation by cross-cultural researchers along such dimensions as stimulus familiarity, functional and conceptual equivalences, and emic versus etic conceptual paradigms.

While cross-cultural research incorporating these components has not yet been done, it has been possible to contrast cultural groups through the study of behavioral, attitudinal, and imaginal correlates of need achievement, comparing these correlates to theoretical patterns derived from the original data base.

Two studies in particular, Nuttall (1964) and Todman (1976), have examined the correlates of need achievement with black populations. Nuttall contrasted northern and southern groups of black men and women along a number of SES, psychological, sociological, and academic achievement dimensions. Of particular note to this discussion were his findings of different patterns of interrelated variables in each group, that is, his northern men high in need achievement looked different from his southern men high in need achievement. Similarly, there were fewer but still significant differences between his groups of northern and southern women high in need achievement. Todman's findings also pointed to cultural variability in the personality, attitudinal, and behavioral correlates of high-scoring black and white college women. As one example, lack of self-confidence was strongly related to need achievement in white women, while the opposite was true for black women.

The important implication of these two studies is that psychological constructs such as need achievement do not have the same meaning or conceptual equivalence in dissimilar cultural groups. Variability can be found among Afro Americans who share a common history but experience regional and cultural differences in life style and values. Nonequivalences may mean simply that the same psychological variable is expressed in different behavioral terms from one group to another. It may also mean that a Western psychological construct has no parallel in another culture.

Although neither of the two studies cited above began from the cross-cultural paradigm, the data base collected through these and other efforts can serve as a foundation for further empirical, cross-cultural study of need achievement and similar constructs.

BEHAVIORAL ASSESSMENT OF SPECIFIC PROBLEMS

Behaviorally-oriented clinical assessment is the most recent of major approaches. Assessment and treatment are tightly interwoven activities for behavior therapists, who have just begun to study assessment in its own right. Partly because of the relatively short history of behavior therapy, and the even shorter history of behavioral assessment as a distinct specialty, little has been written about application to non-Euro-American groups. Accordingly, this section is shorter and more speculative than the previous ones, which drew upon substantial literatures on race and IQ, and race and the MMPI, respectively. The goal of this section is to prompt behavioral assessors to recognize and begin to think critically about hidden uniformity assumptions underlying their methods.

Like behavioral therapy, behavioral assessment seeks to define problem behavior in specific, concrete terms. The implications of this stance have been incisively clarified by Goldfried and Kent (1972). In an article comparing objective and projective assessment with behavioral assessment, these authors highlighted intrinsic differences between methods in their reliance on inference from test-elicited responses. Whereas traditional assessment uses test responses to draw conclusions about a subject's status on an underlying trait, behavioral assessment uses test responses on the level on which they occur, that of specific, concrete actions. Sundberg (1977) has further clarified these characteristics by noting that behavioral assessment data are considered a sample of behavior and are minimally submitted to the psychologist's subjective interpretation.

Inasmuch as behavioral asssessment minimizes abstract categorization, its procedures would seem to be less vulnerable than others to the miscategorization that produces functional, conceptual, and theoretical nonequivalence. However, opportunities for cultural bias to skew the outcome of assessment continue to exist. As we shall see, although behavioral assessment procedures typically make fewer assumptions about the meaning of behavior than do objective or projective procedures, nevertheless, the assessor may easily overlook important cultural subtleties.

In the present section, we shall briefly explore possible cultural effects on the assessment of a particular behavioral problem, assertiveness deficit. The inability to "stand up for one's rights" was an early interest of behavior therapists, who have devised over time various procedures to assess and treat this problem.

Assertiveness training would seem to appeal particularly to blacks and other disenfranchised groups. Such people would be well served by skills enabling them to advocate their legitimate interests in the face of long-standing, entrenched opposition. However, there are cultural twists in realizing this potential, which have been expressed by Dejoie (1979): "The concept of assertiveness, then, can be expressed as a right which people have to appropriately express their feelings (verbally and non-verbally) in an honest, open and direct manner which does not have the intent of denying the rights of others. However, it would seem that the 'rights' which people are entitled to and the 'appropriateness of their expressions' are not constants." (pp. 10-11). The task of this section is to analyze systematically how cultural differences explain some of the variations in human rights and situational appropriateness mentioned by Dejoie.

Initially, it is useful to consider the state of the art in assertiveness. Behavioral approaches to assertiveness have been specific in principle but global in practice. In an incisive critique, Rich and Schroeder (1976) have identified hidden uniformity assumptions underlying much of the research and practice to date. Usually, this work is conducted as if one assertiveness situation is little different from another and improvements in one kind of assertive response will transfer to another kind. To completely explain an assertiveness problem, according to Rich and Schroeder, one must analyze the constraints, opportunities, and general rules operating in a particular social situation and the specific response class (e.g., asking for favors, saying no, expressing positive feelings) and response components (e.g., eye contact, body posture) that will prove effective in light of these rules.

For the practice of clinical assessment, one implication of Rich and Schroeder's position is to make allowance for the diversified nature of assertive behavior. Whether an assertiveness problem truly exists, and the nature of the needed response, may vary considerably according to the situations at hand. Such a recommendation is partly only a restatement of the guiding philosophy that distinguished behavioral approaches from trait approaches to assessment, and the need to express it indicates how easily psychologists overlook variety and rely on oversimplified formulations.

In assessing assertiveness, some of the variety encountered will have cultural origins. Cultural issues in assertiveness are easily encompassed within the general framework outlined by Rich and Schroeder, who indeed mention such issues, and special attention to them may appear unnecessary. However, as we have seen, those evaluating assertiveness are prone to standardize their conceptions of situations and behavior, making unwarranted uniformity assumptions. As cultural differences are only dimly understood, they may be particularly easy to overlook. It is important to describe explicitly how cultural variety might apply to assertiveness, so that assessors will be particularly alert to these possibilities.

In actual practice, the assessor of a black client might begin by distinguishing between assertiveness problems in black versus white relationships. Among other blacks, the black client may encounter culturally-distinctive, assertiveness-demanding circumstances. An adolescent, for example, might profit from learning to "play the dozens," a game of verbal one-upmanship involving the stylized exchange of barbs. For another client, it may be important to insure that the assertive response provided contains response components that are characteristic of black social situations. For example, to effectively and appropriately turn down a request, a black may need to express a unique pattern of wording, eye contact, and posture. Finally, because of particular social conventions, a black client may need to master response classes and patterns of assertiveness that are culturally distinctive. An example of this could occur if, as suggested by some theorists, blacks have particularly important obligations to their extended families. If the client needed to become more assertive in handling requests from distant relatives, for example, the culturally sanctioned response might not be a flat "no." Rather, he or she might not need help with immediate compliance, since this may be somewhat mandatory; but help might be given in asserting his or her right to reciprocated aid, stemming from the bilateral nature of familial obligations. Or, to deny a request in accordance with cultural conventions, he or she might learn to respond with a barrage of favors needed in return, signalling in that culture the degree of imposition the client felt.

The differences described above are truly cross-cultural. They underscore the importance of the basic theme of this chapter, that even in the measurement across cultures of supposedly straightforward behaviors such as assertiveness, conceptual and functional equivalence must be sought.

There is a second kind of black-white difference to be considered, that which arises in evaluating a black client's relationships with white. Within the dominant cultural frame of reference, members of different groups may be required to behave differently. Rich and Schroeder (1976) have discussed this issue as follows: "Societal values suggest different behaviors for different ages and sexes, as well as for different sub-cultures. Research on sex-role stereotypes, for example, suggests that... women may be labelled aggressive for the same responses that would produce a label of assertive for men" (p. 1084). Similarly, what is considered assertive for whites may be considered aggressive for blacks. The assessor and client should be aware of these constraints, whether or not they choose to respect them.

As noted previously, there is nothing in the principles underlying behaviorally-oriented assessment of assertiveness that would interfere with detecting such cross-cultural differences. Indeed, it is a measure of theoretical compatibility with the cross-cultural perspective that Rich and Schroeder anticipate exactly the kind of cultural influences that are indicated above. On the other hand, explicit discussion of cross-cultural issues in this article is limited to one sentence: In order to guarantee that cultural nuances are recognized in clinical practice, formal efforts—theory, research, knowledge dissemination—must be performed.

CONCLUSION

The adoption of the emic-etic paradigm into cross-cultural research is recent, and a number of different models are utilized (Berry, 1969; Brislin, 1976; Price-Williams, 1975; Triandis, 1972). However, underlying each distinct method is the same premise, that of cultural relativity and the validity of cultural differences. This extension of this premise to Afro Americans is a slow process; however, it is increasingly being called for by critics of traditional techniques and methods of investigation.

Even while calling for a new conceptual framework for the assessment of black-white differences, most critics have been unaware of the tradition of cross-cultural investigation and the theoretical premises and methodology associated with it. Adoption of the cross-cultural research paradigm to the issues in psychological assessment confronting blacks would require a major rethinking of the whole argument on genetic versus environmental determinism and of the methods used to settle the question. As we have seen in the case of the SOMPA (Mercer and Lewis, 1978) and the Black-White MMPI Scale (Costello, 1977), it is quite difficult to give up old habits of conceptualizing and investigating differences and to adopt a new paradigm.

For purposes of illustrating the use of a cross-cultural paradigm in psychological assessment, the present authors have chosen to highlight and critique three broad areas: tests of intelligence, tests of psychological functioning such as the MMPI, and the behavioral assessment of assertiveness. These were selected because of their widespread use and/or visibility in the field. However, we wish to suggest that a cross-cultural perspective be adopted as a conceptual and methodological framework for all assessments of populations where the possibility of variability that is culturally rather than socially or environmentally determined exists.

As indicated earlier, such variability can occur even where there is considerable cultural overlap, as exists between blacks, whites, and other broad ethnic groups in the United States. A cross-cultural framework would allow for the existence of such variability without demanding it, document its nature in behavioral and/or theoretical terms, and, above all, provide for the empirical demonstration of functional or conceptual equivalence where such equivalences do exist.

REFERENCES

Abl, T. *Psychological Testing in Cultural Contexts.* New Haven, Conn.: College & University Press, 1973.

Bailey, B.E. and Green, J. Black thematic apperception test stimulus material. *Journal of Personality Assessment* 41 (1977):25-30.

Baratz, S. and Baratz, J. Early childhood intervention: The social science base of institutional racism. *Harvard Educational Review* 4 (1970):29-50.

Bem, D.J. and Allen, A. On predicting some of the people some of the time: The search for cross-situational consistencies in behavior. *Psychological Review* 81 (1974):506-20.

Berry, J.W. On cross-cultural comparability. *International Journal of Psychology* 4 (1969):119-28.

Block, N.J. and Dworkin, G. I.Q., heritability, and inequality. In *The I.Q. Controversy,* edited by N. Block and G. Dworkin. New York: Pantheon Books, 1976.

Brislin, R. *Translation: Applications and Research.* New York: Gardner Press, 1976.

Brislin, R., Lonner, W., and Thorndike, R. *Cross Cultural Research Methods.* New York: John Wiley & Sons, 1973.

Cleary, J.A., Humphreys, G., Kendrick, S.A., and Wesman, A. Educational uses of tests with disadvantaged students. *American Psychologist* 30 (1975):15-40.

Cook, R.A. Identification and ego defensiveness in thematic apperception. *Journal of Projective Techniques* 17 (1953):312-19.

Costello, R.M. Construction and cross validation of an MMPI black-white scale. *Journal of Personality Assessment* 41 (1977):514-19.

Costello, R.M., Fine, H., and Blau, B. Racial comparisons on the MMPI. *Journal of Clinical Psychology* 29 (1973):63-65.

Costello, R.M., Tiffany, D.W., and Gier, R.H. Methodological issues and racial (black-white) comparisons on the MMPI. *Journal of Consulting and Clinical Psychology* 38 (1972):161-68.

Cowan, G. Achievement motivation in lower class Negro females as a function of race and sex of figures. *Representative Research in Social Psychology* 21 (1971): 42-46.

Cowan, G. and Goldberg, E. Need achievement as a function of race and sex of figures. *Journal of Personality and Social Psychology* 5 (1967):245-49.

Cowan, M., Watkins, B., and Davis, W. Level of education, diagnosis and race related differences in MMPI performance. *Journal of Clinical Psychology* 31 (1975): 442-44.

Cronbach, L.J. *Essentials of Psychological Testing.* New York: Harper & Row, 1970.

Davis, W. Race and differential power of the MMPI. *Journal of Personality Assessment* 39 (1975):138-40.

Davis, W. and Jones, M. Negro vs. Caucasian psychological test performance revisited. *Journal of Consulting and Clinical Psychology* 42 (1974):675-79.

Dejoie, M.M. Assertiveness training and the black client. Unpublished mauscript, University of California, Berkeley, 1979.

Gibbs, J.C. The meaning of ecologically oriented inquiry in contemporary psychology. *American Psychologist* 34 (1979):127-40.

Goldfried, M.R. and Kent, R.N. Traditional vs. behavioral assessment: A comparison of methodological and theoretical assumptions. *Psychological Bulletin* 77 (1972):409-20.

Goldschmidt, W. *Comparative Functionalism.* Berkeley: University of California Press, 1966.

Gynther, M.D. Review of the MMPI. In *The Seventh Mental Measurements Yearbook,* edited by D. Buros. Highland Park, N.J.: The Gryphon Press, 1972a.

———. White norms and black MMPI's: A prescription for discrimination? Psychological Bulletin 78 (1972b):386-402.

Gynther, M.D., Altman, H., and Warbin, R. The interpretation of uninterpretable MMPI profiles, *Journal of Consulting and Clinical Psychology* 40 (1973): 80-83.

Gynther, M.D. and Witt, P. Windstorms and important persons: Personality characteristics of black educators. *Journal of Clinical Psychology* 32 (1976): 613-16.

Harrison, R.H. and Kass, E.H. Differences between Negro and white pregnant women on the MMPI. *Journal of Consulting Psychology* 31 (1967):454-63.

———. MMPI correlates of Negro acculturation in a northern city. *Journal of*

Personality and Social Psychology 10 (1968):262-70.

Herrnstein, R.J. I.Q. *Atlantic Monthly* 228 (1971):43-64.

Holtzman, W.H. Projective techniques. In *Handbook of Cross-Cultural Psychology, Volume 2: Methodology,* edited by H.C. Triandis and J.W. Berry. Boston/London: Allyn & Bacon, 1980.

Hunter, J. and Schmidt, F. Critical analysis of the statistical and ethical implications of various definitions of test bias. *Psychological Bulletin* 73 (1976):1053-71.

Jensen, A. How much can we boost I.Q. and scholastic achievement? *Harvard Educational Review* 39 (1969):1-23.

Jones, E.E. Black-white personality differences: Another look. *Journal of Personality Assessment* 42 (1978):244-52.

Jones, E.E. and Zoppel, C.L. Personality differences among blacks in Jamaica and the United States. *Journal of Cross-Cultural Psychology* 10 (1979):435-56.

Kamin, L. *The Science and Politics of I.Q.* Potomac, Md.: Lawrence Erlbaum Associates, 1974.

Korchin, S.J., Mitchel, H., and Meltzoff, J. A critical evaluation of the Thompson TAT. *Journal of Projective Techniques* 14 (1950):445-52.

Light, B. A further test of the Thompson TAT rationale. *Journal of Abnormal and Social Psychology* 51 (1955):148-50.

Lonner, W. An analysis of the pre-publication evaluation of cross-cultural manuscripts: Implications for further research. In *Cross-Cultural Perspectives on Learning,* edited by R. Brislin, S. Bochner, and W. Lonner. New York: John Wiley & Sons, 1975.

McClelland, D.C. Testing for competence rather than for "intelligence." *American Psychologist* 28 (1973):1-14.

McClelland, D.C., Atkinson, J.W., Clark, R.H. and Lowell, E.L. *The Achievement Motive.* New York: Appleton-Century-Crofts, 1953.

Megargee, E. A comparison of scores of white and Negro delinquents on three projective tests. *Journal of Projective Techniques and Personality Assessment* 30 (1966):530-35.

Mercer, J. and Lewis, J. *System of Multicultural Pluralistic Assessment.* New York: The Psychological Corporation, 1978.

Mitchell, H.E. Social class and race as factors affecting role of family in TAT stories. *American Psychologist* 5 (1950):299-300.

Mussen, P. Differences between the TAT responses of Negro and white boys. *Journal of Consulting Psychology* 17 (1953):373-76.

Nuttall, R.L. Some correlates of high need for achievement among urban northern Negroes. *Journal of Abnormal and Social Psychology* 68 (1964):593-600.

Olmedo, E.L. Acculturation: A psychometric perspective. *American Psychologist* 34 (1979):1061-70.

Price-Williams, D.B. *Explorations in Cross-Cultural Psychology.* San Francisco: Chandler & Sharp, 1975.

Rich, A.R. and Schroeder, H.E. Research issues in assertiveness training. *Psychological Bulletin* 83 (1976):1081-96.

Riess, B., Schwartz, E., and Cottingham, A. An experimental critique of assumptions underlying the Negro version of the TAT. *Journal of Abnormal and Social Psychology* 45 (1950):700-9.

Rodgers, D. Review of the MMPI. In *The Seventh Mental Measurements Yearbook,* edited by D. Buros. Highland Park, N.J.: The Gryphon Press, 1972.

Schwartz, E., Riess, B., and Cottingham, A. Further critical evaluation of the Negro version of the TAT. *Journal of Projective Techniques* 15 (1951):394-400.

Shore, R. A statistical note on differential misdiagnosis of blacks and whites by the MMPI. *Journal of Personality Assessment* 40 (1976):21-23.

Snider, J.G. and Osgood, C.E. *Semantic Differential Technique: A Sourcebook.* Chicago: Aldine, 1969.

Sundberg, N. *Assessment of Persons.* Englewood Cliffs, N.J.: Prentice-Hall, 1977.

Thompson, C.E. The Thompson modification of the Thematic Apperception Test. *Rorschach Research Exchange and Journal of Projective Techniques* 13 (1949):469-78.

Todman, P.A. A comparative study of achievement and power motivation in black and white women. Unpublished manuscript, Harvard University, 1976.

Triandis, H.C. *The Analysis of Subjective Culture.* New York: John Wiley & Sons, 1972.

Wiggins, J.S. *Personality and Prediction: Principles of Personality Assessment,* Reading, Mass.: Addison-Wesley, 1973.

Witt, P. and Gynther, M. Another explanation for black-white MMPI differences. *Journal of Clinical Psychology* 31 (1975):69-70.

9   Family Therapy with Black Families

Nancy Boyd

Therapists in a variety of mental health settings in urban areas are in the process of working with families and clients from a number of different ethnic groups. New treatment modalities such as family and network therapy have become accepted forms of treatment in many community mental health centers and clinics throughout the country. It has been said, however, that, if family therapy as a distinct approach is still in its infancy, family therapy with black families is still in the incubator stage (Foley, 1975).

The literature on the treatment of black families in therapy has not been extensive and has been further diluted by the fact that there has been no central forum in the literature for debate on crucial issues such as intervention strategies. It is hoped, therefore, that this chapter will help to fulfill a critical need for clinicians in the family therapy field by providing an overview of the literature on cultural patterns in black families and on family treatment approaches in black communities.

THE NEED FOR EXPOSURE TO CULTURAL PATTERNS

Every clinician who enters a family enters a cultural system that is at least somewhat different from his or her own. The therapist brings a value system, cultural background, personal and professional experiences, many of which may be very different from those of the families being treated. Therefore, it is extremely important for family therapists to explore their own belief systems, perceptions, and prejudices. In addition, it is vital that they become acquainted with the cultural values of the families with whom they work.

This becomes even more crucial when one considers that, for many family therapists working with black families today, their primary exposure to black people and black culture came through the literature of the 1960s. This literature (Moynihan, 1965) adopted a "deficit" view of black families and used such terms as "disadvantaged, disorganized, chaotic, depressed, and deprived" to describe family patterns. This becomes particularly alarming when one examines studies of clinicians' perceptions that have shown that, a decade later, many clinicians still cling to these stereotypic views (Boyd, 1977).

Before a discussion of family therapy with black families can begin the current body of literature on the cultural patterns and life styles of black people must be reviewed. The purpose of this is twofold. First, the current literature is often the only exposure many beginning therapists have to black family life styles. Second, one of the problems in the current work on family therapy is that there has not been sufficient integration of the current sociological research on cultural patterns into the treatment milieu. Clinical training programs and educational institutions have not helped to fill this void. This is particularly unfortunate because it places the burden of the integration of the sociological and clinical literature on each individual clinician. It is a primary assumption of this author that these components cannot be separated and that our intervention strategies and knowledge of family structure must follow from a careful study and understanding of the culture and strengths of the families with whom we work.

THE STRENGTHS OF BLACK FAMILIES: A GUIDE FOR THE FAMILY THERAPIST

In the 1970s black researchers began to challenge the deficit view of black family life and began to explore their strengths. Hill (1972) has identified certain key strengths: strong kinship bonds, adaptability of family roles, strong religious orientation, strong educational and work orientations. In addition, therapists who treat black families have noted that survival and coping skills, in the face of often severe socioeconomic realities, are important strengths (Boyd, 1977). This chapter will use the basic framework of these strengths to illustrate how they can be utilized in family therapy. They will provide the context from which intervention strategies can be further elaborated.

KINSHIP PATTERNS IN BLACK FAMILIES

The nature of kinship patterns in black extended families has been given a great deal of attention in the sociological literature (Billingsley, 1968; White,

1980; Stack, 1975). Hill (1972) states that "kinship relations tend to be stronger among black than white families" (p. 5). As a result of these strong kinship bonds, many black families have become extended families in which relatives of a variety of blood ties have been absorbed into a coherent network of mutual emotional and economic support. Sometimes these networks are formed not by choice but external bonds, e.g., sports peers, etc. This is one of the most important facts many deficit theorists have overlooked in their statements about "the black matriarchy." White (1980) has pointed to "the number of uncles, aunties, big mamas, boyfriends, older brothers and sisters, deacons, preachers, and others who operate in and out of the black home" (p. 45). He makes the observation that a variety of adults and older children participate in the rearing of any one black child. He notes the tendency of various persons to form an extended family—to interchange roles, jobs, and family functions. As a result of this, White points out that the black child does not learn an extremely rigid distinction of male and female roles. For example, men will often participate in child care and in household chores such as cooking when family circumstances dictate. Stack (1975) reports that the black families she studied had evolved patterns of "co-residence, kinship-based exchange networks linking multiple domestic units, elastic household boundaries, and lifelong bonds to three generation households." She states further that "the black urban family, embedded in cooperative domestic exchange, proves to be an organized, tenacious, active lifelong network" (p. 124).

It is important to note that all of the authors who have written about black extended families have stressed that kinship ties are not necessarily drawn along "bloodlines" (Hill, 1972; Stack, 1975; White, 1980). Within the kinship network there may be a number of persons who are not "blood relatives" but who may function in important roles in the family. For example, a neighbor may take care of a close friend's children in times of economic stress or illness. This sort of pattern is often overlooked by family therapists, and important family dynamics are therefore ignored.

Informal Adoption among Black Families

Another strength in black families is the tradition of informal adoption (Hill, 1972). He discusses the fact that black families have historically taken in other children and the elderly and that "doubling up" had been a common practice among these families since the days of slavery. Hill points out that formal adoption agencies have not adequately served blacks. Therefore, black people have had to develop their own means for the informal adoption of children. This has resulted in a tight kinship network among blacks in which children are provided with extra emotional and economic support. This network has extended also to the care of the elderly, who are often absorbed into the homes of family members. Stack (1975) refers to this process as "child-keeping." She sees it as a survival measure that grew out of a recognition in the black community of the problems and difficulties that are inherent in raising children with limited economic resources. She points out that there may be a number of women who act as "mothers" toward black children, some just slightly older than the children themselves. An excellent example of this is the woman who temporarily raises a sister's, or a niece's, or a cousin's child and regards these offspring as much her grandchildren as children born to her own son or daughter.

Kinship Ties and Their Implications for the Family Therapist

What, you might ask, does this have to do with family therapy? When a therapist is working with a black family, is it really important for him or her to know this information? It will be argued here that this information is not only important but an essential part of the treatment of any black family. Since, as we have seen in the literature, many black families have extended family networks in which many individuals interact, family therapy with these families must include a broader "systems" model.

It has become almost a cliche in the clinical field that family therapy is a "system approach." However, with some notable exceptions (Minuchin, 1974; Bell, 1962; Bowen, 1976) that system has been seen as the "nuclear family." The interest in family therapy beyond the immediate confines of the "nuclear family" came first from those who had adopted a "social network" approach. The earliest applications of this network viewpoint occurred as a consequence of the conduct of family therapy in the home of the nuclear family (Pattison, 1976; Perry, 1963; Speck, 1964). Pattison (1976), in his excellent review of this literature, describes the work of family therapists who included friends, relatives, and neighbors in the family sessions when the extra familial person was noted to play an important role in the dynamics of the family.

Pattison also notes another step in which family therapy groups were expanded to include not only the nuclear family, but also persons related by blood, marriage, friendship, neighboring residence, or work association. The clinical pioneers in this effort have reported their work as an attempt to collect, organize, and utilize the total social network of the identified patient. The method, thus far, has been termed "network" therapy, "ecological systems" therapy, and "case linking." Other "network" therapists have also begun to recognize that the nuclear family unit is not representative of all existent family structures (Attneave, 1969; Auerswald, 1968, 1972; Speck and Attneave, 1973). As Pattison (1976) indicates, family therapists have come to recognize that the basic social unit may not be the nuclear family, or even a family kinship per se, but a collage of persons related in an intimate psychosocial kinship network. Very little, however, has been done in terms of applying the systems model to the treatment of black families.

System Approaches With Black Families

Sager and Brayboy (1970) have shown that therapists must expand their traditional definition of family, which often determines acceptance into a family clinic. They note that therapists must reevaluate their definition of the family and abandon such limiting notions as a legally bound couple or a nuclear family definition. The therapist frequently works with only fragments of the nuclear or extended family, or with combinations of relationships.

Minuchin and associates (1967, 1974) represent a notable exception: a beginning approach to the application of a broader model of family therapy with poor, black families. They propose a way in which the family therapist might incorporate important members of the family's network into the change process. As a consequence of their work with different subgroups within the family they began to explore the impact of extended family members and members of the family's social surroundings. They came to the conclusion that an effective therapist, together with the family, must explore its immediate surroundings and involve significant others who may provide support or challenge certain ways of interaction among family members and pull the family to change. Their position represents an important distinction from the social network approach, however. They stress the importance for the therapist of exploring the kinship network with the family and selecting only those relevant to immediate or emerging therapeutic goals. Therefore, unlike network therapists, who often include large parts of the family's social system, Minuchin advocates the careful selection of the "significant others" who will be included.

Another implication of this systems approach with black families is the fact that very often key members of a family's kinship network may not be willing or able to come to the clinic for regular visits. Therefore, it may be necessary on occasion to schedule family sessions in the home. It is important to stress, however, that these home visits should not be made without a clear discussion with key family members beforehand. This is a very sensitive issue with many black families and may be related, at least in part, to their experience of the welfare system in which home visits were often a means of "checking up" on families and considered an invasion of their privacy.

**Use of Genograms in the Exploration of Kinship
Issues with Black Families in Therapy**

Once clinicians began to recognize that it might be important to explore the extended ties beyond the nuclear family, the questions arose of how to gather and organize this kinship information in a meaningful way. A clinical tool was developed known as the "genogram," which is based on the concept of a genealogy or "family tree" and is borrowed from the field of anthropology. Family therapists have begun to explore the ways in which these genograms can be used to introduce important structural questions about the roles of different family members, their relationships, and their conflicts (Guerin, and Pendagast, 1976).

While there has been no literature to date as to the ways in which genograms can be used in the treatment of black families, in my experience they are an essential part of such a treatment process and can provide important kinship information that can be used in the treatment of these families. Although the practice of some clinicians has been to collect the genogram in the initial interview with the family, this can be counterproductive with black families. Many black families are suspicious of what they perceive as "prying" into their lives by well-meaning therapists. Therefore, it is recommended that genograms not be taken in the initial session but only after the therapist feels that he has established a bond and a therapeutic relationship with the family. For many black families issues such as illegitimate births, the marital status of parents, or the paternity of the children may be "family secrets," which the family will be unwilling to discuss with an "outsider" until a relationship of trust has been established.

Another useful concept to keep in mind is that genograms with black families seldom completely conform to bloodlines. They are often extremely complicated if they are accurate. There are usually indications that children or other relatives, at various times, have lived with different members of the extended family.

Obtaining an accurate genogram presupposes a clear understanding of possible kinship patterns in black families. It is essential if the clinician is to formulate the appropriate questions to obtain *accurate* information. For example, Figure 9.1 represents the genogram of the J family (names have been changed in order to insure anonymity).

During an intake interview, Mrs. J. brought her son Johnny, (age 13) stating that he was having difficulty in school and was acting out at home, refusing to obey her. During the course of the first three interviews the therapist asked "who was living in the home?" and learned the following information: Johnny had five siblings living in their home. His "stepfather" also lived with the family. In addition, Mrs. J's sister Mary and her three children had moved in with the family temporarily after a fire in her apartment. The wording of this first question is extremely important. If the therapist had asked the more traditional intake questions such as "how many siblings?" an important pattern of "doubling up" in times of emergency would have been missed.

The therapist, knowing that children are often "kept" by relatives for a variety of reasons, asked if Mrs. J had any other children who were not living in the home. She replied that she had a 20-year old daughter, Carla, who was staying with her aunt in North Carolina. This young woman visits the family in the summer. It is not uncommon when a young woman has a child at a very young age for an older female relative to raise the child. Gradually more

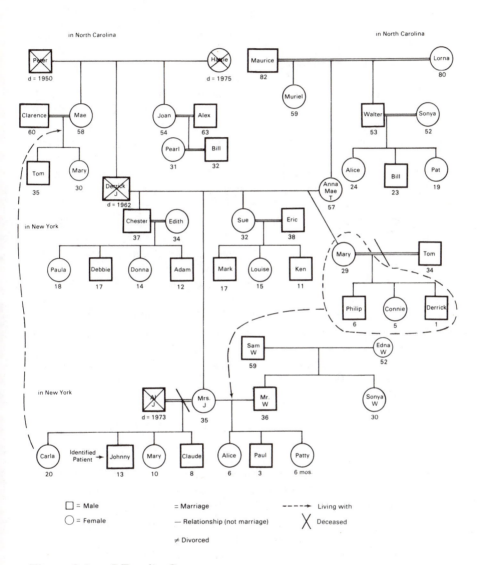

Figure 9.1. J Family Genogram

relatives were added. When asked, "Who helps you out?", Mrs. J replied, "my mother and I don't know what I'd do without my neighbor, Mable C. Her kids have been raised right along with mine and she helps me out plenty of times. She keeps the baby while I'm at work."

When the beginning of Johnny's problems were explored, it became clear that the onset had closely corresponded with the arrival of Mary and her family. Mrs. J reported that prior to that time Johnny had been her "right-hand man." He was essentially a "parental child," or a surrogate parent, who cooked for the younger children and helped with their homework until Mrs. J and Mr. W (the "stepfather") returned home from work. Mary's arrival, with the added burden of three younger children, had placed an additional stress on the family, particularly on Johnny. The course of treatment was as follows: A family network meeting was held, which included Mrs. J and her children, Mr. W, Mary and her children, and Mrs. Anna Mae J, Mrs. J's mother. The pressures on Mrs. J's family since Mary's arrival were discussed. Mrs. J's mother agreed to take Mary and her children to live with her temporarily and to help her find her own apartment. Follow-up meetings were held with the three adult women and Mr. W to monitor their progress and to clarify their own roles within the family system. In addition, a number of sessions were held with Mrs. J, Mr. W, Johnny, and his other siblings to help them reestablish the boundaries of their family unit. Mrs. J and Mr. W discussed areas in which they often disagreed on the disciplining of the children. Within three months, Johnny's school performance had improved and his acting out behavior at home had stopped. Once again, he resumed "helping out" his stepfather and mother with the afterschool care of the younger children. This time, however, it was clear that Mrs. J and Mr. W were in the key parental role.

ADAPTABILITY OF FAMILY ROLES IN BLACK FAMILIES

One of the important responsibilities of the family therapist is the clarification of family roles. There is now a growing body of literature (Hill, 1972; Stack, 1975; Staples, 1971; White, 1980) that supports the flexibility of roles within black families. A misinterpretation of this flexibility has been responsible for many of the deficit views of the 1960s, which stressed the negative role of the "black Matriarchy" (Moynihan, 1965). What many of these approaches failed to see was the underlying strength that allowed black men and women to adopt multiple roles within the family. The concept of this adaptability as a "strength" in black families has been stressed by Hill (1972), who points out that the flexibility of family roles developed as a response to economic pressure. These family roles can take many forms. Hill gives the example of families in which there are working wives, where an older sibling might act as a substitute "parent" for younger siblings. Role flexibility can extend to husband—wife roles also, particularly if both parents are working. In these cases Hill points out that the wife will often act as the "father" or the husband as the "mother." The key aspect of this flexibility is that the sharing of decisions and tasks has always been an important survival mechanisms for black families.

Implications of Role Adaptability for Treatment of Black Families

There are a number of important therapeutic implications of this role flexibility. For example, family therapists in their exploration of role responsibilities and boundaries in the family must be extremely careful to distinguish between functional and dysfunctional systems in black families. This is particularly important for family therapists who were raised in different cultures with much more rigid role definitions.

Second, this strength can be mobilized by the therapist in times of stress such as the hospitalization of a parent or the return to work of a mother after death of the father, or after separation or divorce. Because of the flexibility between households, extended family members can also be mobilized to temporarily fill parental roles.

Although this adaptability is clearly a strength in black families, it can become dysfunctional if boundaries are not clearly defined. Minuchin (1974) looks at two examples of situations where role responsibility and boundaries can become blurred to the point where there is not a clear division of authority within the family. He uses the examples of a parental-child system and a three-generational system containing a grandmother, which are discussed below.

The Parental Child in Black Families

Minuchin (1974) states that "the allocation of parental power to a child is a natural arrangement in large families, or in families where both parents work. The system can function well. The other children are cared for, and the parental child can develop responsibility, competence and autonomy beyond his years" (p. 97). He shows, however, how a family with a parental-child structure may run into difficulty "if the delegation of authority is not explicit or if the parents abdicate, leaving the child to become the main source of guidance, control and decision. In such a case, the demands on the parental child can clash with his own childhood needs and exceed his ability to cope with them. Acting out behavior can often occur among parental children in late latency and in adolescence when the demands of the household conflict with his or her need to be with peers" (p. 98).

Foley (1975) has discussed a pattern in which the oldest daughter is often treated as a surrogate parent. This often leads to an excessive amount of responsibility being placed upon the adolescent girl. He offers the following suggestion to the family therapist faced with such a problem: "In an initial family interview, it is always wise to check out the amount of obligation given to this child, and if overburdened, to suggest a more equitable division of labor" (p. 33).

Because of the role flexibility in black families, the role of the parental child can be filled by boys as well as girls. Minuchin (1974) describes a situation in a black family in which a tight alliance has been formed between the mother and a ten-year old boy, who is the parental child. This subsystem operates to the exclusion of the other children. The identified patient is a seven-year old girl who has been "scapegoated" by the family. Minuchin's strategy is as follows: "In this case, the therapeutic goal is to realign the family in such a way that the parental child can still help the mother" (p. 98). This is an extremely important point for therapists working with black families to remember. When different family structures are encountered, the therapist must use the existing structure and help it to become more functional. The therapist's role is *not* to try to eliminate the parental child role completely because it is essential to the family's survival.

The subsequent steps are as follows: "The boundary between mother and parental child has to be clarified. The boundary between mother and other children has to be modified to allow them direct access to her. The parental child has to be returned to the sibling subgroup though he maintains his position of leadership and junior executive power" (ibid.).

Three-Generational Families: The Role of the Grandmother

A recent study by the author exploring clinicians' perceptions of black families in therapy has shown that the therapists interviewed were very conscious of the role grandmothers frequently play in black families. Fifty percent of the clinicians interviewed discussed such aspects as "very strong ties through the female or maternal line in black families." They gave such answers as: "there were often three generations of women in one house—a grandmother, her daughter and her grandchildren." These therapists discussed the tendency of grandmothers to become involved in "primary child care" or to "help in the raising of children." (Boyd, 1977).

Despite the recognition that this pattern exists in black families, very little emphasis towards application has been given to it in the family therapy literature. This is important because the definition of the grandmother role is a potential problem area, particularly in three-generational, single parent black families.

Minuchin (1974) discusses such a family. The family presents the problem of the youngest daughter, aged ten, who does not obey, wanders away from home, and comes home from school very late. As the therapist explores the problem, it spreads beyond the identified patient. The clinician points out the mother's difficulty with all of her children. When the grandmother is asked to come in, the situation changes, however. It becomes obvious that she is the executive head of the family. The mother's power and competence disappear in the presence of her own mother. The therapist defines his goal as: "joining the mother and grandmother together in the parental subsystem in a position of complementary and mutual support."

This situation can also be present in two-parent black families, where both parents are working and the grandmother is primarily responsible for child care. An example of such a case occurred in the treatment of the F family, in which a ten-year old boy was presented with acting out behavior. In the first session, only the parents and their two children came. Both parents appeared bewildered and unsure of their parenting skills with both children. When it was learned that the grandmother had the primary child care responsibility, she was asked to join the family sessions. It became apparent that the grandmother "ran the household." She had "her way" of handling the children and the parents had theirs. The therapist's goal was to form a working alliance between the parents and the grandmother, so that the children were no longer given conflicting messages. This was accomplished by having a number of joint meetings with the parents and the grandmother to discuss family rules, division of labor, and child care policies. Disputes and differences of opinion were discussed. Later, the children were included in sessions in order to clarify the boundaries in the family.

Once again, it is important to note that the therapist's role was not to evict the grandmother from the system or to alter radically this family's structure. This grandmother was an essential part of the family system. The therapist's goal was to help this dysfunctional system function better by helping the executive members of this family to form a working alliance in which roles and responsibilities were clarified.

Socioeconomic Issues and the Treatment of Black Families

Many black families present a variety of life problems that emanate from their socioeconomic realities. The questions for family therapists arising from these realities are many: What issues should be explored in family therapy? Should the therapist become involved with helping the family navigate the vast social service bureaucracy with which many of our families must contend? Particularly when working with poor black families, one is often called upon by families to help with the negotiation of system issues. These may include problems with the welfare system, housing, child welfare, schools, courts, churches, police, etc. This is particularly true once the therapist has been accepted by the family as a "trusted person," a very valid and legitimate rule for the family therapist working with such families.

Foley (1975) supports this position: "Most black families have a multiplicity of problems. They have been seen often by social workers, school counselors, visiting nurses, and others. To tell such clients that therapy will be long and difficult is self-defeating. What is needed is to pick out a problem that has a workable solution and to set about accomplishing it. This may mean working on an increase in welfare allowance, getting an appointment at a public clinic, or having the house police investigate vandalism. If possible, *the therapist should assist and not replace the family in doing this;* for example, not going with a member of the family to the welfare office but allowing the person to experience success by his own effort." (p. 30).

These issues are important to stress, particularly when one considers the lack of emphasis on the relevance of socioeconomic issues in therapy in many of our professional training programs. The results of this deficiency can be clearly seen in studies that have explored clinicians' perceptions of the most common problems seen in black families who came for therapy (Boyd, 1977). There were clear differences in the clinicians' responses to these questions along racial and professional lines. Social workers tended to discuss socioeconomic issues more often than psychologists. Although black social workers did not differ from white social workers in their perception of socioeconomic problems as important, there were clear racial differences between psychologists. Fifty-three percent of the black psychologists and only 7 percent of the white psychologists indicated that they deal with socioeconomic problems in therapy with black families.

The impact of training programs on the perceptions and strategies employed by family therapists from different disciplines will be discussed below.

MIDDLE CLASS BLACK FAMILIES IN THERAPY

The vast majority of the sociological literature on black families has focused on the poor. Minuchin's work (1967) was a look at the "families of the slums." One might be tempted therefore to ask "What about middle class black families?" Has any research been done to clarify their needs and the issues they bring to therapy? The unfortunate answer to these questions is that very little research or clinical literature has focused on these families.

One of the few researchers who has attempted to look at patterns in black middle class families and raise questions relevant to family therapy issues has been McAdoo (1977, 1978). Her research attempts to answer the questions raised by Stack (1975), by seeming to indicate that only by cutting himself off from his family is the black of poorer circumstance able to raise himself to a more stable level. The implication here was that because of the reciprocal nature of the kinship help systems in black families the upward social mobility of individuals would be limited. McAdoo (1977) sees "the story of the family as not ending with the supportive help that enabled one child to reach higher education and social achievement, but extending indefinitely by means of reciprocal expectations, based on the obligations of providing help in exchange for help received in the past." (p. 78). She goes on to delineate the choice for such an individual as follows: "The mobile individual has two alternatives: (1) he must either continue his participation in the obligatory reciprocity stream or (2) he must isolate himself and his family of procreation from his family of orientation." (ibid.).

McAdoo's (1978) own research with black middle class families shows a different picture. Unlike Stack's (1975) poverty sample, her middle-class group was able to maintain their contract with their extended-kin-help network without sacrificing their own mobility goals. She reports that "many felt that they would have been unable to obtain their educations without extensive kin help." (p. 775).

Education is such an important value in many black families, regardless of social class, that many sacrifices are often made to help at least one family member to go on for higher education. It is not unusual for an older child to drop out of school and go to work in order to help a younger sibling to achieve his or her education. Later, that child may contribute to the education of other children in the family.

The implications of these patterns for the family therapist are many. Often, for black families to maintain middle class income, both parents have to work. This puts considerable strain on family relationships. The family therapist will often have to help a black family in such a situation to renegotiate time for individuals, a new relationship between the couple, and the ever-present demands of parenthood.

Another pressure of mobility is that many black families represent the first generation to achieve some level of higher education and a more comfortable life style. With this new life style come new responsibilities and roles, and the pressures of racism are experienced quite differently. For many, there are no role models, and they are entering into "unchartered territory" in terms of their own family history. External stress from work or educational institutions can place additional pressure on such a black family. A sensitive family therapist must realize that "middle class" or "professional status" for black families does not represent the same level of economic or social security that it does for some of their white counterparts. Often they carry additional financial responsibility for other members of the extended family. The therapist must therefore help family members to resolve the conflicts that arise.

OTHER NETWORKS: THE CHURCHES

Religion has long been recognized as an extremely important strength in the black community. Hill (1972) points out that it was through the church, one of the most independent institutions in the black community, that blacks learned to use religion as a means to survive.

It was therefore very surprising that clinicians utilize these networks so little in family therapy with blacks. In a recent study (Boyd, 1977), the majority of the clinicians interviewed reported that they rarely discuss religious beliefs or church membership in their therapy with black families. There are a number of possible explanations for this finding: (1) religious issues are not seen as important by therapists and are therefore not discussed; (2) black families who use the services of the mental health center or agency may be those who are not well connected to the network of social services provided by black churches; (3) some black clients may dichotomize problems; i.e., they may see some problems as appropriate to discuss in therapy and others to discuss with their minister.

These results have continued to remain a puzzle, however, because they are so contrary to my own experience. Many of the black families with whom I have worked have described elaborate church networks in which their minister and other "brothers and sisters" in the church became their support network. This has been especially true of older black women. My own consciousness in terms of this issue was heightened while working at Harlem Interfaith Counseling Service, a black agency in New York, where it became increasingly clear that the churches provided a very important mental health network for their parishioners. Often these interventions are in times of crisis. It has been particularly striking to me because at other agencies, family therapists who would routinely contact a prior therapist of the patient would not contact a minister who had been seen for pastoral counseling.

The impact of church networks is even more apparent in the inpatient hospital setting where patients are often admitted involuntarily. While working as a psychologist on the family service unit at Bronx Psychiatric Center, I began to pay close attention to the visitors my patients received. In addition to family members and friends, it soon became clear that many of the black patients received visits from their ministers and members of their churches. For example, members of the Jehovah Witness faith, frequently received visits from "sisters" from their hall, who then served as a "community support system" after discharge. Considering the recent attention in the psychiatry literature to support systems for deinstitutionalized patients, it is surprising that this is a network that is rarely tapped.

Another such situation occurred in the case of Ronny T., a young man who had been brought to the hospital for threatening to set himself on fire after a fight with his wife. In family sessions with Ronny, his wife, and his father, it became increasingly clear that Ronny had frequently beaten his wife. She would turn for help to their minister and other church members. They were members of the Church of God in Christ and were involved in a close religious-social network in which their minister frequently provided counseling for his congregation. It also became increasingly clear that the family intended to have no further contact with the mental health services after discharge but would return to their own support network in their church. Through a call to their minister, I learned that, in the past, Ronny and his wife had come to him for help on a number of occasions. This particular instance, because of his threat to ignite himself, a neighbor had called the police, who then brought him to our psychiatric facility. At my invitation, and with the family's enthusiastic approval, the minister agreed to become a "cotherapist" in the family's therapy. Our contract was to work together with the family until Ronny's discharge and for six months after. At that point, the family decided to consult with their minister if needed. In follow-up phone calls six months later, it was clear that the couple was working on this issue and Ronny had not been rehospitalized.

This example is not given to suggest that family therapists must routinely include ministers as cotherapists. However, it is a very striking example of a situation where a therapist was able to mobilize a network and work closely with a patient's "significant others." Another important point is that, if the therapist had not inquired about church networks and other supports, an important resource might have been overlooked.

Just as a family therapist may help a family to reconnect with its kinship network, help might be provided to enable a family or a deinstitutionalized patient to reestablish ties with his or her church network. This whole area of religious beliefs and church affiliation in black families is one that needs further exploration.

"RESISTANCE" TO THERAPY ON THE PART OF BLACK FAMILIES

The issue of the reluctance of black families to enter therapy or their "resistance" to treatment has been discussed by a number of authors (Foley, 1975; Sager and Brayboy, 1970; McAdoo, 1977; Boyd, 1977). For example, Sager and Brayboy have stated that "treatment of the black family is affected not only by the usual resistances that most families bring to therapy but by the specific ones that relate to the fact that the members are black" (p. 233).

In a recent survey of family therapists (Boyd, 1977) 43 percent saw black families as more "resistant" to therapy than white families. Clinicians made such comments as: "Black families do not come in. It's harder to keep black families in therapy"; or, "Black families perceive the therapist as threatening or prying." Other clinicians felt that "Therapy is a new, unfamiliar experience for blacks. They are less willing to talk about their problems with an outsider." (p. 125).

There are a number of possible explanations for these phenomena. One contributory factor is clearly related to the history of institutional racism with which many black families have had to contend in their dealings with the social service bureaucracy. They therefore view the family therapist as "just another caseworker" who is going to pry into their lives.

Another possible explanation may be found in the referral process. Black families are frequently sent by other agencies, such as schools, the welfare department, the courts, and the police, and are often not self-referred. The consensus of many clinicians in the same study by Boyd was that institutions generally force black families to come for therapy.

This condition may account, at least in part, for the perception of black families as more "resistant" to therapy. This is understandable when one considers that a family that is more aware of the purpose of therapy and that comes for treatment on its own will be more likely to be motivated to come for treatment sessions. For many black families, who are often forced to come, the same incentive and motivation are not present. One of the critical issues of which therapists must therefore, be aware is that the process of "joining" with black families and motivating them to keep appointments is an extremely important part of the therapist's job. Treatment of black families often requires a much more active therapist. who is willing to extend himself or herself in order to acquaint the family with the therapeutic process. As Sager and Brayboy (1970) have said: "The family's confidence and trust must be earned; it is not given automatically" (p. 223). During this initial "joining" period the reluctance of individual family members or important "significant others" to become involved must be discussed and their cooperation enlisted.

These issues of suspicion and "resistance" on the part of black families cannot be avoided or denied by the clinician. It can be disastrous for the therapist either to deny the suspicion and hostility of the black patient or to feel guilty about the fact that these sentiments exist. The fact that the word "resistance" has been placed in quotes throughout this chapter is also significant. As Sager and Brayboy (1970) have shown: "Labelling all raising of the black-white issue as resistance is one more expression of the old therapy gambit of blaming the patient for all stalled treatment and using resistance as a ploy to explain it" (p. 224). Closely related to this question of "resistance" is that of the misinterpretation of communication styles in black families.

COMMUNICATION STYLES OF BLACK FAMILIES

The question of communication in black families has been an issue of contention in therapeutic literature. Clinicians frequently describe black clients as resentful and suspicious (Rosen and Frank, 1962), difficult to establish rapport with, untreatable or unreachable (Calnek, 1970), incapable of insight, etc. Since psychotherapy relies heavily on verbal exchanges, this becomes an important issue for many therapists in their treatment of black families. These misconceptions on the part of clinicians are often based on misreading of black communication styles. Also, if a family therapist has not established a sufficient base of rapport with a family, it is very likely that its communication pattern will remain closed to him.

Whitten (1979) and Minuchin, et al. (1967) discuss the overt manifestation of incongruency between the language styles of therapists and black families. Minuchin describes this as a "pseudo-dialogue" in which the therapist and family members talk in parallel monologues, assuming they are communicating and relating with each other. At times, families may attempt to decipher the therapist to no avail. This results in an escape through disruptive actions, mutism, or direct statements such as "I don't understand you" or "I don't know." Minuchin states that some therapists interpret this behavior as "resistance." At the same time, family members often respond to the differences in the therapist language by referring to it as "social worker talk" (p. 247). Thus, both the therapists and the family members derogate each other's communication styles. Whitten (1979) notes that many black families respond to this situation by giving up and dropping out of therapy. She also notes that many mental health professionals do not acknowledge the intimidating influence of white professionals on some black people.

Foley (1975) examines some of the more recurrent patterns of communication among black families that must be explored by the family therapist. His excellent case examples provide extremely useful material for clinicians. He divides his discussion into four types of communication styles that he has seen frequently in black families: (1) incomplete messages, (2) frequent use of nonverbal messages, (3) the need for relabelling, and (4) the all or nothing quality of affective exchanges.

In his first examples of incomplete messages, Foley notes that communication among black families often tends to be in generalities rather than specific instances. He stresses that such generalizations need to be made concrete. He gives the example of a couple who engage in frequent fights and states that it is often very helpful to have the family members or the couple show the therapist a typical fight. The therapist can then stop the fight at various points and help the spouses to clarify their messages to each other.

The second communication style deals with the importance of observing nonverbal communication in black families. This may provide important information that is not said verbally. Foley uses the following case to eloquently illustrate this point. He describes therapy with a black family in which the couples were locked in a battle but neither was willing to discuss it. One of their children was constantly getting into trouble in school. It was clear to the therapist after the initial session that the child's behavior was only a cover for other problems in the family, in particular in the marital relationship. The therapist picked up a number of nonverbal cues such as the way the father sat (slightly turned from his wife) and the fact that he would verbally agree with his wife while inclining his head in a negative fashion. The therapist fed back these discrepancies to the couple as a way of clarifying their communication.

Foley discusses his observation that, due in part to social factors, poor black families often label behavior in negative ways. He describes how he utilizes the therapeutic tool of "relabelling" as a way of introducing positive feedback and the potential for change into the family system. He has shown that the therapist must notice changes in belief or attitude in the family members with whom he or she is working. The therapist's function often is to label changes and credit positive effort. In families where there is an improper feeling response, it is necessary for the therapist to act as a model for the family and to encourage more responsiveness.

SHORT-TERM THERAPY WITH BLACK FAMILIES

One therapeutic strategy that has been extremely useful with black families, particularly poor families, is the technique of contracting for a specific number of sessions in order to resolve a specific set of issues or a crisis. Sager and Brayboy (1970) feel that this short-term therapy or crisis intervention approach is more appropriate and effective than a long-term approach aimed at more fundamental character change. In their family treatment unit, these authors often used a time-limited approach of approximately 15 sessions, during which the presenting disruption and stress are dealt with and the family is helped to reconstitute itself on a more adaptive level of functioning. Because they are aware of the pressure on these families, these therapists stress an "open door" policy, in which family members may contract for more sessions at the end of that time, or they can terminate with a clear understanding that should another crisis arise or should members feel dissatisfied with their family's functioning they can feel free to return.

This kind of flexibility is rare in mental health clinics and hospitals. However, the combination of short-term therapy and an open door policy may be a possible alternative to more traditional methods that often lose black clients before they can become sufficiently connected with the clinic.

MULTIPLE FAMILY GROUPS WITH BLACK FAMILIES

Another alternative form of family treatment for black families is that of multiple family groups. Powell and Monahan (1969) assert that motivating and sustaining treatment with low-income black families can be problematic in that they often withdraw from treatment before goals can be reached. These patients have often been labeled as "rejects" by the mental health establishment. Powell and Monahan question whether professionals have rejected the patients because of the patients' "lack of motivation" or whether they have been rejected by therapists and agencies because the programs have been too rigid and have not been consonant with the particular problems and needs of these clients. Many of these families were perceived by mental health clinics as "isolated." Therefore, it was felt that putting several of these families in a group would help to focus on the life problems they felt were most pressing.

One of the earliest issues Powell and Monahan encountered in the running of this group was that many of the black families involved presented some difficulty with attendance and lateness. They felt that clinic attendance was low on the list of priorities of these families and that the "pressing problems of everyday living took precedence over therapy" (p. 38). The families did not respond to interpretations of "resistance." The therapists therefore decided not to persist in confronting this behavior in view of their commitment to structure the treatment to the needs of this particular group. After about three months, attendance began to improve and soon ceased to be a problem, with the exception of one mother. The therapists felt that the fact that they did not continue to interpret the latenesses and absences as "resistance" was helpful in increasing the involvement of the group with the therapists.

Powell and Monahan feel that the multifamily group provides a continuing source of concrete behavioral examples in place of abstract theoretical concepts. The therapist and family members can delineate and interpret the role of each family member. Whitten (1979) in her review of their work has pointed out that one of the strengths of the approach they outlined is that it is flexible. Rather than interpret the "different" behavior of the families as pathological, they adjust the parameters of the treatment to those differences. They carefully evaluate the situation in order to discriminate between neurotic and realistic needs. They assert that through the sensitivity to the specific needs of the families the therapeutic process became more meaningful and the families were able to feel more involved.

There are other aspects of the multifamily group model that make it a viable intervention strategy with many black families. It borrows closely from the multifamily model of community supports, which many black families have adopted for survival reasons. Many black mothers and fathers feel particulary overwhelmed and desperately need support in the demands of raising children. The multiple family model removes the onus and the emphasis on pathology and focuses on shared common problems. Therefore, members of other families can share similar experiences, and members of different generations can share their views. The emphasis is upon improving communication and trying out new solutions to life problems. It can be a particularly powerful tool in cases where family members have become estranged from contact with their own extended family members or when a black family is suffering from the isolation that results from a move to a new community. In these cases the multiple family group can provide a new support system that is consistent with traditional cultural practices.

USE OF COMMUNITY BASED PARAPROFESSIONALS IN WORKING WITH BLACK FAMILIES

Epstein and Shainline (1974) descibe a one year experimental program designed to provide a paraprofessional parental-aide service to black low income families. They reported that these families often do not make use of office-based clinical services. In their program, parent-aides provided in-home counseling and guidance.

In most cases, the parent-aide provided the sole therapeutic intervention while maintaining consultation with the former office-based mental health professional. It was felt that the parent-aides encountered family situations that would have severely taxed the competence of office-based therapists. They demonstrated that for many families, in-home interventions can be crucial to a successful outcome. They were able to observe interactions that often remained out of the view of the more traditional therapist.

Epstein and Shainline were able to acknowledge the cultural differences of black families. They felt that part of the success of the parent-aides can be attributed to their refusal to label these differences as pathology. The barrier between the parent-aides and the families was easier to surmount because they were not made to feel like "patients" and because many of the aides had survived similar struggles. Epstein and Shainline also noted that while telephone communication is usually kept to a minimum in traditional therapy, it was a vital means of interaction in this program. It increased the availability of the parental-aides; their contracts with the families were not limited to a 50-minute session. This is a crucial form of outreach that must be adopted by all family therapists who hope to be effective with black families. In addition, given the reluctance of many crucial extended family members to come to see a therapist in the clinic setting, home visits may be one of the only ways for a therapist to reach these important members of the family network. Boyd (1977) noted that many therapists in her sample made home visits as a part of their therapeutic intervention. Whitten (1979) in her review of Epstein and Shainline's work cautions that this method should not be adopted simply as a less expensive approach to service delivery but should be incorporated as part of the responsibility and training of all mental health professionals and paraprofessionals. She suggests that families might benefit from mental health teams that combine the services of parent-aides and mental health professionals.

IMPLICATIONS FOR THE TRAINING OF FAMILY THERAPISTS

This chapter raises a number of issues germane to the training of family therapists, particularly those who will work with black and other minority families. It is clear that there must be more systematic exposure to relevant cultural issues, in part through the literature but also through direct cultural contact with minority supervisors during their training years. This is often complicated by the fact that family therapists come from a variety of different disciplines (i.e., psychiatrists, psychologists, social workers, mental health workers, nurses, paraprofessionals, etc.). Many of these training programs have not included minority professors and supervisors to facilitate the training process. Also, very few of the major institutes for training family therapists have made cultural issues an important part of their curriculum. This must change if the goal of cultural awareness on the part of family therapists is to be achieved.

Another training issue has been the tendency of many training programs to focus primarily on the nuclear family, with very little emphasis on extended family networks. This approach needs to be remedied if therapists are to develop a realistic base for expanding their clinical skills for working with black families. Finally, an attempt must be made to recruit and train more minority clinicians who can bring their own unique cultural backgrounds and experiences to their treatment of minority families.

SUMMARY AND CONCLUSIONS

As this chapter has established, therapists who treat black families must be willing to expand their concept of "family" beyond the limits of the nuclear family unit. We must adopt a broader approach to family therapy, which is based on our understanding of the extended family systems in black families. It is critical that we utilize the natural support systems in order to help families in times of stress. We must expand our models of family therapy to include the "significant others" who are extremely important in the lives of many black families.

Alternative methods of treatment such as network therapy, short-term treatment, multiple family groups, and the use of paraprofessional aides, which have been explored in this chapter, must be expanded in order to meet the needs of black families. Finally, there is a need for the expansion of the training of family therapists of all professional disciplines to include training in the cultural issues, which must be acknowledged and utilized if we are to provide viable mental health services in our black and other minority communities.

REFERENCES

Attneave, C.L. Therapy in tribal settings and urban network intervention. *Family Process* 8 (1969):192-210.

Auerswald, E.H. Interdisciplinary versus ecological approach. *Family Process* 7 (1968):202-15.

_____. Families, change and the ecological perspective. In *The Family Therapy Textbook,* edited by A. Ferber, M. Mendelshon, and A. Napier. Boston: Houghton Mifflin, 1972.

Bell, N.W. Extended family relations of disturbed and well families. *Family Process* 1 (1962):175-93.

Billingsley, A. *Black Families in White America.* Englewood Cliffs, N.J.: Prentice-Hall, 1968.

Bowen, M. Theory in the practice of psychotherapy. In *Family Therapy: Theory and Practice,* edited by P. Guerin. New York: Gardner Press, 1976.

Boyd, N. *Clinicians' Perceptions of Black Families in Therapy.* Ph.D. dissertation, Teachers College, Columbia University, 1977.

Calnek, M. Racial factors in the countertransference: the black therapist and the black client. *American Journal of Orthopsychiatry* 40 (1970):39-46.

Epstein, N. and Shainline, A. Paraprofessional parent-aides and disadvantaged families. *Social Casework* 55 (1974):230-36.

Foley, V. Family therapy with black disadvantaged families: Some observations on roles, communications, and technique. *Journal of Marriage and Family Counseling* 1 (1975):29-38.

Guerin, P. and Pendagast, E. Evaluation of the family system and the genogram. In *Family Therapy: Theory and Practice,* edited by P. Guerin. New York: Gardner Press, 1976.

Hill, R. *The Strengths of Black Families.* New York: National Urban League, 1972.

_____. *Informal Adoption Among Black Families.* Washington, D.C.: National Urban League, Research Department, 1977.

Jones, R. *Black Psychology.* New York: Harper & Row, 1980.

McAdoo, H. Family therapy in the black community. *American Journal of Orthopsychiatry* 47 (1977):75-79.

McAdoo, H. Factors related to stability in upwardly mobile black families. *Journal of Marriage and the Family* 40 (1978):761-76.

Minuchin, S. *Families and Family Therapy.* Cambridge, Mass.: Harvard University Press, 1974.

Minuchin, S., Montalvo, B., Guerney, G., Rosman, B., and Schumer, F. *Families of the Slums.* New York: Basic Books, 1967.

Moynihan, D. *The Negro Family: The Case for National Action.* Washington, D.C.: Office of Policy Planning and Research, U.S. Department of Labor, 1965.

Pattison, E. *A Theoretical-Empirical Base for Social Systems Therapy.* Presented at the 33rd Annual Conference of the American Group Psychotherapy Association. Boston, February 1976.

Perry, S.E. Home treatment and the social system of psychiatry. *Psychiatry* 26 (1963):54-64.

Powell, M. and Monahan, J. Reaching the "rejects" through multifamily group therapy. *International Journal of Group Psychotherapy* 19 (1969):35-43.

Rosen, H. and Frank, J.D. Negroes in psychotherapy. *American Journal of Psychiatry* 119 (1962):456-60.

Sager, C. and Brayboy, T. *Black Ghetto Family in Therapy: A Laboratory Experience.* New York: Grove Press, 1970.

Speck, R.V. Family therapy in the home. *Journal of Marriage and Family Living* 26 (1964):72-76.

Speck R.V. and Attneave, C.L. *Family Networks.* New York: Vintage Books, 1973.

Stack, C. *All Our Kin: Strategies for Survival in a Black Community.* New York: Harper & Row, 1975.

Staples, R. *The Black Family—Essays and Studies.* Belmont, Calif.: Wadsworth, 1971.

White, J. Toward a black psychology. *Black Psychology,* edited by R. Jones. New York: Harper & Row, 1980.

Whitten, L. *Black low income families in therapy.* Unpublished paper prepared for "Family Therapy" seminar in the Institute for Advanced Psychological Studies, Adelphi University, New York, 1979.

10   Changing Norms of Hispanic Families: Implications for Treatment

Carmen Carrillo

A varied and complex population, Hispanics number at least 12 million people in the United States. Socioeconomic, cultural, and linguistic barriers have kept Hispanics a medically underserved population. Effective treatment of individuals of Hispanic heritage is predicated on the practitioner's ability to communicate effectively, approach patients with an understanding of their world view, and perceive them in a nonethnocentric and nonstereotypic fashion. This chapter explains the roots of cognitive/affective processes that influence interactional behavior among Hispanics. The harsh realities that form a backdrop for Hispanic behavior are described. Prevalent ethnocentric views of Hispanics and their negative consequences are explored. Suggested approaches for successful treatment are delineated.

HISPANICS AS A MEDICALLY UNDERSERVED POPULATION

Hispanics are not only overrepresented among the poor, they also generally experience a higher degree of unemployment, poor housing, discrimination, poor education, and inadequate nutrition than the dominant population group. Poverty not only limits Hispanics' ability to afford adequate health care, but its environmental correlates create a greater predisposition to illness. Furthermore, discrimination and poverty contribute to inner stress, internal conflicts, and repressed anger. These internalized effects have had severe consequences on Hispanics' mental health. Drug abuse, alcoholism, and suicide have increased among Hispanics.

Despite greater medical and mental health care needs, Hispanics either underutilize available services, seek treatment for disabling illness at later stages than other groups, or are offered inferior quality health care than that offered the Anglo community. Additionally, Hispanics lack the opportunity for adequate health education or access to the technical advances of public health since Spanish language materials are virtually nonexistent.

Even the known health needs of Hispanics have not been adequately addressed. Services to Hispanic communities are deficient in many respects: availability, accessibility, comprehensiveness, continuity, and appropriateness. Furthermore, the quality of service available to Hispanics is often inferior to that available to other groups. The resources to Hispanic communities are inadequate in number for certain care such as alcoholism services, long-term care, and home health services. In short, available programs are insufficient to meet the needs of Hispanic communities. For example, community mental health or mental retardation programs, residential halfway houses or alternatives to hospitalization are not commonly available to Hispanics. Finally, Hispanics for various reasons are served more often by paraprofessionals or others with limited training, rather than by professsionals.

TOWARD EFFECTIVE TREATMENT

As mentioned above, effective treatment of individuals of Hispanic heritage is predicated on the practitioner's ability to communicate effectively, approach patients with an understanding of their world view, and see them as individuals rather than in terms of ethnocentric stereotypes. A lack of sensitivity to racial, cultural, and ethnic factors by practitioners has been identified (Carrillo, in press). This may explain why some services are utilized and others not. For example, there are insufficient health education materials for minorities. For Hispanics in particular, this means an absence of culturally relevant materials and, in some cases, of Spanish language information. Furthermore, there is a reliance in fields like mental health on the traditional medical model rather than an understanding and application of a psychosocial model, which adapts itself more readily to the special needs of Hispanics. The evolution of community mental health theory and practice has been slow to reach Hispanic communities, which stigmatize the consumers of mental health services. As a result, only the most severely impaired avail themselves of the scarce resources available. Psychosocial approaches that address social and cultural realities have not been available to Hispanics. Therefore, participation in individual psychotherapy, marital therapy, or other approaches such as stress reduction or assertiveness training is negligible though desirable.

Knowledge about the health needs and practices of Hispanics is woefully sparse. The small number of culturally sensitive researchers with an interest in Hispanic issues has not been sufficient to generate the necessary theoretical and empirical work required to provide the field with sufficient knowledge to adapt training, curriculum, and practice.

Last, but not least, Hispanics are underrepresented among those who make policy, control budgets, or operate programs. Thus, changes beneficial to Hispanics are few and far between and, therefore, difficult to assess. Effective treatment of Hispanics requires an appreciation of the cultural historical determinants of behavior, knowledge of culturally sanctioned normative behavior, and sensitivity to the personal and interpersonal conflict resulting from changes in those cultural norms.

SUGGESTED APPROACHES FOR SUCCESSFUL TREATMENT

In working with Hispanic groups it is necessary to be familiar with specific behaviors, values, and belief systems. The following is an attempt to outline and describe behaviors that have special connotations to Hispanic groups. The underlying assumption here is that there is a great risk of inaccurate psychological evaluation, resulting in misdiagnosis and ineffective treatment of a Hispanic person or family if the evaluator is unfamiliar with the cultural context of the phenomena in question.

The information presented herein is complex and sometimes seemingly contradictory. The seeming contradictions emerge because culture is a changing phenomenon, with Hispanic culture being a mosaic of rich and shifting characteristics. Hispanic groups will naturally vary according to general status, socioeconomic level, educational level, and regional identification. An understanding of the changing characteristics of Hispanic culture is important for mental health practitioners to be able to eradicate ignorance or stereotypic bias. Adequate diagnosis, treatment, and prognosis of Hispanics requires no less.

HISPANIC FAMILIES

The key to the understanding of any cultural group is knowledge of its family structure and ideology. It is important to note that cultures are constantly evolving, and that the descriptions of behaviors, beliefs, and attitudes that are captured on paper do not reflect the ongoing adaptations made by people as they respond to the environment. Nevertheless, it is useful to trace the evolution of family systems in Hispanic culture.

It is not unusual for Hispanic groups to be characterized by the tradition of an extended family system. The system has been described as a tightly knit organization of family members who provide support and acceptance to one another. A basic point to be considered is that because of the function of the family, an Hispanic individual may not refer himself or herself to a clinic that may be perceived as "ajena" (alien). Where the extended family structure exists, that individual may be more likely to seek out the advice and support of family members or close family acquaintances rather than seek mental health assistance from professionals.

Recourse to family members may denote a certain degree of over-dependence on parents and underdeveloped self-autonomy in other cultures, but this is not necessarily the case among Hispanic groups. On the contrary, reliance on the extended family may be a very adaptive and appropriate response to stress. Where structures for emotional support exist, it is adaptive to utilize them. Caution must be exercised in not pathologizing an Hispanic person's psychological and social interactions with the family. For example, interpretation of the behavior of a male who calls his mother once or twice weekly must include a thorough and sensitive examination of other factors in his life before focusing on oedipal issues. Such behavior must be viewed within the context of the respect and devotion to the mother expected of him by the culture. Conversely, to behave in an aloof and indifferent manner towards a parent might be interpreted within Hispanic culture as indicative of serious pathology.

Socioeconomic changes impact family structure and family dynamics. Migrations in pursuit of better employment disrupt the geographic relatedness of households, until then parts of extended families. Employment patterns or separation can result in changes in family structure, which then alter family dynamics. This alteration can result in interpersonal and intrapersonal conflict. For example, a couple in which the husband is underemployed and the wife has recently entered the labor force will have difficulty maintaining a patriarchal family system.

There is insufficient data in the literature addressing geographic migra-tions, although the Hispanic family in this country is traditionally rooted in a genesis of migration. There are indications, however, that many families tended to settle in particular areas and remain there. There is also some evidence that Mexican-American families tend to be more geographically stable than Anglo families (Keefe, Padilla, and Carlos, 1979). It has also been established that minority health professionals tend to return to their community of origin to practice (Montoya, et al., 1978). Still, little is known about those who choose to leave. Among the reasons for geographic migration are pursuit of educational efforts, job opportunities, and personal relationships. The potential for geographic resettlement is greater among those Hispanic in business, civil service, and the professions. As entry into these categories of employment increases, a corresponding increase in geographic mobility can be expected. Therefore, the stability acquired by settling in certain communities that enabled the maintenance of an extended family system can be expected to suffer disruptive impacts.

Family dynamics based on traditional sex and age roles necessary to the organization of the extended family are changing. The interpersonal and intrapsychic dynamics will be altered when the following conditions exist: (1) unemployed male head of household, (2) employed female (wife/mother), or (3) combinations of the above. Employment implies responsiblity for the maintenance of the household. With that responsibility comes authority. When the traditional structure changes, the responsibility and authority roles are altered. These alterations create interpersonal and intrapsychic conflicts. Clinicians working with Hispanics must be alerted to consider problems presented by an individual, a couple, or a family within the context of changes in the economic system in that family, with its corresponding sociopsychological changes.

Married couples separate for many reasons. Traditionally, the male is the first to migrate in search of financial opportunities, with the female and children to follow. This type of separation can last from a few weeks to a few years. Depending on the length of the separation and other factors in the relationship, the family dynamic will be impacted in various ways. Increasingly, conflicts in the relationship brought about by unmet expectations related to sex-role functions become irreconcilable and result in marital separations. This author has found that in a sample of female community workers in their early 30s, employed in health, mental health, and education settings, the divorce rate is 20 percent (Carrillo-Beron, 1977). Likewise, the topic of women as single heads of household is commanding increasing attention. Sotelo (1978) found that in a bilingual child-care center located in the San Francisco Bay area, 75 percent of the children live in homes in which the head of household is a single Hispanic woman. Although one might expect a high proportion of women in need of child care to be single heads of household, one would not expect to see such statistics describing Hispanic women. These trends indicate role changes and corresponding difficulties in the Hispanic community.

Geographic migrations and structural changes of the Hispanic family change the organization of traditional family systems and the role assignments of its members. These changes bring about a systemic need for the family to restructure, reconstitute, reintegrate, and realign itself so as to meet the needs of its members. Each family member plays a significant role in this endeavor, moving the process from her or his own perspective.

Finally, surrogate extended families are increasingly emerging. For Hispanics who no longer enjoy the advantages of a genetic extended family, the definition of "family" has broadened. A surrogate family can be sculpted with friends who become "tias y tios" (aunts and uncles), children who are adopted, and older persons who are invited to be acting grandparents. The need for these support systems must be recognized and understood in the clinical context. Their existence should be encouraged as part of a prevention strategy in working with Hispanics.

CHANGING NORMS OF HISPANIC FAMILIES

It is important to identify behaviors that can be considered "consistent" and "expected," and thus normative, within Hispanic families. To do this, however, requires that a basis for discussion be established. The discussion can begin with a description of Hispanic families, with the explicit understanding that traditional family structures are on the wane. The descriptions, then, may appear stereotypic and rigid. It is obvious that not all Hispanic families meet the description of the traditional family outlined herein. Variables such as generational status, socioeconomic status, as well as other factors such as upward mobility and divorce rates all contribute to making Hispanic families more diverse than the traditional extended family. Finally, social movements impacting the Hispanic experience, such as the Chicano movement and the feminist movement among Hispanic women, have impacted on the Hispanic family. These impacts have resulted in intra-familial stresses and personal conflicts for the family's members.

An outstanding feature of the literature on Hispanic groups is the agreement among authors concerning the theme of rigid adherence to sex roles and gender-appropriate behavior. Researchers note that sex roles among Hispanic groups tend to be more clearly defined than in other cultures (Madsen, 1964; Rubel, 1966; Tharp, et al., 1968; Murrillo, 1970; Carrillo-Beron, 1974). Hispanic males are defined as being proud, authoritarian, controlled, vengeful when dishonored, possessive in relationships; the Hispanic female is defined as being protected, submissive in relation to the male, sexually pure, and seen as vulnerable to seduction by the sexually aggressive male.

Currently, both men and women are far less insistent upon strict separation of sex roles. Based on recent changes within Hispanic culture, these traditional sex roles have been changing drastically. The impact of political and social movements for greater personal freedom and self expression has altered sex role behavior, especially that of the "submissive female." Additionally, the more urbanized Hispanics become, the greater the possibility is for Hispanic women of reaching economic independence from

men who in the past nurtured and maintained the submissiveness. Nonetheless, one may expect to encounter a higher degree of adherence to sex role
behavior within Hispanic culture than among non-Hispanic groups. The
following is a discussion of sex-role issues in Hispanic cultures. These issues
provide a context for the mental health practitioner seeking to understand
Hispanics.

AUTHORITARIAN FATHER AND MALE SUPREMACY

During the entire childhood of the male, virility is encouraged by stressing
courage to the point of temerity, aggressiveness, steadfastness, and honor.
Boys are taught never to run away from a fight and to honor their word. These
behaviors are rewarded by compliance with his wishes, nurturance by
females, and respect from others. Beginning with adolescence and through
the entire life of the male, virility will be measured, primarily, by sexual
conquests and, secondarily, in terms of physical prowess in relation to other
males. The undisputed authority of the male in the home and in all other
functions in relation to the female may be explained by the simple fact that he
is a man and is expected to conquer through his sexual powers. Authority and
male supremacy is fostered through socialization and child rearing practices
from infancy. Even before a child is born, a set of expectations is already at
work. In Mexico and most Latin American countries, male children are
highly valued and desired. Folklore has it that in the past the virility of the
father who sired a girl was considered questionable. Female infants, however,
were accepted as having merit within the family if they were born after the
birth of several male infants. The girl, in this case, would be seen as desirable
to assist the mother in serving her father and brothers. The girl in turn would
be protected by the males in her family. It was not uncommon for the husband
in a couple that gave birth only to girls to seek other sexual partners in order
to fulfill his own manhood by having a son.

THE ROLE EXPECTATIONS OF THE MALE

Above all, the male child must grow up to fit the dignified role of being a
man. There must be no dolls or pottery for the child to play with. Any
demonstration of feminine interests meets with disapproval by older brothers,
certainly the father, and the mother as well. The Hispanic male is socialized
from an early age to learn appropriate sex-role determined behaviors.

Boys are discouraged from participating in activities that might be
interpreted as "submissive" and unmanly, such as helping with the dishes.
These tasks are "traditionally" female and should be left to the female. Boys

are to be "little men," to come and go as they please, to play with other boys, and to accept responsibility as they grow into their adult roles as "authority figures." Therefore, they are discouraged from showing weakness and should instead strive to be self-controlled and expect females to attend to most of their physical needs. For example, little boys may be specifically trained not to make their beds since this would be contrary to their roles as men and would undermine the male supremacy of the father.

The mother may relate to her son with ambivalent attitudes of veneration in catering to his needs and resentment that she is not given the same privileges. It is most important to note that, despite the emphasis on being "strong," boys are raised with a spirit of enjoying friends, especially male friends, and of valuing warm and expressive interpersonal relations.

The role of the father in relation to child rearing is usually disciplinarian. Children are taught to listen to him and to exhibit fear and respect when around him. This is the model of behavior that boy children are reared with in regard to what will be expected from them as men. The male is seldom questioned by the female, and in traditional Hispanic families males have a great deal of independence, in sharp contrast to the female, who is protected by the family and is not allowed similar freedom.

STANDARDS OF CONDUCT FOR THE HISPANIC FEMALE

The Hispanic woman is introduced to the role expectations of women by observing the behavior of her mother. In Hispanic culture, the mother holds the highest respect. The Hispanic mother models behaviors that define her role as focused around the denial of all her needs and the absolute pursuit of the satisfaction of everyone else. The female is expected to be submissive in relation to the male. She is protected by the males in her family and is expected to be pure and held in high esteem by the extended family and the community. As a mother, she is supposed to be deeply affectionate, tender, and overprotective toward children. Infants are deeply loved, fondled, and admired. Nurturing through feeding is valued, as is close physical contact. The mother is to be the source of all tenderness and sentimentality. Cultural expressions such as writing, painting, sculpture, and religion are saturated with direct or symbolic allusions to maternity, whether religious or secular.

The rearing of females is quite different from the rearing of males. The daughter is raised to see the father as the ultimate authority who can determine her fate in either permitting or prohibiting her from realizing her plans. When she asks her mother's permission, she is told: "Preguntale a tu papa; lo que diga tu Parde." (Ask your father; whatever he says.) Already at a very early age she is trained to believe in the supremacy of the male. As a female, she must learn how to please the family and to be cooperative, thereby avoiding conflicts. She is to be respected because she is a female and is taught to conduct herself as a "lady" in order to maintain that respect. Because women are expected to be ideally "pure" and "chaste" they are frequently protected from men and expected to live more sheltered lives than men.

Presently, it is safe to say that both men and women are less insistent upon strict separation of sex roles. Nevertheless, the role expectations of males and females in the traditional Hispanic culture discussed above continues to be present in some forms. Ramirez (1967) has found that there appears to be definitive agreement by Hispanics of both sexes in respect for authority and relatively strict child rearing practices as compared to a control group of Anglo subjects.

PATTERNS OF NEUROSIS

An individual's failure or inability to accept, conform to, or adhere to sex-role defined standards of conduct can produce psychosocial problems. The following is a schematic guideline to the types of problems that may emerge.

First let us examine prevalent conflicts among males. One can deduce that in the male there can be problems of (1) submission/assertion and compliance/ rebellion in the area of authority, (2) preoccupation and anxiety regarding sexual potency, (3) conflict and ambivalence regarding the need for role consistency at all times, and (4) isolation and depression because of his inaccessibility as a "man who never 'breaks' or falters." Of course, reaction formations and over compensations are not uncommon. Generally speaking, symptomatic behavior emerges in relation to problems associated with sex role and identity.

Females experience other types of conflicts. The main areas of difficulty for the female arise around her expectations to meet the stiff requirements that the cultureal climate demands. Her inability to live up to these standards would lead her to have feelings of failure, leading to depression due to her internalized anger at not being treated equally. Unable to act out her rage or articulate her needs, she will tend to somatocize her complaints and be the victim of ill health.

INTERPERSONAL RELATIONSHIPS

The focus of Hispanic culture is not achievement through competition, but harmony through cooperation. Thus, a critical emphasis in Hispanic cultures is the development, maintenance, and enrichment of interpersonal relations, rather than an interest in mobility through the use of relationships. Hispanic people have developed exquisite ways of relating to one another through the development of social gestures, friendliness, romanticism, sentimentality, and a deep appreciation for light heartedness and humor during conversation. The human potential movement, for example, was well-suited for a culture of alienation but ill-suited for people who freely touch each other, laugh together, sing, and assist each other when in need. Linked to the appreciation of interpersonal relationships is a deep respect for affiliation, affection, and the need to belong to a larger network of family and friends. This network requires lifelong commitments, which include others in a variety of circumstances and settings. There is a delight in conversation, contact, caring, and presence in times of illness, death, or other difficulties.

EFFECTS OF EXTENDED FAMILY SYSTEM

The extended family system has been described as being tightly knit, providing for all of the needs of its members, including close friends in coparenthood (compadrazgo), permissible of emotional displays, promotive of hierarchical role distinctions, and distinct in its child rearing practices. Let us examine these characteristics and their effects on Hispanic individuals.

Even though large, Hispanic families are tightly knit. The presence of many people in the household has discouraged the need for individual privacy and a preference for being solitary. The result of this is that family members have tended to be much more at ease in conversation with one another and comfortable meeting others. It is very unusual, for example, to have structured activities at social gatherings among Hispanics since they are not needed.

As an inclusive network, the Hispanic family traditionally met the various needs of its members. Members are open with one another and seek the support and advice of other family members. Individual family members may earn a place as "expert" in a particular area, such as sex education or fiscal planning. Family mores dictate that Hispanics seek out the advice of a family member or close friend before seeking the help of a professional. To do otherwise would be insulting to the family. Recent studies, however, demonstrate the influence of generations in the United States and educational status on preferred source of advice, with a longer time in this country and higher level of education resulting in advice seeking from professionals (Carrillo and Molina, 1978; Keefe, and Casas, 1978). Nevertheless, help-seeking behaviors by Hispanics will be influenced by the familial resources available and their attitudes towards taking problems outside the family. An institutionalized form of extended family kinship that is prevalent in Hispanic cultures is compadrazgo. Compadre and comadre are titles of formal respect and position granted to members of close friends of the family. Literally, the compadre and comadre are the godfather and godmother of a child who is baptized. The compadres have a very important role within the family; if anything were to happen to the natural parents, the compadres (godparents) automatically become the child's parents and be expected to perform all parental duties. Both terms have been used informally as well to refer to extended friends of the family who, although not formal family members, are held in high esteem and affection and are, therefore, made relatives and integrated into the family system. The titles compadre and comadre, then, extend the concept of family to close friends and distant relatives. This custom, however, is also changing. Keefe, Padilla, and Carlos (1979) report that some third generation Hispanics are not familiar with the concept of compadrazgo.

Hispanic families are very comfortable with affective gestures. The mother has been depicted as often overprotective, freqeuntly using physical gestures of touching when speaking to her children. The father is a very contradictory figure within the affective system. On the one hand, he is described as being aloof, frequently absent from child rearing responsibilities within the home, constantly demanding respect of his authoritarian position within the family, and eliciting fear from family members. On the other hand, the male is also more "open" in his expression of emotion in comparison to males of other cultures. The Hispanic male is able to demonstrate deep feelings of joy, sadness, and excitement and cries easily when he is affected in a positive or negative manner. Also, his most agressive acts are often stimulated by the love and affection that dictates that he protect, defend, or avenge.

Traditional Hispanic culture is affiliative and hierarchical. A clear hierarchy of roles determines status and power relationships within the family and the community. The Hispanic child is reared to develop as an obedient, interdependent individual. The two extremes of the age continuum—the elderly and the very young—hold the highest status in society. They are given respect, power, and love. Babies, for example, are called "los reyes de la casa" (the kings of the household). The elderly grandparents, who traditionally hold power over ultimate decisions, share this status.

The determination of who receives more or less respect is based on roles or social attributes that are predetermined by beliefs and traditions. This is in contrast to status and respect based on accomplishments or academic degrees earned by the individuals (Diaz-Guerrero, 1975). A Pygmalion effect takes place when those who are awarded status and respect, use it, maintain it, and, ultimately, earn it.

Clearly, Hispanics appear to be moving away from such strict concepts of role and authority within the family, and with this movement approaching new normative behaviors for males and females. The mental health professional must be cautious in assessing Hispanic individuals; it is important to clarify the possibility of misdiagnosis in the light of these observations concerning sex roles. Viewed within a cultural context, male domination is not necessarily an indication of psychopathology on the part of either sex. For example, an Hispanic man who prefers the company of other men and who behaves in an authoritarian manner with his wife may be manifesting his "machismo" rather than indictating personal pathology. Such behavior among other cultural groups may imply "latent homosexuality," or an "inferiority complex," or that the woman is masochistic and prefers to be a "martyr." Such is not necessarily the case among Hispanic groups.

It is imperative for persons working with Hispanics in the helping professions to be able to identify behavior that is "normal" or accepted in the culture from that which is "abnormal" in other cultures. The crucial point is that health professionals must be informed of cross-cultural sex-role differences before rendering verdicts concerning psychopathology or appropriateness and inappropriateness of behavior among Hispanic groups.

Effective parenting in Hispanic cultures requires that children master those courtesies reflective of the interpersonal values central to the culture. These values include respect for authority and humility as an expression of the equality of persons in the world. Thus, manners are important. After telling a stranger one's name upon initial introduction, "para servirle" or "a sus ordenes" follows. Translated, this means "to serve you" and "at your orders." Commonly-acceptable use of the Spanish language is saturated with these forms, which reinforce hierarchical relationships. On the one hand, the forms ensure recognition of the dignity of others, but, on the other hand, they connote submission to another. The "Tu" form and the "Usted" form are other examples of race and class distinctions as originally manifested in language. The Spanish colonizer used the familiar "Tu," while the colonized Indian was required to reply with "Usted." When two people meet, the one in the position of submission refers to the other as "Usted," the one in a position of command uses "Tu," a familiar form of you. This practice can be identified in contemporary language use.

In Hispanic culture, the handshake among men, the abrazo (embrace), and the kiss are expressions of love as are cooperation, friendliness, smiling behavior, and other expressions of affection. Cultures influenced by Mediterranean Latin relational styles specialize in this kind of warm proximity-seeking behavior. This type of behavior can be sharply contrasted to cultures where *power* is stressed as the focal mode of communication.

The research in this area (Ramos, 1962) implies that while Hispanic sociocultures have been more efficacious promoting interpersonal relationships, the Anglo-American socioculture has been more efficacious in dealing with problems of authority and power. Because Hispanic culture is primarily a "love culture" and not a "power culture," Hispanics resolve problems by modifying the person rather than modifying the social environment. Cross-cultural research is needed to provide a clearer picture of the ways in which power and love interact in human relations relative to the dimensions of efficacy and inefficacy and of active versus passive reactions to stress and interpersonal relationships.

Diaz-Guerrero (1975) has developed a need hierarchy in regard to the Hispanic worker. He lists self-esteem as extremely low in the Mexican. Guerrero further states that because of the inability to feel self-confidence, the Mexican struggles to value himself or herself highly in relation to others. This problem with self-esteem is frequently dealt with by boasting and bragging rather than making a serious effort to identify the areas in which he or she *does* experience self-value. The lowered self-esteem and the tendency toward boasting is closely linked to exaggeration of virile ability in the male (machismo).

The male child, Diaz-Guerrero believes, has never been totally accepted by the father, who also struggles with his lack of self-esteem and, therefore, sees the son competitively and reacts to him critically, humiliating him frequently in public regarding issues of manhood. The son must, therefore, continuously be "proving himself."

Ramos (1962) offers a further explanation for this lack of self-esteem and attributes it to Mexico's history of conquest. Ramos states that during the conquest, a deep sense of inferiority was ingrained in the Hispanic/Indian by the conquistador who asserted his prowess and deduced superiority from it. The process of mestizaje or cross breeding became, then, a way to "mejorar la raza" (to better the race). This process, he believes, caused the Indian and mestizo to develop "menor valia" or "less worth." The conquistadores' imported machismo, with its gender-defined value system, contributed to assaults on self-esteem.

Sociocultural values, which are ingrained in the Hispanic family, also contribute to problems of self-esteem. For example, abuses or exaggerations of the exercise of authority by a family member can permit the personal or individual dignity of another family member to be trampled upon. For example, the oldest son is left "in charge" of younger siblings, and, if he is an 11-year old in charge of several toddlers, frustration brought about by lack of expertise may lead him to physical or verbal abuse. Also, the father, though always affectionate, is first and foremost a disciplinarian. And, although authority and discipline is necessary, its abuse can be detrimental. In addition, the authority expressed by the father can be irrational and unjust if inconsistent.

From early childhood human beings need to believe in their own self-worth. But if from early childhood there is no logical way to construct self-esteem on a real basis, it can be concluded that the development of self-esteem can be seriously impaired by threats in infancy and childhood. Diaz-Guerrero further develops this premise by explaining contemporary life in Mexico. Because of the prevalent economic conditions, historical as well as present, there has been little opportunity for the Hispanic to develop self-esteem. Not only is the subsistence of the masses of people substandard and precarious, thus endangering individual survival, but Mexicans and other Latin Americans know full well that their countries are sardines (small to medium sovereign entities) coexisting with sharks (the super powers) (Arevalo, 1961).

Individualism is not valued highly in Hispanic culture. Life cannot be enjoyed in a detached sense. The Hispanic expects life to be hard and demanding and, therefore, creates collective celebrations to enhance its quality. There is no notion of individual enjoyment as in the American's "doing one's own thing." If the Hispanic were to adapt such a slogan, it would transform into "doing our own thing." Consider the term "La Raza Unida." This is the opposite of individualism because it stresses a collective unity of the Latin race. Thus, the notions of individual enjoyment or accomplishment are not as sharply demarcated toward the individual as they are in Anglo culture. This may very well be because of the value placed on the family as the main unit of functioning and support.

IMPLICATIONS FOR PROGRAM DEVELOPMENT

The issues discussed here can be translated into clinical applications. With an understanding of the cultural context of the behavior and ideation of an Hispanic individual, evaluations will be more accurate, treatment more effective, and prognoses better. General improvements in the treatment of Hispanics by the society at large are obviously desirable as well.

Health programs must be made relevant to Hispanics. Consideration of Hispanics must be made in planning, training, recruitment, and integration of services to make programs relevant to the Hispanic population. Also, in the development of supportive services, coordination with community support systems as they exist in the Hispanic communities is crucial. Continuity of care and preventive care and health maintenance must be approached from a culturally sensitive perspective.

Government can assist us in these efforts. Federal data collection relevant to minorities and particularly to Hispanics would assist planning for regional national policy that emphasizes the specific health needs of the Hispanic. Program planners at state and local levels could promote and institutionalize pilot projects that have proved effective. Some ways of achieving this are to make available training grants to hospitals, medical schools, and research institutions for programs relevant to Hispanics. Above all, the appropriateness of services to needs must be gauged. Professionals must recognize the special medical and mental health problems of Hispanics and assist in articulating the need for epidemiological and demographic data, as well as program development.

Finally, regulatory and funding bodies should respond to the urgent mental needs of the Hispanic population by taking prompt action in the following areas.

Diagnostic Evaluations

Regulations are needed to ensure that:

1. Civil Commitment evaluations be conducted in the person's primary language, by a bilingual-bicultural mental health professional.

2. Psychological testing be conducted in the person's primary language, or not at all.

Treatment

Regulations are needed for better patient care as regards:

1. Instructions for psychotropic medications should be written in the patient's primary language to prevent inappropriate doses.

2. Community mental health centers and public mental health programs located in catchment areas with substantial percentages of Spanish-speaking residents should be required to adjust their staffing patterns to provide services in Spanish.

3. All mental health services should demonstrate standardized fluency examinations for employees hired to serve the Spanish speaking.

4. All mandated services should be required to demonstrate their capability to serve the Spanish speaking.

5. The Immigration and Naturalization Department should provide mental health services to people in distress in its detention centers.

Monitoring and Evaluation

To ensure the linguistic and cultural appropriateness of mental health programs, state authorities can take leadership in requiring:

1. Integration of federal, state, and county planning efforts as they affect services to the Spanish speaking.

2. Requirements that programs address the needs of the Spanish speaking in their planning efforts if the target population includes 2 percent or more Spanish speaking residents.

3. Patients' rights advocates should be representative of their client population, be autonomous from county programs, and be skilled in working with the Spanish speaking.

4. Community Mental Health Centers Advisory and Governing Boards and Mental Health Advisory Boards should be required to be made up of past or present consumers, to ensure input from Spanish-speaking people who have experienced the services.

The required evaluation of services should include specific reviews of progress, or lack thereof, in remedying the gross underservice of Hispanics by the mental health system.

Unresponsiveness on the part of government and its programs to the needs of the Spanish speaking, clashing with the increased social awareness of the Hispanic population, have produced an unhealthy psychological climate amongst Hispanics. The frameworks and recommendations presented here provide the remedy for a deficient mental health delivery system, which has been unable in the past to respond appropriately to the needs of Hispanics. Only with the proposed changes and a thorough understanding of the changing norms of Hispanic families can the Hispanic individual be understood and be provided with effective services.

REFERENCES

Arevalo, J.J. *The Shark and the Sardines.* New York: Lyle Stuart, 1961.

Carrillo, C. Overcoming barriers to treatment of the Hispanic patient. In *Handbook of Psychological Factors in Health Care: A Practitioner's Text in Health Care Psychology,* edited by M. Tospe, J.E. Nieberding, and B.D. Cohen, in press.

Carrillo-Beron, C. Conflicts, consequences and change in sex-role attitudes among Chicanos. Paper presented at the American Psychological Association Convention. San Francisco, Spring, 1974.

Carrillo-Beron, C. Raza mental health: perspectivas femeniles. In *Perspectivas en Chicano Studies.* Los Angeles: The National Association of Chicano Social Science, 1977.

Carrillo, C. and Molina, F. Attitudes toward healing within Raza. Unpublished manuscript, 1978.

Diaz-Guerrero, R. *The Psychology of the Mexican: Culture and Personality.* Austin: University of Texas Press, 1975.

Keefe, S.E. and Casas, J.M. Family and mental health among Mexican Americans: Some considerations for mental health services. In *Family and Mental Health in the Mexican American Community,* Monograph No. 7, edited by J.M. Casas and S.E. Keefe, pp. 1-24. Los Angeles: Spanish Speaking Mental Health Research Center, 1978.

Keefe, S., Padilla, A., and Carlos, M. The Mexican American extended family as an emotional support system. *Human Organization* 38 (1979):144-52.

Madsen, W. *The Mexican Americans of South Texas.* New York: Holt, Rinehart and Winston, 1964.

Montoya, R., Hayes-Bautista, D., Gonzales, L., and Smeloff, E. Minority dental school graduates: Do they serve minority community. *American Journal of Public Health* 68 (1978):1017-19.

Murrillo, N. The Mexican-American family. Paper presented at The Mexican American Seminars. Stanford University, Stanford, California, April 3-4, 1970.

Ramirez, M., III. Identification with Mexican family values and authoritarianism in Mexican-Americans. *Journal of Social Psychology* 73 (1967):3-11.

Ramos, S. *Profile of Man and Culture in Mexico.* Austin: University of Texas Press, 1962.

Rubel, A.J. *Across the Tracks: Mexican Americans in a Texas City.* Austin: University of Texas Press, 1966.

Sotelo, M.L. Coping: A study of Chicana and Latina single heads of households. Master's Thesis, 1978.

Tharp, R.G., Meadow, A., Lennhoff, S.G., and Satterfield, D. Changes in marriage roles accompanying the acculturation of the Mexican American wife. *Journal of Marriage and the Family* 30 (1968):404-12.

11 Therapeutic Interventions with Urban Black Adolescents

Anderson J. Franklin

The clinical problems presented by black urban adolescents are on the surface no different from those of any other youth population. They include concerns about self-image, achievement of autonomy, sexuality, peer relationships, school life, and vocational aspirations, to name a few. The difference in these concerns is in the intrapsychic and societal resources available to black youth during the process of development. By resources I refer to both psychosocial experiences and those family/community structures engaged for adequate adjustment and goal attainment. For adolescents at this stage of development control over their lives is a central issue. G. Stanley Hall (1905) characterized adolescence as a period of "storm and stress." Such a characterization alludes to the difficulty parents have in managing the adolescent child and the conflicts experienced by the adolescent from growth into adult responsibilities. Too often this period is represented as negative, creating ambivalence and frustration among professionals and parents in the handling of the adolescent.

The black urban adolescent has all of the concerns that characterize development during this life span. In addition, there are unique issues that go with the status of being black in an urban environment. Life for many urban black adolescents is rooted in poverty, illiteracy, unemployment, and racism. Adaptive styles for such social circumstances are often not ideal. What confronts the clinician in work with the urban black adolescent are essentially problems borne out of racism and stressful life conditions masked by common developmental concerns, or vice versa. Given what these youth must cope with, it is not unlikely to find therapists who either disregard the effects of racism on a youth's development, or, as noted by Thomas and Sillen (1974), the therapists believe that "since social norms cannot be changed overnight the individual must learn to conform to the prevailing scheme of things" (p. 141). The prevailing scheme of things for urban black residents is abominable. It is worse as an adolescent. The consequence of such life conditions is reflected in the high rate of institutionalization (psychiatric and correctional) and poor school performances of black youth (Kramer, Rosen and Willis, 1973; Jones, 1973). The U.S. ideal of personal success is known by black youth. It is flaunted daily on television and other forms of mass media. The impact on mental health from the media's conveyance of its embellished form of reality is still controversial (Pierce, 1974). Likewise, the chance of blacks achieving such a norm is equally known from community referents as well as social statistics. The disparity between the ideal and the actual future life conditions for young black adults is discouraging. Unfortunately, there is little in the present that foretells better living circumstances in the future. The urban black adolescent must temper expectations of a better life from that of the average contemporary black family. When we consider the importance attributed to the relationship between vocational aspirations and identity, the frustrating circumstances of life for the black adolescent provides another dimension to understanding an already difficult process in development.

THE STATUS OF BLACK ADOLESCENTS

According to the 1970 census, over 75 percent of the black population resides in an urban metropolis. Youth under the age of 18 years comprises 42 percent of the black population. About 52 percent are females and 47 percent are males. The average black urban family has a mean family income of $7,074 and a per capita income of $3,557. As of October 1977, 24 percent of all blacks ages 18 to 24 years had not completed a high school education. For some urban areas the statistics are worst. For example, a New York Board of Education report estimates that 45 percent of the entering high school students do not complete the fourth year. Over 50 percent of many urban public high schools are black (Crain and Mahard, 1978). In addition, 51 percent of all students enrolled in programs for the educable mentally retarded (EMR), as reported by the 1974 Office of Civil Rights survey were black, whereas they represented only 24 percent of the survey population. Unemployment for black adolescents is 37 percent approximately; if one considers the National Urban League (1979) hidden statistics (includes persons discouraged to work), the employment for black youth climbs to over 50 percent. Of the persons institutionalized in state mental hospitals and correctional facilities approximately 50 percent are nonwhites (note: nonwhites comprise only 12 percent of the total population).

These statistics only partially portray characteristics of the total population of black youth. Certainly, not every urban black adolescent can be characterized by these social statistics. Such data, however, provide a description of conditions in which we as professionals might find an urban black adolescent. None of these statistics capture the social atmosphere or economic stress under which black youth must live. These discouraging statistics allude to environmental conditions but do not describe adaptive styles the person must employ to cope with such life circumstances.

DEVELOPMENTAL AND CLINICAL PROBLEMS

The lack of a comprehensive body of knowledge representing the psychological development of the urban black adolescent makes conclusions in this area difficult. At best, we can draw upon the general literature on adolescence and make inferences about black adolescents. By following this procedure we run the risk of misrepresenting development for the black adolescent. Since the urban black masses are subject to poor living conditions, the urban black adolescent's life must be considered within this context. Dohrenwend and Dohrenwend (1974) have portrayed the consequences of inner city life as contributing to a high incidence of psychopathology. It is certainly apparent that urban life has many levels of stress, which form particular adaptive behaviors (Clark, 1965; Valentine, 1968). In the category of deviant behaviors, juvenile delinquency has been a popular focus of social and behavioral scientists. An examination of the literature will attest to this preoccupation. A dominant theme within the social science and education literature is the description of the broken or parent-absent family, the welfare dependency of the black community, the poor school achievement of black youth, and its overall effects upon the development of black children (Billingsley, 1968). It is not my intent to critique these assumptions or interpretations but to note that the prevalence of such conditions have not been considered in a systematic analysis of their impact on psychological development of black adolescents.

The role of the clinician when confronted with the presenting problems of the adolescent is to distinguish between those personal concerns that are characteristic of average developmental experiences from those that are markedly deviant and possibly pathological. Since so much of adolescent behavior is viewed as alienation from society's roles and parental authority, deviant behavior is often interpreted in psychopathological terms. It is a period of life where there is no clear unanimity among professionals as to allowable levels of personal conflicts before psychopathology is judged present. Weiner (1970) addresses this confusion amply in his discussion of the different views on normality and abnormality in adolescence.

> ...psychological disturbance is so much a normal concomitant of adolescence that its absence is a cause for concern. Beres (1961) suggests that the adolescent who does not experience a state of flux and uncertainty is likely to have suffered a premature crystallization of his response patterns that may
> Jones 11:2

presage serious psychopathology. Anna Freud (1958) contends that teenagers who remain "good children" and fail to show outer evidence of inner unrest are displaying deviant development. In her view such children are responding to their impulses with excessive, crippling defenses that impede normal maturational processes (p. 42).

The clinician's struggle to determine when adolescent behavior is truly pathological must evolve from considering the etiology of symptoms and their developmental history. "It is only when a developmental reconstruction can be made in the course of diagnosis and therapy that a clear distinction between pathology and the normal adolescent process can be attempted" (Sprince, 1964, p. 103). The developmental context becomes extremely important in determining when behavior is pathological. This is a major factor in interpreting the experiences of the black adolescent. Clinicians must be able to not only extract the particulars about early childhood experiences for the black adolescent but comprehend the significance of coping with socioeconomic inequities and racism in terms of their impact on psychological development. To compartmentalize the developmental history of the black adolescent into traditional psychodynamic categories without considering the adaptive forces inherent in the social realities of community life is to forfeit diagnostic precision. Developmental histories must be evaluated within an understanding of the larger social context for proper formulations about behavior. This is a point cogently conveyed by Weiner (1970):

> From the clinical point of view it is unwarranted automatically to interpret model behavior as behavior that does not call for professional assistance.
> Yet judgments about normality cannot be completely independent of the context in which behavior occurs. Few would disagree that ritual suicidal behavior has different implications for psychological disturbance in Japan and the United States, primarily because of the different socio-cultural values attached to such behavior in the two countries. However it is possible to encompass the import of socio-cultural relativism within the normality-as-health perspective. As Romano and others propose, "health" criteria for normality can be defined to include adequate capacity for social interaction, which implies that the individual is in relative harmony with his immediate society. At the same time, by focusing on freedom from pain, discomfort, and disability, the health perspective of normality avoids the error of labeling as abnormal an individual who calmly meets an emergency or crisis that is unnerving most of those around him (pp. 49-50).

The importance of this concept to diagnosis is represented by the inclination to formulate pathology when a black adolescent relates atypical family structure or dynamics. For example, clinicians who have no understanding of some harsh realities in urban life may prejudge psychosocial development upon learning a youth shares a bed with siblings. The hardships of some black families overpower the naive clinician to the point of incomprehension about survival under such conditions and misjudgment about the adaptive styles generated by such an environment (Billingsley, 1968; White, 1980).

The question of when behavior is abnormal and pathological in adolescence is best answered in the scrutiny of the youth's psychosocial history. If there is evidence of patterned maladaptive behavior throughout childhood, there is sufficient reason to conclude that the clinical issue is characterological in substance. On the other hand, if the youth has had a childhood relatively free of psychosocial problems, except for the most recent times, it is likely that current clinical issues are transient. Although simply stated, this judgment is not the easiest to exercise when making a diagnosis. There are those problems that seem transient and symptomatic of the developmental experiences for this age but are in fact masking fundamental characterological issues. Similar to any other age group, there are age-related problems that usually constitute the initial issue for the client. With further clinical interviewing, other issues are exposed. The most common example of this with adolescent patients is the depression associated with the inability to establish affectional ties with peers of the opposite sex. The peer pressure among adolescents to explore sexuality is great. Adolescence is the first time that sexuality becomes a critical conscious concern about the relationships between the sexes (Conger, 1977). Most adolescents are basically naive about the responsible manner in which to integrate the physical, psychological, and emotional demands of this new-found experience. There is very little parental or formal education about sexuality in adolescence. By sexuality I am not limiting this to knowledge about the biological reproductive process. On the contrary, this is only a small part of the dynamics inherent in wholesome heterosexual relationships. We know that in spite of the effort of sex education in the public schools 11 million teenagers become pregnant a year (Planned Parenthood Federation of America, 1976). Black adolescents have a disproportionate number of teenage pregnancies. When interviewed about the incidence of pregnancies, teenagers do not profess much ignorance of the reproductive process in contrast to the responsibility that goes with heterosexual experiences. Very often the dilemma for the adolescent is how to manage the overpowering sex drive within the prevailing social attitudes and sanctions. To some the sex drive is frightening. The complexity of the sex urge is reinforced by peer anecdotes, myths, nocturnal emissions, dreams, and fantasies. The anxiety associated with this experience can greatly hamper the development of self-concept. Contributing to this one issue, for example, are such interrelated concerns as parent-child conflicts, management of peer pressure, comprehension of physiological changes, and self-esteem. An adolescent who has managing heterosexual relationships as a primary concern requires the clinician to discern if the issue is developmental and transient or reflective of characterological issues. The following cases are illustrative of this diagnostic issue.

Mary was brought to the clinic by her parents with an expressed concern about her lethargy and her withdrawn and depressed behavior. She was 15 years old, was in good health, had no previous history of social or psychological problems, and was an excellent student. In appearance Mary was neat, dressed in peer-appropriate stylish clothes, and adult looking in physical development. Both relatives and peers had commented on her attractiveness, as well as her growing sex appeal. In the initial therapy sessions Mary denied her depression as "no big thing," she just felt "unmotivated" except for school work. She portrayed herself as having several girl friends who felt and acted similar to her, but in recent years she found the number of close friends dwindling as their interest in boys developed. Queried as to her interest in boys, Mary skirted the issue for several sessions, until one day in a burst of tears she relayed her confusion about her sexuality. Because Mary had developed at a young age she attracted suggestive comments and approaches from peers and some adults. Her appearance and experiences caused a change in the way her friends and parents reacted to her. In school, boys hovered around her and tried to persuade her into sexual exploits. She attributed her appearance as the basis for some girl friends to "put her down" and others to associate with her because she attracted boys. These days it seemed like her appearance defined the nature of her relationships wtih peers. Conflicts with her parents about her manner of dress and attention from boys were frequent. She felt her parents were ashamed of her appearance because they disagreed with the way she dressed. "Tight-fitting jeans or shirts always seemed to set my folks off." Complicating the matter for Mary was her own positive feelings about her manner of dress and the advances of boys. What contributed to her depression was the unresolved frustration from conflicts with her parents and sexual attraction to boys. The "hassles" forced a solution of disengagement from encounters and depression from growing social isolation.

Mary's physiological changes and emerging sexuality at an earlier age than her peers brought increased pressure to assume the consequences of early maturation. As is often the case, Mary had no preparation for the new demands placed on her relationships with others from her physical changes. Suddenly, new social rules were placed upon her, which became overwhelmingly frustrating to manage. People spent more time responding to her appearance than helping her to gain understanding of how to manage it in a responsible way. In order to minimize the pain and frustration Mary elected to withdraw, thus acquiring new problems from voluntary isolation.

For the clinician treating an adolescent patient such as Mary the major responsibility is determining whether the manifestation of depression is a historical pattern or situationally specific. Because establishing a trustworthy bond with adolescents can be extremely difficult, learning the basis of adolescent depression can be elusive and misinterpretations can result from the youths' reluctance to explain their behavior. In particular, discussion of sex with an adult therapist can be frustrating because adult reactions are frequently the source of the conflict in the first place. "Sex is just something you don't talk to grown-ups about" is the frequent comment of teenagers. Consequently, unless the therapist can get beyond the implicit adversary tradition of adult-adolescent relationships and establish an open and trusting rapport, the basis of clinical problems can be obscured. In the case of Mary it became clear during the course of therapy that her inability to resolve the management of her experiences in adolescent sexuality was the center of her immediate problems. Her solution to withdraw only compounded the situation. As therapy helped Mary become informed of the naturalness of her sexuality and experiences as well as appropriate ways of managing it her depression and relationships with others improved. The concerns of Mary were indicative of issues presented by passage through a development stage. However, if the therapist had been unsuccessful in getting Mary to disclose her true conflicts, it is likely the direction of therapy would have taken a different path. It must be stressed that before clinical formulations become firm about the presenting problems of adolescents the therapist must be confident that a sufficient bond is established with the youth in order to evaluate the integrity of the disclosures.

In another case concerning adolescent sexuality, preoccupation with achieving the ideal adult male role and the concommitant appropriate social skills in heterosexual relationships obscured a more fundamental issue of sexual identity. A 15-year old black male was referred to the clinic because of academic difficulties. After six months of therapy the client reluctantly began to reveal that his school performance was affected by his preoccupation with girls. He had no girl friend and had difficulty establishing any kind of meaningful ties with girls. His naivete about just approaching and talking to girls was indicative of his ineffectual social skills. A high level of enthusiasm to establish relationships with girls led to a treatment plan of discussing boy-girl experiences as well as social skills training. After a short period of working with this treatment plan it became evident that the client repeatedly sabotaged his own efforts. What emerged was the patient's own ambivalence about girls and a haunting attraction to boys. Once this admission occurred the issue of sexual identity became the focus of therapy. A suspicion of an identity issue had been formulated early in the initial sessions, but the youth was adamant in asserting his interest in girls. It was only after carefully and slowly confronting the youth about the identity issue and after the youth's failures in social skills assignments mounted that the therapist was to get the youth to acknowledge a basic conflict.

The significance of this case is in the prevalence of the initial problem. Many adolescents present as the root of their distress the management of heterosexual relationships during the emergence of their own sexuality. Peer and societal pressure force certain conforming behaviors upon adolescents that heretofore were not required. In both cases a therapist can easily succumb to the conclusion that these problems are transient and symptomatic of passage through a developmental phase. In the case of Mary such an assumption would be appropriate, but with the latter example an apparent incompetence in social skills masked a larger issue of sexual identity.

Sociocultural Implications

Although both of the cited cases were with black youths, they contain circumstances that could apply to any group of adolescents. The critical variable in synthesizing these experiences for black youth and making clinical formulations is evaluating the contribution from their social milieu. Comprehension of the social milieu is essential for the development of an effective treatment plan. Given recent reports on the status of black adolescents in the United States, these youths are placed in marginal situations and life conditions. Families of black youth are equally victims of stressful circumstances, in part represented by concerns about economic and educational opportunities for their children (Ogbu, 1978). The stress in black families today, with deteriorating options, is a context within which problems of black youth evolve. Hypertension among black adults and some adolescents is symptomatic of the stress experienced in the black family and communities (Lawson, 1979; Myers and Miles, 1979; Dohrenwend and Dohrenwend, 1974). Likewise, the increasing evidence of health and mental health problems in the black community broadens the view of the problems (Kramer, Rosen, and Willis, 1973). To understand the development of black adolescent self-esteem and adaptive styles, the social milieu of their families must be considered. Consequently, what may be a suitable clinical judgment for white adolescents may not be appropriate to help the black youth.

In the case of Mary, an attractive black adolescent, one of the chief pressures was the encouragement by some peers and school counselors to use her appearance as a vehicle to escape economic hardships through modeling. In spite of her above-average school performance, she was frequently led to believe that her future was dependent on her physical appearance. On the other hand, her parents were apprehensive that her attractiveness and deportment would get her into trouble. They were brutally frank with community examples of how nice looking girls ended up in trouble with boys. As added pressure they emphasized the importance of education, not a flaunting of beauty, as a way out of the ghetto. Consequently, in school her beauty was lauded and a feature of her social status, but at home it was devalued and considered an obstacle to upward mobility.

The case of the 15-year old black male is also an example of how the urban social milieu affects development. He was in a school that reflected many of the problems of contemporary urban high schools. Education and management of the predominantly black student body was minimal. The school environment was greatly defined by interests of student peer groups rather than teachers and school administrators. At this school education was a laissez-faire proposition for students. Classroom time was frequently consumed with maintaining order. Psychological development in this social context is different from a school environment where educational goals determine the climate. For our male patient the school environment forced identifying with the social demands of peer groups as the greater priority rather than working toward educational goals. Because the school was so ineffectual in establishing educational demands, no competing alternative existed for the client. The school was at best performing a custodial function. Therefore, for him negotiating the myriad of school demands from peers became the overpowering need when in school.

GUIDE TO THERAPY

The Initial Interview

Black adolescents referrals in urban areas are often from public agencies such as schools or the court systems. Seldom do youth come of their own volition, and when brought by parents it usually means that parental control has been lost. Given this circumstance, reluctance to participate in therapy is built-in at the initial contact. This attitude is somewhat molded by the image of psychological services imparted by the schools and the community. Within schools, referral to the guidance counselor is often associated with a discipline problem. As professionally compromising as this position may be, it is frequently the responsibility of the school counselor to remedy a bad situation. This sets up the school counselor as the "bad guy" whose actions can place conditions on the school experience of the youth. When the school counselor cannot help the student, referral and/or suspension can result. School counselors are often the ones who contact parents, monitor attendance and truancy, and handle an assortment of behavior problems. The orientation to therapeutic assistance, therefore, is predetermined. It is not evolving from a self-defined need but, rather, from an imposed demand from others.

In addition, the therapist must handle the community image of psychological services as a stigma of defective mental health. Adolescents are just as reluctant as adults to reveal their contact or need of psychological help. Black adolescents indulge in the same patterns of peer deceit about seeing a psychologist as adults. In one instance I had a youth who repeatedly represented his weekly visits to therapy as special coaching in judo to allay the suspicions of peers and excuse his absence from the regular afternoon of playground basketball.

Heretofore, representatives of traditional professions such as the pastor or physician were the principal source of help for black families having trouble with their adolescents. Another alternative is to seek the help of the courts. Through a court order a youth can be placed under the court's authority as a "person in need of supervision" PINS, which essentially absolves the parent from the responsibility of their child's behavior. Parents who resort to this solution have usually reached their limits of control over the youth. Interviewing such parents often reveals that sufficient signs of problems with the youth were known far enough in advance where, if confidence in mental health practitioners had existed, appropriate therapeutic interventions could have stemmed behavioral patterns.

For whatever reasons black youth are not referred for therapeutic assistance until such time that a problem has become severe. Further education of the black community about the utility of mental health services is certainly needed but the reality remains that black youth come to the attention of therapists when their behavior is unmanageable. Because youth will rarely see their behavior as problematic and seek therapy by their own volition, and because parents will wait until their authority and control is strained, the circumstances of an initial contact with the therapist are almost uniformly the same: exasperated parent and an unwilling adolescent. This condition, coupled with the black public attitude toward mental health services, is an issue that a therapist and intake worker must be sensitive to in the development of an adequate initial bond with the adolescent patient.

In the initial contact with the black adolescent there is the issue of whether the parent should be included. As a matter of practice I will see both parent and child during the first session, leaving time to see the adolescent alone. The alone time allows the youth to present his or her interpretation of why he or she is in therapy as well as to answer some questions about the process that were unanswered or unclear. It is important to stress the confidential nature of therapy and the benefits that may be gained from the process. Clarifying the therapeutic process becomes an important part of this initial stage. This does not mean that as therapist one strives to convince the youth why he or she should be in therapy. Rather, assuring the youth about the advantages of therapy should flow from an exchange of information. However, in some instances in the initial session the youth will not engage in any meaningful discussion. If silence with occasional monosyllabic responses is the norm, it is sometimes helpful for the therapist to offer reassurances by anticipating what are the (nonverbalized) concerns for the youth.

Trust is at the basis of any therapeutic relationship, but for adolescents it is a major concern. Since they are usually brought or referred by other authority figures initially, there is little to differentiate the therapist from other adults managing their lives. Talking briefly about the therapist's role is an aid to the black adolescent's understanding of therapy, whether the patient initiates it or not. Another important ingredient in this initial session is to convey the adolescent's responsibility in therapy. Like many patients, the adolescent will expect the therapist to prescribe a quick remedy for the situation. This, of course, has to be dispelled through the educative process on patient responsibility. However, when the youth is brought to therapy based on the motives of others the youth may vigorously disclaim any reason for why he or she may not agree with it. In fact the youth may perceive the requirement to see a therapist as a waste of valuable time. Therapy is interpreted as another adult imposition and reinforces underlying rationale for the acting out behavior. Consequently, the therapy session may constitute another area of resistence to adult authority. Trying to overcome such an attitude to establish a bond is difficult. Yet, that difficulty emphasizes the importance of the initial sessions as a time to build rapport. Without such a tie to the adolescent, therapy will make little progress. Reticence to engage the therapist during the initial sessions may be indicative of all of the above misgivings on the part of the adolescent. This is why a more active role initially may help the youth to change his or her view of the therapist as another imposing adult figure to an empathic and concerned individual.

One advantage of conducting the initial interview with the parents involved is the opportunity to observe the dynamics between parents and child. Because so often the parents are before you in a state of exasperation and possibly desperation, the manner in which they portray issues can be very informative. It is not uncommon for some youth to learn for the first time precisely why their parents are upset with them. In some instances this can lead to a lively debate between parents and child, affording the therapist a glimpse of the interpersonal dynamics. There are those who cower in the presence of the parents and sit meekly, or sullenly while hearing the "charges" against them. On the other hand, there are some youth who will immediately launch into an argument as to the accuracy of their portrayal. A therapist's pitfall in these exchanges is appearing to take sides. The parents will seek affirmation of their child-rearing practices from the therapist, and the adolescent will be assessing how much his or her view is valued.

Once an initial understanding of the presenting problem is acquired the task of developing rapport with the adolescent remains. An important feature of acquiring fidelity and integrity among adolescents is passing tests of confidence. This can assume numerous forms dependent on the circumstances. However, because the adolescent period is a stage at which many adult behaviors are explored and identity is based on sometimes exaggerated or distorted personal notions of adult life styles, the sharing of peer exploits is highly guarded. To be privy to such information requires an understanding and trusting person. For an adolescent this cannot be determined at first contact with anybody, much less an adult. Consequently, various trials to test integrity are presented. Such tests are not restricted to adolescents, but it seems that this age group can devise very creative and provocative forms. There are those who become mummified—a test of strength to endure the stress of silence; you will also encounter the seducer, who seeks validation from you as they do from their peers; the starer, who will rivet you with constant eye contact; and the abuser, who will verbally or physically try to intimidate you. The basic dynamic issue in the first sessions of therapy with the adolescent is one of control. The streetwise kid is very adept at maintaining control over the situation by adopting various roles. This can be deceptive to the naive therapist and lead him or her toward clinical conclusions that are inappropriate. During the early sessions with a streetwise youth the therapist must be vigilant that he or she is not being misled. Until proven worthwhile, the value of therapy sessions to the coerced black adolescent has no more appeal than any other forced obligations. The little appeal it may have is its liberation from class time if so scheduled. It will certainly be alienating if therapy sessions interfered with more important afterschool peer activities.

There are several types of common behaviors seen during the initial sessions of therapy. These take the form of initial resistances to establishing rapport and securing meaningful clinical data. There is the proverbial "reluctant talker." This may be represented by a withdrawn youth whose demeanor may even include physical disengagement (e.g., moving the chair to the other side of the room, turning sideways, and avoiding eye contact by staring at the ceiling or down at the floor). Such disengagement is not unusual by a youth who objects to being brought to the therapist. Because this form of protest can begin before the youth reaches the therapist's office, it is easy to attribute more psychological disturbance than exists. To help discern whether a ploy is being used by the youth to prevent the therapeutic process, the psychological history can be examined to determine how characteristic is this behavior. In addition the therapist can consult with significant others such as parents or teachers to learn whether the observed behavior is typical of the youth in other settings. A most common form of marginal participation in therapy that keeps the therapist at bay is responding in monosyllabic utterances such as "yes," "no," "maybe," "uh huh," etc. Some youth are very adept at limiting their conversation to such responses no matter how skillfully the questions are devised to circumvent them and to open up the youngster to free flowing discussions.

Another type of initial response a therapist might get from a black adolescent is just the opposite of the withdrawn posture. This type might be termed the "babbler," a person who discloses everything, dumping every conceivable grievance. Often the tone of this disclosure is bitter and relates how parents, teachers, siblings, or peers have imposed on the youth. One can get the impression that the youngster is the most misunderstood person in the world. The rapidity of issues presented and their lack of focus can keep the therapist from identifying appropriate therapeutic issues. This can particularly be difficult if the youngster repeatedly dominates sessions with complaints and avoids any one issue. Although a therapeutic objective initially may be to allow the youth to ventilate issues of concern, excessive preoccupation may be a veiled tactic to keep the therapist disengaged. For some black youth who are expansive in this fashion it is easy to provide embellished stories if the therapist has been caught up in the dramatization. Sometimes the content of the babbler's talk can take the form of convincing the therapist that the youth has everything under control in spite of shocking circumstances. Youngsters who focus their discussion to shock and disarm the therapist I call the "impressors."

It is not uncommon for some urban streetwise black youth to begin sessions by relating antisocial exploits such as indulgence in drugs, sex, alcohol, or delinquency. These tactics are attempts to force the therapist into making value statements, verbally or nonverbally. Raised eyebrows, furrowed brows, and shifting in one's seat at sensational points in the story are telltale signs to the youngster that he or she has touched judgmental sentiments in the therapist. When urban black youth meet a white therapist whom they believe is naive and impressionable about street experiences they may try to employ this offensive tactic to either scare the therapist off and/or test sincerity. It is also a device to measure the therapist's knowledge and empathy for the sociocultural conditions of life for the black adolescent.

An example that characterizes this dynamic is the experience of two white therapists who were working with a group of black adolescent girls between the ages of 15 and 18 in a residential group home. Since most of these girls had spent the majority of their lives moving from foster homes to group residential accommodations, they had some sophistication in dealing with the approach of the professional helper. First contacts were received with great indifference on the part of the youngsters. Their indulgence of the administrator's programming of group therapy was met with suffocating apathy and righteous indignation. They were disorderly, assertive, and detached from the therapist's attempts to structure a group. When met individually in order to obtain more specific intake information, one girl related the "horrors" of her circumstances. Her custody had been shifted from one adult to another throughout her childhood by her mother. To her best recollection she was currently in the custody of her mother's pastor, an elderly woman. She was in frequent pain over the past year because of a suspected ovarian cyst, which could not be treated properly because of confusion over who had authority to permit an operation. She had seen her father shot and killed and was with her best girl friend when she overdosed on drugs. Other tidbits along this theme were thrown in for effect. Although these incidents were exaggerated to get a rise out of the therapists, they were basically true. Subsequent sessions and other information revealed that this youth often greeted professional aid in this manner because such services were short term and transient. She did not want to make a personal investment to resolve intrapsychic conflicts under such conditions. But, since she was repeatedly subjected to such transient services by authorities her only recourse was to disarm the therapists and discourage pursuit of therapeutic objectives by creating a feeling of hopelessness in them. It was an overwhelming story for the two white therapists, but with supervision and encouragement they were able to establish rapport with the girls and work effectively with them.

Establishing Rapport

Being candid, direct, at ease, and engaging with black adolescents has proven most effective in establishing rapport; whereas shrouding interaction in clinical jargon and deportment tends to alienate and impede the youth's ability to engage the therapeutic process. This does not mean that therapists should discard clinical judgment or responsibility. It does advocate a more assertive role on the part of a therapist when working with adolescents than one might employ with adults. Usually, a significant segment of therapy with black adolescents is educational, so that the therapist will eventually assume an informative role. Reassuring the patient that the therapist's role is to aid understanding helps to launch the establishment of rapport. Inquiring too early into the rationale of behavior can intimidate and put adolescents on the defensive. It can be perceived as no different from the prying and justifications demanded by parents. Adolescent life is constantly under the scrutiny of adults. The youth's relating of psychosocial experiences are to be encouraged, but deeper exploration should be approached cautiously until such time as rapport is firmly established. A too early exploration of issues in depth can encourage the youth to fabricate information in order to satisfy transparent clinical needs of the therapist. "Giving the therapist what they want to hear" also fulfills the compliant role expected of youth by adults.

Another therapist's aid in establishing rapport is language. Communication among streetwise urban black adolescents is sociolinguistically rooted in the use of slang. Knowledge of how youth use language can be valuable to the therapist. When slang is strategically and unpretentiously integrated into the therapist's conversation with the youth this conveys some understanding of the youth's peer world. It expedites rapport. This ability is often misconstrued by some therapists that they must be facile with "street talk." The biggest error a therapist can make is to try and appear down to earth and fluent in something they are not. Such representations out of ignorance appear as inappropriate as errors made when attempting to speak a foreign language. Knowing the slang of black youth is a helpful but not necessary prerequisite for rapport. The colorful street language of black youth requires more than knowledge of words. Cadence, tone, timing, situationally appropriate usage are also essentials for slang fluency. Employing slang words without such cognizance portrays the therapist as unsophisticated. The best solution for therapists' incompetence in the use of slang is to omit it from their conversation, be honest about ignorance of terms, and encourage their patients to educate them about their meanings. Even for those therapists who once had facility with street slang but have been out of touch with the world of adolescents it would be wise to temper their use of dated idioms until acquiring a grasp of contemporary usage.

Physical Appearance and Deportment in Therapy

Physical appearance and deportment in therapy is another element in the bonding process that is given insufficient attention. Dress for black adolescents is an important dimension of identity. There are instances of black youth not attending school because they cannot afford the clothes required by the peer group dress code. In the black urban high schools it is not uncommon to find youth attired in expensive brand-name clothes. How they are acquired is another issue, but the fact is that possession of fine clothes is a status symbol. Although all youth cannot obtain the best, it is an ideal to strive for. It may be the only ostensible means of declaring self-pride, particularly if the family is part of the working poor. Black adolescent attire must be understood within the context of the dress code. Even looking "bummy" has a code, that is, the type of sneakers (i.e., gym shoes) one may wear, the type of jeans, tops, etc. It can, for example, be as specific as the manner in which one wears socks. In New York having a pair of Puma's (sneakers) with ankle-length socks over calf-length sweat socks is the acceptable way to dress, particularly if one plans to play basketball in the local playground. There are variations on this fashion, including proper color combinations. Extreme deviation from the style is subject to strong sanctions from the peer group.

The importance of dress in therapy is that it can provide the therapist with an enormous amount of nonverbal clues about the black adolescent. By having some knowledge of the popular dress codes among adolescent peer groups the therapist can from observation assess how conforming to youth norms the youngster may be. For example, a therapist may plan to determine how genuine or vicarious is the youth's identification with the peer culture. Attire can provide the therapist with clinical hypotheses about the adolescent. In contrast, attire can impede the establishment of a therapeutic bond if the therapist finds the youngster's manner of dress offensive. The most poignant example that comes to mind is the frequent issue of the "hat" and "coat." Keeping in mind the proposition that attire is frequently an expression of identity or attitude of the youth, a common source of conflict is the manner in which youngsters wear their clothes. In this regard a primary issue between black adolescents and adult authorities is whether they can remain inside a room with their hats and coats on. There has never been one thing that can ignite as much conflict and resistance between adolescents and adults than trying to convince youngsters that they should not sit before them attired in a hat and/or coat. For example a 15-year old black adolescent male was brought to therapy by the parents because of persistent school failures. During the initial family sessions the youth sat with his hooded coat on until commanded by one of the parents to remove it. Whenever seen alone the youth kept his coat on throughout all of the early sessions.

How one interprets this simple behavior rests with the emerging clinical data, but general knowledge about many adolescents is that they will keep outer garments on throughout the day because of no other reason than it is part of the day's uniform. On the other hand, a number of other reasons can exist for this practice. In some instances black youth may keep jackets on because of peer symbolism and conformity. For some youth the outer garment covers other clothes that do not equal the desired quality and value. Remaining in their coats may reflect an attitude toward therapy and the intent to escape it as soon as possible.

Although a therapist may find talking to a youngster while the youth is still fully attired with hat and coat somewhat annoying, the therapist cannot allow this appearance to be overly disconcerting. A responsibility of the therapist is to use all behaviors verbal and nonverbal as aids in clinical formulations. One reasonable formulation about why a youth remains wrapped up in the outer garments is that it constitutes a form of resistance. Another youth who had remained zippered up with his hood over his head and uncommunicative for several sessions was confronted about the loss in benefits from not using therapy. The therapist emphasized that regardless of how he wanted to use the sessions circumstances required that he attend so why throw away a unique opportunity to share his concerns confidentially. Once this message was sufficiently conveyed the young man disclosed how he had successfully frustrated the efforts of another therapist that past year with the same deportment. Although there are possibly other reasons why this youth elected to respond to such overtures from the therapist, the essential point is that use of clothes by black adolescents can be important clues to intrapsychic dynamics.

Another major example of this phenomenon is the wearing of hats by black adolescents, especially males. The type of hat a black youth wears can represent an integral part of identity. Again keeping such an apparel on may be more a part of "the uniform" than intended disrespect. Careful probing about this behavior can reveal vital information about the character of the peer group the youth identifies with as well as self concept.

The importance of clothes for some black adolescents extends to the therapist's attire. One black adolescent who infrequently came to sessions was confronted by his residential counselor about his attendance record. After encouragement the youth revealed that he was offended by the casual appearance of the therapist. The therapist did not measure up to the youth's perception of how a professional should appear. To this youngster, who was a stylish dresser even when casual, the attire of the therapist was a statement of attitude towards him. Although there were other issues of resistance involved, the therapist's clothes played a part in the dynamics of the bonding process. In general, parents have rarely been free of comments from their adolescent children on how they are dressed. Because this is a frequent exchange between adolescents and parents (or significant other adults) therapists should be aware of how dress affects youthful attitudes. As a black therapist working with black adolescents I have found that physical appearance and deportment can be intricately linked to the issue of "role model." If a black therapist is too casual in manner and dress, this creates a paradox for the presumed professional stature. Since clothes are a materialistic symbol of achievement, the youngster may view informality as a contradiction of professional status. It can translate as "he must not be that important nor his job that profitable." Nevertheless, this does not diminish the significance informality can play in the therapeutic process with black youth.

INDIVIDUAL THERAPY FOR BLACK ADOLESCENTS

Adolescence is a critical period of development in the life span. There are many crises experienced during this age without the appropriate level of maturity. Many clinical problems in adults are unresolved conflicts from adolescence. The physiological changes that occur during adolescence for boys and girls provide unique demands upon personal adjustment (Katcha-dourian, 1977). The inadequacy of schooling in urban centers raises issues of personal competency and self-worth. The disillusionment experienced by black adolescents when confronted with their lack of marketable skills on leaving school is great. Anger, depression, and despair are characteristic symptoms presented by some youth in these circumstances. Acting out behavior for the preservation of a self-image assumes many forms. In some instances it is the basis for the pursuit of illegitimate careers and/or self-destructive behavior. Black youth are desirous of all the trappings of success propagated by the media about the "American dream" (Pierce, 1974). When the reality of unfulfillment is recognized, bitterness ensues.

An example of this is the case of an 18-year old black male brought to my attention by school authorities for loitering and disruptive behavior. Upon examination of records by the guidance counselor it was discovered that the youth had been enrolled in the school for four years with accumulated credits equal to two years. This youth was a classic "drop in," one who attends school but not classes with any regularity. School authorities paid little attention to this youth's lack of school progress and apparently that of many others like him. At the point of this incident the youngster was acting out his depression through harassment of younger students. Underneath this behavior was his resentment of younger students attaining a functional level equivalent or better than his. In addition, many of his friends had either dropped out of school or graduated. The loss of his original peer group was increasingly isolating him from the new social order established by a younger student body. To compensate for this loss he maintained self-esteem through control and domination of other students. He cultivated a cadre of followers who indulged in various illicit activities. His older appearance and demeanor made him an attractive leader to a number of students following the same pattern. The initial sessions were dominated by attempts to establish rapport and the ventilation of vituperative rage. Depression was exacerbated by family pressures to get a job and/or leave home. Upon discovering that his ability would yield only marginal employment the youth vacillated between dejection and disparagements. Those of his peers who had left the school were either incarcerated, lost to idle unemployment, in college, or employed. None of these alternatives were appealing or within realm of his capability. Frustrated, he sought solace in the security of familiar and negotiable surroundings. The high school was a home away from home. The demeaning lack of opportunities in the world of work was avoided as long as he could remain in school. It was extremely difficult to gain the trust of this youth because of a pattern of resisting assistance from adult authorities. Once confidence was achieved the youth was slowly guided into recognizing the realities of his circumstances and seeking remedies. Ultimately, the youth was enrolled in a high school equivalency program. While his educational needs were attended to, therapy continued to allow the youth to focus on his anger and channeling such energy into constructive goals.

The process of arriving at such an untenable position for this youth is common in urban public schools. Immersed in counterproductive school climates, black adolescents are lost to neglect. There is little monitoring of academic progress of black youth. Repeated failure experiences and accumulated skill deficiencies result in frustration and depression. Reconstructing some of the classroom experiences of black adolescents reveals a combination of contributing factors. Teachers are frequently portrayed by urban black adolescents in therapy as disinterested in them and teaching. In a number of intances teachers have told classes they were not fit for an education or have conveyed the same message through indifferent instruction.

The social disorganization in urban high schools is also at the root of truancy. Truancy cases referred for individual therapy often reveal instances of school phobia. In several cases black adolescents were disoriented by the lack of structure in the schools. The impact of the transition from the elementary school structure to the changing classrooms schedules of secondary school create an adjustment problem for some youth. Overwhelmed by a new school plus the conformity pressures by older peers sometimes causes black youth to avoid attending school. The chaotic decorum of the high school is frightening. Consider the case of Carol.

Carol, an attractive 14-year old, was referred for poor school attendance. It was also reported that when she did attend her participation was minimal and she was withdrawn. She was frequently observed sucking her thumb. Carol was very reticent during the first sessions and restricted herself to monosyllabic responses. Her responsibilities at home were great, and she often functioned as a surrogate parent to the younger children. Because of poor school performance, authorities placed her in remedial classes, although her prior elementary school record was satisfactory. Although distressed about Carol, both parents were unable to attend to the problem adequately because of inevitable loss of time and money when absent from the job. School authorities interpreted this as a sign of disinterest on the part of the parents. Although Carol eventually expressed an understanding of her parent's dilemma, she felt conflicted by the need for their support and the real necessity to maintain a level of family income for survival. Pressured to be a model for the younger children by both parents, Carol felt an inability to relate her school problems. Carol reported experiences of sweaty palms, body tremors, racing heart rate and dizziness whenever she had to change from one class to another. Since her first days of high school the pandemonium of changing classrooms provoked discomfort. Moreover, the majority of students were complete strangers. She also frequently went the entire day without going to the lavatory because the toilets were the place where girls frequently congregated to smoke marijuana and coerce others to join them. On one occasion she actually wet herself; thereafter she drank little for the entire day. The combination of problems led to an increased withdrawal from school and, subsequently, frequent incidents of truancy.

Carol was taught some relaxation exercises to be employed whenever she experienced anxiousness. Some desensitization routines were also used to help reduce the fear of changing classrooms. In addition, role playing to increase social skills for establishing peer contacts was performed. As Carol gained better control over her behavior it became clear that part of her fear was rooted in the pressure to be a proper role model for her younger siblings. Several sessions with the parents helped to reduce the pressure from home and encouraged a more supportive environment.

The extent of truancy and disruptive behavior as a mask for school phobia is unknown. For some black adolescents the social disorganization that prevails in urban high schools is a source of phobic responses. Fitting into the peer social structure of a school can be a stressful experience for adolescents, especially if the youngster is timid about establishing new relationships. The effect of the urban school environment on personal adjustment is a critical clinical issue to discern during treatment. Frequently, black youth must manage both the pressures from home as well as the school. The therapist must also view how both of these settings are affected by racism.

GROUP THERAPY WITH BLACK ADOLESCENTS

Group therapy in counseling black adolescents is effective because it allows the youngster to learn that problems of adjustment are not unique but shared by many. One of the first realizations acquired by adolescents in group therapy is the commonality of concerns. Although the group session allows shared problems to be exposed, it takes time before admission of adjustment issues are disclosed. This is due to the black youth's need to protect the image of competency. Self-effacing comments in front of peers is not desirable. The therapist's ability to get beyond the posturing and bravado to the vulnerability of adolescence is crucial. A therapist must be cognizant of the adolescent's need to maintain and protect a carefully cultivated peer image. The early sessions of group therapy are replete with youngsters playing the roles they are noted for. If the youths are familiar with one another, then their public image is strongly projected. They cannot appear to be any different from when they are outside of the group. If the youths are unfamiliar with each other then several role possibilities emerge. They can be themselves if basically they are satisfied with the level of acceptance currently given to their image. On the other hand, entering a group with new peers allows an opportunity to alter or modify self-presentation according to the purpose of impression. A scrutiny of psychosocial history and a conference with parents or teachers can determine the discrepancy between projected group therapy image and the image projected in other contexts. There is merit in obtaining this type of clinical data because they disclose the youth's stability and consistency in presentation of self. A youth who is repeatedly changing in character from one type of situational context to another has questionable emotional stability. Although adolescence is a time in which many roles are assumed, something of the basic identity persists. Acquiring an awareness of the consistency of self-presentation in the group in contrast to other social contexts facilitates identification of strengths and weaknesses in the adolescent's identity. One of the objectives of group therapy is to allow the adolescent to feel acceptance by others (MacLennan and Felsenfeld, 1968).

Achieving group therapy goals with adolescents is not the easiest task (Berkovitz, 1972). Although adolescents grow in groups, the formation of new groups is approached with caution. Alliances among friends can inhibit or facilitate the functioning of the group during its early sessions. Likewise, the experience of other adolescents as strangers can produce a variety of coping behaviors, such as wisecracking, incessant laughter, profanity, seat squirming, jostling, bullying, or silence. The range of behaviors is often presented in a dynamic display of expressions in every group. The activity level of adolescents is high. This energy is usually brought into the group situation. A therapist can expect youth to be restive in group sessions.

Because of this usual decorum I believe that an active therapist is necessary. Such a therapist engages the youth and sets limits and goals in therapy. A too passive therapist with the average urban black youth will encourage group disorganization. Although interpreting the group's response to a passive therapist may have merits, the lack of structure in general is counterproductive. Groups for black adolescents should be psychoeducational in objective. There should be allowance for disclosing psychological issues and experiencing an educative process in behavior management (Stuart, 1977). With this as an objective the active therapist must be deliberate in some interventions (Anderson, 1972). In my experience, establishing some ground rules in the first session helps to structure the group and makes expectations clear.

The first area of discussion is confidentiality. It is important that youth learn to respect the privacy of others. If this issue is not handled in the initial sessions, it encourages the youth to conceal feelings for fear a breach of confidence will occur. Although no insurance about confidentiality can be given, establishing this as a major agreement allows the therapist and group to handle instances in which confidence is violated. Additional rule settings should be a combination of the therapist's and the group's priorities. For example, some statement about decorum should be made within the context of respecting the participation of others. Youth should learn that as much as they dislike "disrespect" so do others. If no control is exercised over the activity level during the group process, youth who want to participate will become discouraged and submit to disruptive behaviors.

The manner in which ground rules are presented and enforced should be consistent with the therapeutic process. Being an active therapist does not mean assuming the role of a severe parent. However, a therapist exhibiting responsible guidance can be a positive role model. Identity achievement is a process that considers many role models; therefore, a decisive and responsible therapist-group interaction can be a learning experience for youth. It is particularly important in work with black youth that a male therapist exhibit strength and empathy. I am aware of several instances in which a passive, easily intimidated male therapist became repugnant to black male adolescents. It contradicted their notions of "machismo" or masculinity. The therapist posture must be flexible to adapt to whatever arises in the group process.

Handling the assertive black male in group therapy can be an arduous endeavor. Moreover, when disruptive behavior is the presenting problem, the purpose of the group acquires a special focus. For some youth the role of the disruptive person is a mask for a variety of inner conflicts. It manifests as a "camouflaging syndrome" to deceive others about insecurities (Franklin, 1977). Group members with this behavioral manifestation are going to resist strong exposure of inadequacies. There is usually peer support for a youth's deviant behavior. Group therapy can serve as an "alternative peer reference group" to counteract the pressures of buddies. As a youth engages new forms of behavior the therapy group can provide support in the face of adversity. Within the nurturing environment of the therapy group the youth can begin redefining his or her self-image. There is greater freedom to experiment with more constructive roles.

THE PSYCHOEDUCATIONAL APPROACH

The plight of the urban black adolescent is poignantly represented by the poor quality of education. It remains a national concern. Nevertheless, many black youth referred for therapy have deficiencies in the basic ability to read, write, and execute mundane arithmetical problems. Many are simply functionally illiterate. Because of these circumstances intrapsychic conflicts are exacerbated. Therapy to be effective must be combined with corrective educational measures. If tutoring can be an adjunct to therapy, this can enhance the achievement of developmental goals. A more effective and comprehensive approach is a programmatic effort combining a curriculum of instruction and personal development in the therapeutic processes. This is a psychoeducational approach and is represented by the programs offered by alternative schools for adolescents. The development of the Street Academy by the Urban League a decade ago is an exemplary institutional strategy (National Urban League, 1977). This program serviced dropouts who voluntarily solicited educational assistance. Subsequently, several urban public school systems have developed programs based on the Street Academy model.

The intent of the alternative school is to reduce the impersonality of education and to increase opportunities for individualized or small group instruction. Curriculum objectives are to improve competency in basic skills. The assumption is that the level of basic skill deficiencies is related to the level of self-esteem and deviant behavior. Black youth in such positions have been alienated from formal education. Many students bring with them the self-defeating behavior patterns that disengaged them from school in the first place. The stigma of expulsion, or dropout, creates resistance in the youth to attempt any corrective efforts. This is particularly the case when youth realize the magnitude of their inabilities.

In the development of a psychoeducational program, therapy and instruction are an integrated experience infused in classroom tutorial and therapy experiences. Youth enrolled in psychoeducational programs must be assessed for both their educational competencies and emotional stability. The extent of personal adjustment to this program is linked to the kind of experiences the youth had in the public school. For some youth the change to a personable environment induces different behaviors. I have known youth to express satisfaction from a level of personal attention theretofore never experienced. Some youth who were thought incorrigible by public schools became task- and goal-oriented students. On the other hand, there are those who are continually frustrated by their skill dilemma. They may be motivated to improve their skills, but the requirements to achieve this improvement are perceived as overwhelming. The unattractive aspect of the "catch-up" game in remedial work is the humiliation of not possessing the competence. In some instances a youth's sense of pride would inhibit instruction at levels below self-expectations. For these youth the input of therapy is critical. The self-concept of the youth must be adjusted to allow him or her to capitalize on the instructional services. Because it is recognized that the adolescent population referred to the alternative school is acting out and resistent to program goals, one strategy adopted by a program was to structure the first weeks to developing "school readiness" (National Urban League, 1977).

Upon entering the program students were engaged in an agreement to participate fully and obey the ground rules. Those persons who felt an inability to comply were free to leave. The youth who remained were exposed to approximately six weeks of intensive personal exploration about their school experiences. Respect for the views of others was insisted upon and reflected an individual's commitment. Teachers, therapists, administrators, and peer aides all participated in the orientation phase. Each morning students and staff engaged in a meditation period in a large, hand-linked circle. Afterwards the ensemble would divide into "rap groups" to discuss personal experiences of managing school life. Skits were eventually developed to represent the range of scenarios in school life. These were dramatically produced and videotaped by the students for later viewing in group sessions. In one skit students were encouraged to demonstrate the multitude of ways a disruptive student could control a teacher and the class. Through group process students discussed how such behavior was injurious to self and counterproductive. Students were instructed in the positive attributes of assertive behavior: while assertive behavior could be employed to disrupt, it could also be utilized to demand a proper education. Skits were then developed around how assertive behavior could be used constructively and under what kind of circumstances. Group therapy was also videotaped as a source of feedback on interpersonal interactions. Skits were also created around this theme. Encounters with teachers, peers, and family in the student life were also developed into a variety of scenarios and videotaped. Videotaping the kinds of experiences the youth would face in the pursuit of their education and the proper management of behavior was the substance of the school readiness phase of the first weeks. During this period there was very little formal instruction. The assumption was that, until the student learned about his or her own counterproductive behavior and the underlying reasons for that behavior, formal instruction would be ineffective. After the orientation phase the curriculum was introduced, with the group process integrated into a period of the daily schedule.

The important feature of the psychoeducational approach is the linking of therapy to educational objectives. In this regard therapy had an explicit goal. Although focused on behavioral management for educational objectives, all of the usual issues raised in therapy were entertained. There was a specific life context—"the schooling process"—for the youth to concentrate on, and it provided a unique clarity to other intrapsychic issues. For example, the inability to live harmoniously with parents or siblings was connected to effects on educational achievement. Acquiring a perspective on how to manage behavior in the school context aided students in other domains, such as the home.

The psychoeducational approach blends the goals of formal education and personal development. Several domains in the youth's life are simultaneously treated to maximize self-actualization. A key factor in the effectiveness of the psychoeducational model is the youth's recognition of the interdependence of issues. For example, achieving educational goals was related to control of disruptive behavior, the management of peer pressure, the resolution of family conflicts, and/or acceptance of individual responsibility. Time and staff assistance allowed for continual focus on these issues. Intervention was comprehensive. All professional assistance was related to the goals of the program. As an added inducement to attaining program objectives, graduates were employed as paraprofessionals. These youth not only served as role models, but as cotherapists; they quickly could disclose the dynamics preventing alienated peers from engaging in this "last chance" opportunity. After a while, graduates conducted most of the school readiness orientation phase of the program freeing professional staff to concentrate on individual student needs.

A difficulty with this type of psychoeducational approach is the financial cost of implementation. There is a small student-staff ratio and considerable concentration on individualized remedial assistance. In spite of these drawbacks, there is some evidence that suggests that proper programmatic leadership by administrators can overcome the economic obstacles. For example, the school readiness orientation has given some students a sense of individual responsibility that transfers to other settings. Students returning to local schools have made adjustments in behavior management to concentrate on school work.

SUMMARY AND CONCLUSION

The problems of black adolescents are reflective of their age group. However, the dynamics underlying their behavior must be interpreted within the realities of their life conditions. Many of the families of urban black adolescents exist within marginal socioeconomic circumstances. This creates a social context that contains numerous stressful conditions. Indicative of the situation is the disproportionate incidence of health and mental health disorders in the black community. Consequently, in order to understand black adolescent development and behavior disorders, the conditions of their life and the management of racism must be an integral part of clinical formulations.

Social statistics support the marginal life circumstances for many families of black adolescents. However, in the diagnosis of behavior disorders the clinician, in spite of the social conditions, must discern if the presenting problem is a by-product of common age-related issues or symptomatic of persistent characterological factors. It is crucial that the clinician in making this determination is informed of the social milieu of the black adolescent. Sensitivity to the adaptive styles generated by the social milieu will facilitate clinical formulations and the therapeutic process. For example, the disruptive behavior of the black adolescent in school may mask a variety of inadequacies emanating from inequities experienced in an oppressive and racist school environment. A black adolescent's acting out behavior may directly result from the stigma of placement in low achieving classes, functional illiteracy, and/or no job opportunities. Knowing the parameters of normal and abnormal behavior within the prevailing social context of the black adolescent refines clinical assessments.

Comprehending the psychosocial background for the average black adolescent is an important aspect of the initial interview and early therapy sessions. Like many adolescents, black youth are commonly referred to therapy by educational or judicial institutions. When parents bring adolescents, often such institutions have recommended them. Control of the black adolescent is a primary reason parents solicit clinical assistance. Because referral is usually based upon one of these circumstances, resistance by the black youth is often great. The form resistance takes can be characterized by withdrawal, excessive babbling, monosyllabism, yarn spinning, or aggression. Many times youth will challenge the clinician to demonstrate trustworthiness. Candor and active confrontation of the black youth's resistances have proven an effective manner of establishing a bond. Until trust of the black youth is gained, rapport and therapeutic goals cannot be achieved. Therapy for black adolescents is often an educative as well as clinical process. The credibility of mental health services is suspect in the black community. Black adolescents will reflect this attitude. It is important, therefore, that the advantages of therapy and the ground rules for participation are conveyed early in initial sessions. The therapist's deportment and manner of dress can be important agents in establishing rapport with the black adolescent. Casual dress and knowledge of slang can be useful so long as it is not superficial. Likewise, awareness of dress codes, language usage, and activities of the black adolescent peer world can facilitate assessment of the youth's self-concept and peer status.

Individual and group psychotherapy are traditional and appropriate forms of intervention with black adolescents. In addition, special interventions such as psychoeducational programs can combine many services to focus upon multiple problems. Working with black adolescents in individual therapy provides several unique pitfalls. The therapist must be cognizant about his or her own feelings about the adolescent experience and those that might be associated with black adolescents in particular. Equally important for the therapist to be aware of is (un)conscious racism. A by-product of this dynamic is for the therapist to succumb to stereotypes of black adolescent life and/or attempt to encourage the youth to accept oppressive life circumstances. When in a group, therapists must be aware that youth will indulge in face-saving behavior in front of peers. Establishing ground rules for the group process is essential in the early sessions. The group experience can provide the black youth with information about managing interpersonal relations with peers as well as developing strategies for coping with adult authorities. For youth involved with counterproductive peers the therapy can act as an "alternative reference group" to support disengagement from delinquency and injurious behaviors. Different from the traditional forms of therapy is the psychoeducational approach. An example of such an approach is an alternative high school for dropouts. This program combines services to assist both educational and related psychological needs. Black youth who have been disruptive and unproductive in traditional school settings are provided first with a concentrated school readiness experience before formal instruction. In the school readiness experience black youth and staff examine the dynamics of disruptive behavior or the alienation process. With the aid of group sessions and psychodrama, insight into behavior management is sought. Upon achievement of adequate awareness and control of productive behavior, formal instruction for skill deficiencies is incorporated into the daily activities.

The development of black adolescents within the context of limited social and economic opportunities is insufficiently understood. There is no comprehensive body of knowledge that clearly delineates the consequences to socioemotional and intellectual growth. The disproportionate number of black children who are tracked into educable mentally retarded (EMR) classes or low achieving classes or who are socially promoted in spite of functional illiteracy must experience a devalued self-esteem as well as a substandard overall state of psychological well-being. Likewise, growing up in a community subjected to numerous insufficiencies—socially, economically, and politically—must have a unique impact on black adolescent development. Exactly how black youth internalize the pressures of their life conditions is speculative. There has been no systematic study of the common parameters and processes of mental health development for black youth. The social science literature has given much attention to the deviancy in the life of black youth but little concern to the average experiences of development for the masses. A paucity of scholarship in this area relegates social services to black youth to evolve from superficial and racist impressions. In order to improve the delivery and effectiveness of services to black adolescents it is imperative that more adequate knowledge of average development be obtained.

REFERENCES

Anderson, R.L. The importance of an actively involved therapist. In *Adolescents Grow in Groups: Experiences in Adolescent Group Psychotherapy,* edited by I.H. Berkovitz. New York: Brunner/Mazel, 1972.

Beres, D. Character formation. In *Adolescents: Psychoanalytic Approach to Problems and Therapy,* edited by S. Lorand and H.I. Schneer, pp. 1-9. New York: Hoeber, 1961.

Berkovitz, I.H., ed. *Adolescents Grow in Groups: Experiences in Adolescent Group Psychotherapy.* New York: Brunner/Mazel, 1972.

Billingsley, A. *Black Families in White America.* Englewood Cliffs, N.J.: Prentice-Hall, 1968.

Clark, K.B. *Dark Ghetto.* New York: Harper & Row, 1965.

Conger, J.J. *Adolescence and Youth,* 2nd ed. New York: Harper & Row, 1977.

Crain, R.L. and Mahard, R.E. *The Influence of High School Racial Composition on Black College Attendance and Test Performance.* Washington, D.C.: National Center for Educational Statistics, U.S. Department of Health, Education, and Welfare, January 1978.

Dohrenwend, B.P. and Dohrenwend, B.S. Psychiatric disorders in urban settings. In *American Handbook of Psychiatry,* 2nd ed., vol. 2, edited by S. Arieti and G. Caplan. New York: Basic Books, 1974.

Fanon, F. *Toward The African Revolution.* New York: Grove Press, 1967.

Franklin, A.J. Counseling youth in alternative schools. *Personnel and Guidance Journal* (March 1977):419-21.

————. Ethnocultural considerations in the delivery of mental health services. Unpublished manuscript. Department of Psychology, City College of the City University of New York, 1979.

Freud, A. Adolescence. *Psychoanalytic Study of the Child* 13 (1958):255-78.

Gartner, A. and Riessman, F. The performance of paraprofessional in mental health fields. In *American Handbook of Psychiatry,* 2nd ed., vol. 2, edited by S. Arieti and G. Caplan. New York: Basic Books, 1974.

Hall, G.S. *Adolescence* vol. 1. Englewood Cliffs, N.J.: Prentice-Hall, 1904/1905.

Hill, R.B. *The Strengths of Black Families.* New York: National Urban League, 1972.

Jones, R.L. Racism, mental health, and the schools. In *Racism and Mental Health,* edited by C.V. Willie, B.M. Kramer, and B.S. Brown. Pittsburgh: University of Pittsburgh Press, 1973.

Katchadourian, H. *The Biology of Adolescence.* San Francisco: W.H. Freeman, 1977.

Kramer, M., Rosen, B.M., and Willis, W.M. Definitions and distributions of mental disorders in a racist society. In *Racism and Mental Health,* edited by C.V. Willie, B.M. Kramer, and B.S. Brown. Pittsburgh: University of Pittsburgh Press, 1973.

Lawson, W. Hypertension and diabetes mellitus: A challenge for black behavioral scientists. In *Research Directions of Black Psychologists,* edited by A.W. Boykin, A.J. Franklin, and J.F. Yates. New York: Russell Sage Foundation, 1979.

MacLennan, B.W. and Felsenfeld, N. *Group Counseling and Psychotherapy with Adolescents.* New York: Columbia University Press, 1968.

Moynihan, D.P. *The Negro Family: The Case for National Action.* Washington, D.C.: U.S. Department of Labor, Office of Planning and Research, March 1965.

Muuss, R.E. *Theories of Adolescence,* 3rd ed. New York: Random House, 1975.

Myers, H.F. and Miles, R.E. Life change stress; somatization and blood pressure in blacks. In *Fourth Conference on Empirical Research in Black Psychology,* edited by W.E. Cross, Jr., and A. Harrison. Washington, D.C.: Center for Minority Group Mental Health Programs/NIMH, 1979.

National Urban League. *Rethinking Alternatives: The New York Urban League Street Academy Story—10 Years of Progress.* New York: National Urban League, 1977.

National Urban League. *The State of Black America 1979.* New York: National Urban League, 1979.

Ogbu, J.U. *Minority Education and Caste: The American System in Cross-Cultural Perspective.* New York: Academic Press, 1978.

Pierce, C. Psychiatric problems of the black minority. In *American Handbook on Psychiatry,* 2nd ed. vol. 2, edited by S. Arieti and G. Caplan. New York: Basic Books, 1974.

Planned Parenthood Federation of America. *11 Million Teenage Pregnancies.* New York: the Allan Guttmacher Institute, 1976.

Sprince, M.P. A contribution to the study of homosexuality in adolescence. *Journal of Child Psychology and Psychiatry* 5 (1964):103-17.

Stuart, R.B., ed. *Behavioral Self-Management.* New York: Brunner/Mazel, 1977.

Sue, S., McKinney, H., Allen, D., and Hall, J. Delivery of community mental health services to black and white clients. *Journal of Consulting and Clinical Psychology* 42 (1974):794-801.

Thomas, A. and Sillen, S. *Racism and Psychiatry.* Secaucus, N.J.: Citadel Press, 1974.

Valentine, C.A. *Culture and Poverty.* Chicago: University of Chicago Press, 1968.

Visher, E.B. and Visher, J.S. *Stepfamilies: A Guide to Working Stepparents and Stepchildren.* New York: Brunner/Mazel, 1979.

Weiner, I.B. *Psychological Disturbance in Adolescence.* New York: John Wiley & Sons, 1970.

White, J.L. Toward a black psychology. *Black Psychology* 2nd ed., edited by R.L. Jones. New York: Harper & Row, 1980.

Yamamoto, J., Quinton, C.J., Bloombaum, M., and Hattem, J. Racial factors in patient selection. *American Journal of Psychiatry* 124 (1967):630-36.

12   Life Enhancement Counseling: A Psychosocial Model of Services for Cuban Elders*

José Szapocznik, David Santisteban,
William M. Kurtines, Olga E. Hervis, and Frank Spencer

❋

Whether a characteristic is defined as a virtue or a defect is largely a matter of perspective. The very same characteristics that make Cuban elders appear as poor candidates for many traditional psychotherapies can also be incorporated as components of alternate treatment strategies in improving their condition.

Life Enhancement Counseling is a psychosocial model of service developed by the Spanish Family Guidance Center in Miami, Florida to enhance the meaningfulness of life in the Hispanic elderly. Life Enhancement is accomplished by building on the elder's strengths, reducing environmental sources of conflict and stress, and facilitating acceptance of past life experiences. This model of counseling was designed to treat depressed individuals who have lost their sense of purpose in life, usually as a reaction to physical, personal, or material losses, progressive isolation, displacement, learned helplessness, and/or ageism. In practice, Life Enhancement Counseling utilizes a life review approach (Butler, 1963) to facilitate completion of unfinished business and resolution of regrets and self-reproachments and to identify capabilities or interests that have been historically available to the

*This work was partially supported by the Administration on Aging Grant No. 90-A-1209. The authors wish to express a special note of gratitude to the counselors who so marvelously performed in this project—Angel Perez-Vidal, Alejo Vada, Maria de los Angeles Coton, and Javier Lasaga—and to Marta Larrazabal for her assistance in the initial stages of implementation. This work would not have been possible without the valuable assistance of our Director of Community Services, Angela Rodriguez. Finally, a special note of acknowledgement goes to Mercedes Arca Scopetta for her contribution and vision during the initial conceptualization of the Life Enhancement Model.

elder but are currently not used. Once these strengths have been identified, the potential for reenacting them in the context of current conditions is assessed. Depending upon these assessments, directive counseling and ecological intervention strategies are carried out that may lead to a reenactment of past strengths.

The Life Enhancement Counseling Model was developed specifically for the treatment of the problems of meaninglessness and purposelessness among depressed Cuban elders. Within the context of Life Enhancement Counseling, meaninglessness and purposelessness is defined as the lack of sense of positive direction and challenge. The problem of meaninglessness and purposelessness is not confined to Cuban elders; it is widespread and shared by elders throughout the United States. Therefore, basic concepts encompassed by the model address the problem of elders in general. For this reason, important aspects of Life Enhancement Counseling should readily generalize to other elderly populations, although specific cultural idiosyncracies must be considered. Before outlining further the Life Enhancement Counseling Model, a description is presented of the context and population for which this model was developed.

THE CUBAN ELDER

Estimates of the number of Cubans in the United States tend to indicate that over 750,000 Cubans have settled in this country. Most of these individuals, over one-half million, live in the greater Miami–Dade County area of south Florida. In the migration waves of the early 1960s many middle- and upper-class Cubans left their country to seek political asylum in the United States. By 1978, however, the demographic distribution of Cuban exiles was reported by Clark (in press) to be representative of the Cuban population of the island in the late 1950s in terms of socioeconomic states. Regarding age, however, approximately 17 percent of this population is over 55 years of age; 7.8 percent is over 65, which overrepresents the elderly population.

The Cuban's exile in the United States has been a mixed blessing. While it provided for the opportunities that many Cubans sought for an alternate political reality away from their homeland, it has had its complications. In general, large sectors of the Cuban population have been highly successful in their adaptation to U.S. life. Particularly, many Cubans have had remarkable economic successes. Their impact on the Miami area has been quite noticeable; they have contributed significantly to the revitalization of the sagging Miami economy, which previously depended almost solely on tourism.

Moreover, many Cuban elders have also adapted remarkably well. While some elders have suffered considerably with the disappearance of the extended family, many have adjusted well to peer group support systems. Their adjustment to these new forms of support systems is, indeed, remarkable given elders advanced age and reduced resiliency. Others who have been less fortunate have required mental health or other supportive services to assist them in their transition and adjustment to the kinds of peer and social service support systems that are most prevalent in the United States. Thus, while there have been successes, there have also been difficulties. Adaptation to the United States has required the development of new styles of living that are faster, more impersonal, and individualistic. The rapid rate of change has caused dislocations: Some, such as the young, may have rushed into assimilation, cutting off their roots and cultural heritage; others, particularly the elders, have been most affected by migration because of their lesser ability to adapt and have suffered the most. Cuban elders, in fact, face double jeopardy (cf. Szapocznik, Faletti, adn Scopetta, 1978): (1) the mental health of this population is seriously threatened by the usual predicaments confronting older citizens; (2) there are specific mental health hazards affecting Cuban elders.

Mental Health Problems of the Elderly

The elderly constitute about 10 percent of our national population. Of this group, it is estimated that 25 percent suffer from significant mental health problems, and over 25 percent of suicides reported are committed by the elderly. The mental health problems of elders are complex in their origins, including financial worries, unhappiness over the loss of social status, grief over death of loved ones, physical ailments, and physical degeneration. In view of the dire mental health needs of elders, it is unfortunate that the necessary support and mental health services are alarmingly unavailable. For instance, only 2 percent of all the patients seeing private psychiatrists are elders, and less than 3 percent of the budget of the National Institute of Mental Health has been spent on the plight of older persons (Carter, 1979).

Among the elderly, there are two major mental health problems: senile dementia and depression. Senile dementia is the most terrifying mental health problem of the elderly, reported to be the fourth leading cause of death (Cohen, 1979). Depression, on the other hand, is the most widespread mental health hazard affecting elders. It is considered to be a major factor in the very high levels of suicides among elders. The Life Enhancement Counseling Model presented in this chapter is primarily aimed at the treatment of depression among the elderly, with special emphasis on the enhancement of meaning and purpose in life.

Specific Mental Health Hazards of Cuban Elders

In addition to the usual problems of old age, Hispanic cultural background and the effects of force migration and political exile conspire to produce especially complex and severe problems of adjustment for the Cuban elderly population of Dade County. Some of the major problems that have been identified are: (1) lack of knowledge of the language, the culture, and the social service delivery system in the United States, (2) social isolation and loneliness, (3) loss of country and status, (4) effects of transplantation and other complications of old age that would not have happened to these immigrant elders had they stayed in their country of origin, and (5) differential rates of acculturation in Cuban families. All of these interrelated sources of psychosocial stress work together to threaten the mental health of the Cuban elder.

A study conducted by Hernandez (1974) among Cuban elders in Miami has revealed that the psychosocial problems represented by language barriers, discriminatory institutional policies, and mental illness have impacted with substantial intensity on the Cuban elderly. Language seems to be the major problem affecting this population, rendering them ill equipped to interact effectively with the host U.S. culture.

Social isolation and loneliness have been generally identified as major problems among the elderly (Smith, 1976). With the Cuban population, Hernandez (1974) also found that one-third of the sample surveyed reported feeling lonely and isolated. Clinical experience at the Spanish Family Guidance Center suggests that these feelings seem to be rooted in the isolation of elders that has resulted from the breakdown of the extended family. As revealed by the authors' own acculturation studies (e.g., Szapocznik, Scopetta, Kurtines, and Aranalde, 1978), isolation may also occur because of the Cuban elders lack of acculturation, which limits their mobility within the host U.S. social structure.

Unresolved losses and grief reactions, as Patterson (1969) reports, are also a source of depression in the elderly. Clinical experience at the Center corroborates the generalizability of Patterson's findings to the Cuban-American elderly population. With Cuban elders, in addition to the losses typically experienced by other elders, the loss of country and status is usually a source of anguish and grief, which needs to be treated in therapy.

For many elderly persons, the expectation of a respected and dignified role within the extended family was a major source of meaning. They had expected that in their sunset years they would be the ultimate authority figures and major contributors to their family's well-being. The reality, however, has turned out to be very different from these expectations. What was once a valued role for the elder, to be an authority figure in the family, is now considered by their modern Americanized children and grandchildren interference in their internal affairs. Furthermore, confronted by the many additional stresses that exile has brought on older persons, they are often perceived as a burden to their families rather than as a source of support.

The effects of transplantation in old people—depression, withdrawal, and other passive behaviors—are counterproductive in facilitating adjustment to a foreign land. The Cuban elder's forced migration to a new environment, thus, functions to foment passive behaviors and to inhibit initiative and other behaviors necessary for a more effective adaptation to the new environment.

The differential rates of acculturation across generations of Cuban family members represents another threat to mental health and psychosocial adjustment among the immigrant elderly. The findings from an acculturation study by Szapocznik, Scopetta, Kurtines, and Aranalde (1978), taken in the context of clinical experience with Cuban families with elderly members, suggest that intrafamily differences in acculturation contribute to the disruption of the nuclear and extended family. Experience also reveals that this familial disruption is an important etiological source of despair, depression, and feelings of meaninglessness and purposelessness in elderly persons. These problems become exacerbated when supportive systems other than the family are not available, either because the elder is unable to seek other alternatives, because community support systems do not exist in sufficient quantity, or because existing social programs discourage, through culturally insensitive institutional practices, their use by Hispanic elders.

Among Hispanics, the extended family has always been a major strength. Now, however, because of the intergenerational differential rates of acculturation, the extended family itself can become disrupted and in those cases become a major source of stress for the elder. Exposure to these above-mentioned sources of stress results in anxiety, depression, withdrawal, meaninglessness, anomie, and a loss of a sense of purpose in life.

THE NEED FOR POPULATION-SPECIFIC TREATMENT

The unique needs, characteristics, and problems of this population presented a dilemma concerning appropriate treatment modalities. Should existing community and mental health approaches be utilized with this population, or should a specific strategy be developed to address the uniqueness of this population? This latter concept of matching treatment modalities with client variables has been discussed frequently by mental health treatment methodologists and has received widespread endorsement (Bergin, 1971; Kiesler, 1971; Paul, 1969; Sloane, et al., 1974). Paul (1969), for example, has argued that mental health treatment research should be directed toward ascertaining which procedure is most effective for a person with specific characteristics and problems in a given set of circumstances.

The proper procedure for matching clients and treatment methods, however, has been a matter of debate. There are those who advocate that alternate treatment methods can be developed to match client characteristics (e.g.,

Hunt, 1960; Lorion, 1974; Magaro, 1969) and those who argue that traditonal psychotherapy can be effectively extended to different client populations via special techniques that facilitate a therapeutic relationship (e.g., Gould, 1967; Heitler, 1976; Orne and Wender, 1968; Terestman, Miller, and Weber, 1974).

As Heitler (1976) points out, there are important ethical considerations to both solutions. If alternative treatment methods are developed for special populations, then they will be receiving separate and unequal therapeutic modes (cf. Lerner, 1972; Lorion, 1973). Yet, if the second solution is adopted, there is the risk of forcing these unique populations into a mode of problem solving that does violence to their cultural expectations and life styles (cf. Goin, Yamamoto, and Silverman, 1965; Lorion, 1974).

The philosophic and operational orientation of the Spanish Family Guidance Center has been based on the premise that psychosocial services should take into consideration the specific characteristics of the treatment population and should address the particular mental health hazards confronting each population group. Thus, treatment is adapted to the client rather than attempting to force clients into preestablished treatment modes. In the case of Cuban elders, there are two sets of characteristics that must be considered: one related to their ethnicity and cultural background, and the other to their advanced age.

Cultural Sensitivity

Clinical experience and previous research (Szapocznik, Scopetta, Aranalde, and Kurtines, 1978) suggests that Hispanic and Anglo Americans differ along several important dimensions. Some of the most basic differences between these groups can be understood in terms of their value orientations (cf. Kluckhohn and Strodtbeck, 1961). Relative to Anglo Americans, Cuban immigrants tend to value lineality and a present-time orientation and lack the orientation to attempt to exercise control over natural forces and environmental conditions (Sandoval, 1976; Szapocznik, Scopetta, Aranalde, and Kurtines, 1978).

The differences in basic value orientations between Cuban immigrants and Anglo Americans have implications for the delivery of mental health services. As Heitler (1976) points out, mutuality of patient-therapist expectations is crucial. If basic value orientations are indeed as fundamental as Kluckhohn and Strodtbeck (1961) postulate, value structure must be matched by a similar set of service delivery assumptions. Indeed, *a culturally sensitive service delivery modality can be defined as one built on a set of assumptions that complement the client's basic value structure* (Szapocznik, Scopetta, and King, 1978). The problem of developing a service delivery modality that is sensitive to Cuban value structure has been discussed extensively elsewhere (cf. Szapocznik, Scopetta, Aranalde, and Kurtines, 1978; Szapocznik, Scopetta, and King, 1978). For our present purposes, it is sufficient to note that the Life Enhancement Counseling (LEC) Model was designed to be culturally sensitive to the following four basic value orientations identified in our previous research (Szapocznik, Scopetta, Aranalde, and Kurtines, 1978).

First, the LEC Model takes into consideration the Cuban elder's preference for a lineal relationship style. The Life Enhancement counselor relates to the client hierarchically, recognizing that the counselor's role is perceived by the client as a position of authority. With this recognition the counselor takes responsibility and charge of the newly formed "therapeutic system." Conceptualizing in terms of a therapeutic system, the emphasis is placed on the systematic contribution of the counselor as well as the client, with the counselor carrying a major share of the responsibility. The counselor capitalizes on the Cuban elder's preference for lineality to place herself or himself in a position of authority, which she or he later uses to move the treatment plan forward through strategies such as directive reinterpretation and restructuring maneuvers (defined below).

Second, the LEC Model also considers the Cuban elder's sensitivity to environmental social pressures as documented by findings of high levels of need for approval among Cubans (Tholen, 1974) and the field dependence of Hispanic groups in general (Ramirez and Castañeda, 1974; Witkin and Berry, 1975). Given this characteristic of the population, it is important to conceptualize psychosocial functioning within a broad ecological framework (Auerswald, 1971). Ecological theory is discussed in a subsequent section.

Third, Cuban clients tend to perceive themselves as unable to control natural forces or modify detrimental environmental conditions (Santisteban, 1975). For this reason, when confronted with environmental pressures or tensions, the Cuban elder frequently adopts a passive, fatalistic attitude. The therapist uses his or her position of authority to create new client-environmental transactions that will give the elder a greater sense of mastery.

Finally, services for Cuban clients must be present-time oriented. The Cuban client is usually mobilized to seek services by the onset of a crisis and expects the counselor to provide immediate problem-oriented solutions to the crisis situations. The Life Enhancement Counseling Model capitalizes on crises to engage clients and to promote restructuring of interpersonal relations and ecological conditions. For this reason, it is standard procedure to schedule the admission interview session within three days of initial contact with the Center to more effectively engage clients closest to the time when they feel the greatest sense of urgency. Further, in order to maximally utilize this characteristic of the Cuban population, the culturally sensitive service provider is not only cognizant of how to use crises to engage clients but also knows how to create them within a therapeutic structure to promote change.

In addition to these basic value orientations, there are various customs, habits, and mores that must also be considered by culturally sensitive counselors. For example, in Cuba it was customary for patients to give presents to their physicians. Cuban elders commonly continue this custom and generalize from physicians to their mental health counselors. Within the context of certain theoretical treatment approaches such as the psychoanalytic therapies, accepting presents from a patient is considered counterproductive. However, the culturally sensitive counselor needs to recognize that for Cuban elders, giving presents to their "healers" is a time honored tradition that need not be challenged, but simply and gracefully accepted.

Age Appropriateness

Clinical experience and research on the elderly reveal a set of age-related characteristics and problems. The problem of meaninglessness and purposelessness, already mentioned, is one characteristic of elders. It is noteworthy that struggles for meaning and purpose occur at various developmental crossroads in life. The adolescent, for example, seeks to develop a sense of direction and purpose where none previously existed. The middle-age adult confronting a mid-life crisis seeks a redirection in meaning and purpose. In contrast to these struggles for meaning and purpose that occur at earlier developmental periods, the elder's sense of meaninglessness and purposelessness is usually a consequence of a *loss* of meaning and purpose.

The loss of direction and challenge is most frequently related to Sigmund Freud's two areas of successful adult functioning: work and love. Losses related to work come about by such events as mandatory retirement or physical disability. Losses related to love come about through such events as death of one's spouse or close friends. In the case of Cuban elders, a third type of loss compounds their sense of meaninglessness and purposelessness: loss of country.

In addition to the problem of meaninglessness, there are also other characteristics of elders that have provided a basis for the Life Enhancement Counseling Model. For instance, central to the strategie chosen for inclusion in Life Enhancement Counseling is making therapeutic use of the characteristic of elders to reminisce about their life experiences. Since reminiscence occurs spontaneously and is well accepted by elders, it is readily available for therapeutic use through a life review procedure—a therapeutic strategy that has been used widely with elders (Butler, 1963; Lewis and Butler, 1974).

Since elders tend to be plagued by social problems, the model was also designed to allow the therapist access to the elder's social environment through the use of an ecological approach to conceiving of problems and their solutions. Isolation, for example, is more typical among elders than other age groups because of their lesser physical mobility and their difficulties in using transportation. Moreover, some elders because of their greater passivity tend to be less effective in controlling/regulating/dealing with their environment.

Finally, the concepts of life review and ecological intervention are utilized to draw on the elders' past strengths. In the course of life review the therapist identifies past strengths and interests, which can be reenacted within the context of current ecological conditions. The focus on reenactment of past strengths is based on the recognition that, on the one hand, elders have a vast pool of experiences and, on the other, they are unlikely to adopt totally new interests at an advanced age. For this reason, it is felt that creative reenactments of past strengths and interests are more feasible therapeutic strategies with elders than attempts at growth in totally new and foreign areas. An example is the case of the Cuban elder who as a younger woman had been a teacher and enjoyed caring for children. Upon immigration to the United States, she was no longer able to work as a teacher because of the language barrier and was forced by economic circumstances to work in a factory. Upon retirement she became depressed and had frequent emotional outbursts. Through the life review process, this elder's former interests in child care were discovered. As part of the treatment plan, ecological interventions by the counselor included arranging for her to work as a volunteer teacher in a daycare center for Hispanic children. Thus, by enabling her to reenact past and cherished interests and competencies, Life Enhancement Counseling restored an important source of purpose and meaning. This regained sense of purpose in life was a crucial factor in ameliorating conditions that were sustaining her earlier depression.

The Life Enhancement Counseling Model as described below is intended to match the needs of Cuban elders as a mental health treatment population. It is noteworthy that the unique needs and characteristics of Cuban elders would typically appear to make this population poor candidates for psychotherapy. However, our effort in this section has been to demonstrate that whether a characteristic is defined as a virtue or a defect is largely a matter of perspective. The very same characteristics that make Cuban elders poor candidates for many traditional psychotherapies can also be incorporated as components of alternate treatment strategies in improving their condition and ameliorating their problems.

LIFE ENHANCEMENT COUNSELING MODEL

Basic Concepts and Assumptions

Life Enhancement Counseling was developed to meet the unique needs of Cuban elders while providing services in an age appropriate and culturally sensitive fashion. The Life Enhancement Counseling Model attempts to integrate two basic theoretical orientations: psychosocial developmental (Erickson, 1950) and ecological (Auerswald, 1971), with the latter borrowing heavily from general systems theory (von Bertalanffy, 1968). Life Enhancement Counseling aims primarily at developing strengths within the elder and his or her life context. The assumption underlying this approach is that for many elders psychosocial maladjustment and psychiatric symptomatology results from a sense of meaninglessness and purposelessness rooted in the loss of a positive direction and challenge in life that is characteristic of old age in today's society. In general, the basic problems of meaninglessness and purposelessness at the root of the depression in many Cuban elders can be treated successfully with Life Enhancement Counseling. It must be noted, however, that for some elders who manifest extremely high levels of depression/anxiety at admission, it might be advisable to use antidepressive medication as an adjunct to Life Enhancement Counseling. Since the Life Enhancement Counseling Model is specifically designed for treating elders whose depression is a consequence of a feeling of lack of meaning or purpose in their lives, this aspect of the approach receives primary emphasis in this chapter. The following basic concepts and assumptions provide the conceptual foundation for the Life Enhancement Counseling approach.

To begin with, it is stipulated that the parameters of meaningfulness are encompassed within a person's total experience, both past and present. For the past experiences of an elderly person to be a source of meaning to him or her, a basic level of acceptance and ego integration (Erickson, 1950) of the past must be achieved. For the current experience to be meaningful, ecological theory (Auerswald, 1971) would predict that current transactions must be fulfilling in the here and now. Thus, meaning and fulfillment arises from acceptance of the past as well as from the nature of the current transactions of the elderly person with his or her environment.

Borrowing from Erickson's psychosocial theory of life-span development (1950), it is a basic tenet of this model that a person's sense of meaning emerges from his or her past history when ego integrity is achieved. Ego integrity emerges with the acceptance of one's past as something that had to be and, in fact, was no other way. Without such acceptance, unresolved feelings about past events result in negative affective responses that block the emergence of meaning. This lack of acceptance by the elder of his or her life experience leads to despair. It is our contention that as completion is brought to these unresolved feelings, the meaning of past experiences gains clarity and areas of meaningfulness emerge.

Ecological theory (Auerswald, 1971) suggests that psychiatric symptomatology results from dysfunctional relations between the person and his or her ecology. In the case of depression in elders that is rooted in a lack of a sense of meaning or purpose, ecological theory would suggest that such feelings and behaviors are maintained and supported to some extent by the total ecology, either through actual suppression of meaningful behavior or by the unavailability of opportunities for meaningful behavior.

The basic tenet of the Life Enhancement Counseling Model that *integrates* these two theoretical orientations, psychosocial developmental and ecological, is the assumption that what is fulfilling and how fulfillment and meaning can be obtained currently by an elderly person have already been established by the time the person has reached an advanced age. Therefore, it is assumed that the definitions of meaningfulness for each elderly person can be found within that person's past history. Thus, in order to enhance life's meaningfulness in older persons, new definitions of meaning need not be created. Rather, if each elderly person's own definition of meaning is accepted, then it is possible to create new environmental circumstances that allow important features of meaning to emerge in new behaviors and/or experiences that can be maintained by the current environmental circumstances. Ecological theory (Auerswald, 1971) suggests that these new experiences can be obtained by creating a new interplay between a person's behavior and the environmental response to this behavior. Since the sense of purposelessness and meaninglessness is conceptualized as rooted in a lack of positive direction and challenge, one aim of Life Enhancement Counseling is to change the interactions between the individual and the social context in such a way as to provide the individual with a restored sense of direction and challenge.

Application

In applying the Life Enhancement Counseling Model, it is essential to take into consideration that individual elders do not usually fit the model perfectly. The Life Enhancement Counseling Model, in fact, is merely a set of guidelines—a working model comprised of a set of assumptions intended to represent the modal treatment characteristics that apply to this particular population. Using these guidelines as a reference point, the actual application of Life Enhancement Counseling has to be individually tailored to each elder's needs and conditions. What follows is a brief discussion of some of the techniques used in the application of the model to clinical cases.[1] The model encompasses two major concepts: (1) life review and (2) ecological assessment and intervention.

Life Review. The life review procedure involves having an elder recount his or her life events and experiences. The life review procedure uses standard interviewing techniques and clinical methods to elicit reminiscenses in elders. The procedure is administered flexibly and in such a fashion that the counselor encourages a general recounting by the elder of his or her life experiences. The counselor, however, using clinical judgment may decide to probe for further exploration in areas either not covered or not sufficiently covered. This procedure has been widely used as a therapeutic tool in mental health treatment with the elderly (e.g., Butler, 1963), although typically limited to recounting life experiences. The life review procedure is usually considered a therapeutic technique in itself: it has cathartic value because it allows expressions of fears, frustrations, and misgivings, and it also facilitates achievement of ego integrity by helping to organize memories in a way that brings closure to these experiences. However, as incorporated in Life Enhancement Counseling, life review is extended beyond the simple recounting of life experiences. As used here, it incorporates three additional strategies: (1) enhancing meaningfulness of positive memories, (2) facilitating acceptance of unresolved incidents that interfere with ego integration, and (3) rediscovery of past strengths, capabilities, or interests that can be reenacted as part of the treatment program.

Enhancing the Meaningfulness of Positive Memories. The emphasis in this strategy is on identifying events, incidents, relationships or periods in the elder's life that were filled with meaning and raison d'etre. Once these significantly meaningful aspects of life are identified, there is an effort to expand them and to gain clarity on them. Clinical techniques are used, as appropriate, "to bring to life" these meaningful life segments, creating a here and now experience around them. This strategy is particularly useful in the initial stages of treatment with the depressed elder for establishing an immediate sense of therapeutic efficacy, which is of critical importance with present oriented Hispanic patients who expect immediate therapeutic gains. For example, in the case of an 80-year old widower who became depressed after his wife died, happy memories of his married life could be used to counter his present sense of abandonment.

Facilitating Acceptance of Unresolved Incidents. For many despairing elderly persons, the meaningfulness of their past history is often stored behind a wall of unresolved negative feelings. In these cases, clinical techniques are employed to facilitate acceptance of these feelings and events in order to achieve ego integrity. For this purpose, a number of clinical techniques have been found helpful, including gestalt and psychodynamic methods. Particularly useful in working with this population has been a technique we have termed directive reinterpretation (cf. *Life Enhancement Counseling Manual,* in preparation). Levine and Padilla (1980) reported that directive styles of therapy are generally preferred by Hispanic clients and, as noted above, are consistent with Cuban value orientations. Directive reinterpretation, as used here, refers to providing the elder with an alternative interpretation of events or experiences that helps to move the client toward some therapeutic goal. When used as part of life review, the therapeutic goal involved is the acceptance of past events or experiences.

An example of the use of directive reinterpretation to facilitate acceptance of unresolved incidents is found in the case of Elvira. Elvira sought treatment for a reactive depression, which was precipitated by the death of her parents within the last year in Cuba. In the course of life review, it was discovered that she felt responsible for the death of her parents, whom she had left in Cuba several years before. In her view, she had abandoned them at the time when they needed her most. In order to facilitate resolution of these feelings, the counselor used directive reinterpretation to provide her with an alternative understanding of her behavior toward her parents: she had left Cuba because political circumstances endangered the life of her husband and the future of her children and grandchildren. Whereas her decision to leave Cuba had in effect forced her to leave her parents behind, the intent of her decision, the counselor explained, was not to abandon her parents, but rather to save her husband, children, and grandchildren. Thus, by emphasizing that her decision to leave Cuba was, as a responsible wife and mother, the only decision that she could have made under the circumstances, the counselor directed her toward a more realistic interpretation of her decision, i.e., that it was inconceivable that she could have done otherwise.

Rediscovery of Past Strengths, Capabilities, or Interests. The aim of this strategy is to identify themes that run through the elders' history that have provided them with meaning and purpose throughout their lives and can be reenacted as part of the treatment program. Throughout the life review, the counselor listens for features of these experiences that reflect each elder's values and definition of meaning. Later the counselor using ecological interventions will attempt to reenact in the present these meaningful experiences, with meaning defined uniquely by each elder through the life review. Work with clients in the demonstration activity discussed here has taught the authors that themes amenable to reenactment are varied and may have had lesser or greater centrality in elders' lives. In some instances, the most relevant and reenactable themes derive from experiences that were centrally meaningful, such as a lifetime of work or a lifetime of dedication to raising a family. In other instances, however, old age provides the unique opportunity to develop areas that may have played a secondary role in an individual's earlier life, such as an interest in gardening, cooking, painting, fishing, or cultivating friends.

An example of a reenactment of a central theme is found in the case of Marta, who had dedicated her life to raising children and who had thoroughly enjoyed caring for her many children. At the time that she sought treatment, her children were already grown and were out of the house. In this case her own children felt that it was an imposition on her to have her care for the grandchildren. Reenactment of her interest in caring for children was accomplished by family counseling, by formulating an understanding within the family that for Marta to take care of her grandchildren was not an imposition but, rather, a joy. Moreover, it was arranged for Marta to receive some remuneration for taking care of the children so that she would not feel used.

A second example of reenactment that involves a theme that had been of secondary importance is provided by the case of Pedro. Pedro had been a simple, illiterate fisherman in Cuba. When he came to the United States he was so depressed shortly after arrival from Cuba that his landlady became concerned with his severe withdrawal and referred him to our program. In the initial session, Pedro was so severely depressed that he was not able to verbally communicate with his counselor. After a while however, he did express himself through a short folksong ("Punto Guajiro"). Upon further exploration, the counselor learned that Pedro, while fishing, would always sing to himself, and he would freely compose as he went along. For the second session, the counselor obtained a tape recorder and, with Pedro's permission, taped one of his spontaneously constructed songs. For the third session, the counselor had had the song typed and provided Pedro with a copy. From then on, the treatment revolved around the compilation of a set of Pedro's folksongs with the notion that perhaps they might be published sometime in the future. As the reader might imagine, for an illiterate man to see his own creation prepared into a book format was a great source of excitement and provided him with a renewed source of purpose and meaning. Thus, through the process of reenactment, what had seemed so secondary and what had never received very much attention now became—in old age—a source of pride and a source of hope that it might even produce a small amount of income.

Ecological Assessment and Intervention. The ecological approach is derived from systems theory, which focuses on interactions between the individual and the extrapersonal environment. An ecological approach conceives the problem of meaninglessness as rooted in the pattern of transactions between elders and their environment. This approach assumes that the person and the environment share the responsibility for the initiation and maintenance of the transactions that occur between them. Thus, in the ecological model of service delivery, the focus is on changing the *transactions* between the person and the environment. In the case of elders, the intended direction of change is from less to more meaningful and fulfilling transactions. An example can be found in the case of Rosa, an elderly woman who had become isolated and spent most of her time in her room in a boarding house. She had recently moved to this boarding house in a neighborhood new to her and had become frightened of going out because of the reported high crime rate in the area. In this case, Rosa's transactions with the outside world were extremely limited. Within walking distance of the boarding house there was a church with various group activities. As part of treatment, the counselor facilitated a meeting between Rosa and the priest of the church at Rosa's house. In a subsequent session, Rosa was invited to attend a church activity, accompanied by her counselor. At this gathering, the counselor facilitated her meeting a group of elders who also lived near the church. Arrangements were made for two of these elders to come by Rosa's house and pick her up to attend the next group meeting on the following week. In this fashion, the counselor brought about a change in the way in which Rosa and the church group interacted without changing either her or the church group. Thus, the focus is not on intrapersonal or social change, but on changing the transactions between the person and the social environment. Note that within this approach, the counselor is viewed as a catalyst who precipitates change in transactions by creating new situations. The intention is to manipulate the parts in order to bring about new transactions that will maintain themselves, thus creating a new structural arrangement in the person-social environment.

The ecological work of the Life Enhancement Counseling Model can be conceptually explained in two parts: assessment and intervention. In practice, these parts are closely interrelated and they occur throughout the entire treatment process.

Assessment. Following or concurrent with the life review process, an assessment of the elder's ecological situation is conducted. Its purpose is to identify: (1) environmental sources of stress and (2) the resources that are available to each elder. The objective of the ecological assessment is to ascertain the ecological possibilities of effecting current life experiences that are meaningful. The determination of what is meaningful is obtained in each case from the life review.

Within the Life Enhancement Counseling Model the scope of assessment is limited to identifying those transactions that contribute to the elderly patient's current conditions and those resources that could facilitate improvement in the person-social transaction. For this reason, the assessment does not dwell on the intrapersonal or the macrosocial condition, but on the interface between these as they affect the elderly patient. In the example of Rosa, the initial presenting problem was one of unmet emotional needs related to isolation. An important source of environmental stress was assessed to be Rosa's fear of going out because of the reported high crime rate in her new neighborhood. The symptom of isolation was a function of the stress produced by the environmental conditions of high crime rate. Neither Rosa's fear, an intrapersonal variable, nor the crime rate, a macrosocial variable, were targets of intervention. Within the Life Enhancement Counseling Model, the target of intervention was to change the relation between the elder and her environment in such a way that her fear of crime no longer resulted in her isolation. Thus, the second step in the assessment involves the identification of resources that could be utilized to achieve desired changes.

In the case of Rosa, an assessment of available resources was aimed at identifying community support systems that could be mustered on behalf of the isolated elder. For the Cuban elder in general, the most frequently available support systems are the family, the church, volunteer groups, and senior centers. An important part of this phase of the assessment is determining which of these support systems are most appropriate for each determining which of these support systems are most appropriate for each individual elder. This is an aspect of the work in which clinical judgment Typically, the counselor will explore with the elder his or her openness to each of these support systems as well as the relative availability of the various support systems to each elder. While the Hispanic family is often considered the most basic support system in our work, conditions may not always make it a viable support for a particular elder. The family itself, for example, may be so disrupted that engaging the family might hinder rather than facilitate problem resolution. In the case of Rosa, an assessment of resources revealed that a nearby church had an ongoing group that was available as a support system and acceptable to the elder. Hence, the ecological assessment of the problem of isolation revealed something about the source of the problem; the ecological assessment of the environmental resources revealed support systems that could be utilized in problem solving during the next phase of treatment, ecological intervention.

It is noteworthy that the assessment is focused in that (1) it is intimately linked with the nature of the presenting problem, (2) it yields specific treatment goals and a sense of how to achieve them, and (3) it is limited to understanding the nature and source of the transaction that can sustain or change the presenting problem, without probing into intrapersonal or macrosocial dynamics.

Intervention. Ecological intervention can be conceptualized in terms of three phases: (1) testing the viability of the identified resources, (2) developing an ecological treatment plan, and (3) restructuring.

Concurrent with the identification of resources through ecological assessment, the counselor begins to test the viability of these resources. In this case, testing refers to determining the flexibility or rigidity of existing transactional patterns between the patient and the resources identified as potential support systems. For example, in the case of Rosa, several resources were identified by the counselor that had potential for extricating her from her isolated position. As the counselor identified each of these resources, he discussed with Rosa her willingness to change her transactions and explored the willingness of persons representing these resources to reach out to Rosa. Through this exploration, the counselor was able to assess the client's interest in church activities and, subsequently, the priest's willingness to reach out to her. Hence, because of the possibility for change in this direction, this was an area with potential for restructuring the transactions between an isolated woman and her environment.

Once one or more potential directions for changing transactions have been identified, the counselor attempts to develop an ecological treatment plan to restructure the person-environmental transactions. This phase of planning the restructuring strategies is closely interrelated with the previous and the following phases in the sense that testing, planning, and restructuring are all part of an ongoing process. As a rule, the entire process is handled with utmost clinical judgment. Each step of movement toward change in person-environment interaction is a test of flexibility in the direction of movement. The movement process, in turn, is incorporated into a treatment plan that is, in effect, developed "on the march" as each test for flexibility is passed. The restructuring that occurs represents the successful and full completion of the movement process from isolation to person-environmental interaction. The underlying assumption is that changes in transactions can take place; the testing process is aimed at identifying an appropriate path to follow for each individual client.

The case of Rosa provides an example of the interrelatedness of the testing, planning, and restructuring phases. Initially, the counselor was able to assess the woman's interest in church activities and the priest's willingness to reach out to her. On the basis of this information, the counselor planned to use the church as a vehicle to bring Rosa out of her isolation. The first and least threatening step, getting the priest to visit Rosa, was accomplished successfully, and the counselor was ready to test Rosa's willingness to take the next step of visiting the church. However, because she was still afraid of going out alone, the counselor had to modify his plan and accompany her on her first visit. Having accomplished that step successfully, the counselor tested Rosa's willingness to return to the church and again found that she continued to be afraid of going out alone. In order to successfully restructure her interactions with the environment, it was necessary to modify the plan in order to sustain the restructured transactions once the counselor moved out of the situation. This was accomplished by arranging for some elders from the church group to regularly walk her to the church.

There is one other aspect of the treatment of Rosa that merits discussion. Why was the church explored in her case as a potential resource? The counselor's attention was directed toward this potential ecological resource during the life review process. Rosa had on several occasions mentioned that she had always enjoyed attending church regularly. From this information obtained through the life review process, the counselor identified the church as a potential source of strength that could be reenacted. The ecological intervention in the case of Rosa was, thus, directed toward the reenactment of a past source of strength.

The Case of Miguel

The Life Enhancement Counseling Model can be perhaps best illustrated by a complete case history. The case of Miguel illustrates many of the most important features of the model. Miguel is an 80-year old Cuban man exiled in Miami. His two daughters and youngest son live in Miami. He lives with his wife in a run-down, two bedroom house.

In spite of an extremely successful life history, Miguel's later years have been marked by psychiatric impairments. His psychiatric history reportedly began with a series of myocardial infractions in 1971. In 1975 he had a cerebrovascular accident, which left him with a residual right hemiparesia and motor dysphasia. There was one reported suicide attempt in 1976. At the time of admission into the counseling services in 1978, the client had been under psychiatric treatment since early 1974. The psychiatrist's evaluation of the client included the following observations: history of physical ailments, blunting of interest, and continual worsening of memory and intellect; complaints of nervousness, tension, depression, insomnia, and periods of confusion and disorientation along with numerous somatic complaints. The psychiatrist also reported unkept appearance, difficulty in hearing, and profound physical decay; labile mood; slow, broken, and hesitant speech; defective judgment and insight. The diagnostic impression from previous psychiatric evaluations was: organic brain syndrome, with depressive features. Accordingly, the prognosis given with this earlier diagnosis was poor.

An evaluation of the client at the time of admission indicated that Miguel hardly ever left his room, reportedly having lost all interest and motivation toward life. Miguel's wife reported that whereas he had always strived to be the center of attention, this characteristic had become an obsession in recent years. This condition was particularly burdening to Miguel's wife, who was forced to remain home nearly all the time tending to her husband.

Life Review. A comprehensive life review indicated that events that had been particularly satisfying and meaningful to Miguel involved a high degree of innovation and creativity. Some included a touch of nonconformity and defiance, such as his interest in journalistic writing, in which he was engaged in Castro's Cuba against the advice from Castro's secret police. Miguel particularly delighted in the challenge involved in such activities, as well as the artistic value of the end product.

Ecological Assessment. A review of the immediate ecology of Miguel indicated a lack of extended family support. At the time, Miguel was receiving little support from his children. In addition, Miguel was confronted with a poor economic situation, which was best reflected in substandard living conditions: living in an old house with holes in the ceiling, defective air conditioners, jammed windows, and a leaking roof.

Treatment Plan. In view of the results of the life review and ecological assessment, a treatment plan was developed for Miguel. The treatment plan included Miguel and his wife, with the children living in Miami as relevant support systems. In order to draw him away from his inertia at admission, it was necessary to engage Miguel in an activity that was meaningful to him. Based on the information gained through the life review, this activity appeared to have to be creative and productive, preferably even an obstacle-defying activity—that is, one that at first appeared difficult, at least to the client. One of Miguel's previously successful activities was painting. At the time of admission, he insisted that he would never be able to paint again, providing the counselor with a welcome "obstacle" to be overcome. A major aim in the treatment plan was, therefore, defined as providing Miguel with the self-esteem and confidence necessary to return to this most satisfying activity. A secondary aim was defined in terms of pooling together the efforts of the immediate family in order to better the client's living conditions.

Rediscovery of Past Strengths. The positive aspects of Miguel's life review were constantly reenacted during the early counseling sessions, with subsequent sessions turning attention gradually to the present situation, also emphasizing the positive aspects of his current condition. In this regard the first two counseling sessions were devoted to a review of Miguel's collection of articles on Cuba, with emphasis not only on the subject matter, but also on his taking an active, tutorial role within the relationship.

Counseling also addressed Miguel's lack of mobility and "walking habits." For over two years prior to admission into the program, Miguel refused to walk out of his house. During a session conducted in the client's home, the counselor, using the excuse that he had had such a big Latin lunch that he needed to walk a bit in order to "walk off" some of the heaviness caused by the food, casually asked Miguel if he would oblige him and walk with him while they talked. Miguel did and has since continued to walk outside the home at least once daily. At first Miguel dutifully dragged his right foot (due to hemiparesia and motor dysphasia, according to his physician), but recently he has started to pick up his foot and walk properly. Had the counselor asked Miguel to walk for his own good, he probably would not have complied. However, since the need was presented as being the counselor's, Miguel happily obliged, consequently restoring his own ability to walk again.

Miguel's interest in scientific discovery was also rekindled, mostly by setting up situations that, within a supportive environment, allowed his scientific curiosity to reemerge. The counselor casually took Miguel and his wife to a beautiful botanic park located near their house but unknown to them. Typical of Miguel's depressed condition, he initially insisted that he was not up to par and could not go. At the park, Miguel immediately set out to look for snails, his specialty within the field of zoology, and to self-gratifyingly lecture on their behaviors.

These reenactments of Miguel's past strengths and interests were based on information revealed by Miguel's life review. They were aimed at placing him in situations that demanded the very kind of competency that Miguel had insisted was "all in the past, now." The counselor attempted to create situations where Miguel had an opportunity to behave competently and to perceive his strengths in areas that he believed had been eroded by old age and infirmity.

Ecological Intervention. The immediate aim of the ecological intervention was to improve Miguel's living conditions. The counselor began by obtaining an application for public housing and helping Miguel and his wife to fill it out, subsequently presenting it at the appropriate agency with an accompanying statement regarding the urgency of the petition. However, recognizing the time it takes to process such an application and for vacancies to occur, the counselor immediately turned to the problem of the present living conditions. Working largely through Miguel's wife—who generally kept good relations with the entire family, including Miguel's siblings—one of Miguel's brothers was engaged to fix the leaking roof and a hole in the kitchen ceiling. In addition, a friend of the family was engaged to repair the faulty plumbing. Finally, and perhaps most satisfying to Miguel, the counselor also mobilized the family to clear out their garage, which was to be used as an art/work room by Miguel.

Generally, Miguel's living condition will truly improve only when he and his wife move to a better house under public housing, but improvements in his present condition have indeed been notable and have had a noticeable positive effect on Miguel.

The process of improving Miguel's current housing conditions had a twofold purpose. On the one hand, it was necessary to improve the living conditions, but this could have been accomplished in several ways. The counselor chose to engage the family and friends in this process to use the existing circumstances to promote their involvement with Miguel in a fashion that would be supportive.

At the time of Miguel's termination from treatment, considerable progress could be observed. Miguel was at the point where he had engaged in a number of activities that he had previously abandoned. He had become more active at home, having regained interest in his physical appearance—as evidenced by his shaving and showering daily and also by being more careful about his choice of clothing. His motor functioning had also improved to the extent that he could prepare breakfast, and walk to nearby stores. The client had also become less demanding of others and was taking more care of himself. He had even reactivated some of his creative abilities, having sketched a bouquet of flowers brought by a friend. This was a most significant expression of progress since Miguel had ceased to paint over six years ago.

In terms of his psychiatric symptomatology, Miguel still complained much about his condition, but he no longer "lived for his illnesses" in order to draw attention. He reported less nervousness and anxiety, very slight insomnia, and hardly any numbness in his right limbs. Improvement had particularly been observed within the realm of interest and motivation, with consequent improvements in memory, intellect, and speech quality. Self-esteem and confidence had been largely regained and were beginning to find expression again. Miguel, his wife, his daughters, and his counselor all agreed that prognosis at that point had been greatly improved.

There are several aspects of the treatment process illustrated in the case of Miguel that are typical of the innovative approach to counseling elders presented here. One of these is the lack of emphasis on insight or the development of knowledge and understanding on the part of the client of his own dynamics. Intrapsychic awareness is eliminated as an intermediary step to a better life. Rather, the therapeutic strategies were aimed, on the one hand, at alleviating *real* ecological stresses and, on the other, at setting up the situations that allowed the client to circumvent his *imagined* shortcomings. Another aspect of the Life Enhancement Counseling Model that this case illustrates is its simplicity. For elders who are neither technologically nor psychologically wise, a simple approach to treatment is necessary. What is needed is an approach that capitalizes on their wisdom without trying to teach them our technological understanding of their situation. Life Enhancement Counseling, thus, attempts to create with great simplicity situations from which the elder can profit from his or her strengths given the current physical, personal, and ecological conditions.

RESEARCH AND EVALUATION OF LIFE ENHANCEMENT COUNSELING

Life Enhancement Counseling was developed as part of a three year (1977-80) demonstration model project funded by the Administration on Aging. The research reported in this section was conducted to ascertain the overall effectiveness of Life Enhancement Counseling applied to Cuban elders, to identify the specific treatment components that contribute to its effectiveness, and to determine the parameters of the population for which this approach is appropriate.

Client Characteristics

In an earlier section, it was noted that Dade County has a large elderly population, including a sizable group of Hispanic elders. The elders involved in the demonstration activity reported here were identified through agency referrals and self-referrals. Self-referrals were encouraged through a systematic community outreach program that included public service announcements, newspaper articles, television and radio talk shows, as well as presentations to community and elderly groups. At the time of this writing, 175 elders had sought the services of the demonstration project. Not all of these elders seeking assistance from the program met the criteria for admission to treatment. Of the total 175 elders seeking assistance from the project, 141 were admitted to treatment. At the time of this writing, of those admitted to treatment, 30 had not continued in treatment for various reasons, 43 were still in treatment, and 68 had completed all preevaluation and postevaluation measures.

As the project proceeded, clinical experience indicated that Life Enhancement Counseling was most appropriate for the treatment of depressed individuals, particularly those presenting depressions that had developed as a reaction to, or were compounded by, various aspects of aging. Experience with the treatment population further revealed that Life Enhancement Counseling was not entirely appropriate in the treatment of advance senile dementia, psychotic, terminally ill, or very frail debilitated elders. Based on the clinical observations, a procedure was developed to identify those patients whose characteristics made them appropriate for Life Enhancement Counseling: depressed, purposeless individuals were considered appropriate; organic, psychotic and very frail elders were not considered appropriate. This procedure was used to identify the 44 Cuban elders considered appropriate and used in the evaluation research reported here. The 44 Cuban elders included 10 males and 34 females. The average age was 67.5 with a standard deviation of 9.1 and a range of ages from 51 to 85. There was a wide spread in the time spent in the United States by these elders, ranging from three months to 26 years, with a mean of 12.9 years and a standard deviation of 5.7 years. The overall education level of the sample was relatively low, with a mean of 7.2 years of education, a standard deviation of 4.8, and a range of from zero to 18 years. Fully 57 percent of this sample had never gone beyond elementary school, and 80 percent never finished high school.

Counselors

Three counselors conducted the Life Enhancement Counseling procedures. These counselors were bilingual and bicultural (Cuban and American). There were two men and one woman. Their levels of training varied to include one bachelors degree in social work, one masters degree in social work, and one doctorate in counseling psychology. Their clinical experience was also varied, ranging from two to 15 years of clinical experience. The counseling supervisor was a bilingual, bicultural individual with a masters degree in social work who had previous experience in directing demonstration and clinical research services. Extensive training in providing Life Enhancement services was conducted by the Principal Investigator at the beginning of the project and the Clinical Director later on. Case supervision and case conferences were used as mechanisms for training. The counselors were also trained in administration of the Psychiatric Status Schedule (PSS) and the Older Americans Resources and Services Project's Multidimensional Functional Assessment Questionnaire (OARS) until they reached acceptable interater reliabilities among each other and with other professionals knowledgeable in the administration of these instruments.

Evaluation Measures and Variables

Outcome Measures. The literature available on service delivery to the elderly (e.g., Pfeiffer, 1975) emphasizes the need to examine the elderly within the context of their ecology. This requires taking into consideration the different systems that impact upon the elderly and the different levels and areas of functioning of this population.

As noted by Pfeiffer (1975), the range of problems experienced by older persons include mental health problems, social and economic problems, and impairments in capacity for self-care. Moreover, different areas of functioning influence each other. For instance he notes that physical illness in the elderly person can lead to depression. On the other hand, ample social resources can positively influence mental status and assist the individual in obtaining appropriate health care services.

Taking these factors into consideration, the choice of measures was guided by an attempt to obtain a fairly comprehensive profile of the project's elderly clients. The two outcome measures chosen were the OARS Multidimensional Functional Assessment Questionnaire (OARS) and the Subjective Distress macroscale of the Psychiatric Status Schedule (PSS).

The OARS Multidimensional Functional Assessment Questionnaire. This instrument was designed to evaluate the extent and degree of impairment of older persons. It was developed by the Older Americans Resources and Services Project, a division of the Duke Center for the Study of Aging (Pfeiffer, 1975). According to Pfeiffer, older persons who have problems tend to have multiple problems in multiple areas of functioning. The OARS represents a technology for assessment of multiple areas of functioning simultaneously, thereby providing a comprehensive profile.

The OARS measures an elder's functional level at the time of administration in each of the following areas: social resources (extent, quality, and availability of social interactions), economic resources, mental health, physical health, and capacity for self-care in activities of daily living (Pfeiffer, 1975). Its emphasis on current functioning makes it an excellent instrument for outcome evaluation. Utilization of services is the focus of the remainder of the questionnaire. It collects information about a variety of services that elderly or impaired individuals might require. Data is systematically obtained regarding services the client is currently receiving and also those services she or he feels she or he currently needs.

The Psychiatric Status Schedule. This instrument (Spitzer, et al., 1970) has been recommended by the National Institute of Mental Health (Waskow and Parloff, 1975) as one of the best measures of treatment outcome of its kind. The Psychiatric Status Schedule (PSS) is an instrument designed to improve the research value of clinical judgements of psychosocial functioning. The interviewer uses the PSS interview schedule to elicit information needed to judge the items of the inventory, most of which are brief nontechnical descriptions of small units of behavior. The focus is upon the subject's symptoms and functioning during the past week. The emphasis, therefore, is on current functioning.

Spitzer and his collaborators summarized the schedule into four factorially derived macroscales: Subjective Distress, Behavioral Disturbance, Impulse Control Disturbance, and Reality Testing Disturbance. Because of the nature of the present demonstration project, only the Subjective Distress section of the PSS is used in evaluating changes in psychosocial functioning. Five symptom scales comprise the summary symptom scale of Subjective Distress: Depression-Anxiety, Daily Routine/Leisure Time Impairment, Social Isolation, Suicide/Self-Mutilation, and Somatic Concerns. These five symptom scales tap problem areas that are frequently encountered in elderly patients. In particular, it would seem that these five scales evaluate symptoms that would be expected to be negatively correlated with a feeling of meaningfulness in life and a joy of living.

Counselors' Global Ratings. Because it is desirable to obtain outcome assessments that reflect various perspectives (Waskow and Parloff, 1975) in addition to the more standardized outcome measures, a global rating of improvement was also obtained from the counselors. The counselors' ratings were made at the time of termination. The ratings used a 1-5 scale: 1 = worse, 2 = no worse, 3 = slight improvement, 4 = considerable improvement, and 5 = best outcome.

Adaptation of the Measures. With the permission of Drs. Spitzer and Endicott, the PSS was modified to make it more suitable for administration to an Hispanic population. The schedule itself was completely translated into Spanish. In addition, the administration of the schedule was modified to make it more culturally sensitive and appropriate to an Hispanic population. Similarly, the OARS was translated into Spanish. In the case of the OARS translations, studies have been conducted to ascertain the reliabilities of the language parallel forms (Santisteban, Szapocznik, and Kurtines, in preparation). These reliabilities were found to be consistent with the original interater reliability studies reported by Pfeiffer (1975).

Independent Variables. The basic independent variable of the evaluation study is treatment effectiveness as measured by pretest and posttest scores on the outcome measures. In addition, four other measures were obtained to serve as predictors of treatment effectiveness: (1) level of acculturation, (2) extent of Life Enhancement Counseling, (3) medication, and (4) total number of sessions.

Acculturation Behavioral Scale. The level of acculturation was measured by the Acculturation Behavioral Scale (Szapocznik, Scopetta, Kurtines, and Aranalde, 1978). This scale is a 24-item, factorially derived instrument designed to measure individual language usage, customs, habits, and preferred idealized life style. Szapocznik and his associates (ibid.) report high levels of reliability (internal consistency, retest, and parallel forms), and there is evidence for construct validity as well (cf. Kurtines and Miranda, in press).

Extent of Life Enhancement Counseling. Whereas all the cases reported in the analysis below received some degree of Life Enhancement Counseling, the extent of Life Enhancement Counseling as defined by the model and provided to each elder varied from individual to individual. To account for these between-subject differences, ratings of the "extent of Life Enhancement Counseling" were obtained. Each of the case histories were reviewed by four members of the professional staff who were not involved directly in the delivery of services. Each rater made an independent judgment using the following scale: 1 = slight Life Enhancement Counseling, 2 = moderate Life Enhancement Counseling, and 3 = excellent example of the Life Enhancement Counseling Model.

Medication. After the initial admissions interview, the counselor determined if a psychiatric evaluation was necessary. In those cases in which the psychiatric evaluation indicated it necessary, appropriate medication (usually elavil, serentil, or norpramine) was prescribed. Medication was regularly monitored by a psychiatrist.

Total Number of Sessions. The total number of sessions refers to all sessions with the counselor and/or psychiatrist, including admission and evaluation as well as treatment sessions.

Procedure

Pretreatment measures obtained during the admission interview were the OARS, the PSS, the Acculturation Behavioral Scale, and demographic information. All the pretreatment measures were administered by the same individual who would become the elder's counselor. Experience in previous studies revealed that continuity of contact with one person is vital to maintaining clients engaged in treatment. In fact, in previous studies when pretreatment assessment was handled by a person different from the counselor, a high attrition rate occurred between admission and the first counseling sessions.

Clinical procedures in providing treatment to this largely Hispanic population required that the initial admission session be scheduled soon after initial request for services. Consistent with the crisis orientation of this population, in all cases initial admission sessions were scheduled within three working days of initial contact.

In order to enhance the objectivity of the evaluation procedure, it was necessary to have someone other than a client's counselor administer posttreatment outcome measures. The posttreatment outcome administration was performed by counselors who were in the same Life Enhancement Counseling unit but who had not been directly involved in the treatment of the client being posttested.

RESULTS

The data on Cuban elders constitute the core of the findings reported in this section. Two main sets of analyses will be reported: (1) pretreatment and posttreatment analyses on the outcome measures, and (2) regression analyses to determine parameters of treatment effectiveness.

Outcome Analyses

The data on the outcome measures for the 44 Cuban elders who had completed the study at the time of this writing were analyzed as follows. Two tailed, t-tests were calculated to compare the mean pretest and posttest scores on the OARS and the Subjective Distress PSS macroscale. The mean, standard deviation, t-values, and levels of significance for the pretest and posttest scores are presented in Table 12.1

As Table 12.1 depicts, mean posttest scores for all OARS variables were significantly lowered, reflecting significant improvements in the multiple dimensions of functioning assessed by this instrument. While significant reductions occurred for all variables, the most dramatic improvement is not in any one area, but in overall functioning as assessed by the OARS total score. The largest improvement for a single scale was predictably, Mental Health. Table 12.1 also reveals that there were significant improvements in all areas evaluated by the Subjective Distress macroscale of the PSS. It is noteworthy that the single largest improvement on the PSS was obtained for the Depression-Anxiety subscale.

Table 12.1
Means, Standard Deviations (S.D.), t-values, and Levels of Significance for OARS and PSS Scales for 44 Cuban Elders

	Pretest		Posttest			
	Mean	S.D.	Mean	S.D.	t-value	Level of Significance
OARS						
Social Resources	2.66	.89	2.20	.95	3.81	.000
Economic Resources	3.20	.82	2.39	.78	6.66	.000
Mental Health	3.02	.55	2.20	.51	7.50	.000
Physical Health	2.64	.86	2.16	.74	4.53	.000
Activities of Daily Living	2.32	1.14	1.68	.91	4.88	.000
OARS Total	13.84	2.71	10.64	2.49	9.37	.000
PSS Subjective Distress Macroscale*						
Depression-Anxiety	52.52	14.05	33.91	5.66	8.86	.000
Daily Routine/Leisure Time Impairment	44.48	13.16	39.09	4.18	4.85	.000
Social Isolation	46.36	12.20	41.16	3.19	3.31	.002
Suicide/Self-Mutilation	45.95	8.77	42.00	0.00	2.99	.005
Somatic Concerns	56.39	19.45	45.02	5.45	3.66	.001
Subjective Distress Total	51.14	16.49	33.93	4.76	6.91	.000

*The small amount of variance in posttests of the PSS Subjective Distress subscales was due to floor effects at the normal end of these scales. It should be noted that one finding of this study was that the PSS, which was originally validated on inpatient populations, displays a floor effect when used with outpatient populations, thus limiting its use as an outcome measure with outpatient populations.

Although the thrust of this chapter has been to document the effectiveness of Life Enhancement Counseling with Cuban elders, analyses of the data obtained from a second sample on non-Cuban elders (comprised of seven non-Cuban Hispanics and three non-Hispanic whites) provide some tentative evidence for the generalizability of Life Enhancement Counseling as an effective intervention modality with non-Cuban elders. As with the Cuban elders, the pretest-posttest differences on overall OARS and the total PSS Subjective Distress were significant, reflecting the effectiveness of Life Enhancement Counseling with the non-Cuban elders. However, for this sample, not all of the individual scales reflected significant improvement. The improvements were greatest in OARS Mental and Physical Health and in PSS Depression-Anxiety and least noticeable in OARS Social Resources and Activities of Daily Living and in PSS Daily Routine/Leisure Time Impairment. Hence, the greatest improvement for this group took place in the mental health area and the least improvement in daily routine and social resources.

While it appears that Life Enhancement Counseling is highly effective with depressed elders, the data from the project indicates that it is not generally recommended for the treatment of certain types of impairments common to the elderly. In fact, the model was specifically designed for enhancing meaning of life, thereby assuming meaninglessness to be a critical target problem. Clinical experience suggests that, while Life Enhancement Counseling can be an adjunct to the treatment of elders with other impairments, it does not directly apply to the treatment of organic or psychotic disorders, or of frail or debilitated elders. In order to assess the impact of treatment on such individuals, outcome analyses were conducted on the sample of clients (N = 14) who had completed treatment but who had been excluded from the previous analyses because the nature of their impairment went far beyond problems of meaninglessness. Generally, this sample was more impaired than the other samples at the time of admission *and* at the time of termination. Generally, there was overall improvement as assessed by the total OARS and PSS scales. However, in many of these cases the degree of Life Enhancement Counseling that was possible to conduct was limited because of the deteriorated state of the clients. What is critical to point out here is that in some of the areas that represented crucial target problems for these individuals, such as physical health and impairment in activities of daily living, little improvement was achieved through our treatment. Hence, Life Enhancement Counseling does not appear to affect some of the most critical target problems of severely deteriorated elders.

Regression Analyses

The analyses reported in this section aim at identifying variables that are predictive of success in Life Enhancement Counseling. In order to conduct these analyses it was necessary to develop a composite measure of treatment effectiveness by factor analyzing the outcome measures. The factor analysis revealed the existence of two distinct outcome factors. One factor was the Composite Score of OARS Gain scores and Clinical Global ratings. The second factor consisted of the Subjective Distress Gain scores.

Client Variables. A stepwise regression analysis was conducted using the OARS and Global Rating Composite Score as the dependent variable, and acculturation, age, sex, number of years in the United States, and education as independent variables. The results of this regression analysis indicated that none of these client variables were significant predictors of improvement as measured by this factor. A second regression analysis was conducted, this time using Subjective Distress Gain as a dependent variable. Again, the results of this analysis suggested that none of these clients' variables were significant predictors of Subjective Distress Gain.

Treatment Variable. A stepwise regression analysis was conducted using the treatment effectiveness Composite Factor (OARS Gain and Clinical Global ratings) as the dependent variable and (1) extent of Life Enhancement Counseling, (2) medication, and (3) total number of sessions as predictor variables. The result of this analysis indicated that the single significant predictor of treatment effectiveness on the Composite Factor was the extent of Life Enhancement Counseling: $F(1,42)^2 = 21.21$, $p < .001$. A second regression analysis was conducted, this time using Subjective Distress Gain as the dependent variable. The results of this analysis indicate that the single significant predictor of improvement on this factor was medication: $F(1,42) = 5.28$, $p < .05$.

The regression analyses of the effect of treatment variables upon outcome revealed that extent of Life Enhancement Counseling was the best predictor of OARS gain, while the use of medication was the best predictor of improvements in levels of subjective distress. These findings would suggest that each of these two treatments have differential effects on different types of problems: Life Enhancement impacts on multidimensional functioning; medication relieves subjective distress. Further analyses were conducted to examine in closer detail these interesting effects and their interaction.

The first set of analyses was designed to determine whether Life Enhancement was also effective in reducing subjective distress in those clients who received *no* medication. From the total sample of 44 Cuban elders, 17 received no medication. Analyses conducted on pretest and posttest scores of subjective distress revealed a significant improvement in total Subjective Distress macroscale scores: $t(16) = 3.39$, $p < .01$. The Depresson-Anxiety subscale decreased significantly: $t(16) = 4.01$, $p < .001$. The remaining subscales (Suicide/Self-Mutilation, Somatic Concerns, Social Isolation, and Daily

Routine/Leisure Time Impairment) did not improve significantly. However, an examination of the pretest and posttest means indicated that the lack of apparent improvement was a result of very low initial scores, which were already close to the "floor" in each of these scales. Thus, although medication was the best predictor of improvement in subjective distress, clients who received no medication, but did receive Life Enhancement Counseling, improved in subjective distress generally and depression/anxiety specifically.

A second set of analyses examined the interaction between the two treatment variables under discussion, Life Enhancement Counseling and medication. Two 2×2 analyses of covariance were conducted separately on post-OARS Total and PSS Subjective Distress Total, with pretreatment scores as covariates. The independent variables for these ANACOVAs were (1) low vs. high levels of Life Enhancement Counseling and (2) medication vs. *no* medication. For the OARS variable, there was a significant trend for level of Life Enhancement, $F(1,39) = 3.24$, $p < .08$, and a significant Life Enhancement x medication interaction effect, $F(1,39) = 4.51$, $p < .006$.

Plotting of these data revealed several interesting findings. First, patients who tended to receive medication also tended to be the most dysfunctional on all measures at admission. Second, patients who received no medication improved significantly with counseling alone. Finally, and perhaps most interesting, is the finding that, among those subjects on medication, those who received extensive Life Enhancement Counseling improved more than those subjects who received little Life Enhancement Counseling, indicating that medication alone is not the most desirable treatment strategy.

COUNSELING AND THE ELDERLY: THE LIFE ENHANCEMENT MODEL IN PERSPECTIVE

For too long, mental health services have been unavailable to the elderly. Although there are many reasons for the present state of affairs, perhaps the most important reason has been the dearth of appropriate treatment procedures. This dearth is rooted in a lack of understanding of the ways in which elders function and the unavailability of creative strategies for turning elder's characteristics, typically perceived as weaknesses, into their strengths. Too often, the many psychological symptoms of the elderly are viewed as inevitable aspects of growing old, rather than as symptoms of psychosocial problems that are reversible once appropriate interventions are identified. In this section, Life Enhancement Counseling is presented within a broader perspective, and its potential and limitations discussed.

Life Enhancement Counseling represents an attempt to redirect the mental health service delivery effort along new lines by offering an alternate model for conceptualizing counseling for the elderly. This approach builds on elders' strengths and natural proclivities, while utilizing environmental resources to buttress elders' functioning. It has been developed specifically for the treatment of the most pervasive mental health problem confronting the elderly: a problem that is typically diagnosed as depression but is conceptualized here as a loss of meaning and purpose in life. As an intervention approach, Life Enhancement Counseling has been designed to provide a replicable intervention methodology, with clearly delineated steps and procedures.

Life Enhancement Counseling for Whom?

When Life Enhancement Counseling is applied to a depressed population, it is effective for a broad range of clients. Within the Cuban sample included in the results section above, for example, regression analyses using client characteristics as predictors of treatment effectiveness reveal that this approach was effective for a wide range of ages: The Cuban elders in this sample ranged from a relatively young age of 51 to a very elderly 85. Treatment was also equally effective along a wide range of levels of acculturation and years in the United States, the latter ranging from three months to 26 years. Similarly, while there tended to be more women than men, the results showed that treatment was equally effective for both groups. Remarkably, Life Enhancement Counseling was equally appropriate for a wide range of educational levels, ranging from illiterates with no education to an elder with a doctoral degree.

Life Enhancement Counseling was also found to be effective when applied to a group of ten non-Cuban elders (seven non-Cuban Hispanics and three non-Hispanic whites). This finding has important implications for the generalizability of the counseling model to non-Cuban elders and warrants further investigation. Replications on this work with non-Cuban elderly populations should be encouraged.

The clinical experience and research findings suggest that Life Enhancement Counseling is not entirely appropriate for elders with senile dementia, for the terminally ill, or for frail or handicapped elders. For these individuals, the improvements were limited, and Life Enhancement Counseling functioned best as a supportive therapy. For this group, gains were usually not as impressive as with the depressed-only patients.

Implications for Treatment

The work reported in this chapter has important implications for mental health treatment of elders. The most clinically relevant findings can be summarized as follows:

1. Life Enhancement Counseling is an acceptable and effective method in the treatment of depressed elders, particularly those who have lost their sense of meaning and purpose in life.

2. Life Enhancement Counseling is effective with a wide variety of elders across age, sex, socioeconomic status, education, acculturation level, and ethnic background.

3. Life Enhancement Counseling is particularly effective in bringing about multidimensional improvement in the areas of social resources, economic resources, mental health, physical health, and activities of daily living.

4. Life Enhancement Counseling should be used in conjunction with antidepressant medication with clients who present severe levels of subjective distress. With these clients, the medication was highly effective in reducing subjective distress, although Life Enhancement Counseling had a substantial effect beyond that of the medication alone.

5. Life Enhancement Counseling by itself (i.e., without medication) is effective in reducing subjective distress, particularly depression/anxiety in those clients presenting initially moderate levels of dysfunction.

Conclusions

The Life Enhancement Counseling Model described in this chapter represents an innovative integration of treatment strategies for providing mental health services to elders. This approach utilizes elders' natural proclivity to reminisce and recognizes the significance of their current ecological conditions. Life Enhancement Counseling, thus, draws on elders' past strengths and competencies and reenacts these in the present in an effort to ameliorate those conditions that contribute to elders' mental health distress. The development of this method is rooted in a philosophic orientation of service delivery that encourages tailoring treatment to client characteristics and needs, rather than forcing clients into preexisting treatment modes.

NOTES

1. A more detailed presentation of application procedures is available in the form of the *Life Enhancement Counseling Manual*. A copy of the manual can be obtained from the Spanish Family Guidance Center, University of Miami, 747 Ponce de Leon Blvd., Suite 303, Coral Gables, Florida 33134.

2. One subject was deleted from the analysis because of missing data.

REFERENCES

Auerswald, E.H. Families, change, and the ecological perspective. *Family Process* 10 (1971):263-80.

Bergin, A.E. The evaluation of therapeutic outcomes. In *Handbook of Psychotherapy and Behavior Change,* edited by A.E. Bergin and S.L. Garfield. New York: John Wiley & Sons, 1971.

Butler, R.N. The Life Review: An interpretation of reminiscence in the aged. *Psychiatry* 26 (1963):65-76.

Carter, R. Opening address. National Conference on Mental Health and the Elderly, Select Committee on Aging. Washington, D.C., April 23 & 24, 1979.

Clark, J. The Cubans of the island and of the exile: A comparative sociodemographic analysis. In *Cubans in the United States,* edited by M.C. Herrara, J. Szapocznik, and J.I. Rasco. in press.

Cohen, G. Report to the National Conference on Mental Health and the Elderly, Select Committee on Aging. Washington, D.C., April 23 & 24, 1979.

Erickson, E.H. *Childhood and Society.* New York: W.W. Norton, 1950.

Goin, M., Yamamoto, J., and Silverman, J. Therapy congruent with class-linked expectations. *Archives of General Psychiatry* 13 (1965):133-37.

Gould, R.E. Dr. Strangeclass: Or how I stopped worrying about the theory and began treating the blue-collar worker. *American Journal of Orthopsychiatry* 37 (1967):78-86.

Heitler, J.B. Preparatory techniques in initiating expressive psychotherapy with lower-class, unsophisticated patients. *Psychological Bulletin* 83 (1976):339-52.

Hernandez, A.R., The Cuban minority in the U.S.: Final report on need identification and program evaluation. Office of Research and Demonstration, Social and Rehabilitation Service, U.S. Department of Health, Education, and Welfare, Grant Number 08-P-55933/3-02, 1974.

Hunt, R.G. Social class and mental illness: Some implications for clinical theory and practice. *American Journal of Psychiatry* 116 (1960):1065.

Kiesler, D.J. Experimental designs in psychotherapy research. In *Handbook of Psychotherapy and Behavior Change,* edited by A.E. Bergin and S.L. Garfield. New York: John Wiley & Sons, 1971.

Kluckhohn, F.R. and Strodtbeck, F.L. *Variations in Value Orientations.* Evanston, Ill.: Row, Peterson, 1961.

Kurtines, W. and Miranda, L. Family role perception among acculturating Cuban American college students. *International Journal of Intercultural Relations,* in press.

Life Enhancement Counseling Manual. Spanish Family Guidance Center, in preparation.

Lewis, M. Butler, R. Life-review therapy: Putting memories to work in individual and group psychotherapy. *Geriatrics* (November 1974):165-73.

Lerner, B. *Therapy in the Ghetto: Political Impotence and Personal Desintegration.* Baltimore, Md.: The John Hopkins University Press, 1972.

Levine, E.S. and Padilla, A.M. *Crossing Cultures in Therapy: Pluralistic Counseling for the Hispanic.* Monterey, Calif.: Brooks/Cole, 1980.

Lorion, R.P. Socioeconomic status and traditional treatment approaches reconsidered. *Psychological Bulletin* 79 (1973):263-70.

_____. Patient and therapist variables in the treatment of low-income patients. *Psychological Bulletin* 81 (1974):344-54.

Magaro, P. A prescription treatment model based upon social class and premorbid adjustment. *Psychotherapy* 6 (1969):57-70.

Orne, M. and Wender, P. Anticipatory socialization for psychotherapy: Method and rationale. *American Journal of Psychiatry* 124 (1968):88-98.

Patterson, R. Grief and depression in old people. *Maryland State Medical Journal* 18 (1969):75-79.

Paul, G.L. Behavior modification research: Design and tactics. In *Behavior Therapy: Appraisal and Status,* edited by C.M. Franks. New York: McGraw-Hill, 1969.

Pfeiffer, E. OARS Multidimensional Functional Assessment Questionnaire. Duke University for the Study of Aging and Human Development, 1975.

Ramirez, M. and Castañeda, A. *Cultural Democracy, Bicogniture Development, and Education.* New York: Academic Press, 1974.

Sandeval, M.C. Ethos and Cubanos. *Krisis* 1 (Spring 1976):?.

Santisteban, D. Locus of control as a cross-cultural variable. Masters thesis, University of South Florida, 1975.

Santisteban, D., Szapocznik, J., and Kurtines, W. A Spanish translation of the OARS Multidimensional Functional Assessment Questionnaire. In preparation.

Sloane, R.B., Staples, F.R., Cristol, A.H., Yorkston, N.Y., and Whipple, F. Patient characteristics and outcome in psychotherapy and behavior therapy. *Journal of Consulting and Clinical Psychology* 44 (1974):330-39.

Smith, J.E. The elderly Florida in the year 2000. Unpublished paper. The Institute for the Study of Aging, University of Miami, March 1976.

Spitzer, R.L., Endicott, J., Fleiss, J.L., and Cohen, J. The psychiatric status schedule: A technique for evaluating psychopathology and impairment in role functioning. *Archives of General Psychiatry* 23 (1970):41-55.

Szapocznik, J., Faletti, M.V., and Scopetta, M.A. Psychological social issues of Cuban elders in Miami. Spanish Family Guidance Clinic and Institute for the Study of Aging. Technical Report, 1978.

Szapocznik, J., Scopetta, M.A., Aranalde, A., and Kurtines, W. Cuban value structure: Treatment implications. *Journal of Consulting and Clinical Psychology* 46 (1978):961-70.

Szapocznik, J., Scopetta, M.A., and King, O.E. Theory and practice in matching treatment to the special characteristics and problems of Cuban immigrants. *Journal of Community Psychology* 6 (1978):112-22.

Szapoczik, J., Scopetta, M.A., Kurtines, W., and Aranalde, A. Theory and measurement of acculturation. *Interamerican Journal of Psychology* 12 (1978):113-30.

Terestman, N., Miller, J., and Weber, J. Blue-collar patients at a psychoanalytic clinic. *American Journal of Psychiatry* 131 (1974):261-66.

Tholen, J.F. An interactive approach to the study of outcome in group counseling: Matching conceptual level with degree of structure. Master's thesis, University of Miami, 1974.

von Bertalanffy, L. *Organismic Psychology and Systems Theory.* Worchester, Mass.: Clark University Press, 1968.

Waskow, J.E. and Parloff, M.B. *Psychotherapy Change Measures.* Report of the Clinical Research Branch Outcome Measures Project, NIMH U.S. Department of Health, Education, and Welfare, Publication No. (ADM) 74-120. Washington, D.C.: U.S. Government Printing Office, 1975.

Witkin, H.A. and Berry, J.W. Psychological differentiation in cross-cultural perspective. *Journal of Cross-Cultural Research* 6 (1975):4-87.

13   Psychopathology, Psychotherapy, and the Mexican-American Patient

Arnold Meadow

INTRODUCTION

Two previous papers have compared the frequency of types of psycho-pathology in Anglo-American and Mexican-American adult and child patients (Meadow and Stoker, 1965; Stoker and Meadow, 1974). These papers were based on the statistical comparison of clinical descriptions of patients included in official hospital and clinic files. Although the two studies demonstrated major differences in psychopathological behavior between ethnic groups, they were insufficiently detailed to provide guidelines for differential therapeutic interventions. The present chapter is designed to link with a single theory the results reported in the earlier papers in order to provide a more reasoned basis for suggestions regarding the delivery of mental health services to the Mexican-American group. In addition to the findings of the earlier studies, this chapter will draw upon other relevant investigations and excerpts from the therapy protocols of a 23-year old Mexican-American community college student.

A basic hypothesis of this study is that the most frequent types of psychopathological behavior of the patients in a culture are intensified forms of the most frequent types of psychopathological behavior in the general population of that culture. More specifically, the theory is proposed that psychopathological behavior that is more frequent in Mexican-American than Anglo-American patients is similarly more frequent in a milder form in the Mexican as compared to the Anglo-American general populations.

The theory further postulates that the hypothesized similarity in behavior is produced by idiosyncratic Mexican cultural and social structural factors. It assumes that each culture is characterized by different values and social structures, which produce typical behavioral reactions to stress. Thus, to cite a well-known example: the Jew in reaction to stress will react with excessive eating, the Irishman with excessive drinking. Each culture, in turn, may have different cultural values and social structures that produce the stress. Thus, for the Jew stress may be produced by anti-Semitism or an overprotective mother who stuffs the child with food; for the Irishman a similar amount of stress may be produced by a potato famine or a family attitude that bemusedly tolerates the old boy who has had a little too much to drink.

In the present chapter an attempt is made to describe three behaviors that are hypothesized as appearing more frequently in an intense form among Mexican-American than among Anglo-American patients and more frequently in a milder form among Mexican as compared to Anglo-American general populations. The behaviors are: (1) hallucinations, (2) passive behavior of males in a sober state, and (3) verbal and/or physical aggression of males in the alcoholic state. The chapter will also attempt to delineate some of the cultural and social factors that appear to be at least in part producing the described behaviors.

HALLUCINATIONS

An Arizona state hospital study revealed significantly more auditory and visual hallucinations among Mexican-American than among Anglo-American patient groups (Meadow and Stoker, 1965). The differences reported were not only significant but great in magnitude. For the visual hallucinations variable the frequency of symptom occurrence expressed as a percentage of the sample was 28.3 percent for the Mexican-American males and 8.3 percent for the Anglo-American males. For auditory hallucinations the percentage was 71.6 percent for the Mexican-American males and 41.6 percent for the Anglo-American males. Cultural differences in the frequency of hallucinations were also reported in the child guidance clinic study, although the symptom was relatively rare (Stoker and Meadow, 1974). For Mexican-American male child patients hallucinations were reported as 4 percent, for Mexican-American female child patients as 3 percent, for Anglo-American male child patients as 0 percent and for Anglo-American female child patients as 0 percent.

The state hospital study results were obtained from a sample that was predominantly schizophrenic. Ninety-one percent of the Mexican-American males and 81 percent of the Anglo-American sample had been assigned a schizophrenic diagnosis. The results, thus, indicate that the symptomatology of schizophrenia may be importantly determined by a cultural factor.

The high frequency of hallucinations among Mexican-American patients is influenced by the widespread belief in the Mexican culture of the occurrence of supernatural phenomena. Mexican-Americans are aware of this fact and, accordingly, do not regard a report of an hallucinatory experience as an indication of mental illness. Torrey (1969) has reported data indicating that 90 percent of Anglo residents in psychiatry associate the phrase "hears voices" with the word "crazy"; in contrast, only 10 percent of Mexican-American high school students make the same association.

The widespread cultural belief in supernatural phenomena makes it necessary for the therapist working with Mexican-American patients to carefully investigate the meaning and function of an hallucinatory experience. The report of the return of a dead person to the earth to carry on conversations with the living is frequent. A famous contemporary Mexican novel, *Pedro Paramo,* contains many incidents of this kind (Rulfo, 1959).

Some Mexican-American hallucinatory experiences may simply reflect a cultural belief and occur in persons completely free of psychopathology. In other cases Mexican-American hallucinations may have the same significance as those reported by Anglo-American patients. There exists an intermediate group of Mexican-American patients in which the hallucination may be interpreted as a symbolic expression of a wish fulfillment or as a sign of a warded-off superego criticism. For these patients the hallucination is a symptom of psychopathology, but it does not signify the serious break with reality that would be implied if it occurred in an Anglo-American case. An hallucination described by a 23-year old Mexican-American patient can be assigned to this group. An excerpt from his therapy protocols will illustrate their function and meaning:

THERAPIST (T): You seemed to question me at the beginning of the session; do you have confidence in me?
PATIENT (P): Yes, 90 percent.
T: 90 percent?
P: Well, you're human. You may get mad. Many times people in a power position get mad. You can say, well, this guy doesn't know psychology. How can he question me. (long pause)
T: Well, I can understand how you can have doubts; after all, you couldn't have confidence that the members of your family would accept you.
P: You know, there's something I haven't told you. Grandma always loved me a lot but at 14, I turned bad. Really bad. I was strong. I'd fight with Grandma. Then Grandma got sick and went to the hospital. My mother took me to the hospital to see her. My mother said, "Grandma, look who is here. It's Carlos!" "Carlos!!¹ I don't want to see him," she said, turning away from me. "Mama, please don't be mad!" "Get away from me, cabron," (goat) she said. And then three days later she died.
T: And how did you feel?

P: It made me feel guilty. You know there are many levels of reality including the supernatural. I heard my grandmother's voice, "Carlos! ven! ven! ven!" (Carlos! come to me! come to me! come to me!)

T: When did that happen?

P: Several times. The last time was about one year ago. Inside of me, I feel there is another reality. In our everyday life we just see one level. There are really other levels.

T: Can you tell me more about that?

P: Well, when we are scared, we can get in touch with other levels. Like that time I told you. I was 17 and I ran away from home and I went into that cave with some other boys and we had silvysyhin, the mushrooms. I had that weird feeling. Even the animals in the cave were acting weirdly. The animals also felt we were not in everyday reality. I was really scared. I never believed in telepathy, but since that time I do. You can know, for example, what is going on with somebody 3,000 miles away, if you have a close emotional tie with them.

T: Can you give me an example?

P: Well, like the time I had the mushrooms. I became so scared. So I began thinking of my mom. I began thinking it would be so nice to be with my mom. Suddenly, I saw her. She was wearing a pink nylon robe. She was talking and I could hear her say, "I am worried that something is happening to Carlos." And then she lighted a candle and began to pray for me.

When I came back to Mexico City I asked her. I said, "What were you doing last Thursday at 9 p.m.?" And she replied, "I was worrying, worrying about you, Carlos." "But what were you doing?", I persisted. "I lighted a candle and prayed for you." "And were you wearing a pink robe?," I asked. "Yes," she said.

You think I'm crazy. Well, all my nervousness started after that!

The patient's first hallucination occurred in the form of a vision of his mother. It appeared while the patient was under the influence of the mushrooms. Although the mushrooms provided a somatogenic precipitating factor, the content of the hallucination reflected the patient's psychological needs at that time: he was 17; he had run away from home and was thinking how nice it would be to be with his mother. The visual hallucination had obvious wish fulfilling determinants.

The report of hearing the voice of the dead Grandma had no precipitating organic factor associated with it. In the interview, the patient directly linked it with a psychological factor when he described the feelings of guilt he had experienced as a result of his adolescent rebellion against Grandma and her refusal to talk to him on her death bed.

The Mexican-American patient who reported the hallucinations had been seen for a total of ten hours over a period of five months at the time this report was written. There were absolutely no indications from the material he presented of any past or present psychotic functioning. The patient had previously been seen at a university medical center for a series of three interviews. The psychiatrist who interviewed him also reported an absence of psychotic signs and assigned him a primary diagnosis of "anxiety neurosis in a passive dependent character" and a secondary diagnosis of "episodic alcoholic addiction."

PASSIVE BEHAVIOR

Clinical observations of Mexican-American patients in clinics and hospitals reveals a striking passivity of behavior. The passive behavior occurs irrespective of the diagnostic group to which the patient is assigned. A statistical confirmation of this statement is provided by the study of the case files of 152 Mexican-American and 152 Anglo-American patients in three southwestern child guidance clinics (Stoker and Meadow, 1974). One of the behaviors rated in the inspection of the case file records was "passivity." The results indicated that the percentage of "passive" behaviors was 7 percent for Anglo-American boys and 21 percent for Mexican-American boys. The results were significant at the 5 percent level.

Oscar Lewis' classical study of the Mexican town of Tepoztlan describes the passivity of Mexican adolescents and links their behavior with an authoritarian family:

> The strongly authoritarian family and other factors have tended to produce passive, dependent youths rather than youths noted for initiative, ambition, drive and independence....
>
> In contrast with our own society there is in Tepoztlan, with the outstanding exception of courtship and elopement, a noteable absence of open "revolt" against the authorities and example of parents or against local tradition....(1951, p. 395).

A strong statistical confirmation of the existence of a child training pattern emphasizing passivity, at least in the early years of childhood, is provided by Minturn and Lambert's (1964) comparison of mothers' restriction and inhibition of children's aggression in six cultures. Basing his conclusions on data abstracted from a factor analysis of interview data, this investigator describes the percent of cases with factor scores on maternal restriction of peer directed aggression for the six cultures studied.

The percent of cases with maternal restriction of peer directed aggression was 8 percent for Orchard Town (New England), 57 percent for Tarong (Philippines), 63 percent for Nyagsongo (Kenya), 63 percent for Khalapur (India), 63 percent for Taira (Okinawa), and 91 percent for Juxtlahuaia (Mexico). The results, thus, reveal a dramatically greater inhibition and restriction of aggression in the Mexican mothers as compared with that of the mothers from the five other cultures.

In a study of a small town in Morelos, Mexico, Fromm and Maccoby (1973) have similarly described a child training pattern that inculcates passivity:

> The data...present a surprising picture. In contrast to what one could expect, the process of education in the home as well as in school tends to weaken rather than strengthen the character of the child. From 6 to 16 years there occurs an increase in the predominance of submission, receptivity and the capacity to permit oneself to be exploited (p. 253).

Fromm and Maccoby also report that the most frequent mode of relationship of a Mexican adult male to others in the Morelos town they studied was that of passivity. Twenty-four out of 46 male heads of family whom these investigators studied were characterized by the phrase "passive-receptive" (ibid., p. 186).

Diaz-Guerrero (1975) has described the passive behavior of the Mexican and the active behavior of the Anglo Americans as expressions of contrasting sociocultural premeses (SCP). The former is designated as a passive endurer of stress (PES), and the latter as an active endurer of stress (AES). He writes:

> Mexicans, we said, then, are passive endurers of stress and Americans are active endurers of stress. Suddenly, I, a Mexican, and my Australian-American wife, could understand many incidents of total misunderstanding between Mexicans and Americans, the most common being the scandalized "Why don't they do something about it!?" in the presence of too many ill-fed children, poverty, dirt, or sickness of Mexicans. But their virtue is that they can, whereas the Americans could not, passively endure all such misery. It was as if the Mexicans held as an SCP the following: "Life is a rough proposition, and the best way to deal with it is to passively endure what it brings." Soon I realized that such an approach to life in Mexico is solidly backed. It is virtuous; abnegation, obedience, self-sacrifice, submission, dependence, politeness, courtesy—all forms of passive endurance—are Mexican sociocultural virtues. The prevalent religion at the pre-Cortesian agreed that "This is a valley of tears." The prevalent easy adjustment of the Mexican to tragedy, even death; the ni modo ("What can anyone do, there is

no way"); the widespread use of proverbs, stories and jokes of a quasi stoic philosophy; the strong fatalistic attitudes—all these are beautiful examples of a well-integrated and well learned philosophy indicating that the very best way, indeed the righteous way to endure stress is passively. I do not have to say that the prevalent American philosophy makes a virtue of the active endurance of stress and considers it the best possible way "to face reality." Life is lived best in constant activity. This is the solution to the problem of life, and even the travel agencies know about this. Keep them happy having fun....(ibid., p. 121).

There are three components to Professor Diaz-Guerrero's statement. The first is that Mexicans differ from Anglos in being more passive. The second is that Mexicans view passivity as a positive value. Finally, there is the implication that the value placed by the Mexican on passivity is equal or perhaps even superior as a guide to living that the value the Anglos place on activity.

The statement that Mexicans are more passive than Anglos agrees with the other research cited in this chapter. Evidence that supports the statement that Mexicans value passivity is more equivocal. There is some data indicating that traits such as passivity, submission, and dependency are valued in Mexico for women but are strongly repudiated for men (Paz, 1961).

The question as to whether passivity or activity is superior is an ethical one, which is more difficult to answer. If one restricts the qustion to the more limited one of whether passivity or activity is conducive to better mental health, much depends on the meaning and context of the passive behavior. If by passivity one means a broad stoic philosophy that attempts to weather the inevitable slings and arrows of outrageous fortune with courage and resignation, Mexican passivity may be viewed as one of the possible valuable philosophic solutions to living. This conclusion is particularly valid in a country in which the social and economic barriers to mastery of the environment have been tragically limited. Octavio Paz puts the matter well with the following comment:

Stoicism is the most exalted of our military and political attributes. Our history is full of expressions and incidents that demonstrate the indifference of our heroes towards suffering or danger. We are taught from childhood to accept defeat with dignity, a conception that is certainly not ignoble (ibid., p. 31).

Diaz-Guerrero's suggestion that the Anglo-American emphasis on activity as an end in itself does not represent the summum bonum of human aspiration is a wise one. It is a world of the perpetual jogger condemned to run forever without surcease. Certainly the human organism requires times for passivity, repose, and contemplation. However, there is another context of passivity that is probably not as valuable from the view of mental health. We refer to passivity that is used as a defense mechanism. Passivity in this sense is a behavior adopted by the organism in response to anxiety, a behavior that reduces the capacity of the organism to express other basic needs.

The suspicion that some Mexican passive behavior is defensive in nature is aroused by the fact that in some Mexican males the customary pattern of passive behavior is often punctuated by episodic violence committed under the influence of alcohol. Depending upon the year of the comparison, Mexico's homicide rate ranks as either the highest or the second highest in the world. Details of violent behavior under the influence of alcohol will be described in a subsequent section.

AGGRESSIVE BEHAVIOR

The child guidance clinic study (Stoker and Meadow, 1974), which indicated a significantly greater amount of passivity in Mexican-American than in Anglo-American boys, also indicated differences between the groups on several other dimensions. Mexican-American boys were significantly higher than their Anglo-American male counterparts in the variables of agitation, fighting, passivity, hostility, impulsivity, irritability, negativism, obstinancy, and defiance, stealing, and temper tantrums. In contrast, Anglo-American boys had significantly greater amounts of affect hunger, anxious biting of nails, compulsive enuresis, masturbation, nervousness, no or few friends, poor social relationships, sucking of thumb, desire for attention, and dropping out of school.

The state hospital adult patient study (Meadow and Stoker, 1965), similarly, showed a greater amount of violence among Mexican-American males as compared to Anglo-American male patients. The Mexican-American males significantly exceeded the Anglo-American males on the variables "total of single threats" and "attempts to hurt others."

A comparative study of ethnic hostility has also been reported for delinquent groups. Swickard and Spilka (1961) compared groups of Spanish-American and non-Spanish-American delinquent males on probation from similar class backgrounds on the Siegel Manifest Hostility Scale, the Social Desirability Scale, the MMPI Lie Scale, and the Rosenzweig Picture Frustration Study. The results indicated that the mean Siegel hostility score of the Spanish-American groups, adjusted for social desirability, was significantly greater than the similarly adjusted non-Spanish-American group mean.

To summarize, Mexican-Americans when compared to Anglo-Americans show greater amounts of hostility among groups of (1) child guidance patients with mixed diagnoses, (2) adult state hospital patients with predominantly schizophrenic diagnoses, and (3) delinquents on probation. The behavioral difference, thus, occurs irrespective of diagnostic label.

AGGRESSIVE BEHAVIOR AS A DEFENSE AGAINST PASSIVE DEPENDENCY

The mere statistical statement that passive behaviors and aggressive behaviors are more frequent in Mexican-American than Anglo-American patients does not reveal the relationship between them. Clinical experience with patients reveals that in the sober state Mexican-American males tend to be passive. The ingestion of drugs and alcohol often represents an attempt to overcome passivity with more outgoing aggressive behavior. The following therapy excerpt from the protocols of the 23-year old Mexican-American patient illustrates this motivation.

P: The guy in the cave gave me the mushroom. Immediately he began to appear to me like the Devil. He offered me something more. It was marihuana. I already had taken the mushroom and I didn't want to take anything more. The guy said, "What's wrong with you? Here, take it! I made it for everybody!"

I had taken the mushroom to be in with the guys and then when I refused the marijuana they rejected me.

We were all under the effects of the mushroom. We started playing with the dogs, without words. "Vete! Vete! (Go! Go!)" we would think and then the dogs felt it. They began to bark and left the cave.

The guys began to act aggressively towards me.

T: Why was that?

P: They felt I had bad vibrations. I didn't go along with their trip. I kind of got scared. The mushrooms made me feel scared.

One of the guys said to me, I wasn't macho enough. Another said, "Hey, Carlos! Somebody is thinking about you. Rosa is thinking about you."

It's a funny thing, I met those guys on the bus. They didn't know me, And yet he told me "Rosa is thinking about you." Rosa is my mother's name!

This guy's message was "I was dependent on my mother and would always be." He said, "Estas pensando (you are thinking of your mother)" and I said, "Yes, I am."

And then he replied, "You always will, you want to go back to your mother. You always will be dependent on her, Carlos. You always will be around her."

That really got me. When you're under mushrooms, it's incredible. When he said that, I felt very scared—as if he kind of cursed me. "You will never be able to break that dependency feeling," I thought. You see, I felt he was under the effect of the mushroom and had the power of a guru.

T: What does all this have to do with macho?

P: I felt I was a coward and couldn't handle either dope or drink. I felt inferior.

T: Can you explain further?

P: Macho is the opposite of dependency. When he said "You won't be able to break the dependency," I felt I didn't want to be with mom. My mom is nervous. She is like me. She has many things that I don't like. I felt that I couldn't go out, leave her, be myself, be independent!

The patient's verbalizations suggest that at least part of his motivation to take the drugs was that of overcoming his passive dependent relationship to his mother. The patient perceives the process of ingesting drugs and alcohol as being macho, which in turn is perceived as being the polar opposite of the state of being dependent on mother.

RELATIONSHIP BETWEEN ALCOHOLISM AND VIOLENCE IN THE GENERAL POPULATION

A high correlation between crime and alcohol ingestion has been noted in Mexico for over a century. The historian, Cosio-Villegas (1973) observes that sociologists at the turn of the century reported that 85 percent of those arrested and confined to the Mexico City jail were drunk when they committed their crime. The same author cites an 1899 Mexico City study that reported a correlation between the number of bars and eating houses (figones) and the number of registered arrests.

One of the best contemporary studies of the relationship between alcohol ingestion and violence is that reported by Lola Romanucci-Ross (1973). This investigator compiled careful lists of "alcoholics," "heavy drinkers," and those who had committed "serious violence" during a period of participant observation residence in a Morelos village. The results indicated that, of 67 men on the violent list, 97 percent were on either the alcoholic or heavy drinker list. In contrast, only 34 percent of the men of the total male population were on either of these lists. The author concludes that the tie-in between aggressive violent behavior and alcoholism is nearly complete; that is, the aggressor is almost always a heavy drinker or an alcoholic and is in most cases intoxicated when the aggression is committed.

Positive correlations between crime and alcoholism have been reported for the United States. However, the correlations are not as high as those reported in the Mexican studies (Wolfgang, 1958). On the other hand, high correlations are reported for other countries. Veli Verkko (1951) has reported particularly high correlations between violence and crime in Finland. Nevertheless, alcoholism is not always associated with crime or violence. Many individuals who drink are perfectly law abiding. In a cross-cultural survey, MacAndrew and Edgerton (1969) have reported that in some societies heavy drinking is accompanied by peaceful behavior.

RELATIONSHIP BETWEEN PASSIVITY, VIOLENCE, AND ALCOHOLISM IN PATIENT POPULATIONS

The Arizona state hospital study indicated that, in addition to receiving significantly higher designations in alcoholism, a greater proportion of Mexican-American male patients received significantly higher scores than the Anglo-American male patients on the variable "threatening or attempting to hurt others" (Meadow and Stoker, 1965). The statistical data provide no detailed information about the psychological relationship between drinking and violence in the populations described. We turn again to the therapy protocols of the 23-year old Mexican-American patient in a search for explanatory hypotheses.

T: Can you tell me why you drink?

P: Well, one reason is that I am shy. With booze inside of me I can say things.

T: Can you give me an example of how you are when you are sober?

P: Say I have some opinion which disagrees with yours—well—when sober I don't say anyting. I might say to myself, well, everybody has their faults. Besides you might not like what I'd say. So I accept what you say.

Like when I'm with a guy who is one of those macho types. So I just say, yeah, yeah. And they keep on saying they did this and they did that—to impress.

"Oh, really! That's good!", I say—just to go along. For example they say, "I slept with three or four girls last week." And I know they haven't and haven't even had one girl. I still accept it. I say nothing. (Accepto. No digo nada.)

T: And when drunk?

P: When drunk I say, "Man why don't we face reality? Why should we always try to be first?" You see, I know that they're saying lies (mentiras). I don't take so much bullshit when I drink. I am more sincere (sincero) and honest (honesto). I tell them the truth when I drink and they don't get mad because they know you're drunk. I tell them they haven't even had one woman, and since I'm drunk I'm excused.

T: Can you tell me a bit more how you feel and act when drinking?

P: When I drink I am wild, rebellious, strong, savage; I am thirsting for life, women, good food, and music. That's the way I am when I drink. I dance. I'm a good dancer. I sweet talk the ladies. When I used to drink, I'd go to bed with a different girl every night. Drinking makes me more alive. It gives me more imagination. I used to make poetry when I had a few drinks.

The patient feels that his true self emerges when he's drunk. In his sober state, although he may disagree with one of his companions, he is passive and does not challenge him. He believes, however, that when he does not drink he is dishonest and dismisses his real feelings. In describing the behavior of the Mexican male in the general population, Oscar Paz (1961) has also observed that the Mexican expresses his "real" feelings when he is drunk. "It is revealing," Paz writes, "that our intimacy never flowers in a natural way, but only when involved in fiestas, alcohol, or death." (p. 70) The Mexican's belief that his true self emerges when drunk contrasts with the Anglo-American belief that the drunken state is abnormal. Indeed U.S. society has officially reinforced the view of the drunken state as pathological, with its classification of alcoholism as a mental disease.

The Mexican-American patient's phrasing suggests a moral approval of drinking and the activities that accompany it. The words communicate a Rabelaisian gusto; the patient celebrates the pleasure of wine, woman, and song; he seduces not one but several women. Moreover, he boasts of these activities. The Anglo-American's attitude is noticeably different. Although he may, when drunk, indulge in similar pleasures, they are often tinged with guilt; drinking per se may be regarded as sinful.

The Mexican-American patient describes a sharp contrast between the sober and the alcoholic states. Without alcohol he is shy, he cannot "say things." In the subsequent discussion, it becomes clear that the "things" that are said when drunk are challenging, competitive, and aggressive. In fact, the patient is describing a kind of competitive jousting, a trial by verbal battle, which is enacted with fatal regularity in Mexican-American and Mexican bars. Two Mexicans who are drinking together not only boast of their real or fantasized sexual prowess, but each in turn may attempt to denigrate the potency of the other. It is this attitude that the patient is expressing when he says, "Why should you always be first!" and "I don't take so much bullshit when drunk."

RELATIONSHIP BETWEEN ALCOHOLISM, PASSIVITY, AND VIOLENCE IN THE MEXICAN GENERAL POPULATION

Lola Romanucci-Ross (1973) has described a similar competitive drinking contest in the general Mexican population. She writes:

The typical murder—typical insofar as it reflects the social image of such events—involves jealousy, anger, and intoxication, although in its "pure" form it may be motiveless, the grotesque result of a drunken quarrel over nothing. There is a Mexican joke to this effect. A group of men begin drinking together in a bar. After a few drinks they call each other "friend." After a few more they call each other "compadre." Another round and they have become "brothers," embracing one another with protestations of affection. After more drinking one says to another, "Yo soy tu mero papa" ("I am your very father") and then there is a killing (p. 144).

The relationship between a passive character structure and alcoholism has been discussed for the general population of a Mexican town by Fromm and Maccoby:

> Our study demonstrates the connection between a receptive character orientation and vulnerability to alcohol. Although 79% of the men have receptive tendencies and 57% are predominantly receptive, this orientation is more characteristic of the alcoholics than of the heavy drinkers, more than 80% of the alcoholics, 60% of the heavy drinkers, 47% of the moderate drinkers and only 37% of the non-drinkers were classified as predominantly receptive in their type of assimilation (1973, p. 219).

Finally, Lola Romanucci-Ross (1973) in her reports of subjects of the same town presents data that lead her to conclude that most of the violence in the town involves either temporary or chronic intoxication.

The material provided by the description of Mexican behavior under the influence of alcohol can now be used to explain the paradox of the characterization of Mexican behavior as being both passive and aggressive. The passive behavior is emitted in the sober state. The aggressive behavior appears under the influence of alcohol.

Two alternate theoretical interpretations may account for the determinants of Mexican violent behavior in the drunken state. The first assumes that alcohol releases lower centers from cortical control, thus allowing the free expression of aggressive impulses. This theory is impugned by the fact that Mexican women when they do drink do not act aggressively like men. For example, Oscar Lewis describes the women of Tepoztlan as follows: "In contrast to men, they do not respond to intoxication with aggression or impulsiveness but with self pity" (1951, p. 329).

An explanation in terms of a cognitive theory is more compatible with the facts. The patient states in his therapy session that he *expects* that his drinking companions will be more tolerant of his behavior when he is drunk. Although formal Mexican law does not excuse a person from punishment for a criminal act on the basis of voluntary intoxication, in practice, Mexicans and Mexican-Americans act as though aggressive behavior under the influence of alcohol is justifiable. In his sober state the Mexican-American does not assert himself for fear of reprisal. The culture defines the drinking situation, however, by implicit rules that permits a certain amount of self-assertion.

Jane Collier has noted a similar attitude among the Mexican inhabitants of Zincanteco:

> Only the stupidest of Zincantecan defendants at a hearing before a mediator would admit to being guilty without some effort to reduce the plaintiff's demands. Even when his guilt is undeniable, he will plead drunkenness or dredge up stories from the past to show some justification for his actions (1973, p. 98).

The drinking situation, thus, provides to the Mexican an opportunity to convince himself and others that he is macho—an opportunity that is not available to him in the sober state. In most cases the protagonists have a reasonably accurate idea of how far they can go and control their behavior accordingly. Sometimes there are errors. Thinking becomes befuddled. The tolerance of the adversary is underestimated. The high, male adult murder rate in Mexico is one result of this miscalculation.

FAMILY DETERMINANTS OF MEXICAN PSYCHOPATHOLOGY

A complete discussion of the structure and functioning of Mexican and Mexican-American families is beyond the scope of this study. Selective features of the family related to the prediction of psychopathology will be discussed.

There are, of course, differences between Mexican and Mexican-American families, but there remains a core of identity between the two family variants. On the positive side, both families have mothers who are warm, giving, and protective during the first year of childhood. It is perhaps for this reason that the incidence rate for psychoses for Mexican Americans in Texas was considerably lower than that of other groups in the population (Jaco, 1959). In both groups the grandmother also takes an active, positive role in childrearing. This fact not only adds to the security of the child but provides to the older Mexican or Mexican-American woman an important function in life. Jaco also reports that the incidence of functional old age and organic psychosis is also lower for the Texas Mexican-American group. The Mexican family also tends to have more solidarity. Siblings, for example, will provide more support to each other. The more extended family frequently provides more support than its Anglo-American counterparts.

The normal Mexican father "listens" to his son. He gives him counsel (da consejos). He "orients" him and "educates" him.

The behavior of the normal Mexican father should not be misinterpreted. There is a tendency in the United States to view the ideal father as nondirective, as a parent who just lets his son grow. In adolescence the motto is frequently "let him sow his wild oats." Americans sometimes identify all authority with tyranny. They accordingly find it difficult to empathize with the more directive stance of the normal Mexican father.

On the negative side, three family characteristics may be identified as productive of psychopathology: (1) the tendency in *some* Mexican and Mexican-American families for the father to ignore and/or tyrannize the son, (2) the effect of the sibling position of the eldest girl, and (3) the effect of the stepfather family.

In some Mexican and Mexican-American families the son cannot assert himself vis-à-vis the father, and this situation becomes one of the important breeding grounds of the son's passive-aggressive behavior. An additional excerpt from the therapy protocols of the 23-year old Mexican-American patient will exemplify this constellation of factors.

P: At 12 they moved me in with my mother and stepfather. They told me to say I was my mother's brother and never to tell my stepfather I was really her son. Even now I don't call her mom. I treat her like my sister. We never had a relationship like mother and son. I never remember her giving me a kiss. My mother lied; she said I was her brother.

She was 15 when I was born. She didn't love me. I felt unwanted. I was an accident. My parents married because my mother was pregnant. My father left when I was two months old.

At the home of my stepfather I felt rejected as compared to my stepbrothers. I was the last to be fed. Sometimes they told me to eat in the kitchen. I felt my stepfather didn't want me. Some people told him I wasn't my mother's brother. He probably was mad and jealous. When he'd fight with my mother he'd say, "If it wasn't for this so-called brother of yours...!" or "You like Carlos better!" I felt I didn't have a home there. With my grandmother when I was younger, yes. With my mom I always felt I was in the middle.
T: How did you feel towards your stepfather?
P: I felt resentment (resentimientos). I was angry. He'd pick on me as an excuse to fight with my mother. He felt bad because she had lied to him. She was not a virgin. He tried to make her suffer for what he felt was a sin. And he treated me as a black sheep. During their fights my mom would always tell him, "You take advantage of me, now, I have nobody. Wait 'til Carlos is older." At 16 I was very rebellious. I did threaten to hit him, but I didn't. Now that I'm stronger than him, what would be the use. I love my halfbrothers. They love him, me, and my mother. With the exception of that time at 16, I always respected him.

In a subsequent interview, the patient described the fear and guilt he experienced as his stepfather entered the house.

P: If my stepfather was coming down the hall, mother would say, "Carlos, quick! He's coming." She'd put fear into me. She'd make me feel very nervous when he came home. "Carlos! He's coming!" I'd say, "So what?" Then she'd say, "Go away! He'll be here in a minute." I think she made me feel guilty. I'd feel it was my fault that things did not go smoothly, that it was because of me.

The patient would sometimes feel anger at the stepfather but felt he could not express it.

P: My stepfather would sometimes say to my mother, "You take care of your brother better than you take care of my kids."
T: And how would you feel when he'd say that?
P: I'd say inside of me, "F... you!" But I was young, I couldn't stand up to him and say, "You are full of bullshit. You are lying!"

Homes with stepfathers may cause special problems with the children in the United States. Moore and Holzman's (1965) study of a sample of 13,000 Texas high school students indicates that a home containing a natural parent and a stepparent, particularly a stepfather, appeared to produce more family tension than a home with a single natural parent or a home with both natural parents. This result was especially conspicuous among the better-educated families. The analysis of the present case and other stepparent families among normal and patient Mexican and Anglo-American families suggested the hypothesis that the stepfather may be peculiarly rejecting in the Mexican culture. The rationale supporting this hypothesis is based upon the observation of the special value placed by the Mexican male on his wife's virginity. The thought of her sleeping with another man appears to be particularly repugnant to the Latin male. The Mexican stepfather is accordingly more likely to reject the stepson, the persistent reminder of his wife's previous liaison.

The feelings of our patient about the virginity of one of his former girl friends provides an excellent example of the Mexican attitude. In therapy session IV the patient describes the beginning of the disintegration of a relationship with an Anglo woman with whom he had lived for several years before he migrated to the United States.

P: She started talking about her sexual affairs before she met me. I was hurt. In my culture we cannot accept these things. I loved her, I didn't want to leave her, but I was hurt and had resentment. In my head I said it was okay. The Anglos do these things. It's only a difference in cultures. So, I never told her not to talk to me like that, and I started to go out and began to drink.

The difference between the psychological impact of the Mexican and Anglo-American stepfather is further demonstrated by a study reported by

Rosenquist and Megargee (1969). As part of a larger research project, these investigators compared the relationship to delinquency of single parent families and single parent-stepparent families in three cultural groups: Mexican, Mexican American, and Anglo American. The results indicated that among the single parent Mexican families nine out of 18 were delinquent; among the single parent plus stepparent Mexican families nine out of nine were delinquent. Corresponding figures for the Anglo were eight out of 13 for the single parent families and 13 out of 17 for the single parent plus stepparent families. The difference between the proportion of delinquents in the single parent and single parent plus stepparent families was significant for the Mexican group but failed to reach a requisite level of significance for the Anglo-American and Mexican-American groups.

The absence of a significant difference in the Mexican-American sample perhaps reflects the influence of acculturation factors.

According to the theory proposed in the present chapter, the single parent plus stepparent family exacerbates a constellation that is hypothesized as a core Mexican problem, the passive-aggressive response to a male authority figure.

Maldonado-Sierra and Trent (1960) have also characterized the central problem of the Puerto Rican patient as an inability to express unconscious resentment towards a dominant and authoritarian father. They have developed a method of group therapy in which one of the therapists assumes the benign role of the sibling in the Puerto Rican family.

It is of interest that these Puerto Rican investigators have arrived at a formulation of the problem of their patients similar to that formulated by our team on the basis of work with Mexican-American patients.

SOCIOCULTURAL ORIGINS OF PASSIVE-AGGRESSIVE REACTION TO AUTHORITY FIGURES

In Mexico the fear of asserting oneself against authority is the product of three centuries of oppression by Spanish colonial governments and the continuing exploitation of the majority of the population by the small governing elites of the postcolonial political regimes (Hansen, 1975). Octavio Paz captured the essence of the Mexican reaction to the Spanish authorities when he wrote: "The Indians and Mestizos had to sing in a low voice, as in the poem by Alfonso Reyes, because 'words of rebellion cannot be heard well from between clenched teeth'" (1961, p. 143). In the United States the historically conditioned passive-aggressive behavior towards authority figures was reinforced by the prejudice and/or ignorance of Anglo teachers and other adults, who treated Mexican Americans as inferiors.

SIBLING POSITION AND PSYCHOPATHOLOGY

An important determinant of psychopathology in Mexican culture is sibling position. The relationship has not been noted by other investigators because the usual practice in sibling position studies is to designate position without taking into account sex role. This practice is not appropriate for Mexican culture because of the sharply segregated sex roles in the Mexican family. Thus, the oldest girl in the Mexican family has very specific responsibilities regardless of whether she is first, second, or third born.

In the Arizona state hospital study (Meadow and Stoker, 1965) and the child guidance clinic study (Stoker and Meadow, 1974) when the sibling position of the patient was defined in terms of position relative to the total number of siblings in the family, no difference between the number of oldest children and the expected frequency of oldest children was found for either the Mexican-American or the Anglo-American group. In contrast, when the sibling position was defined in terms of position among same-sex siblings a significantly greater proportion of patients occupied the first sibling position among the Mexican-American females of both studies. A similar analysis for the Anglo-American females of both studies revealed no significant difference.

The greater amount of psychopathology associated with the role of the oldest female child may be ascribed to the excessive responsibility assigned to her in the Mexican-American family. The family is frequently large, and the oldest girl is often overburdened with household work and with the care of numerous children.

In the general Mexican population the oldest girl frequently is placed under greater pressures than her younger siblings. Most oldest girls in the general population do not develop serious mental illness, but they may manifest minor disturbances and resentments. Oscar Lewis describes the role of the older daughter in the Tepoztlan general population as follows:

> When a girl is at home, she is at the complete disposal of her mother. The mother is in a position to exploit the daughter and frequently does, especially the eldest daughter. Many girls marry to escape the hard work at home, and some of our case histories reveal the resentment daughters sometimes hold in retrospect toward their mothers. The following was told by a woman forty years of age.
>
> When I was nine we went to Tacubaya because it was the time of the Revolution....I made tortillas when I wasn't going to school. I went to school for four years and each morning I got up at 5 A.M. and ground corn and made coffee for my mother, brothers and sister. I never ate breakfast before school for lack of time. I also made the tortillas for the family for lunch and supper.

I cut and sewed the clothes, washed and ironed and did all the work of the house when I was fourteen. I also milked the cows. My mother was always a merchant. Since I was such a hard worker, men began to ask for my hand but my mother and brothers didn't want me to marry. I, poor thing, loved my mother and didn't understand how mean she was. She didn't love me because she made me work so hard when she had enough money to hire a maid. I took care of my mother but when I was twenty, I was fed up with it and eloped with my novio (1951, p. 342)

It may be useful at this point to examine the logic of the argument that has been presented. At the beginning of this chapter the hypothesis was proposed that a cultural factor that produces pathology in a patient population will produce a similar but lesser degree of disturbance in the general population. In the present section an initial datum was described that indicated that the role of the oldest daughter in the Mexican-American population was associated with greater psychopathology than the role of younger siblings. A description was then presented from Lewis' Tepoztlan, Mexico community study that indicated two items of data. The first indicates the nature of the oldest daughter role, which turned out to require excessive amounts of work. The second indicates that daughters reacted to these role demands with resentment.

The argument thus links Mexican-American psychopathology with Mexican role expectations and Mexican behavior derived from a community study. There are several gaps in the extant knowledge. There is no data available indicating the relationship of Tepoztlan culture to the general Mexican culture. Neither is there data relating the Mexican to the Mexican-American culture. If no empirical relationships were found, the proposed hypothesis could not accordingly be rejected. However, the fact that some meaningful relationship exists between the Tepoztlan data and the Mexican-American patient data suggests that at least come confidence can be placed in the proposed hypothesis. Cultural and general population data were taken from the Mexican rather than the Mexican-American culture because several excellent studies have been executed by anthropologists on Mexican culture, while there are no comparable studies on Mexican-American culture.

The sibling position data for the adult patients were based on a sample of predominantly schizophrenic patients; data for the child patients were based on a sample of patients with a wide variety of predominantly nonpsychotic diagnoses. The fact that the incidence of pathology was increased in both samples for incumbents of the eldest daughter role suggests that the cultural role stress determinants of schizophrenia may be nonspecific in nature. This conclusion would drive an additional nail in the lid of the coffin of those theories that postulate specific types of etiological stress factors in schizophrenia (Bateson, et al., 1956; Lidz, 1957).

THERAPY FOR MEXICAN AMERICANS

This section will present certain suggestions for the delivery of mental health services to the Mexican-American population based upon a knowledge of their more frequent types of psychopathology.

Mexican and Mexican-American male patients manifest some initial resistances towards coming to therapy, which have not been sufficiently explored. An understanding of these attitudes provides data that facilitate the formation of procedures for effective modification. The initial resistance towards coming to therapy is based in part on the cultural assumption that males should not share personal secrets. A brief excerpt from the protocols of the 23-year old Mexican-American patient will serve to introduce the problem.

P: How then do I get better, Doctor?
T: The idea is to say whatever comes to your mind. By talking freely, you will gradually become aware of your real thoughts and feelings and thus be better able to handle them by reason.
P: But I've read that some people have secret things that they don't share with anybody.
T: They are the patients who don't get well.

The form in which that patient betrays his reluctance to reveal his secrets is characteristically Mexican. The patient does not directly challenge the therapist's instruction. Instead he uses a form of indirection; he says that he has *read* that people don't share some secrets with anybody. In this phrasing the patient does not fully oppose the therapist's suggestion. It is not he, the patient, who is proposing concealment, it is people. It is not even the patient's idea, but one that has appeared in a book. Nevertheless, despite his indirection, it is perfectly clear that the patient is reluctant to discuss his secrets.

Octavio Paz has described with considerable insight the penchant for secrecy in Mexican culture:

> Every time a Mexican confides in a friend or acquaintance, every time he opens himself up, it is an abdication. He dreads that the person in whom he has confided will scorn him. Therefore, confidences result in dishonor, and they are as dangerous for the person to whom they are made as they are for the person who makes them (1961, p. 30).

One possible source of Mexican reticence is the shame pattern, which Mexico shares with other countries of the Latin world (Peristiany, 1966). For the Latin, it is not so much the evil deed that one does that is of decisive importance, but the other person's knowledge of it. Calderon, Spain's greatest playwright, once wrote a play in which the protagonist takes elaborate pains to disguise the vengeance that he is undertaking for an insult. The play expresses in dramatic form the theme that insult does not bring shame to a person unless it is known by others.

A second possible determinant of Mexican secrecy is the role attitude that only women reveal personal secrets. Two clinical examples may serve to demonstrate the way in which this phenomenon influences a patient's attitude towards therapy. The first dialogue is quoted from the therapy protocols of a 44-year old Mexican-American male schizophrenic patient:

T: The reason you hear that voice is that you have a mental illness.
P: Mental illness! I didn't know, doctor, that men can have mental illnesses.

The following excerpt from a therapy session with the 23-year old Mexican-American patient demonstrates a less absurd but, nevertheless, similar conception of the incompatibility of the idea of being a male with that of having a mental problem.

T: How are you this morning?
P: Asi, asi (so-so). I'm still worried. Worried about my heart. I feel like fainting. When that happens it makes me scared. I don't know why. I just don't know what is going on. I want to break the circulo (the circle) of being afraid—of being nervous. Every day I'm afraid I have this feeling of losing balance. I made an appointment with the eye doctor to see if I need glasses. (long pause)
T: What are you thinking?
P: I feel embarrasssed. I feel ashamed.
T: Why is that?
P: I'm always complaining. I'm embarrassed[2] even though you are a doctor. I should be more macho. I should try to work out my own things. I don't complain, however, to people outside the clinic. They are not doctors. But even with you I feel ashamed.
T: You feel you are not macho?
P: A macho person doesn't get sick. A macho person is always strong. He feels good all the time.

But I am scared. I have pains.

I'm kind of embarrassed as my feelings don't fall into the true natural feelings of logic.

The exquisite sensitivity of Octavio Paz could also not fail to register the underlying connection between Mexican secrecy and an overexaggerated fear of femininity:

The speech of our people reflects the extent to which we protect ourselves from the outside world. The ideal of manliness is never to "crack," never back down. Those who "open themselves up are cowards." Unlike other peoples, we believe that opening oneself up is a weakness or a betrayal.... The man who backs down is not to be trusted, is a traitor of doubtful loyalty; he babbles secrets and is incapable of confronting a dangerous situation. Women are inferior beings because in submitting they open themselves up. Their inferiority is constitutional and resides in their sex, their submissiveness, which is a wound which never heals (1961, p. 30).

Whatever its origins, the Mexican emphasis upon secrecy is often a potent weapon against therapeutic intervention. It is not only a factor that increases resistance within the initial therapeutic hours, but it is often a principle determinant of a decision not to come for therapy at all.

Karno and Edgerton (1969) have reported that the percentage of Mexican Americans receiving treatment in California is much less than their proportion in the general population. Padilla and Ruiz (1976) ascribe this phenomenon to four types of factors: (1) geographic isolation, (2) language barriers, (3) middle-class attitudes of therapists, and (4) culture-bound attitudes of Anglo therapists. One suspects that the Mexican male's phrasing of secrecy as an index of masculinity is also an important determinant of the Mexican-American patient underrepresentation problem.

The Mexican-American male's resistance towards therapy often influences his wife's therapy attendance. Some Mexican-American unacculturated males disapprove of their wives going anywhere alone outside the home. There is an implicit assumption that even if a woman visits another woman she may be arranging to meet with another man. The attitude is aptly expressed by the old Spanish proverb, "A woman should remain at home—preferably with a broken leg."

A female Mexican-American patient reported to the therapist the following remark of her husband: "Why do you go to see Dr. Meadow with your problems? I'm your husband! If you have problems come to me."

In addition to the male perception that going to therapy means that one is "female" there is the assumption by both males and females that therapy attendance signifies that one is crazy (loco).

MODES OF COPING WITH INITIAL RESISTANCE TO COMING TO THERAPY

Certain procedures are available that in our experience have been helpful in reducing resistance to coming for therapy. A helpful emphasis appears to be that of describing the problem as a medical one. Although reluctance towards seeking medical treatment exists among Mexican-American unacculturated groups, it is not nearly so strong as that towards psychological treatment. Mexican-American patients will accept the necessity of consulting a doctor if they feel they are sufficiently ill. The phrasing of the patient quoted earlier is relevant. Observe that the patient is embarrassed to state his complaints "even to a doctor." The implication is that, although a doctor does not remove the shame of complaining completely, the medical context provides at least a mitigating circumstance.

If the therapist is a Ph.D. no great problem is usually introduced. The word doctor appears to have the effect of reducing the shameful implications of consulting a therapist with a mental problem. For similar reasons it is often more useful to incorporate psychological services for Mexican-American patients in a general medical clinic.

The approach that is advocated is neither a "medical model" nor a "psychological model." It can most appropriately be labeled a model that "begins where the patient is at." The Mexican-American patient often does not have a separate concept in his mind for psychological illness. If he initially views his symptoms in somatic terms it makes sense not to attempt to initially challenge his defenses. Padilla and Ruiz have similarly commented on the Spanish-speaking subjects' (SSSS) perception of his problem as follows:

> However, the Spanish equivalent of mental health, salud mental, does not exist as a separate concept for the SSSS, for the SSSS there is no separation between the psychological and total well-being of the individual. Thus the SSSS is more likely to express his condition of well-being in terms of "estar saludable," "ser feliz," "sentirse o estar como un cañon," or "estar sano o fuerte" all of which imply a physical as well as a psychological component. The difference in what constitutes well-being is important because it may explain in part the underutilization of mental health care by the SSSS. Specifically, the SSSS person "que no se siente sano" (who doesn't feel well) is more likely to consult a physician or folk healer for a physical basis for his condition (1976, p. 14).

Similar approaches have proved to be effective with Mexican-American female patients. In these cases, the fear of not being macho is, of course, not present, but the onus of being crazy remains. Going to a doctor means one is ill, and this condition can be readily accepted by most Mexican-American women. The medical emphasis, however, may be more important with the male patient. Fabrega, Ruebel, and Wallace (1967) in their study of working class Mexican outpatients report that Mexican-American men tend to use medicosomatic descriptions, whereas women allow affective and psychosocial considerations to intervene.

An additional procedure has proven helpful with female patients. In the case of married women it is most important to obtain the initial approval and at least partial participation of the husband. In most cases I will invite the husband to visit me at the office and conduct a joint session with wife and husband. I will then ask the husband if he will give his permission for the wife to come to therapy. Direct contact with the husband often reduces exaggerated fears. In addition, requesting his permission acknowledges what he perceives as the rights of the male in this situation. In some of the more acculturated cases the therapist will attempt to enlist continued participation of the husband in the therapy process. This goal is often difficult to achieve, and one must often be content with at least reducing active resistance towards the wife's entering therapy.

Active case finding pursued by indigenous mental health workers is a sine qua non of an efficient mental health service for Mexican-American groups. These workers introduce the patient to the physician and help to establish personal rapport between them. The Mexican, even in his native land, finds an impersonal relationship between patient and physician requgnant. In 1976 this author visited a group of small neighborhood government health clinics in the impoverished migrant neighborhoods of Monterrey, Mexico. Each clinic was manned by a small medical team headed by a young physician-resident. The clinics were designed to replace a large hospital the government had previously constructed to provide medical services to the people. The hospital had been a complete failure. The migrants and their families could not be persuaded to visit a large impersonal institution. The provisions of the newly formed small clinic project stipulated that the members of the medical team were required to live in the community they served. Many established close personal contact with their patients. The government supplied materials for constructing the clinics, but they were built by members of the community. The latter also subsequently furnished maintenance services to the clinic buildings. The supervising physician of the federal government, who was the head of the new clinic program in Monterrey, stated that the new small clinics had attracted many more patients than the large hospital it had replaced.

The Anglo-American therapist working with Mexican-American patients must guard against his or her own cultural counter-transference feelings. A frequent type of case is the Mexican-American woman who comes to the clinic complaining that her husband has recently begun to drink heavily; she further adds that he comes home, drunk, at 3 o'clock in the morning with lipstick smeared all over his collar; he then wakes her up, beats her, and accuses her of infidelity. She has asked him to come to the clinic, but he refuses. This is the kind of story that is likely to arouse the righteous indignation of an Anglo-American male therapist, who is not without his own brand of macho in certain areas. The female Anglo-American therapist, who may be a leader of a rape prevention clinic or a woman's consciousness group, may be similarly incensed, The Anglo-American therapist may accordingly, consciously or unconscioulsy, encourage the patient to leave her husband. This denouement may represent the best possible outcome for a case, but, then again, it may not. The important point is that the clinician in this situation should make an all-out attempt to contact the husband. The wife can often persuade the husband to agree to a home visit from the therapist.

As the therapist develops his or her knowledge of a case of this kind, he or she may find that the exacerbation of the husband's drinking and violent behavior was instigated by a loss of job. Losing one's job can be a threat for anybody in our culture. It may become a special trauma for a Mexican-American male. The Mexican-American husband may not have the Calvinist attitude that work in and of itself is an unmitigated good. He does feel, however—and the Anglo-American culture is frequently unaware of this attitude—that an adequate male has a strong duty to support his family. Being a "trabajador," (a worker) is a phrase of great praise in this culture. Losing a job may accordingly represent an even greater threat to the Mexican American's feeling of being a man than it would be for an Anglo American. The family situation may have been further disturbed by an upset of the traditional male dominance/female submission pattern, a reversal that might occur if the wife obtained a job or even welfare. In this situation, aside from family therapy, the most helpful step may be that of referring the husband to an agency equipped to help him get a job.

The therapist should consider using family therapy more often than he or she does with an Anglo-American group. The reason is that the Mexican American is more often directly involved with his family. Siblings, for example, often take greater responsibility for another sibling than in the Anglo-American family. When one comes to a waiting room to greet a Mexican-American patient, a frequent experience is that of finding two, three, or even four family members accompanying the patient.

RELATIONSHIP OF ANGLO THERAPISTS TO THE MEXICAN COMMUNITY

If the therapist treating the Mexican-American patient is Anglo American, special problems may arise as a result of the complex interrelationship of the Mexican-American and Anglo-American communities. The Anglo therapist must keep in mind that he is not only treating an individual patient but a patient interacting with his community. If the therapist ignores this principle, a serious misinterpretation of the patient's problems may occur.

An example from a recent Mexican-American patient I treated comes to mind. The patient was a seriously disturbed schizophrenic who was making very little progress in treatment. He was living at home in a small Mexican-American suburb of Sacramento and was engaging in all kinds of disruptive practices in the community. His most recent caper was a call to the police department to come immediately to his home because voices were talking to him from behind the refrigerator.

I discussed with the patient and mother the possibility of the patient moving to a board-and-care home. The patient violently opposed moving away from his mother. The mother indicated her willingness to continue to care for the patient. The Mexican-American community worker, however, strongly advised me to attempt to seek a guardianship for the patient and force a commitment to a board-and-care home. I resisted the suggestion because I felt it was in the best interests of the patient to remain at home.

Later, I discussed the matter with the Mexican-American community worker. After some initial hesitation, she told me that her recommendation was prompted by the fact that many of the Mexican-American citizens in the community were murmuring that since the patient was not improving we were not providing him adequate care. The problem was solved by arranging for a meeting with members of the Mexican-American community at an elementary school. At the meeting, the topic of treatment of the chronic schizophrenic patient was discussed.

A THERAPEUTIC METHOD OF REACTING TO A PATIENT'S CONFLICT ABOUT AUTHORITY

Therapists can enhance the effectiveness of treatment by knowledge of typical Mexican-American reactions to authority figures and the ways in which they are expressed in the therapy situation. In psychoanalytically oriented therapies this knowledge may ultimately be used for interpretation. In other therapies the knowledge may be used as background information, which serves as a basis for supportive or other treatment aims.

The following therapy excerpt from the protocols of the 23-year old Mexican-American patient illustrates the type of patient reaction one might expect and one possible therapeutic response.

P: I was hoping that you would be giving me more information than you have.
T: What kind of information?
P: That you'd tell me what I had. What was my diagnosis. That you'd tell me what to do to get over this fear and the feeling that I can't catch my breath and was going to die.

Maybe you can give me some light. You're a professional. I don't have the background. I don't have the tools with which to excavate.

(Long pause)

(Hesitatingly) Sometimes I get the feelings I've been here five times—still you haven't said much. You take notes and I wonder what you do with them—whether you even look at them—whether you may even throw them away. Sometimes therapists just do this for money. (Long pause)
T: What are you feeling now?

P: Sometimes I feel very guilty. Many of my beliefs are in conflict with the Bible, and the Bible says you will be punished.

Most people are religious. They accept...I question. I question God and then I fear God will punish me for questioning him. (Long pause)

T: Go ahead—just tell me what you are thinking.

P: I was just wondering how you work. You see I don't know how therapy works, you didn't tell me.

T: Perhaps you just felt a little guilty about asking me that? Don't you have a right to question me? Do you feel I will punish you or disapprove of you because you ask questions like that?

P: Well, I didn't really know you, maybe you will. Many people act that way.

T: You feel you are helpless and passive in coping with my reaction?

P: No. I feel....

The patient begins the discussion by questioning the techniques of the therapist, culminating with the accusation that the therapist may be working with the patient for his own financial gain. This thinly veiled attack on the therapist is followed by a long pause. When the patient resumes talking he completely changes the topic to that of religion. In the ensuing discussion of beliefs the patient states that he questions God and fears divine retribution. Finally, in the last sentence the patient returns again to his questioning of the therapist.

The long pauses and sudden shifts of topic suggest that the patient experiences guilt about questioning the therapist and fears retribution from him. The patient is not quite conscious of his conflict between wanting to question the therapist and his fear of retribution. Distantiation of the conflict into the religious area protects him from the anxiety he would otherwise experience if he were directly aware of his motives.

The therapeutic response to the patient's guilt about questioning God does not require a challenge of the patient's religious beliefs. One must be very cautious in the interpretation of defenses, especially in the early phases of therapy. In the instance of this case it suffices that the therapist understands that fear about questioning God also means fear about questioning the therapist. The remark, "Perhaps you feel a little guilty about asking me that?" is designed to give permission to the patient to express his feelings towards the therapist.

The use of religion as a symbolic expression of conflict between aggression towards authority figures and guilt about this aggression is a frequently observed mechanism in therapeutic work with Mexican or Mexican-American patients. One reason is that Mexican parents often invoke God or his worldly representative, the priest, as a threat in their interactions with children. An adolescent's rebellion against his parents in the religious sphere is often fostered by the lay teachers of government schools who inculcate him with atheistic ideology. The scepticism of the present patient towards his parents' religious beliefs was perhaps greater than that for the majority of Mexican-Americans because his mother and grandmother were Catholic and his stepfather was Protestant.

In the following excerpt, the patient provides data describing his experiences with mother, father, and grandmother that illuminate at least part of the origins of his present obsessive religious concerns and attitude towards the therapist.

P: Probably I will be punished as I question God's existence.

T: You seem very guilty.

P: My father told me there is a God and he'll punish you if you're bad. Then my high school teachers told me there is no God.... "You get what you work for," they said, "Don't pray for bread! Make it." It would be easier if I wouldn't question so much. I should just work and live. But something inside of me is always questioning, questioning, questioning....

The Bible says at one point, "The sun stops." That's impossible.

T: And what would your father say in response to your arguments?

P: He'd say, "You're crazy. God will punish you. You are arrogant (arrogante) and vain (vanidoso)."

T: What was your grandmother's reaction to religion?

P: When I was 13 or 14 years old I was very rebellious. Once my grandmother took me to the priest and said, "Kiss his hand." I said, "No, it may be dirty." Grandmother then said, "Cabron (goat)." Then I went to my father and he said, "You don't have to kiss the hands of the priest." I carried at that time a little metal image of the Virgin of Guadalupe. My father said, "Give it to me." He threw the image on the floor and stepped on it. He looked upward to the sky and said, "Now punish me." And nothing happened.

T: What would you say then?

P: I'd say I didn't believe in either one....

Then I came home and Grandma asked me where was my image of the Virgin. I said my father destroyed it. Grandma then seized the Bible my father gave me and threw it on the fire.

She then came at me with a broom saying she was going to beat the Devil out of me and I broke the broom.

Mother then came in and said, "Don't talk that way to your Grandma." And I said. "Pinche madre!" (F... you mother)

Mother would ask God to punish me as I wouldn't let her hit me. I then left the house for a few days. After 14, I wouldn't let anybody hit me.

At 17, I began to smoke marihuana.

The fact that the grandmother supported Catholic and the stepfather supported Protestant beliefs probably decreased the patient's faith in either religion. Nevertheless, both authority figures described God as an all-powerful figure who would ultimately punish the patient for his sins.

The patient was raised in a family environment in which he could not question his stepfather. Repression of his questioning tendencies towards the stepfather is generalized to repression of questioning tendencies towards the therapist. The resultant conflict is projected and expressed in the form of obsessive religious ruminations.

CONCLUSION

In conclusion, the therapist should take into account the special strengths of the Mexican-American group. For example, the Mexican male is not plagued by the bond of puritan prudery that is still found in some Anglo-American male patients. For the most part, he accepts his sexual instincts as natural. He is seldom haunted by the sense of horror about sex that exists in males in Spain. The Mexican-American male may sometimes be worried about his potency; he does not have the attitude that male sexual drives per se are evil.

In addition, once the initial resistances towards therapy have been overcome he is able to form a warm relationship with the therapist. The Mexican-American does not have the tight-lipped Hemingway attitude towards words encountered in some Anglo-American patients. He is often amazingly eloquent, a gift demonstrated by the 23-year old patient quoted in the present chapter. He is thus often a good candidate for verbal psycho-therapies. In his celebration of fiestas, in his aesthetic sensitivity manifested in his architecture, painting, crafts, and literature, the Mexican brings to the world—and gradually begins to express in therapy—a joy in living that may well be emulated by people of other cultures.

To summarize, the present chapter has attempted to demonstrate that forms of psychopathological behavior that frequently appear in male patients of Mexican-American origin represent intensified forms of psychopathology present in milder forms in the Mexican population. Some of the family and other cultural sources of Mexican psychopathology have been described. On the basis of this assessment certain suggestions were made for the more effective delivery of mental health services to this group.

NOTES

1. The name of the patient has been changed to preserve anonymity.
2. The patient uses the phrase "me siento avergonzado," which may be translated "I feel embarrassed" or "I feel ashamed."

REFERENCES

Bateson, G., Jackson, D.D., Haley, J., and Weakland, J. Towards a theory of schizophrenia. *Behavioral Science* 1 (1956):251-64.

Collier, J.F. *Law and Social Change in Zincantea.* Stanford, Calif.: Stanford University Press, 1973.

Cosio-Villegas, D. *Historia Moderna de Mexico.* El Porfiriato Vida Social Tercera Edicion Editorial Hermes, Mexico, 1973.

Diaz-Guerrero, R. *Psychology of the Mexican.* Austin: University of Texas, 1975.

Edgerton, R.B. and Karno, M. Mexican-American bilinguilism and the perception of mental illness. *Archives of General Psychiatry* 24 (1971):286-90.

Fabrega, H., Jr., Ruebel, A.J., and Wallace, C.A. Working class Mexican psychiatric outpatients. *Archives of General Psychiatry* 16 (1967):704-12.

Fromm, E., and Maccoby, M. *Sociopsicoanalisis del campesino Mexicano: Estudio de la economia y la psicologia de una comunidad rural.* Av. de la Universidad 975, Mexico 12, D.F., Fondo de Cultura Economica, 1973.

Gonzales Pineda, F. *El Mexicano: Su dinamica Psicosocial* (segunda edicion revisada). Rep. Argentina, 9; Mexico 1, D.F., Editorial Pax-Mexico, Libreria Carlos Cesarman, S.A., 1961.

Gruening, E. *Mexico and Its Heritage.* New York: Appleton-Century-Crofts, 1928.

Hansen, R.D. *La politica del desarrollo Mexicano.* Cerro del Agua 248, Mexico 20, D.F., Siglo Veintiuno Editores, S.A., 1975.

Jaco, E.G. Mental health of the Spanish American in Texas. *Culture and Mental Health: Cross-Cultural Studies,* edited by M.K. Opler, pp. 467-85. New York: MacMillan, 1959.

Karno, M. and Edgerton, R.B. Perception of mental illness in a Mexican American community. *Archives of General Psychiatry* 20 (1969):233-38.

Lewis, O. *Life in a Mexican Village: Tepoztlan Restudied.* Urbana: University of Illinois Press, 1951.

Lidz, T. The intrafamilial environment of schizophrenic patients: II. Marital schism and marital skew. *American Journal of Psychiatry* 114 (1957):241-48.

MacAndrew, C. and Edgerton, R.B. *Drunken Comportment. A Social Explanation.* Chicago: Aldine, 1969.

Madsen, W. Value conflicts and folk psychiatry in south Texas. In *Magic Faith and Healing,* edited by A. Kiev, pp. 420-40. New York: The Free Press, 1969.

Malonado-Sierra, E.D. and Trent, R.D. The sibling relationship in group psychotherapy with Puerto Rican schizophrenics. *American Journal of Psychiatry* 117 (1960):239-44.

Meadow, A. and Stoker, D. Symptomatic behavior of hospitalized patients. *Archives of General Psychiatry* 12 (1965):267-77.

Minturn, L. and Lambert, W.W. *Mothers of Six Cultures: Antecedents of Child Rearing.* New York: John Wiley & Sons, 1964.

Moore, B.M. and Holzman, W.H. *Tomorrow's Parents: A Study of Youth and Their Families.* Austin: University of Texas Press, 1965.

Padilla, A.M. and Aranda, P. *Latino Mental Health: Bibliography and Abstracts.* NIMH, U.S. Department of Health, Education and Welfare Publication No.

(ADM) 76-317. Washington, D.C.: U.S. Government Printing Office. Reprint, 1976.

Padilla, A.M. and Ruiz, R.A. *Latino Mental Health: A Review of Literature.* NIMH, U.S. Department of Health, Education, and Welfare Publication No. (ADM) 76-113. Washington, D.C.: U.S. Government Printing Office. Reprint, 1976.

Paz, O. *The Labyrinth of Solitude: Life and Thought in Mexico,* translated by L. Kemp. New York: Grove Press, 1961.

Peristiany, J.G. *Humor and Shame: The Values of Mediterranean Society.* Chicago: University of Chicago Press, 1966.

Ramirez, S. *El Mexicano: Psicologia de sus motivaciones* (tercera edicion). Rep. Argentina 9, Mexico I, D.F., Editorial Pax-Mexico, Libreria Carlos Cesarman, S.A., 1961.

Romanucci-Ross, L. *Conflict, Violence, and Morality in a Mexican Village.* Palo Alto, Calif.: National Press Books, 1973.

Rosenquist, C.M. and Megargee, E.I. *Delinquency in Three Cultures.* Austin: University of Texas Press, 1969.

Rulfo, J. *Pedro Paramo.* Letras Mexicanas, 1959.

Stoker, D. and Meadow, A. Cultural differences in child guidance clinic patients. *International Journal of Social Psychiatry* (Winter 1974):187-201.

Swickard, D.L. and Spilka, B. Hostility expression of minority and majority groups. *Journal of Consulting Psychology* 25 (1961):216-20.

Torrey, E.F. The case for the indigenous therapist. *Archives of General Psychiatry* 20 (1969):365-73.

Verkko, V. *Homicides and Suicides in Finland and their Dependence on National Character.* Kobenhavn, G.E.O. GAD, 1951.

Wolfgang, M. *Patterns in Criminal Homicide.* Philadelphia: University of Pennsylvania Press, 1958.

14   The Spanish-Speaking Consumer and the Community Mental Health Center*

Ricardo F. Muñoz

The Community Mental Health Centers Act (Public Law 88-164) was a call:

> to bestow the full benefits of our society on those who suffer from mental disabilities;
> to prevent the occurrence of mental illness and mental retardation wherever and whenever possible;
> to provide for early diagnosis and continuous and comprehensive care, in the community, of those suffering from these disorders;...and to reinforce the will and capacity of our communities to meet these problems, in order that the communities, in turn, can reinforce the will and capacity of individuals and individual families (Kennedy, 1963)

The regulations for Title II of Public Law 88-164 specified that all services of community mental health centers would be made available without discrimination because of race, creed, or color. In addition, these facilities were charged with providing "below cost or without charge a reasonable volume of services to persons unable to pay therefore" (U.S. Department of Health, Education, and Welfare, 1964).

The intended availability of these services makes them especially significant resources to groups that are largely unable to afford mental health care in

*The author received constructive comments on an earlier version of this manuscript from Manuel Barrera, Jr., Guillermo Bernal, Teresa Ramirez-Boulette, Fernando Cordero, Renaldo Maduro, Ed Morales, A. Michael Rossi, Lonnie Snowden, and the editors. They raised many important issues, some of which I have probably not addressed to their satisfaction. Nevertheless, the many changes stemming from their suggestions improved the chapter considerably and I want to express my appreciation to them.

the private sector. One such group is the Spanish-speaking population of the United States.

Estimates of the size of this group vary from 11 to 16.5 million (Meyer, 1977). Many important factors differentiate this large population, as is evident by the large number of terms that have been used to describe its members: Mexican Americans, Mexicans, Chicanos, Latinos, *La Raza,* Puerto Ricans, Cubans, Central and South Americans, Hispanic Americans, Hispanos, Spanish Speaking/Spanish Surnamed, and so on. Many of these labels are tied to country of origin, which is an important source of identification for Spanish-speaking persons. Linguistic differences among different countries serve as quick clues for recognizing compatriots. Another major source of differences is level of socioeconomic status. In fact, members of high social classes from different countries may have more in common with each other culturally and linguistically than with members of other social classes from their own countries. In addition, the amount of *mestizaje,* i.e., the mixture of European (mainly Spanish) and indigenous American (Indian) races, varies substantially, creating Latinos who are descendants of light-skinned Europeans and Latinos who are primarily descendants of the native peoples of the Americas. The infusion of African and Asian populations into Latin America has added even more variety to *La Raza,* the term used to describe the new ethnic group that resulted from the *mestizaje.*

A few words about the nuances of each of the major terms in use to describe *La Raza* may be helpful here. The most straightforward terms are those that refer to the individual's country of origin. For example, many people identify themselves principally as Argentinian, Cuban, Dominican, Mexican, Panamanian, Peruvian, Puerto Rican, and so on. The hyphenated terms, such as Cuban-American and Mexican-American, reflect a "melting pot" consciousness, in that they emphasize the view that "we are all Americans" while modifying this with one's national background to acknowledge the concept of diversity. Descriptive compound terms, such as Central American, South American, or the all-inclusive Latin American, are terms that are in common use throughout the Spanish-speaking countries. (It should be mentioned here that in Latin America the terms "America" and "American" refer to the entire continent and not just to the United States of America and its inhabitants. Thus, there is some resentment toward the appropriation of those terms to refer exclusively to the United States of America.) There are a number of other terms that have specific, and sometimes controversial, meanings.

Chicano (and its feminine form, *Chicana*) refers to people of Mexican ancestry who live in what is now the United States, most of whom were born here, and whose families may have been in the United States for many generations, perhaps as far back as when the Southwest was Mexican territory. The term was formerly an insulting term, and thus many older individuals do not like it. It has also taken on a connotation of raised consciousness regarding the political and institutional disenfranchisement of this group (which is the largest of the groups that comprise *La Raza* in the United States), and a commitment to obtain their full share of rights as citizens.

Nuyorican is a term that refers to persons of Puerto Rican background who were born and/or raised in New York. Both Chicanos and Nuyoricans face the dilemma of not being fully accepted in Mexico (or Puerto Rico) or in the United States.

Hispanic, a word that is being used by the federal government and has thus gained much prominence of late, refers to the Spanish roots of Latin American cultures. However, there is a significant amount of negative feeling throughout Latin America about being considered "Spanish." Spain conquered and looted much of Latin America, Spaniards represent the white European colonists, and their racist practices, which gave those with whiter skin more power and privileges, were and still are found in many Latin American countries. The Indian roots of most *mestizos* are not acknowledged at all by this term. Thus, many members of *La Raza* do not consider "Hispanic" an acceptable descriptor for themselves. The term "Spanish" is, of course, even less acceptable and should really only be used to refer to people from Spain itself. (There *is* a sizable number of "Hispanos" in the Southwest, especially New Mexico, who are descendants of the original Spanish settlers and have lived there through the territorial transitions from Spain to Mexico and to the United States.)

Spanish Speaking/Spanish Surnamed is a term that attempted to encompass all the above groups by acknowledging that many of their members did not speak Spanish but belonged to the group culturally, as easily shown by their last name. The term is too complex to have gained much acceptance outside academic circles.

La Raza refers to the union of the European (principally Spanish) and Indian (indigenous American) peoples. Many Latin American countries celebrate October twelfth, the day the Spaniards discovered America, as *El Dia de La Raza,* to commemorate this momentous occasion in human history in which a new people began to form. *La Raza* (literally "the race") refers to this new ethnic group, also known as *mestizos* (part Indian, part white). This term has great symbolic importance and has been used by many community leaders as a unifying term that includes people with ancestry from all the Latin American countries. Because of its political implications, it has been used mainly by individuals active in trying to change social and institutional conditions of *La Raza.*

Latino (and its feminine form, *Latina*) refers to people of Latin American origin. Technically, it can encompass all of the above groups, since it includes people who live or have lived in or whose ancestors come from any of the Latin American countries, whether or not they are *mestizo,* Spanish surnamed, or, at this point in time, Spanish speaking. It thus reflects biculturality without specifying racial or linguistic characteristics. Unfortunately, this term developed a negative flavor because it was used by some Latinos to set themselves apart from some other Latino groups. For example, in some parts of the Southwest anti-Mexican prejudice is so intense that non-Mexican Latinos used to emphasize their Latin American background to avoid being discriminated against. Whether this ploy had its intended effect or not, it did produce resentment between the two groups. At this time, for example, many Chicanos prefer not to be identified as Latinos.

As can be inferred from the material above, there is no term that is acceptable to all members of these groups. This has made it hard to bring about a united movement that advocates for all of them. In this chapter, I have chosen to use the term Latino as defined above. I am thus referring to individuals with origins (ancestral or personal) in Latin American countries. As the title indicates, I am focusing primarily on those Latinos who are Spanish speaking, since I believe they are generally less acculturated.

(I have chosen not to address the Spanish-speaking groups from outside the Western Hemisphere primarily because I am not as familiar with their historical and socioeconomic realities. I am sure, however, that many of the services provided for Latinos could be also utilized by other Spanish-speaking groups.)

Members of the widely diverse Latino group who reside in the United States are supposed to be served by community mental health centers. Obviously, the challenge inherent in this charge is one of great magnitude. To paraphrase Kluckholm and Murray (1953), all Latinos are in certain respects (1) like all other Latinos, (2) like some other Latinos, and (3) like no other Latino. And, as a group, they differ from the mainstream culture of the United States along a number of dimensions. It is not surprising that the community mental health centers, an invention of the U.S. culture, have found it hard to respond to this group's needs (Barrera, 1978).

This chapter will list the services that community mental health centers are required to provide and suggest specific issues that must be considered in serving the Spanish speaking. Many of the suggestions made here may be considered applicable to other groups in the United States, since it is expected that there will be common elements with other cultural groups.

The regulations for Title II of Public Law 88-164 (U.S. Department of Health, Education and Welfare, 1964) list five "essential" elements of comprehensive mental health services: (1) inpatient services, (2) outpatient services, (3) partial hospitalization services (at least daycare), (4) 24-hour emergency services within at least one of the first three services, and (5) consultation and education services available to community agencies and professional personnel. Five additional services necessary for "adequate" mental health care are also listed: (6) diagnostic services, (7) rehabilitative services, including vocational and educational programs, (8) precare and after-care services in the community, including foster home placement, home visiting, and halfway houses, (9) training, and (10) research and evaluation.

Before these services can be utilized, of course, consumers must find their way to them. So we will begin our exposition with a look at referral patterns.

MAKING CONTACT WITH THE MENTAL HEALTH SYSTEM

There are three stages involved in becoming a user of mental health centers:

1. Identifying the mental health system as an appropriate source of help for the problem the individual is facing.
2. Contacting the mental health center in person or by phone.
3. Coming to the first appointment (the "intake"), after which the consumer decides whether or not to continue.

The first stage is influenced by the person's experience with mental health concepts, whether through reading knowledge or experience (personal or vicarious) with the benefits that can be expected from psychological interventions. In addition, family, friends, and representatives of other systems (e.g., the medical, educational, or legal system) may serve as referral sources, suggesting or demanding that the person get in touch with a mental health professional. In either case, the probability that an individual will consider using the services of a mental health center at all is related to the amount of visibility the center and its staff project. In the case of Latinos, experience with psychological help is generally significantly less than for middle-class whites, partly because mental health systems are not as developed in their countries of origin. It is thus particularly important that the kinds of problems that are amenable to mental health intervention be clearly defined for the Spanish-speaking consumer. But this is not enough. It is also important that the availability of Spanish-speaking staff be made known explicitly. This can be done through written descriptions of services offered but even more effectively through personal appearances at community meetings, media presentations dealing with Latino topics, and concerted efforts to make personal contact with the more important referral sources in one's community (e.g., teachers, doctors, priests, and other parts of the mental health system).

It has been my experience that when one makes it known that one is Spanish speaking and that one is motivated to work with Latinos, the frequency of referrals increases rapidly. Sometimes the response is overwhelming, even in a setting where formerly Latinos came only rarely. Reasons for underutilization may, thus, be more a factor of availability and visibility of Spanish-speaking staff than of lack of need by the Spanish-speaking community.

The second stage, the process of initial contact with a social service agency, is sometimes the biggest obstacle for the consumer. This is particularly true regarding mental health contacts, which are oftentimes preceded by grueling decision making about one's need for "help." The need for sensitive, bilingual, preferably bicultural, receptionists is obvious but not always heeded. Imagine, for example, an outpatient unit that receives 85 percent of its first contacts over the phone but does not have even one bilingual person answering the phones. Despite a sizable Spanish-speaking population in its catchment area, Latinos rarely call. The low utilization rate is then used to justify the lack of Spanish-speaking staff.

When the client comes to a center personally, the relief at being welcomed in one's own tongue is sometimes quite visible: an immediate relaxation of the facial muscles, especially the forehead, and a broad smile. (I have seen similar reactions in English-speaking tourists when they meet someone who *really* speaks English abroad.) A quick but complete explanation of what they can expect can diminish anxiety dramatically. Spanish-language magazines in the reception area can add to the message that it is OK for Latinos to be there, that they are not intruders, and that their language and culture are acknowledged and respected.

When these basic elements are not provided, we can expect that there will not be an influx of Spanish-speaking clients. The structural obstacles are there, whether or not they are intended. Only the more acculturated and bilingual Latinos will use the center, and this fact can be erroneously interpreted to mean that most Latinos can speak English, so that there is no urgency to hire bilingual staff. Though no solid statistics are available regarding the percentage of Latinos whose primary language is Spanish, a recent national Gallup Poll of Hispanic Catholics found that 56 percent of persons interviewed preferred to be interviewed in Spanish (Our Sunday Visitor, 1979).

A Latino mental health worker in an agency that has the above-mentioned obstacles can help to temporarily alleviate them by giving his or her name and work number as the referral phone when making community contacts and by explicitly offering the receptionists help in handling calls in Spanish. It is imperative, however, that this arrangement be made in a formal way and that its temporary nature be agreed upon with the administration. Otherwise, the arrangement will be seen as sufficient and no Spanish-speaking receptionists will be hired. An accurate record of the nature and number of calls in Spanish ought to be presented to the administration periodically. The Latino mental health worker can also offer assistance to those engaged in hiring in screening job applicants for Spanish fluency and for familiarity with basic polite interpersonal interchanges that are part of Latino culture. Though some systems may respond to this offer in a defensive or outright negative way, most will be cooperative. Most de facto discrimination is considered by mental health professionals to be unintentional on their part. This may be in certain ways more harmful than clear racism, because it makes it harder for the consumer to attribute his or her discomfort to the agency's shortcomings. Instead, the consumer may feel that it is his or her "ignorance and stupidity" that is to blame. The mental health contact, instead of being therapeutic, becomes one more noxious stimulus in the client's life.

The third stage, the first interview, is perhaps the most crucial test that the mental health center must pass if it is to be considered helpful by the Latino client. Miranda, et al. (1976) report that 60 percent of Mexican Americans drop out following the initial interview, compared to 35 percent for non-Mexican Americans. I believe that, in some cases, the major reason for this high dropout rate is not being understood, in the linguistic sense. I have been approached by patients who complain that their "Spanish-speaking" therapist doesn't quite understand what they say because the therapist is not really fluent in Spanish. Similar complaints, in the cultural sense, are often voiced. Older people sometimes feel that their therapists' suggestions are contrary to their religious, moral, or "politeness" values. Younger people phrase this in more political or socioeconomic terms.

But bilinguality and biculturality are not sufficient to totally counteract the cultural influences that may lead to quick termination. Miranda, et al. (1976) found that Mexican-American clients who continued for five or more visits were more acculturated than those who only had two or fewer visits. For example, 23 percent of the former group was born in Mexico, compared to 78 percent of the latter. Interestingly, level of education and occupational status were not significantly related to continuance in therapy. Since all subjects interviewed for this study were seen by bilingual-bicultural therapists, the results cannot be attributed to effects of Anglo therapists. It may be that many of the therapeutic approaches that even bilingual and bicultural therapists are trained to offer are not congruent with Latinos' expectations or do not adequately address their problems.

Implications of these data, combined with personal observations, point to the following suggestions: Difficulties in language facility must be acknowledged to the client and permission explicitly given the client to correct or clarify linguistic misunderstandings. The therapist must also ask for clarification when something is not understood. Obviously, therapists of both Anglo and Latino background who do not speak Spanish fluently should not delude themselves into thinking they can conduct psychotherapy in Spanish. But even persons fluent in Spanish will sometimes run up against regionalisms that are literally foreign to them. I have found that letting the client know that I am from South America but that I have lived in the United States since age ten allows me to easily inquire about Mexican or Central American idioms in the course of therapy. (At the same time, that information lets the client know that I am going through the acculturation process with which so many of them are struggling.)

Politeness symbols must be used consciously and discriminatingly. The less acculturated and older the client, the more formally these symbols must be used. For example, late adolescents and adults might be greeted with a formal self-introduction, a handshake, and the polite form of the pronoun "you" (i.e., *"usted"* instead of *"tú"*) and the appropriate form of the verb (e.g., *"En qué puedo servirlo?"* instead of *"En qué puedo servirte?"*). The immediate use of the familiar form of "you" has repeatedly been mentioned to me by clients as a source of irritation in working with some Latino mental health personnel. Similar issues govern the use of the first name versus the last name. Latino therapists whose Spanish is rusty can let the client know that they can understand more than they can speak and explain that they may say things awkwardly without meaning to offend.

Correct pronunciation and spelling of proper names is particularly important. Even if clients speak English, it is hard to communicate a genuine concern for them if every time you address them by name they wince inwardly. Requesting clients to write their names down and to pronounce them slowly for you will show that you are concerned and are trying to pronounce their name correctly.

The first session should include a clear description of what therapy will consist of, a summary of the problems as the therapist has understood them, and a request for prioritization of the problems by the client. The possible participation of family members in therapy should be discussed, if appropriate. The family's cooperation with therapy, their acknowledgment that a certain problem needs work, and, one hopes, their sanction for the therapeutic alliance can in itself be an active ingredient in successful therapy.

When meeting with the family for the first time, in addition to the usual introductions, I generally make sure to indicate that the family knows the situation much better than I do, and, in order to best undertand what is occurring, I need to obtain their assistance. Similarly, I underscore the fact that their coming together is a good sign of family strength. If there are expressions of anger during the session, I restructure their cognitive set by pointing out that when loved ones behave in ways that are hurtful to us our anger can be quite extreme. It is precisely because we care for them that their actions can affect us so strongly. Expressions of caring usually follow this intervention, and I follow them up with a relabeling of the situation as that of a family (if appropriate, I'll use the adjectives "united" or "strong") facing a difficult problem, which I hope to be of some assistance in helping them solve. The tone at the end of the session should encourge a feeling of unity, an acknowledgement of the problem at hand, and hope that something can be done to improve matters.

The cost and payment of the intervention must be clear in the therapist's mind, including sliding scale arrangements or financial assistance arrangements. This financial information must be specified to the client.

Moderate amounts of self-disclosure are generally advisable. Remember that professional psychotherapy as it is practiced in the United States is not a highly valued activity in the Spanish-speaking world. The frustrations caused by a traditionally trained clinician who merely reflects or interprets the client's questions may be enough to discourage further sessions. In addition, in order to be able to trust the therapist *(tenerle confianza),* the client must see both professionalism and respected personal characteristics.

THE "ESSENTIAL" ELEMENTS OF A COMMUNITY MENTAL HEALTH CENTER

Inpatient Services

Most Latino families will attempt to take care of their relatives at home if at all possible and will seek hospital services only as a last resort (Bruhn and Fuentes, 1977). This may explain, in part, the underrepresentation of the Spanish speaking in inpatient wards (Padilla, Ruiz, and Alvarez, 1975).

The therapist's efforts at the beginning of the hospitalization must take into account such possible feelings as the patient's desire to leave the hospital and the family's guilt about bringing their relative (or allowing him or her to be brought). Clarity regarding the hospitalization process, the therapist's desire to make the patient's stay as short as possible, and the authoritative recommendation that hospitalization is indicated at present (if that is the therapist's assessment) can reduce feelings of uncertainty. Assurances that the family can visit the patient daily and that they will be involved in treatment and discharge plans can help bring a cooperative flavor to the therapeutic endeavor.

It is essential that acute inpatient wards provide 24-hour, Spanish-language coverage. At least one member of the nursing staff should be able to communicate with acutely suicidal or psychotic individuals at all times. The experience of a psychiatric crisis can be even more damaging if the environment has no one to speak with. When a person is the only Spanish-speaking patient on a psychiatric ward, the sense of isolation can exacerbate the feelings of dread, distance from others, and strangeness produced by the disorder.

I have found that Spanish-speaking patients respond well to the structure provided by a therapeutic community program on an inpatient ward. The cooperative expectations of such a system allow these patients to gain a sense of being needed and belonging. A "self-improvement level system" based on the patient's behavior allows for rewards based on his or her own efforts and provides tangible, concrete symbols of progress. In an ironic way, the inpatient ward becomes a social system in which its members enjoy a kind of equality not usually found outside of "total institutions."

However, this advantage can become an obstacle to discharge, in that some Spanish-speaking patients become too well socialized to the ward. Their personal involvement with staff and other patients can lead to a reluctance to make discharge plans. Their hard-earned status level may become a source of major reinforcement. And, if added to this, they face a grim economic or social situation in the community, their motivation to leave may be small. The dangers of becoming dependent on the ward must be openly discussed with them at this stage.

Throughout the patient's stay on the ward, the Spanish-speaking therapist carries an even greater responsibility than is true when his or her patients are English speaking. The severity of thought disorders or suicidal intentions in Spanish-speaking patients with little or no fluency in English will be verbally evident primarily to the Spanish-speaking therapists. Explanations of ward procedures, reasons for medication and possible side effects, and legal matters such as involuntary holds can effectively be given to these patients only by or through a Spanish-speaking therapist. At times the therapist may have to institute legal procedures to keep the patient hospitalized against his or her will, explain to the patient how to go about legally resisting involuntary hospitalization, and serve as translator when the patient communicates with a public defender. Obviously, this situation, in which the therapist controls the patient's communications, could be easily abused. Some therapists refuse to place themselves in such a dual role and insist that a translator be obtained.

In addition to basic interviewing and counseling skills, work with inpatients or ex-hospital patients requires becoming familiar with major diagnostic questions, major medications and their side effects, and legal rights of patients.

Outpatient Services

These services are the bulk of mental health center activities. They include brief interventions of one or two sessions, limited-therapy arrangements, or open-ended therapy, which could last months or even years. The level of pathology stretches from minor situational difficulties to chronic psychotic states. Modes of treatment include individual, couple, family, or group therapy. Most outpatients come for therapy voluntarily, though, of course, they may have been influenced to a greater or lesser extent by friends and families.

It has been my experience that Spanish-speaking patients who use mental health centers come with a specific problem in mind and they want and expect the therapist to deal with that problem. They expect the therapist to be directive. They expect their presenting complaint to be taken seriously. And they expect reasonably quick results. In addition, the therapist's demeanor must encompass two important aspects: professional excellence (including reliability, resourcefulness, and self-confidence) and personal warmth (including a genuine concern, caring, and confidence in the client's ability to improve). This combination results in the kind of therapist who is able to provide *consejos,* i.e., advice, who can clearly explain why he or she is suggesting these *consejos,* and who can resist giving advice when this is not indicated.

The outpatient therapist does not have the kind of environmental support that is present in inpatient work. There is no ward, no other support staff to socialize the client into the role of receiver of services. The context and the working arrangement with the client have to be defined completely. Knowing the above-mentioned usual expectations of Spanish-speaking clients, one can begin to structure the work from the first moment:

1. Engaging in a friendly, respectful, mutual introduction.
2. Mentioning briefly one's role or professional title and an explanation of the confidentiality involved in your work.

During the first phase of the therapeutic contact, attention must be paid to the patient's anxiety, uncertainty, and confusion. During this time the proper response might be to meet his or her need to be listened to, reassured, and comforted. This phase of the therapeutic work may need to last a few minutes or go on for one or two full sessions before moving on to the necessary next steps:

3. Outlining briefly what will happen in the following sessions.
   a) Gathering information in the client's own words.
   b) Formulating a treatment plan (which could include acquiring more information) in collaboration with the client.
4. Pinpointing the client's presenting complaint and making sure (through paraphrasing) that the client knows you have understood it.
5. Trying to refine or restructure the problem if it appears that this is clinically necessary. Once again, this must be done in undertsandable language. Necessary technical terms must be defined.
6. Negotiating an acceptable length for therapy, together with a rationale for the proposed treatment, and the obligations of the therapist and the client in the treatment.

The process involved in pursuing this approach is at least as important as the content. The therapist should express concern for the patient in a personal way. There must not be a bureaucratic tone to the interaction. By the time he or she reaches the Latino therapist, the Spanish-speaking client has probably been exposed to a multiple dose of alienating experiences: language and cultural barriers, possibly institutional and personal racism, and, finally, bureaucratic red tape. The therapist needs to diminish these sources of distance and of frustration. A Latino therapist, in particular, will be seen by the client as a source of support in a foreign culture. The need to be accepted by a member of one's own group is generally a factor in the building of rapport from both the therapist's and the client's perspective. This factor can increase the rapport, allowing a stronger therapeutic alliance. However, it can also become an obstacle. Perceived lack of acceptance can be much more devastating for both patient and therapist, and exaggerated expectations of assistance can be so high as to be insatiable—and thus continually frustrating.

The amount of assistance that a therapist should provide to a client experiencing frustrations in dealing with social agencies is a great source of debate. Theoretical, practical, and personal factors combine in determining each therapist's involvement. In general, my own involvement tends to be a direct function of the client's difficulty with English. My previous experience of not being able to communicate in English has sensitized me to the desperation-engendering qualities of such a situation. The added dimensions of institutional inertia and the difficulty of finding the appropriate channels to obtain adequate responses to one's requests prompts me to offer assistance for clients in such ways as translating key correspondence to social agencies (e.g., requests for economic support, for change of schools or classrooms, and so on), serving as interpreter-advocate (e.g., at juvenile court hearings, school board conferences, housing authority requests, and so on), and sometimes as would-be arbitrator (e.g., in disputes between the patient and non-Spanish-speaking persons who play an essential role in their environment).

A specific example may help give a flavor of what a therapist may need to do when working with a Spanish-speaking patient.

A divorced Central American mother of three was admitted to the inpatient ward of an urban mental health center because of a major affective disorder with psychotic symptoms. She was hearing voices telling her to kill herself and had stopped functioning at home, unable to sleep, eat, or care for the children. Her medical records showed that for the past two years she had had recurring episodes of a similar nature. She had been hospitalized locally repeatedly and even sent to the state hospital once. A letter from a psychiatrist who had treated her two years prior to the present admission presented an important piece of evidence. The letter was directed to the housing authority of the city, requesting a change of residence for the family.

Further fact finding revealed that the patient lived in "the projects," in a public housing area where there were few Latinos, where she had apparently made some enemies, and where she was afraid of having her children beaten up when they played outside the home. Her attempts to move had failed. She was feeling quite helpless.

In addition to the use of antidepressants, antipsychotics, and psychotherapy, all of which had been tried before, of course, a major effort was made to budge the housing authority and bring about a change to a predominantly Latino project. This took months to accomplish, during which time efforts to send the lady back home, even with professional companions, resulted in multiple suicide attempts (drug overdoses). Her apartment was broken into twice, most valuables were stolen, and when the police were notified, neighbors accused other members of her family of having been the culprits. The patient, whose English was marginal, could not defend herself properly and decompensated several times.

The therapist continued to advocate for the patient until, finally, an apartment was found. However, during a home visit soon after the family moved in, the therapist discovered that the toilet didn't work and, thus, the family was using the bathtub (covered with newspapers) to defecate, then throwing out the excrement in the garbage. They had been complaining to the main office of the housing complex with no results for weeks. The toilet was fixed hours after the therapist personally filed a complaint.

At a year and a half follow-up, there has been no recurrence of either the psychotic symptoms or the suicide attempts. Many crises have intervened, including quarrels with the neighbors, but now the ex-patient is able to argue with them in Spanish, and the sense of utter helplessness has been reduced to a manageable, if far from ideal, level.

This kind of activist role is not always necessary or appropriate. I believe, however, that it is more often appropriate when working with people who are not fluent in English and who are not familiar with this culture's social and institutional practice. Factors such as low levels of education, poverty, and consequent powerlessness also enter into this decision. Of course, clients of any background can be manipulative and dependent, and this must always be a concern of the therapist. On the other hand, not every manipulative act is unjustified or maladaptive. The therapist, especially the Latino therapist, needs to consider the factors that discriminate between appropriate responsiveness to realistic difficulties and personal crusades that may merely benefit the therapist's self-image.

The kinds of interventions that are appropriate to Spanish-speaking clients are as varied as those that are appropriate to any client. Assertive training has been found helpful with low-income Mexican-American women (Boulette, 1976). Group therapy has been successfully applied with women's groups (Hynes and Werbin, 1977) and mixed (male and female) groups (Herrera and Sanchez, 1976). And from a Jungian perspective (Maduro, 1976; Maduro and Martinez, 1974), behavioral counseling has also been espoused as an approach that can be made culturally relevant (Casas, 1976; Ruiz, Casas, and Padilla, 1977).

The Spanish-speaking therapist ought to remain well informed about the relative efficacy of varied approaches and adapt proven methods to his or her clients. Unfortunately, many of the contemporary advances in short-term psychotherapy are developed only in English. Evaluation instruments, treatment manuals, and self-administered treatments are often unavailable for use with Spanish-speaking consumers. Obviously, there is a great need for research-trained Latino clinicians to begin to develop therapeutic interventions bilingually—that is, to advance the field in both languages simultaneously, so that effective methods can be made available to both English- and Spanish-speaking populations at the same time.

In the meantime, clinicians should consider the following factors in deciding on the approaches to be used:

1. Demonstrated effectiveness (for example, research data versus anecdotal evidence).
2. Comparative risk levels (for example, the use of medication if it has side effects versus the use of a psychological intervention).
3. Length of treatment (for example, a time-limited intervention versus open-ended therapy).
4. Amount of dependence produced in the patient (for example, a self-control approach versus an approach that necessitates ongoing therapist involvement and support).
5. Probability that patient will follow through with treatment (for example, a culturally/religiously relevant intervention versus a foreign, possibly objectionable suggestion).
6. Therapist's own training and personal qualities.

Finally, outpatient therapists could benefit our field immensely by collecting and publishing carefully-quantified data on the outcomes of therapy with Spanish-speaking clients. This could be done both in the form of single case studies or group data.

Partial Hospitalization

There are cases of disturbance severe enough to require greater supervision than that provided by therapy sessions alone, but not severe enough for hospitalization. In addition to the expense of hospitalization, there are other factors that make a partial-care program more appropriate. Two of the main factors are (1) the risk of "institutionalizing" the patient, that is, making the patient so dependent on the hospital that he or she finds it hard to adapt to the outside environment upon discharge, and (2) the risk of the "closing-the-ranks" phenomenon, in which family and friends take over the functions or roles of the patient within their social networks, thereby excluding him or her from their ranks both emotionally and practically.

In the case of the Spanish-speaking consumer, the family generally wants to keep close contact with the patient throughout the period of crisis and to care for the patient as much as possible. It is not unusual for Latinos to request to spend the night in the hospital with even adult children or spouses when these loved ones have undergone surgery, for example. The partial hospitalization program allows the patient or client to receive intensive attention, while at the same time allowing the family to remain together during evenings and weekends.

Partial hospitalization is generally used as part of the after-care following hospitalization for an acute psychological disturbance. However, it can also be used to prevent the need for hospitalization, saving both human suffering on the part of the patient and the patient's family, and saving substantive amounts of money. Both outpatient and inpatient therapists working with Latinos should become familiar with partial- (especially day-) treatment programs in their area. Personal contact with Spanish-speaking staff in the day-treatment program can expedite acceptance and facilitate coordination of goals and treatment approach. Efforts should be made to maintain at least weekly phone contact with day-treatment therapists during the early stages of the patient's entrance into the program.

The kinds of services afforded day-treatment consumers usually include group and individual therapy, arts and crafts, exercise and relaxation groups, and planning for social, economic, and job needs after the patient graduates from the program. Day-treatment programs geared to Spanish-speaking consumers should consider the fact that many of them have a linguistic barrier that makes them more isolated than an English-speaking person. In addition, demographic information reveals that the average Spanish-speaking individual has a very low educational, economic, and employment level. Both of these factors suggest that day-treatment programs should offer English language classes and vocational rehabilitation services or establish a referral system for such services. The Latino client is usually motivated to learn and to "better" himself or herself through education and skill learning. Many have come to the United States in search of opportunity. Often the stress of isolation, combined with economic difficulties, triggers the psychological disorder. A focus on these issues is sure to have a significant effect on preventing further problems.

Twenty-four Hour Emergency Services

The emphasis in these services is on speed and efficiency in initially evaluating the client's problem and making an appropriate referral for services. Emergency crisis intervention teams do not have the luxury of long hours or days of observation. They are called on to make quick decisions regarding how to manage a person who is either in acute distress or in a state of lack of control. They need to make quick but accurate diagnostic decisions. And they usually deal with both clinical and administrative dispositions, that is, providing the person in crisis with information about the most appropriate, presently available resource to meet the client's needs. This may be a clinical service, including the usually scarce inpatient beds, or it may be a nonclinical service, such as lodging, food, money, or a return to the family after the family has been given consultation and reassurance about how to best deal with the problem at hand.

In addition to the diagnostic question, evaluating the risk of suicide, of homicidal intent, and of capacity to obtain food, clothing, and shelter for oneself is uppermost in the minds of emergency service personnel. These factors are, in turn, connected to the possibility of involuntary detention for psychiatric evaluation and treatment. The task, then, is basically one of information gathering and decision making under severe time constraints. The need for linguistic compatibility is obvious under these conditions.

Twenty-four hour emergency services in catchment areas with significant proportions of Spanish-speaking consumers should provide 24-hour, Spanish-speaking coverage. Ideally, this would mean trained therapists or counselors who can interview the person in crisis, gather clinically relevant information, determine the most likely diagnoses (including "no psychological problem"), and consider the most appropriate dispositions. Clinically untrained translators are not acceptable substitutes because the nuances of meaning and associated feelings that are so helpful in forming a diagnostic impression are necessarily distorted in the translation. In addition the calming reassuring intervention of the clinician is much harder to bring about through a person who may not understand the reasons for specific comments.

The most common difficulties I have encountered in cases of Spanish-speaking consumers served by non-Spanish-speaking staff include 1) over-reaction, such as using major tranquilizers for transient situational disturbances, 2) underreaction, such as sending a woman who had taken sleeping pills in a suicide attempt to a place for overnight lodging, without learning that she had *already* taken the pills, and 3) not using support networks. The latter point refers to therapists' neglect of including the family or friends and neighbors in the decision-making process. In some cases, the person is brought to the emergency service by his or her extended family, close friends, *compadres*,[1] and so on. These people expect to be informed of what the mental health workers have determined, and they feel that they have a right to have a say in the disposition. When the clinician excludes these "significant others," he or she is wasting valuable resources and helping to drive an even larger wedge between the client and the client's family. Sometimes this exclusion is occasioned by the clinician's lack of fluency in Spanish or his or her discomfort in dealing with a group of "excitable," "intrusive" Latinos. This is another reason to encourage bilingual and bicultural staff in 24-hour emergency services. Such a staff person is more likely to share in the belief that the family not only *can* but *should* be involved, especially in obtaining history and understanding the problem, and thus involve them more naturally and appropriately.

After a decision has been made concerning an appropriate service referral for the client, the Spanish-speaking clinician should provide an orientation to what the client and his or her family can expect next. For example, if an inpatient stay is appropriate, the procedures of such a ward should be explained, the kinds of other patients who will be sharing the ward need to be described, and the patient's legal rights should be listed—in written form as well as orally. When medications are used, reasons for their need, the possible side effects, and hoped-for results should be carefully explained.

The middle of a psychological crisis is a time when all reassuring symbols are of the utmost importance. Caring, skilled, confident clinicians are one such symbol. If such clinicians are, in addition, culturally and ethnically similar to the client and fluent in the client's mother tongue, the process of bringing order and a sense of safety to the client can be much enhanced.

Consultation and Education Services

The main focus of this service is to provide advice and information to community agencies and professional personnel, as well as to provide nonclinical, educational services to the consumer. Although preventive interventions are generally expected to be part of this service, most consultation is clinical case consultation (Snow and Newton, 1976). There are few, if any, mental health centers that have systematically implemented and evaluated a prevention program to determine if participation reduces the probability of later dysfunction when compared to a control group that does not participate in the program.

Consultation and education can be very useful in improving services for Spanish-speaking consumers in the following ways:

1. Bringing the latest mental health innovations to the clinicians in the "front lines," who generally do not have the time to keep up with the scientific literature.

2. Providing information regarding cultural factors in treatment and maintenance and providing consultation regarding specific cases or specific interventions geared to Spanish-speaking consumers. The main such intervention is generally how to inform Latinos about the services available in a way that makes it clear that they are welcome to use them and that there are staff available who can work effectively with them.

3. Supporting the efforts of Spanish-speaking staff within their individual agencies. Because of the scarcity of Spanish-speaking personnel, there are many therapists who are isolated from Latino colleagues. As the professional becomes better known in the community, his or her case load increases. At some point, the therapist needs to learn ways to limit involvement to prevent burnout. In addition to clinical involvement, however, the systemic need to respond to Spanish-speaking issues, such as affirmative action, usually places the therapist in a position of

having to speak for the continuing efforts to provide more Spanish-speaking personnel and services, and this sometimes antagonizes non-Latino colleagues who may not share this perspective. The consultant's job, then, is to help maintain the Spanish-speaking mental health worker's enthusiasm and self-esteem and to suggest effective strategies for intervention, both with clients and the system within which the therapist works.

THE ADDITIONAL SERVICES FOR "ADEQUATE" MENTAL HEALTH CARE

Diagnostic Services

The assessment of each client's difficulties and assets is a basic requirement of good mental health work. There are many ways to assess individual or group functioning. One such way is psychological testing. There are three concepts that are very important for the mental health worker to understand about psychological testing: reliability, validity, and utility.

Reliability refers to comparability of test scores when given under different conditions. In other words, if we were trying to assess, say, intelligence, would we get similar IQ scores if different testers administered the test? Good assessment instruments are supposed to be very reliable. If they are not reliable, of course, we won't be able to take their results very seriously. The problem with reliability when it comes to testing Spanish-speaking clients is that tests that have been shown to be reliable in English may not necessarily be reliable when given in Spanish. Such factors as familiarity with cultural differences and regional vocabulary on the part of the tester may influence the kind of response elicited from the testee.

Validity refers to how closely results from the test are related to what the test is supposedly measuring. In other words, does the test really measure what it is supposed to measure? Even if the test is very reliable and always gives the same score on the same client, that score may have little or nothing to do with what we are trying to assess. One major example of difficulties with validity is the IQ tests. These tests are generally adequately reliable. They also appear to be valid, in that a high IQ is usually related to good performance in school. However, there is a question about whether IQ tests measure "intelligence" in the sense of "the ability to learn" or in the sense of "being able to get good grades in a middle-class oriented, English-language classroom." Obviously, Spanish-speaking children with little English ability are going to perform poorly on English-language IQ tests, even if they are very intelligent. The same argument holds for other types of tests: scores that deviate from the norm may do so because the testee has personal characteristics that are deviant, or because he or she belongs to a group that, as a whole, deviates from the group for which the test was designed. Because the Spanish-speaking population varies so greatly in terms of customs and language ability, it is hard to find tests that have been standardized on the precise group to which one's client belongs. Most tests are constructed for English-speaking populations. Tests that have been translated into Spanish are not necessarily standardized on Spanish-speaking populations. And those that do have norms for Spanish-speaking populations may still be inappropriate. For example, a test standardized on middle-class, well-educated Spaniards in Madrid may have little validity for poor, uneducated Latin American immigrants in San Francisco. Both the vocabulary and the type of responses that are common to one group may be unfamiliar to the other.

Utility refers to whether test results will have a significant impact on the treatment plans for the client (Mischel, 1968). Even if the tests used are reliable and valid they may be a waste of time and money if the therapist is going to proceed according to his or her "clinical intuition" anyway. The same is true if there are few services available to the client, thus making test results superfluous since they will not influence the services a client receives. When tests are not reliable and/or valid, it is better not to administer them since many people, including professionals, tend to put much more confidence in numerical scores than is appropriate. Erroneous decisions can, therefore, be made, which may be detrimental to the well-being of the client.

One assessment method that avoids many of the pitfalls alluded to is behavioral assessment. This is an individualized problem-oriented approach to assessment that blends easily with treatment. Specifically, the quantity or intensity of the presenting complaints are recorded (usually by the patient or with his or her cooperation). Then a treatment plan to reduce the severity of the problem is formulated and recording of the problem continues. Thus, the treatment plan can be continued if it is working or modified if it is not (Hersen and Bellack, 1976).

Other kinds of clinical assessment include the psychiatric evaluation, including the mental status exam, and the social history. Although there is some controversy about the reliability of psychiatric diagnoses, specific impairment found in the mental status exam can serve as a guide to problem formulation. In addition to the language problems, educational and cultural differences must be taken into account when making these determinations. For example, recent immigrants are not likely to remember more than one or two past U.S. presidents in a memory test, English language proverbs may not be translatable into Spanish in a meaningful way and thus do not serve to test abstractive ability, and it is possible that some individuals may not be able to do "serial 7's" (subtracting a chain of sevens from one hundred) even when at their psychological best due to little or no schooling.

The social history is probably the single most important assessment tool in trying to understand someone from another culture, especially if the interviewer engages the client in descriptions of the norms in their own family or town for such things as marital customs, schooling and employment, problem solving, and so on. A clear picture of the client's level of functioning in his or her original environment and in the present environment prior to the dysfunction is particularly useful in determining treatment goals.

Rehabilitative Services

The need for vocational and educational programs is great for many users of community mental health services. The need is greatly exacerbated for members of the Spanish-speaking population, which has one of the lowest educational and economic levels of any group in the United States.

Clients of Latino background are generally very motivated to use services that provide education or training. Many of them come from families who immigrated to the United States in search of opportunity. The motivational structure is part of their world view. What is needed to trigger it is careful cooperative analysis of the client's situation and the services available.

Lack of English capability is one of the greatest drawbacks to Latinos trying to use these services. English classes (which are helpful in themselves) are often required before entering other training programs. It is clear that the extra step of learning a second language can be a major stumbling block in clients' progress. Spanish-language training programs are sorely needed to allow clients to begin their activities directly in their native tongue. Job and volunteer programs that utilize monolingual Spanish-speaking individuals can help increase these clients' self-esteem, as well as mobilizing human energy that now generally remains fallow.

Precare and After-care Services in the Community

These services include foster home placement, home visiting, and halfway houses. Their purpose is to attempt to prevent hospitalizations in people who are beginning to show signs of deterioration or to avoid relapses in people who have suffered acute episodes of dysfunction.

The halfway houses and three-quarter-way houses (which are midway between a halfway house and a hospital) that have been most helpful with Spanish-speaking clients under my care have emphasized a home atmosphere with a clearly visible Latino atmosphere, such as Spanish names for the house, Spanish-speaking staff, and Spanish-language orientation materials. These places are used as alternatives to hospitalization, so that people who would ordinarily be admitted to inpatient wards are instead accepted into such houses.

Many Latino immigrants arrive in the United States as lone individuals or lone nuclear families. The support of extended families and friends who shared value systems, concepts, and historical realities is not immediately available to them in their new country. When the stresses of psychological problems beset such people, their support systems are not there to help.

Therefore, these community services must do what they can to diminish the possibility of total isolation in their clients.

Acute intervention centers (three-quarter-way houses) with short-term stays and quick disposition back to the client's home and job can be backed up with longer-term care (halfway houses) for those who need more extended periods of stabilization.

Home-visiting teams are extremely important for clients who cannot or will not come to mental health centers. Mothers with many young children, teenagers who are reluctant to make active efforts at obtaining help but who respond well to mental health workers who take the trouble to follow through, and persons in isolated rural areas have made good use of periodic home visits. Many times these consumers can use the visit to diminish growing pressures that would otherwise lead to full-blown crises. This can be accomplished through clarification of issues that were becoming overwhelming to the client when thinking about them by himself or herself, or through simple family negotiation to defuse a current conflict.

Training

As the most pervasive provider of mental health services in this country, the community mental health center (CMHC) can potentially provide the largest proportion of training in mental health interventions.

Training that focuses on the Spanish-speaking consumer should have three targets: (1) the continued training of bilingual, bicultural mental health workers with the explicit purpose of helping them climb the career ladder, (2) the training of non-Latinos at every level to sensitize them and make them more effective in dealing with Latinos, and (3) the continuing education of Latino mental health staff by each other to share information, technique, and motivation.

The first target reflects the reality that our ranks are thinnest at the higher echelons of the mental health system. To meet the great need for Spanish-speaking services, the mental health system has utilized volunteers, translators, paraprofessionals, and others who have then been kept at these levels because of the lack of realistic access routes to more influential positions in the system. Many of these people have accumulated vast experience in mental health, which they cannot transform into policy because they do not have the necessary titles or positions to be influential. It is imperative that those staff members who are interested in pursuing further education be identified, encouraged, and given the opportunity to pursue such studies. Specifically, flexible scheduling, searches for possible funding sources, and arrangements with learning institutions in the community should be fostered by the CMHC administrative structure. Individual supervisory arrangements for developing clinical skills would be of great profit both to the mental health workers and to the clients they will be working with. Specific training in focused clinical interventions that have been tested and found to work well when administered by paraprofessionals should be routinely taught to community mental health center staff.

The second target, training of non-Latinos to work with Latinos, should emphasize cooperation between bilingual and monolingual staff as well as bicultural and monocultural staff. The espousal of efforts to provide Latino staff for Latino clients does not imply that non-Latinos are incapable of rendering helpful services to Latinos. This type of rejection of interested and motivated staff serves little purpose. Ideally, providing scheduled case conferences on Latino clients as well as consultation and supervision on Spanish-speaking cases will serve to increase non-Latinos' awareness of helpful approaches, of their own limitations, and of issues that must be taken into account. By uniting our efforts to provide consumers who are members of *La Raza* the best possible services, we may gain non-Latino support for more relevant staff and program development.

The third target of training, namely, the mutual consultation among bilingual-bicultural therapists, should be a focus of greater activity. Most clinicians, especially those with advanced degrees, have gone through an educational system that ignored or, at best, could not train us to work from a Latino/Chicano perspective. The content matter, the authors of the texts we read, and the faculty who trained us were for the most part alien to our language and our culture. In many cases, we had to journey to geographically distant locations, where we ourselves grew away from our communities' realities. As we return to work with our people, it is important to recognize that we have few models for providing mental health services to Spanish-speaking populations. We have learned methods and techniques that were developed on middle-class whites. As we adapt our knowledge to the conditions of Latinos in the United States, it is incumbent upon us to obtain feedback from each other about how we are going about doing this. All of us have blind spots, and supportive criticism can be a great source of assistance. In general, I have found that the Latino mental health workers with advanced degrees can contribute information on therapeutic technique, diagnosis, innovative treatment approaches, and evaluative methodology. Paraprofessional community workers can shed light on the practicalities of everyday existence in their particular neighborhood, on system resources and obstacles, and on the relevance of new approaches to consumer perspectives. Avenues for mutual continued education include workshops, case conferences, study groups, support groups, consultation networks, newsletters, and so on.

Research and Evaluation

The evaluation of mental health services for the Spanish-speaking population is in its infancy. The fact that this area of activity has a very low priority in CMHCs makes it difficult to believe that any recommendations will be carried out. Nevertheless, there are four areas that need to be considered by evaluation research teams: client entry into their system, therapy effectiveness, possible outreach programs, and who can provide services effectively.

The entry question can be addressed by obtaining the following information: (1) percentage of Latinos in their catchment area and percentage of primarily Spanish-speaking individuals, (2) percentage of service providers at each level who are bilingual or bicultural, (3) percentage of Latino staff who control entry into the system, such as receptionists and intake workers, and (4) percentage of Latinos who utilize the facility. This is the minimum information needed to determine whether the Spanish-speaking consumer has a reasonable chance of gaining entry.

Therapy effectiveness comprises at least five factors:

1. Dropout rate, which can be evaluated by identifying the factors that increase the probability of continued treatment. This kind of information can be helpful in increasing different therapists' ability to engage the client using their colleagues' input.

2. Improvement rates by approach, that is, the theoretical and practical advantages of different therapeutic modalities for different problems. The evidence for superiority of certain modalities over others is very much in dispute (Parloff, 1979). It is important that CMHCs examine which therapies work most effectively with which problems for which clients.

3. Time-effectiveness, that is, given two modalities that show similar results, which one utilizes fewer sessions.

4. Maintenance rates, that is, continued improvement after termination versus "revolving door" effect as another factor in gauging therapy effectiveness.

5. Consumer satisfaction with the way they were treated, such as respect shown to them, availability of bilingual staff, materials, etc.

In all five areas, the research data should analyze Latino responses separately to detect any differences in sevice effectiveness with this group.

Methods of increasing outreach refer to ways in which mental health services can be made to reach consumers who need them but who are reluctant or afraid to use them. For example, if we assume that there are many Spanish-speaking individuals in need of mental health care who do not want to become "cases" but who are eager for information to deal with their difficulties, we might begin a series of problem-oriented mental health classes.

Topics may include marital conflict, child behavior, depression, sexual difficulties, assertion, anxiety reduction, alcohol abuse, social skill training, and so on. The kinds of questions an evaluator would have to answer are: Would more Spanish-speaking consumers be attracted to these classes than to therapy? How distressed are these students as compared to therapy cases? Would we be reaching people who are significantly impaired but who are not using the usual service avenues? How effective are the classes in reducing levels of dysfunction? Or, more realistically, what kind of consumer can use the classes effectively? How can we modify these classes to make them useful to most consumers? Which psychological problems are most amenable to an educational approach? Last, but not least, the evaluator would have to grapple with how these classes would be funded; that is, given that they would not be "therapy," and thus would not fit under the usual case "head count" billing procedures, how could the CMHC get credit for the service?

Provider effectiveness refers to evaluating which disciplines and what levels of training are required for which problems with which population. For example, once the classes discussed above are standardized, could trained community volunteers implement them as effectively as advanced degree therapists?

The bottom line in research and evaluation is to identify the most effective intervention for a certain problem in a certain population. Cost effectiveness is a mandatory factor in a world with limited resources. Latino mental health will profit from clearly evaluated work that shows what kind of services are most effective for bilingual and bicultural consumers. Research-trained Latino clinicians would do well to invest a good portion of their energies into this area if they want to contribute to good services for their people. As policy decision makers exert more and more influence on third party reimbursement patterns, they will be looking for research evidence on which to base their decisions. Unless those of us who are personally involved in the well-being of Latinos contribute to the research, we will have to rely on the good will of others.

BEYOND THE COMMUNITY MENTAL HEALTH CENTER: PROVIDING MORE THAN MERELY "ESSENTIAL" OR "ADEQUATE" CARE TO LATINOS

The bulk of this chapter has been devoted to examining the basic services that CMHCs are mandated to provide to all consumers, especially as they apply to the Spanish-speaking consumer. The remainder of the chapter looks at areas beyond the minimally acceptable level of care. Latinos cannot afford to spend all their energy playing "catch-up" with the rest of the country. It is essential that at least some of our efforts be given to charting our own course, to providing leadership in the field of mental health by developing services for Latinos that will serve as models for mainstream practices.

One of the major areas in which we can show leadership is in changing the emphasis of mental health service delivery from reducing pathology to promoting psychological well-being. The idea is not new. It was known as "mental hygiene" earlier in this century (Lemkau, 1955) and is termed "primary prevention" in current usage (Cowen, 1973; Kessler and Albee, 1975; Muñoz, 1976). What would be new, if we can do it, is to change the proportion of services that are now devoted to therapy into educational, preventive, problem-oriented services where evaluation shows that this is feasible and effective (Muñoz, et al., 1979).

The rationale for this is particularly relevant to the Latino community. Many Latino families are immigrants or descendants of immigrants. They came to the United States in search of a better life. Consequently, they grew up with their parents' explicit goals of learning more, becoming more educated, having a more independent standard of living, and gaining more control over their own lives. This willingness and eagerness to learn forms a key concept, which opens up the door to properly packaged and presented educational programs.

When one combines this characteristic with the cultural reluctance to become "mental patients," we can begin to see that Latinos have been offered services most of them do not want and have not had services available that are needed and that would be more readily received if offered as education rather than therapy. The way services are provided at present, an individual must be in enough distress to overcome the fear of becoming a "patient" to be helped. This means that people who may be confused, in early stages of dysfunction, or merely in a life crisis are not likely to come to CMHCs.

By opening up the door to people who see themselves as needing information and advice but not treatment, we may multiply our effective reach. If evaluation data show that "information and advice" leads to reduction of stress and distress, and symptom improvement in addition, we will have learned that limiting our interventions to "therapy" has no great value in itself. Obviously, therapy would still be an option for those people for whom the educational approach alone would be insufficient.

The relative effectiveness of educationally-oriented interventions as compared to clinically-oriented therapies have obtained good results within a clinical framework. They are now being adapted to an educational, self-management approach, for example, in the areas of anxiety (Rosen, 1976), insomnia (Coates and Thoresen, 1977), drinking problems (Miller and Muñoz, 1976), smoking (Danaher and Lichtenstein, 1978), relaxation (Rosen, 1977), weight problems (Jeffrey and Katz, 1977), sexual dysfunction (Heiman, LoPiccolo, and LoPiccolo, 1976; Zeiss and Zeiss, in press), and depression (Lewinsohn, et al, 1978). The existence of these manuals, which are designed to be used by individuals themselves or under the direction of a teacher, makes the possibility of establishing such educational programs much more realistic. The problem facing Spanish-speaking therapists is that these resources are in English and have generally been written for educated, middle-class audiences. Adapting the approaches to the Spanish language and to individuals who are not used to academic activities represents a major enterprise. Nevertheless, if this is a promising direction, the resources to bring it to fruition must be found.

Another reason to look toward prevention when working with Latinos is that a significant proportion of them are faced with the problems of dealing with a foreign environment. Whether they are recent immigrants, young U.S.-born people leaving their Latino homes and neighborhood for school or work, or adults who, for whatever reason, have to deal with the larger U.S. society after years of living in a protected Latino/Chicano enclave, they are faced with a different set of environmental contingencies, which increase psychological stress, placing them in a high-risk category for emotional problems.

David (1976) has delineated some of these changes and possible ways of diminishing their noxious effects. He points out that, as persons enter a new culture, they immediately lose many of the daily reinforcing events that make life satisfying. This may include something as basic as the ability to communicate. Many Spanish-speaking parents, for example, are reduced from being the clear heads of their family to having to rely on their children for translation and explanations of "how things are done" here. The many sources of social support, including friends, family, familiar institutions, and a recognized place in one's community are no longer available. Music, food, clothing, holidays, and even climate change radically.

The preventively-oriented planner could focus on helping individuals to transfer reinforcing events into the new environment, as well as providing opportunities to develop new reinforcers. Thus, orientation to organizations or institutions that keep alive cultural traditions, to markets and restaurants that provide familiar food, and to media channels that specialize in Spanish-language programming would be ways of transferring treasured reinforcers into people's present environment. English classes, job-finding services, and introductions to entertainment available in the surrounding community would be ways of developing new reinforcers.

David (1976) also refers to the increase in aversive events that are part of joining a new culture. For the Latino student attending the university, it may be a particularly gruesome registration procedure. For a family originating from a rural area, it may be the smog, crime, and crowded conditions of urban living. For an individual who grew up in a well-integrated city, it may be the blatant prejudice (or at least the curious stares) he or she perceives in a predominantly Anglo part of the country.

Aversive events can be planned for in two main ways: avoiding them or neutralizing them. When working with a group, it is possible to make a list of aversive events that are commonly experienced. This list should also include a section on behavior that is acceptable in the home culture but aversive to members of the host culture, that is, aversive events that are innocently performed by the newcomer. Once this list is prepared, methods of circumventing these events or coping with their occurrence can be discussed.

Techniques that are useful in increasing reinforcing events and decreasing aversive events include simulation, modeling, and densensitization. In simulation, the purpose is to provide safe practice, For example, if our goal is to teach school children how to take standardized multiple choice exams like the PSAT and the SAT, we can administer practice exams to the children, go over the exams, and explain the best strategy for going through the exam (e.g., when guessing makes sense, etc.). Modeling involves observation and imitation of the desired behavior in someone who performs adequately. It is important in choosing models that one pay attention to implied messages in the type of model one chooses. For example by using Latino models who are handling their personal or professional worlds competently one reinforces the message that the Latino observer can perform as well. Use of only Anglo models could be counterproductive, in that the observer could attribute the models' mastery of the situation to their ethnicity and not to their behavior. Desensitization involves deep muscular relaxation and systematic gradual presentation of a feared stimulus or situation either in imagination or in reality. The technique is used to diminish fear or anxiety of engaging in a particular behavior. For example, it could be used in helping Latinas to feel comfortable in engaging in assertive behavior, which is necessary for their survival in this country.

All of the above efforts could be part of routine preventive services available to Latinos who are new to the community.

ONE APPROACH TO THE PROBLEM OF LIMITED RESOURCES

The suggestions made above add up to providing more than merely "essential" or "adequate" care. But the upgrading of mental health services means a greater strain on an already strained system. The current need for services in the population as a whole surpasses the delivery capabilities of available or projected personnel (Matarazzo, 1971). The need for Spanish-speaking services is even greater, with an even smaller available or projected supply of bilingual, bicultural staff. How, then, can we propose to increase the breadth of services when we are not even meeting present demands?

In a 1978 article in *Professional Psychology,* Christensen, Miller, and Muñoz described a framework that may provide the kind of quantum leap in delivery potential that would be required to meet the admittedly ambitious goals already listed. The article defined three levels of intervention: prevention, treatment, and maintenance. It also listed five types of adjunct agents that could help in expanding mental health service delivery within those three levels, namely (and alliteratively): paraprofessionals, partners (nontrained helpers), peer-clients, paraphernalia (equipment, tapes, gadgets) and print (written materials).

Underlying the proposal to utilize these therapeutic adjuncts to their fullest demonstrable potential were the following ideas:

1. Adjunctive agents are more plentiful and less expensive than are mental health professionals.

2. Adjunctive agents maintain greater contact with clients in their natural environment and emphasize clients' responsibility for their own changes. For these and other reasons, therapeutic adjuncts have the potential of being equally or even more effective than direct professional services.

3. The role of the mental health professional should not be limited to direct service but, rather, should include significant time devoted to supervision, program development, training, diagnosis, and evaluative research. (Christensen, Miller, and Muñoz, 1978, p. 250).

Table 14.1 is an adaptation of the original model as it applies to Spanish-speaking consumers. The present version includes a row for professionals in addition to the five rows for the adjuncts. Examples within each cell are meant to have direct relevance to Latino-oriented services. Ideally, services should be found on the left-most portion of the table, that is, in the prevention end of the spectrum. Greater attention than is presently being given to maintenance is implicit in this model by its receiving equal space as treatment, which now absorbs most of the mental health budget.

Cost-effectiveness issues are also explicit in the arrangement of the table. The lower rows are the least expensive, while, at the same time, the most available both in terms of amount of contact per person as well as number of persons reached.

Evaluative factors are impacted as follows:

1. Any procedure must be tested at each level; i.e., effectiveness when implemented by a professional does not imply effectiveness when implemented by a paraprofessional, a peer, or printed matter. Conversely, it must not be assumed that providers in higher rows are necessarily the most effective for any procedure. It may be that peers or paraprofessionals are more effective than professionals for certain problems and certain people.

Table 14.1
Expanding Mental Health Service Delivery for the Spanish-Speaking Consumer: An Adaptation and Extension of the Christensen-Miller-Muñoz Model

Type of Service Provider	Prevention	Treatment	Maintenance
Professionals	Develop, test, adapt, and evaluate programs that may have preventive effects in each of the rows below. Provide supervision, diagnosis, triage.	Reconceptualize, restructure, and experiment with new, problem-oriented, short-term methods acceptable to and effective with Latinos. Evaluate their effect when implemented in each row below.	Evaluate and oversee the long-term effects of interventions, specifically on Spanish-speaking clients. Implement follow-up services where needed.
Paraprofessionals	Participate as indigenous agents. Bilingual and/or bicultural counselors trained to do life, educational, career, or retire-	Act as therapist/educators for well-tested therapy packages; consultants during therapy development; consultants to	Lead bilingual/bicultural maintenance groups or "booster" sessions. Keep track of high-risk clients by means of home-

ment planning; nutrition education; paralegal and red tape troubleshooting	clients attempting self-control procedures. Trained parents and teachers could implement treatment in community settings.	visiting teams. Trained parents and teachers could continue to provide environmenatal support.	
Partner-helpers	Serve as models; e.g., immigrants who have coped well could share what they have learned. Big brother programs. Sponsor-protegé (or protegée) programs in business, industry, academia, and so on. Grandparents serving as advisors for your families.	Provide training in basic skills necessary for client well-being. Become companions for clients' practice sessions in handling difficult situations (e.g., looking for a job, finding an apartment, and so on).	Students, community leaders, neighborhood friends, and so on act as support persons for ex-patients. Partner-helpers can also provide resources for economic and educational pursuits.
Peer-clients	Form groups for new immigrants, young people contemplating marriage,	Form self-help groups such as Alcoholics Anonymous, weight-	Conduct "graduate" groups of ex-clients who provide motivation for continued

Table 14.1 (continued)

Type of Service Provider	Prevention	Treatment	Maintenance
	newly married couples, new parents, consumer groups, university student support groups, consciousness-raising groups to further pride in Latino culture.	change programs, depression-control groups, assertiveness groups . . . and so on.	improvement. Organize "payment-in-kind" programs where ex-clients serve as support persons for newer ex-clients.
Paraphernalia	Mass media mental health programs in Spanish. Bilingual videotapes of basic orientation to community resources. Games to teach children to maintain their bilinguality. Computer	Event counters to keep track of frequency of adaptive or maladaptive responses (self-monitoring). Relaxation tapes in Spanish. Biofeedback instruments for somatic complaints,	Checklists, charts, alcohol-content measuring devices, and other gadgets that help monitor continued improvement. Take-home tapes on relaxation, depression-control, and so on.

	programs that translate, teach, inform, and develop job or survival skills.	such as headaches, tension, and so on.	
Print	Materials that describe cultural sources of pride, instruct regarding survival skills in the United States, list economic and educational opportunities, such as grants, scholarships, free education, etc. Information about common psychological questions and preventive techniques.	Bilingual information manuals explaining mental health services and how to use them. Drug and alcohol facts. Well-tested, Spanish-language self-management manuals on relaxation, anxiety reduction, depression, assertion, and so on.	Sources in Spanish on economic, educational, and social sources of support. Life-planning manuals that deal realistically with options available to Spanish-speaking individuals and that go beyond the treated problem.

Source: Christensen, A., Miller, W.R., and Muñoz, R.F. Paraprofessionals, partners, peers, paraphernalia, and print: Expanding mental health service delivery. *Professional Psychology* 9 (1978):249-70.

2. When two or more of the rows have been shown to be comparable in results obtained, it makes practical sense to utilize the lower and less costly type of provider on a regular basis.

3. Adjunctive procedures lower in the table can be used as minimal standards against which to judge the effectiveness of interventions higher in the model.

In terms of the use of available personnel, the model provides a practical and justifiable way to utilize the energies of Latinos at every level to the best of their abilities.

The question of paraprofessional providers of service becomes no longer a matter of guild interests or degreed versus nondegreed personnel. It becomes, instead, an empirical matter. Persons trained to deliver specific services at the preventive, treatment, or maintenance levels would earn their qualifications from the outcomes they obtain.

Latino individuals who want to be of service to their people but who do not want to train and work as paraprofessionals could offer their services as partner-helpers. They would be able to share the skills they already have, thus obtaining positive feedback and concommittant boosts in self-esteem. This would be of particular use for monolingual Spanish-speaking individuals, who, for whatever reason, have not learned English but remain superbly competent in interpersonal skills. This segment of our population is presently ignored and their potential contributions wasted. This is a serious lack of resource conservation, in that we do not benefit from their help and they do not obtain the feeling of being needed that is so important to one's emotional well-being.

Peer-clients who are undergoing the same experience as their fellow clients can benefit from being given explicit responsibility for the mutual improvement of the group. It is while teaching others that we learn most fully.

The use of paraphernalia in work with Latinos is an area in dire need of development. We have not yet made use of this great source of potential aid in disseminating mental health services to our people. The use of the mass media is a readily available channel for education. Audio and video tapes can reach people who have trouble reading in English *and* Spanish. Equipment such as biofeedback machines and response counters can be made less intimidating once they are properly demonstrated and their rationale carefully explicated.

Print is another medium that has not been used enough for mental health education of Latinos. The vast amount of bibliotherapy available in English (Glasgow and Rosen, 1978) gives some perspective to how little is available to the Spanish-speaking consumer.

In each of these types of service provision, it must be remembered that we are talking about evaluated efficacy of particular approaches for particular problems in particular classes of consumers. Nevertheless, in order to have something to evaluate, we must redouble our efforts to produce methods that can be clearly defined and are, therefore, replicable.

Herein lies the role of the professional. As the model is put into effect, three functions will gain prominence for the professional (Christensen, Miller, and Muñoz, 1978):

1. Providing the adjuncts: developing procedures, writing materials for client use, training and supervising providers, coordinating resulting programs, writing grants, and engaging in administration.

2. Matching clients and services: making differential diagnoses, making referrals, setting priorities, sequencing services, evaluating and conducting research on differential responses to various interventions.

3. Evaluating the effectiveness of different types of service providers: evaluating the long-range effectiveness of primary prevention programs, doing treatment-outcome studies, assessing maintenance of gains after treatment, and conducting cost-effectiveness and program evaluation studies that take into account the various combinations of available alternatives.

In short, the Latino professional would act as consumer advocate, asking: what evidence is there that this is an effective procedure for Spanish-speaking persons—and is it more effective than less expensive and more readily available methods?

Admittedly, this framework appears much more complicated than the practices commonly used today. If individual therapy is considered adequate treatment for all ills, for example, the task of providing such a service seems more straightforward. However, what Latino mental health personnel are striving for are relevant, effective interventions that are accessible to any and all Spanish-speaking people who could benefit from them. This is a major undertaking. Meeting the challenge will not be a simple task.

CONCLUSION

We have discussed the legal mandate given to the community mental health centers. We included the five "essential" services and the five added services needed for "adequate" coverage. We have pointed out issues in each of them that relate to the Spanish-speaking consumer.

The chapter ended with a call for services beyond the "essential" and the merely "adequate." In particular, the need for Latinos to take the leadership in the promotion of preventive services was argued. In addition, a model for expanding mental health service delivery was advanced.

The history of the struggle for access to opportunities open to members of majority groups has been long and arduous for members of *La Raza.* We are still struggling for adequate services for our people. Nevertheless, it is of the utmost importance that individuals in policy-making positions, Latinos and non-Latinos alike, reserve part of their efforts and resources for the development of systems of services such as those outlined here. Partly because we have so few Latinos in traditional positions of power within the mental health establishment, we are in a position to implement the most innovative and scientifically supported interventions available. We do not have to deal with the inertia of well-ensconced professionals for whom change is threatening. This assumes, of course, that services for Latinos will be primarily in the hands of Latinos, a questionable assumption at present. The best way to influence the future so that this will become reality is for Latino mental health personnel, especially professionals-in-training, to become knowledgeable in two areas in addition to their clinical training. One is the area of program evaluation and psychotherapy outcome research. The other is the area of social policy. Scientific evidence does not necessarily determine decision making. But a professional with good credentials who is aware of both can exert more influence than one who remains aloof from either.

NOTES

1. A *compadre* (literally "cofather"; the feminine form is *comadre* or "comother") is one's child's *padrino* ("godfather"; the feminine form is *madrina* or "godmother"), although a close friend may be bestowed that title without meeting the formal requirements. The relationship designated by this term, which is used for both parties (the child's parent and the godparent), is supposed to be as close as that of blood relatives. Thus, *compadres* and *comadres* are part of the *familia* (a term that refers to the extended family).

REFERENCES

Barrera, M., Jr. Mexican-American mental health service utilization: A critical examination of some proposed variables. *Community Mental Health Journal* 14 (1978):35-45.

Boulette, T.R., Assertive training with low income Mexican American women. In *Psychotherapy with the Spanish Speaking: Issues in Research and Service Delivery,* Monograph Number 3, edited by M.R. Miranda. Spanish Speaking Mental Health Research and Development Program, UCLA, 1976.

Bruhn, J.G. and Fuentes, R.G., Jr. Cultural factors affecting utilization of services by Mexican Americans. *Psychiatric Annals* 7 (1977):20-29.

Casas, J.M. Applicability of a behavioral model in serving the mental health needs of the Mexican American. In *Psychotherapy with the Spanish Speaking: Issues in Research and Service Delivery,* Monograph Number 3, edited by M.R. Miranda. Spanish Speaking Mental Health Research and Development Program, UCLA, 1976.

Christensen, A., Miller, W.R., and Muñoz, R.F. Paraprofessionals, partners, peers, paraphernalia, and print: Expanding mental health service delivery. *Professional Psychology* 9 (1978):249-70.

Coates, T.J. and Thoresen, C.E. *How to Sleep Better.* Englewood Cliffs, N.J.: Prentice-Hall, 1977.

Cowen, E.L. Social and community interventions. *Annual Review of Psychology* 24 (1973):423-72.

Danaher, B.G. and Lichtenstein, E. *Become an Ex-smoker.* Englewood Cliffs, N.J.: Prentice-Hall, 1978.

David, K.H. The use of social learning theory in preventing intercultural adjustment problems. In *Counseling Across Cultures,* edited by P. Pedersen, W.J. Lonner, & J.G. Draguns. Honolulu: The University Press of Hawaii, 1976.

Glasgow, R.E. and Rosen, G.M. Behavioral bibliotherapy: A review of self-help behavior therapy manuals. *Psychological Bulletin* 85 (1978):1-23.

Heiman, J., LoPiccolo, L. and LoPiccolo, J. *Becoming Orgasmic: A Sexual Growth Program for Women.* Englewood Cliffs, N.J.: Prentice-Hall, 1976.

Herrera, A.E. and Sanchez, V.C. Behaviorally oriented group therapy: A successful application in the treatment of low income Spanish-speaking clients. In *Psychotherapy with the Spanish Speaking: Issues in Research and Service Delivery,* Monograph Number 3, edited by M.R. Miranda. Spanish Speaking Mental Health Research and Development Program, UCLA, 1976.

Hersen, M. and Bellack, A.S. *Behavioral Assessment: A Practical Handbook.* Elmsford, N.Y.: Pergamon Press, 1976.

Hynes, K. and Werbin, J. Group psychotherapy for Spanish-speaking women. *Psychiatric Annals* 7 (1977):52-63.

Jeffrey, D.B. and Katz, R. *Take It Off and Keep It Off: A Behavioral Program for Weight Loss and Healthful Living.* Englewood Cliffs, N.J.: Prentice-Hall, 1977.

Kennedy, J.F. Message from the President of the United States relative to mental illness and mental retardation. 88th Congress, First Session, U.S. House of Representatives Document No. 58. Washington, D.C.: U.S. Government Printing Office, 1963.

Kessler, M. and Albee, G.W. Primary prevention. *Annual Review of Psychology* 26 (1975):557-91.

Kluckhohn, C. and Murray, H.A. Personality formation: The determinants. In *Personality in Nature, Society, and Culture,* edited by C. Kluckhohn, H.A. Murray, and D.M. Schneider. New York: Random House, Alfred A. Knopf, 1953.

Lemkau, P.V. *Mental Hygiene in Public Health.* New York: McGraw-Hill, 1955.

Lewinsohn, P.M., Muñoz, R.F. Youngren, M.A., and Zeiss, A.M. *Control Your Depression.* Englewood Cliffs, N.J.: Prentice-Hall, 1978.

Maduro, R. Journey dreams in Latino group psychotherapy. *Psychotherapy: Theory, Research and Practice* 13 (1976):148-55.

Maduro, R. and Martinez, C. Latino dream analysis: Opportunity for confrontation. *Social Casework* 55 (1974):461-69.

Matarazzo, J.D. Some national developments in the utilization of nontraditional mental health power. *American Psychologist* 26 (1971):363-72.

Meyer, G.G. The professional in the Chicano community. *Psychiatric Annals* 7 (1977):9-19.

Miller, W.R. and Muñoz, R.F. *How to Control Your Drinking.* Englewood Cliffs, N.J.: Prentice-Hall, 1976.

Miranda, M.R., Andujo, E., Caballero, I.L., Guerrero, C.C., and Ramos, R.A. Mexican American dropouts in psychotherapy as related to level of accultura-tion. In *Psychotherapy with the Spanish Speaking: Issues in Research and Service Delivery,* Monograph Number 3, edited by M.R. Miranda. Spanish Speaking Mental Health Research Center and Development Program, UCLA, 1976.

Mischel, W. *Personality and Assessment.* New York: John Wiley & Sons, 1968.

Muñoz, R.F. The primary prevention of psychological problems: A review of the literature. *Community Mental Health Review* 1 (1976):1-15.

Muñoz, R.F., Snowden, L.R., Kelly, J.G., and Associates. *Social and Psychological Research in Community Settings: Designing and Conducting Programs for Social and Personal Well Being.* San Francisco: Jossey-Bass, 1979.

Our Sunday Visitor. A Gallup study of religious and social attitudes of Hispanic Catholics. 1979 (Available from Noll Plaza, P.O. Box 920, Huntington, Indiana 46750).

Padilla, A.M., Ruiz, R.A. and Alvarez, R. Community mental health services for the Spanish-speaking/surnamed population. *American Psychologist* 30 (1975): 892-905.

Parloff, M.B. Can psychotherapy research guide the policymaker? A little knowledge may be a dangerous thing. *American Psychologist* 34 (1979):296-306.

Rosen, G.M. *Don't Be Afraid: A Program for Overcoming Fears and Phobias.* Englewood Cliffs, N.J.: Prentice-Hall, 1976.

Rosen, G.M. *The Relaxation Book.* Englewood Cliffs, N.J.: Prentice-Hall, 1977.

Ruiz, R.A., Casas, J.M., and Padilla, A.M. Culturally relevant behavioristic counseling. Occasional Paper No. 5. Spanish Speaking Mental Health Re-search and Development Program, UCLA, 1977.

Snow, D.L. and Newton, P.M. Task, social structure, and social process in the community mental health center movement. *American Psychologist* 31 (1976): 582-94.

U.S. Department of Health, Education, and Welfare. *Mental Health Activities and the Development of Comprehensive Health Programs in the Community.* PHS Publication No. 995. Washington, D.C.: U.S. Government Printing Office, 1963.

————. Regulations, Title II, P.L. 88-164. *Federal Register,* May 6, 1964, 5951-956.

Zeiss, R. and Zeiss, A. *Prolong Your Pleasure: A Couple's Treatment Guide for Premature Ejaculation.* New York: Pocket Books, in press.

Index

ABOUT THE EDITORS
AND CONTRIBUTORS

ENRICO E. JONES received his Ph.D. from the University of California, Berkeley. Currently Associate Professor at Berkeley, he has published in the areas of clinical intervention and cross-cultural psychology. The focus of his psychotherapy research has been on the impact of race, gender, social class status, and other cultural and social psychological factors on treatment processes and outcome. He has served as a research consultant to the National Institute of Mental Health and as consulting editor to a number of journals. He has been the recipient of a number of fellowships, most recently a National Science Foundation International Exchange Fellowship, for cross-cultural studies at Ecole des Hautes Etudes en Sciences Sociales, in Paris.

SHELDON J. KORCHIN, Professor of Psychology at the University of California, Berkeley, coauthored *Anxiety and Stress* (1955) and authored *Modern Clinical Psychology* (1976) as well as a number of research papers, book chapters, and other contributions. Now on the American Psychological Association's Board of Social and Ethical Responsibility, he served earlier on other major committees of national, regional, and state organizations, as consultant to foundations and governmental agencies, and on the editorial boards of several journals. He has held Fulbright appointments for research and teaching abroad and received various other honors, including the American Psychological Association's Division of Clinical Psychology award for "Distinguished Contribution to the Science and Profession of Clinical Psychology."

W. CURTIS BANKS received his Ph.D. from Stanford University. He is presently a Senior Research Scientist and Director of the Social Learning

Laboratory at the Educational Testing Service, where his work is devoted primarily to the study of personality and social behavior in black children.

NANCY BOYD is Clinical Assistant Professor at the College of Medicine, New Jersey Medical School, where she serves as supervisor in the Child and Adolescent Unit. She is also affiliated with the Center for Family Studies of New Jersey and is Adjunct Assistant Professor at Adelphi University, where she teaches family therapy.

CARMEN CARRILLO is currently Director of Mission Mental Health Center in San Francisco. She specializes in mental health administration, community psychology, and the psychology of Third World peoples. She has published several papers on the treatment of the Hispanic patient.

GEORGE A. DEVOS is Professor of Anthropology and Research Associate at the Institute of Personality Assessment and Research of the University of California, Berkeley. As a psychologist and anthropologist, he has spent over 30 years in the field of culture and personality, with major emphasis on psychological problems related to deviancy, minority status, and ethnic interaction. He has authored over 100 books and articles.

ANDERSON J. FRANKLIN is Associate Professor at the City College and Graduate School of the City University of New York. A coeditor of *Research Directions of Black Psychologists* (1979), his research interests are in adolescent cognitive and social development and ethnographic issues of mental health.

HARRY H. KITANO is currently Professor of Social Welfare and Sociology, and Co-Director of the Alcohol Research Center, University of California, Los Angeles. He has authored numerous articles and books, including *Race Relations* (1980) and *Japanese Americans: The Evolution of a Subculture* (1976).

ROGER G. LUM is presently Executive Director of Asian Community Mental Health Services in Oakland, California and is part-time lecturer in psychology at San Francisco State University. He has served as a consultant to the National Institute of Education on the psychological aspects and instructional features of bilingual education.

ARNOLD MEADOW is Professor of Clinical Psychology in the Department of Psychiatry at the University of California School of Medicine, Davis. His major research interest has been the cultural determinants of psychopathology, and he has contributed over 50 scientific papers to a broad range of psychological, sociological, psychiatric, and legal journals.

RICARDO F. MUÑOZ is Assistant Professor in Residence at the University of California, San Francisco, in the Social and Community Psychiatry Program at the San Francisco General Hospital. He has done work in social learning approaches to self-control with special interest in the treatment of depression and has coauthored *Social and Psychological Research in Community Settings* (1979).

HECTOR F. MYERS is Associate Professor of Clinical Psychology at the University of California, Los Angeles and a Scholar in Residence at the Fanon Research and Development Center. He has authored several research papers and chapters in the area of psychological stress and essential hypertension and is the Associate Editor of the new *Fanon Center Journal: Perspectives on the Mental Health of Black Persons.*

LONNIE R. SNOWDEN, currently Assistant Professor in the School of Social Welfare at the University of California, Berkeley, has published in the areas of social and community interventions, psychological assessment, and the assessment of treatment of drug and alcohol abuse. He is coauthor of *Social and Psychological Research in Community Settings* (1979), serves as consultant to the National Institute on Alcohol Abuse and Alcoholism, and is consulting editor to a number of journals.

STANLEY SUE is currently Professor of Psychology at the University of California, Los Angeles. His research interests include Asian-American mental health, community mental health services, and social support systems. He has served on the editorial boards of several journals, as well as on major committees of national organizations, including the President's Commission on Mental Health.

JOSÉ SZAPOCZNIK is Research Professor at the Department of Psychiatry, University of Miami School of Medicine. A Cuban born psychologist, he has published widely on Hispanic mental health issues, including research on acculturation, biculturalism, cross-cultural values, and their implications for treatment. He has served as research consultant for the National Institute of Mental Health, the National Institute on Drug Abuse, and the Administration on Aging and is Director of the Spanish Family Guidance Center in Coral Gables, Florida.